THE ENVIRONMENTS OF AGEING

Space, Place and Materiality

Sheila Peace

D1613192

P

First published in Great Britain in 2023 by

Policy Press, an imprint of
Bristol University Press
University of Bristol
1-9 Old Park Hill
Bristol
BS2 8BB
UK
t: +44 (0)117 374 6645
e: bup-info@bristol.ac.uk

Details of international sales and distribution partners are available at
policy.bristoluniversitypress.co.uk

© Bristol University Press 2023

British Library Cataloguing in Publication Data
A catalogue record for this book is available from the British Library

ISBN 978-1-4473-1055-6 hardcover
ISBN 978-1-4473-1056-3 paperback
ISBN 978-1-4473-2162-0 ePub
ISBN 978-1-4473-1057-0 ePdf

Cover design: Bristol University Press
Front cover image: Getty/Boris SV

Bristol University Press and Policy Press use environmentally responsible
print partners.

Printed in Great Britain by CPI Group (UK) Ltd, Croydon, CR0 4YY

For my family past and present
Johannah and Reginald
Steve, Tom and Amy
Lynn and Martin
Rosemary and George
Caroline and the children

Contents

List of figures and tables

Figures

Tables

Research summaries

List of acronyms

AFCC	Age-Friendly Cities and Communities
APPG	All Party Parliamentary Group
CQC	Care Quality Commission
DH	Department of Health
DHSC	Department of Health & Social Care
DHSS	Department of Health & Social Security
EHS	English Housing Survey
ELSA	English Longitudinal Study of Ageing
EPSCR	Engineering and Physical Sciences Research Council
ESRC	Economic and Social Research Council
EU	European Union
HA	Housing Association
HAPPI	Housing our Ageing Population: Panel for Innovation
HRP	Household Reference Person
ILC-UK	International Longevity Centre – United Kingdom
IPCC	Intergovernmental Panel on Climate Change
MDP	Migration Data Portal
MHCLG	Ministry of Housing, Community and Local Government
MHLG	Ministry of Housing and Local Government
MoH	Ministry of Health
NGO	Non-Governmental Organisation
NHS	National Health Service
OECD	Organisation for Economic Co-operation and Development
ONS	Office for National Statistics
P–E	Person–Environment
RIBA	Royal Institute of British Architects
UKRI	UK Research and Innovation
UN	United Nations
UN, DESA	United Nations, Department of Economic and Social Affairs
UN, DESA, SDG	United Nations, Department of Economic and Social Affairs, Sustainable Development Goals, 2020
UN-HABITAT	United Nations Human Settlement Programme
UNHCR	United Nations High Commission for Refugees
WHO	World Health Organization

About the author

Sheila Peace is Emeritus Professor of Social Gerontology within the Faculty of Well-being, Education and Language Studies at The Open University. A social geographer by first discipline, she gained her PhD in the field of environment and ageing in 1977 at the University of Swansea. Sheila has maintained an ongoing research career – funded by the Department of Health, the Economic and Social Research Council (ESRC), Research Councils United Kingdom (RCUK), Help the Aged, Anchor Housing, Joseph Rowntree Foundation, Thomas Pocklington Trust and local authorities. Her research concerns many aspects of the person–environment relationship, including design and quality of life issues for older people living in care homes, mainstream housing and supportive housing as well as intergenerational social interaction within community public spaces. She was the first international intern for the International Federation on Ageing based at the American Association of Retired Persons in Washington DC, 1980/81. Throughout the 1980s, she was co-founder of the Centre for Environmental & Social Studies in Ageing at London Metropolitan University (former Polytechnic of North London). She joined The Open University in 1991 where, as part of the Centre for Ageing and Biographical Studies, she contributed to the development of participatory research involving older people. She was Associate Dean (Research) within the former Faculty of Health & Social Care for over ten years until 2009. Her recent research has included collaborative work concerning the kitchen with ergonomic/design colleagues from Loughborough University within the ESRC led New Dynamics of Ageing programme; the lives of people with high support needs for the Joseph Rowntree Foundation, and the needs and aspirations of visually impaired older people for the Thomas Pocklington Trust. More recently she has been a research advisor for the team evaluating the Older Women's Cohousing Community project and consultant for a British Academy study concerning older couples living apart – in a care home and in the community. Sheila was President of the British Society of Gerontology 2014–16 and is a Fellow of the Academy of Social Sciences. Widely published, she co-authored the important study of local authority care homes *Private Lives in Public Places* in 1987; *Environment and Identity in Later Life* in 2006 and was co-editor of *Ageing in Society: European Perspectives in Gerontology*, now in its third edition, where she contributed work on environment and ageing with German colleagues Hans-Werner Wahl, Frank Oswald and Heidrun Mollenkopf. More recent publications in journals such as the *International Journal of Design* have focused on the Transitions in Kitchen Living study (Maguire et al, 2014); the relationship between design and caring (Peace, 2017); age-friendly living for older people with vision impairment (Peace et al, 2018) and in 2020 home adaptation/modification, in the special cross-national issue of the *Journal of Aging and Environment* that she co-edited with Robin Darton.

Acknowledgements

Over the past several years, this book has been central to my thinking, and there are many colleagues, friends and loved ones without whom it would not have been written as it draws upon many aspects of my working and family life.

My thanks go to those whom I have worked with over many years. Across these pages you will find the skills, knowledge and valued thoughts of colleagues and friends, especially Leonie Kellaher and Dianne Willcocks, co-founders of CESSA, Bill Bytheway, Joanna Bornat, Andrew Clark, Manik Gopinath, Caroline Holland, Julia Johnson, Jeanne Katz, John Percival and Richard Ward, formerly and currently at The Open University, Tony Warnes, University of Sheffield, Martin Maguire and colleagues from Loughborough University and Karen West and Melissa Fernández Arrigoitia from Bristol and Lancaster Universities. The voices of participants are central, and I am always grateful to those people who give researchers their time and experience. I thank also, for their kind permission to reproduce visual and textual representation of their own work, Dr Sophie Handler and Professors Habib, Iwarsson, Oswald, Slaug and Wahl. As well as all those whose learning and knowledge I value, I rely on the expertise and resource of the Centre for Policy on Ageing, the Housing LIN and the Centre for Ageing Better.

For greatly valued comments on the manuscript at different stages and on completion, I would like to thank the encouragement and endorsement of Norah Keating, Caroline Holland, Jeanne Katz and book series editor Tom Scharf, without whom I know this book would not have finally emerged. They have been supported by the truly professional and reassuring team at Policy Press: Emily Watt commissioned the book while Laura Vickers-Rendall has spurred me on during lockdown and most recently Caroline Astley, Alice Greaves and Elizabeth Stone managed production with good grace.

Lastly, as sole author, I wish to thank my family to whom this book is dedicated. In particular, special thanks go to Tom for keeping my spirits up, Amy for developing all the figures with great commitment, patience and skill, and finally my husband Steve, whose support never fails.

Series editors' preface

Chris Phillipson (University of Manchester, UK)
Toni Calasanti (Virginia Tech, USA)
Thomas Scharf (Newcastle University, UK)

Demographic ageing and the increasing numbers and growing diversity of older people across world regions are raising new issues and concerns for consideration by academics, policy makers and health and social care professionals around the world. *Ageing in a Global Context* is a book series, published by Policy Press in association with the British Society of Gerontology, that aims to influence and transform debates in what is a rapidly changing field in research and policy. The series seeks to achieve its aims in three main ways. First, the series publishes books which set out to re-think some of the fundamental questions which shape debates in the study of ageing. This has become particularly important within the context of the restructuring of welfare states, especially in the Global North, and the growing complexity of population change. Each of these elements opens up the need to explore themes which reach beyond traditional perspectives in social gerontology. Second, the series represents a response to the impact of globalisation and related processes, which are contributing to the erosion of the national boundaries that originally framed the study of ageing. This is reflected in the increasing scope and breadth of issues that are explored in contributions to the series, for example: the impact of transnational migration, growing ethnic and cultural diversity, new types of inequality, changing personal and family ties and themes relating to ageing in different environmental contexts. Third, a major concern of the *Ageing in a Global Context* series is to explore interdisciplinary connections in gerontology. Contributions to the series provide a critical assessment of the disciplinary boundaries and territories that influence the study of ageing, creating in the process new perspectives and approaches relevant to the 21st century.

Against this background, we are delighted that Sheila Peace has written an exciting book that responds so well to the overarching aims of our series. As might be expected of a scholar whose work has helped to shape the interdisciplinary field of environmental gerontology since the 1970s, *The Environments of Ageing* breaks new ground in conceptualising the spatiality of later life. Its focus is on the contrasting environments, ranging from the specific characteristics of spaces within the home setting to key features of global cities, which influence personal experiences and have a powerful bearing on wellbeing in older age. The book is notable in considering the impact on the environments of ageing of major contemporary trends, including climate change, digitalisation, the restructuring of welfare states and, more recently, the COVID-19 pandemic. With its strong empirical foundations and fascinating insights into the methods used by researchers to generate evidence, the book is set to make a lasting contribution to conceptual, empirical and policy-relevant understandings of what has become a central topic in social gerontology. We anticipate that the book will be read very widely and become an orientation point for academics, policy makers and professionals who share a passion to study and understand better how the environments of ageing are changing within an increasingly globalised context.

Preface: understanding the structure

The 21st century has seen environmental gerontology recognised as a valued field within the multi- and interdisciplinary study of social gerontology. This domain evolved through the last century as researchers recognised the importance of person–environment interaction to understanding ageing and later life. Now it takes into account the complexity of human lives and the environments of the everyday, not only in the immediate and local but also within national and global contexts. Here, context includes the social, political, material, physical, psychological, economic and cultural elements of the society in which discussion is based. The motivation for this book comes from my desire as a white British woman in her late 60s to make a lasting contribution to this field, drawing on more than 40 years of research experience that embraces international scholarship. The aim is to discuss the environments of ageing through the relationships between milieu, behaviour and well-being, and while I focus on the second half of life, the value of life course experience and historical perspectives is recognised as fundamental.

Although I am a human/social geographer by first discipline, my academic work in gerontology commenced before the emergence of geographical gerontology (see Peace, 1977, 2018; Warnes, 1981; Harper and Laws, 1995; Andrews et al, 2007, 2009; Skinner et al, 2018), and I value the intellectual challenge of working with colleagues across the social, human and design/engineering sciences (Peace, 2018). Even so, unsurprisingly when considering environment and ageing, I embed the 'spatial turn' in this text by referring to three levels of spatial scale – pictured in Figure 0.1 – macro- (global), meso- (national) and micro- (local), which I see as essential to discussion within environmental gerontology. This is a project that began some years ago, and during that time I have realised that while my own research addresses important issues at micro- and meso-levels, the fundamental importance of macro-concerns are central. These diverse spatial environments enable attention to be drawn to issues that span the global to local and local to global context.

Across this text, I draw upon a diverse literature based primarily in England and the UK, with international comparison given where appropriate. Across the ten interconnected chapters, I aim to assimilate knowledge, theory and method. The first three chapters provide the necessary foundation through which to consider different perspectives regarding the person–environment relationship in later life. Chapter 1 begins with the central constructs of the person (P) and the environment (E), and I use the short-hand of P–E to denote relations between person and environment throughout the text. The heterogeneity of people in later life, now embracing 40 or 50 years, is captured in this discussion, alongside an understanding of environment that

Figure 0.1: Levels of spatial scale

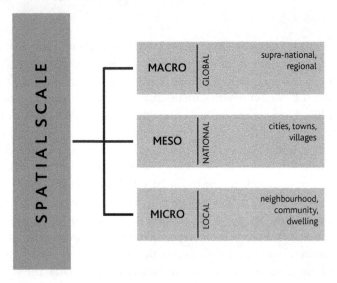

draws upon my appreciation of space, place and materiality. The dichotomy of person and environment then coalesces to consider how older people in specific circumstances find their environment enabling or disabling. Chapter 2 considers theoretical development from both social gerontology and geographical gerontology, providing the framework for assessing the current position of environmental gerontology. Here, the emergence of theory that relates to the 'near environment' in which older people live is seen to dominate social gerontology, whereas the different spatial scales suggested in this text demand a broader conceptual understanding. To complete this first section Chapter 3 introduces the global context where parallel challenges of population ageing, urbanisation, climate change, migration, technological development interact. These issues are part of the 'big picture' impacting at all spatial scales and raising initial concerns regarding the social inclusion of older populations. The content is drawn primarily from the western developed north with some comparison with developing countries.

Next the discussion moves to meso- (national) and micro- (local) levels of spatial analysis, providing a UK/British platform for research regarding P–E interactions, including my work with key colleagues. I call this environmental living, and concepts of home, community and homeland are introduced and discussed across Chapters 4 to 8, which capture the breadth of place and settings. Environment spans the rural to urban continuum – cities, towns and villages – alongside more detailed focus on interactions in communities, neighbourhoods and within living arrangements both age integrated and segregated. Chapter 4 introduces population ageing within the UK, focusing specifically on England, and explores issues of everyday living in rural and urban communities. The global World Health Organization initiative developing the Age-Friendly City or Community is discussed here, and current British initiatives are explored. In Chapter 5, I turn to general housing, the dwellings of most older people, focusing on development, type and tenure, with brief discussion of national policy initiatives and current concerns.

Chapter 6 provides a bridge between the circumstances of the majority who live in age-integrated housing as part of the wider community, many ageing in place, and those who have made a move to age-related settings; to specialised housing or to a care home. Here, different scenarios from empirical research are presented and the issues raised when people make these decisions are debated. I then turn to collective living environments, primarily age-related. Chapter 7 considers specialised housing and alternative environments in later life; while Chapter 8 addresses living within care homes – residential and nursing. The ongoing theme of the meaning of home cross-cuts these chapters, with further reflection in Chapter 10.

The final chapters draw upon the earlier text to bring together issues seen as central to the future development of environmental gerontology. Chapter 9 focuses on research methodology, and attention is paid to the development of participatory (action) research, interdisciplinarity and innovative forms of measurement, with implications for policy and practice. I consider how the ongoing involvement of older people as co-researchers advances this field, the value that is developed through working across disciplines and the applied nature of research that can impact on professional practice.

To conclude, Chapter 10 returns to the diversity of spatial environments outlined in Figure 0.1 – showing how life-changing experiences are seen within and between levels, and what the future may hold. I consider that now is the time to bring to environmental gerontology this broader understanding of the interaction between person and environment. Reflection is given to issues raised across the book, theoretical development is reconsidered and future questions are raised.

Sheila Peace, October 2021

1

Person and environment

Introduction

Environmental gerontologists who are concerned with researching the context of adult human experience and behaviour in later life regard person/environment (P–E) interaction as pivotal to ageing well. Consequently, Chapter 1 opens with the actor and their stage – the separate characteristics of older *people* and their *environment* based on lives in Western developed countries. By discussing these separately, they are then brought together to recognise interaction between them in everyday experiences. Finally, we move beyond this individualised interaction within specific contexts, recognising that P–E also must be addressed at a collective level. This has implications both in terms of levels of interaction and the methodology by which the evidence base and research methods, particularly participatory studies, are supported.

Under the heading of Person (P), attention is paid to the boundaries of ageing, in other words how an older person is defined in this text. Consideration is given to 'successful' or 'active' ageing and proposed definitions of 'third' and 'fourth' ages. Such definitions are grounded in a heterogeneity that sees each individual as uniquely gendered and ethnically, sexually and culturally distinct. Late life experience is built on an understanding of the self that takes a wider life course perspective. All these characteristics have implications for P–E interaction, and awareness of this diversity is necessary before underlying theoretical perspectives are addressed in Chapter 2. Environment (E) then comes to the fore, with the central concerns being space, place and materiality. The underlying relationship between space and place as social, economic, psychological and cultural is unpacked before public and private domains are examined. The issue of materiality is then considered through both material and immaterial worlds, leading to personal experiences of the attachment to place. This discussion captures both global and local contexts.

The chapter ends by bringing the two main components centre stage to discuss their interface – how an older person and their particular spatial environment come together through everyday living. Behaviour is examined at a local or 'micro-' level and yet by using a biopsychosocial approach, a person's well-being subject to varied concerns relating to their physical and cognitive health is experienced wherever they are. These are embodied understandings, a part of a person's sense of being, and personal behaviour relates to a culturally specific environment that may or may not be enabling. The aim here is to provide examples that ground the theoretical perspectives discussed in Chapter 2.

Person (P)

Labelling later life

Across the second half of the 20th century, debates that began in the US focused on how older people may come to disengage from or engage with wider society. These debates were at the root of disengagement theory (Cummings and Henry, 1963), in which it was argued that society and the aged withdrew from each other. Later, this position was challenged through activity theory and successful ageing (Havighurst, 1961; Rowe and Kahn, 1998; Bengtson, 2016), for which agency, control, personal engagement and participation were key terms. The latter more positive view influenced the policy framework for active ageing, which has been defined as follows:

> The word 'active' refers to continuing participation in social, economic, cultural, spiritual and civic affairs, not just the ability to be physically active or to participate in the labour force. Older people who retire from work and those who are ill or live with disabilities can remain active contributors to their families, peers, communities and nations. Active ageing aims to extend healthy life expectancy and quality of life for all people as they age including those who are frail, disabled and in need of care. (WHO, 2002, p 12)

This comment defines 'active' as living in an enabling world where people in later life feel empowered to participate, if that is their wish, and to have the resource and social capital within communities (see Putnam, 2000) to make that choice. The resources needed for those living with long-term health conditions or growing cognitive impairment is acknowledged in later World Health Organization (WHO) reports, in which the concept of healthy ageing is recognised (WHO, 2015a, 2015b, 2017a).

Recent critiques of the concept of successful ageing have revealed its complex and contradictory nature. While this positive approach is based within a neoliberal tradition that supports individualisation within consumer societies, it neglects to understand the social inequality faced by those experiencing poverty and discrimination (see Katz and Casalanti, 2015; Rubinstein and de Meideros, 2015). This critique is relevant to the question posed here: how are ageing and later life defined within a discussion of the environments of ageing? To explore this further, we engage with the sociological debate from developed nations where extended life expectancy has led to a discussion of life stages that are defined as the third and fourth ages. It is argued here that these stages impact on how society and individuals view P–E interaction in later life.

The starting point is the market for retirement housing provided by the independent/commercial sector within the UK, an income-rich, consumer-oriented country, where advertising can be aimed at those aged 55 and over. Here is an anonymised example:

Set on Beechwood Avenue in Notown, Heresville is nestled in a seemingly rural location within 0.8 miles of a station for trains to the city for theatres, galleries and shops. These are shared ownership luxury apartments at their best for those aged 55 and over who aren't seeking to buy outright.

Family and carers may come and visit, and younger family are of course welcome.

Such advertising targets specific groups, commonly couples or singles who have retired from paid employment with financial assets, and may aim to provide a 'home for life' – which could be 30–40 years. This situates particular people within an environment where their stage of life is based not only on chronological time but also on generational, cohort, socio-economic, heterosexual and ethnic differences within an extremely heterogeneous population. While advertisements may be aimed at those who are aged 55 and over, in the main new residents are commonly in their late 70s (Park and Porteus, 2018, p 28). Darton et al's (2012) comparison of those living in extra-care housing (ECH) and care homes shows how over 65 per cent of those living in ECH are women, with nearly 60 per cent widowed, divorced or separated, compared with 73 per cent of care home residents being in those categories. These forms of communal living are predominantly a women's world, a point that is returned to in later chapters concerning the meaning of home. As this age-related community ages in place, they experience blurred boundaries between their ages and needs – an issue that is picked up in Chapter 7.

Before returning to the environments in which people age, the issue of age labelling should be discussed. This is where divisions are made between those identified as baby boomers or third agers, often equated, or fourth agers; this is visualised stereotypically in Figure 1.1 and from a life course perspective in Figure 1.2. These divisions are simple and allied to other stereotypes – the young old and the old/oldest old, and statistical divisions between those who are 65 and over or 85 and over. This rhetoric is commonplace, and the typology needs to be considered alongside a global policy framework that emphasises successful and healthy ageing within all societies, as outlined

Figure 1.1: Labelling later life

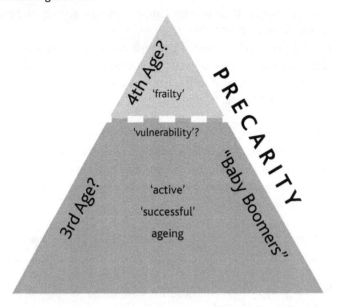

earlier (WHO, 2002, 2015a). How is successful ageing seen in relation to the lives of people who are in deep old age (see Grenier et al, 2017, 2020) and often at the end of their lives?

The expression baby boomers is a socially constructed term that is given in many developed nations to birth cohorts born during the post-Second World War period of population expansion (Phillipson, 2007b). This has temporal variation internationally: for example, in the US and Australia it refers to people born in 1946–64 (Biggs et al, 2007), while two 'waves' are noted in the UK – the first 1945–55 and the second 1956–64, reflecting different peaks in the birth rate (Phillipson et al, 2008).

Drawing on the work of Laslett (1989, 1996) concerning the third age, Gilleard and Higgs consider how demographic, socio-economic and cultural change since the Second World War has led some to a lifestyle that is personally agentic and fulfilling after retirement from paid employment (Gilleard and Higgs, 2002). They comment that 'The baby boom generation broke the mould of the modern lifecourse' (2002, p 376). This group is seen to underpin the third age, a part of the consumer society that embraces new technology, and people with 'greater education, income, social and material security and free time in and out of work' (p 377). This position has also been noted in the US and other Western developed countries (Katz, 2005; Jones et al, 2008).

The positive lifestyle noted for baby boomers has not been the experience of all, and there are cultural, gendered, generational and locational (health, economic) inequalities across developed countries that impact on particular groups such as divorced men, those who never married, ethnic minorities and those with limited education (Dannefer, 2003a; Evandrou and Falkingham, 2006). Phillipson et al (2008), through a review of academic, literary and media sources, consider the advantages and disadvantages faced by first-wave UK baby boomers, then aged 54–63. While they comment on media rhetoric, which portrays the baby boomers as a selfish generation who have benefited from living through a particular historical period, and as consumerists with little concern for the global environment, they also identify this group as coping with working beyond retirement age, caring for parents and partners, offering intergenerational support in times of austerity and being involved in voluntary community work (Ogg and Renaut, 2006). Additionally, they raise societal concerns such as the impact on pensions provision and the pressure on funding health and care services. These are issues that have also been raised in other countries. For example, Putney and Bengston (2005) comment on boomer stress through dual employment and caring responsibilities in the US. While Atsushi (2005) notes how baby boomers in Japan (born 1947–49), who became the wealthier members of corporate enterprises, were faced with a rising pension age and extended working life as the country became a super-aged population.

Although it can be seen that some of the boomer generation may have a higher standard of living than their parents, there is a diversity of experience. Of value to the discussion of environments and ageing, even though it relates to a UK-based study, is Phillipson et al's (2008) comment on how first-wave boomers continued to nurture the development of the nuclear family, their lifestyle influenced by 'first, the surge in popularity of marriage during and immediately after the second world war, this providing the basis for high levels of domestic consumption (Sandbrook, 2005); second, the steady growth of owner-occupation during the 1950s and 1960s; third, the rapid growth of suburban living' (2008, p 9). The influence of this housing history is seen in Chapters 5 and 6.

After this discussion of a third age, we focus on the fourth age, although recognising the dangers of compartmentalising people in these ways where a tension may exist at all ages between a loss-deficit model of ageing and a more positive approach. Again Gilleard and Higgs (2010, 2011, 2013; Higgs and Gilleard, 2015) are authors who address the 'cultural field' of the former and the 'social imaginary' of the latter, contrasting lives with social agency and lives that experience personal dependency through increased disability. This brings us to the lives of those experiencing deep old age and those caring for them, where attitudes underpinning a social imaginary take us to different levels of explanation.

I find the following definition truly negative: 'the fourth age can be better understood as representative of a feared "state of becoming", an ascribed community of otherness, set apart from the everyday experiences and practices of later life' (Gilleard and Higgs, 2013, p 368). These authors take into account issues of 'abjection' of the body, senility, the medicalisation of ageing and what they call 'the "densification" of disability within long term care settings'; the latter predominantly affecting older women (Gilleard and Higgs, 2013, p 374).

I would argue that the labels of the third and fourth age mark a fluid boundary within the life course rather than something more inflexible that exists in the thoughts of some academics and policy makers. Figure 1.2 aims to capture the ways in which older individuals, although living with vulnerability that may lead to frailty, may be recognised as successful individuals and in their own way active. So, while there is always an element of truth in ideas surrounding the fourth age, it should never be seen as just a period of frailty, vulnerability, ill health and dependence.

Lloyd (2015) highlights the importance of enabling self-identity at times when being agentic may become less possible and have to be delegated to others within interdependent relationships (Leece and Peace, 2009; Lloyd et al, 2014). The context in which one lives becomes crucial here in terms of facilitating levels of personal and delegated autonomy (Collopy, 1988). At a time of life when cognitive impairment is increasing, we should seek new ways to exploit the interaction between environment and ageing, building on ways of maintaining the self through person- and relationship-centred care and dementia-friendly environments. Indeed, Grenier et al (2017) take the incidence and experience of cognitive impairment in advanced old age

Figure 1.2: A life course perspective

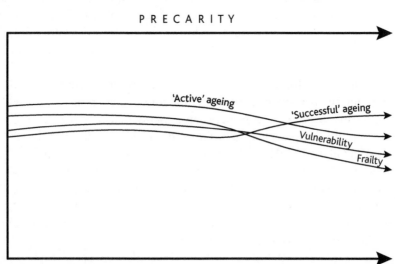

as an example of living without personal agency, utilising the concept of precarity, which indicates situations of insecurity and uncertainty that can be challenged and supported (Grenier and Phillipson, 2013; Grenier et al, 2020). In adopting a radically different approach, they look at the vulnerabilities that people face and how to address them.

The typology of ageing discussed here influences the ways in which people are identified in particular situations and settings, how older people perceive themselves and how they interact with others.

Understanding the person

Variations in personal experience, competence or ability over time change depending on life's gains and losses, and these are influenced by gender, ethnicity, socio-economic status, education and culture (Dannefer, 2003a). In later life, competency is often related to health, well-being and subsequent behaviour, reflected in the earlier labelling of the third and fourth ages. In Figure 1.3, these aspects are brought together with social factors to indicate the set of issues that contribute to the personal.

The life course is added to the divisions and concepts outlined earlier to indicate the importance of personal development over time. Individual ageing does not have normative patterns and will therefore be unique.

Figure 1.3: Facets of person (P)

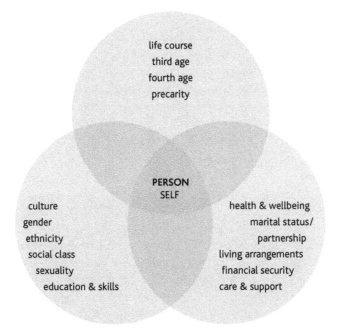

Nevertheless, as Dannefer and Settersten (2010) discuss, there are different ways in which a life course perspective can contribute to understanding the ageing process through historical time. For those who have lived across the 20th century, they show how it can:

- enable appreciation of social change over time, eg the coming of computerisation;
- provide recognition of diversity, inequality and variability among older people through biography embedded within social structure;
- foreground 'linked lives' – how life is 'shaped by the needs, circumstances and choices of others'; and
- allow understanding of age-stratification through institutions such as education, employment or retirement; and how segregating older people from participation is being challenged during recent times of de-institutionalisation and individualisation.

(see Dannefer and Settersten, 2010, pp 12–19)

These issues underpin the approach known as Cumulative Advantage and Disadvantage, in which experience across time contributes to expectations and inequalities (Dannefer and Uhlenberg, 1999; Dannefer, 2003a, 2003b).

Other authors contribute additional views. For example, there is seminal and ongoing work by developmental and lifespan psychologists who are considering universal and individual internalisation and adaptation to continuity and change over the lifetime (e.g. Erikson, 1982; Erikson et al, 1986; Baltes and Baltes, 1990). Grenier (2012) critiques current models of the life course and develops the subject of transitions to question successful ageing in relation to the fourth age. The important perspective of Rubinstein and de Medeiros (2004), who review the relationship between ecology and the self, also needs to be considered: they identify the importance of self, cultural and personal meaning and embodiment; this analysis is considered in Chapter 2.

Within this wider perspective, we can continue to contextualise the older person, unpacking the social to consider the where, why and how of everyday lives.

Social issues

Social issues that underpin people's living environments are discussed here through a consideration of family change, living arrangements, financial circumstances and housing tenure. As a brief examination of complex topics, it draws on texts from a number of international edited collections (Johnson et al, 2005; Dannefer and Phillipson, 2010; Twigg and Martin, 2015a). Where statistics are presented they focus on the UK or England.

Ways of living

> Parallel to population ageing, marked changes [have] occurred in families: in timing of family transitions; in family structures; in patterns of family formation and dissolution; ensuing diversification of families and household forms. (Lowenstein, 2005, p 403)

Over the past century, while heterosexual marriage remains central to family formation, family structure has changed through early and late parenthood, childlessness, increasing rates of divorce, separation, remarriage and singlehood, and a greater number of civil partnerships and arrangements where people have a relationship but live apart for some or all of the time (see Bildgardt and Oberg, 2019). Acknowledging how these changes affect those retiring from paid employment in their mid- to late 60s, particularly in Western developed countries, an increase in all forms of coupledom, including co-habiting and lesbian, gay, bisexual, transgender and queer (LGBTQ) partners, is noted (Tomassini et al, 2004; Lowenstein and Katz, 2010; King et al, 2020). Gender differences also vary in relation to marital status, and in countries where divorce/separation has increased, remarriage may be more common for men than for women, although same-sex partnerships and caregiving roles are also acknowledged (Calasanti, 2020). Basic statistics concerning marital status and household composition for the UK are given in Research summary 1.1.

Research summary 1.1: Social characteristics of older people in the UK

At the time of writing, available demographic data is based on the 2011 census, with more recent reports based on population estimates and projections given by the Office of National Statistics (ONS) (e.g. ONS, 2018a). Data from the 2021 census will be published by ONS in 2022/23.

Data (000s) (%) for those aged	65–74	75–84	85+
2014	6,195 (9.6%)	3,708 (5.7%)	1,503 (2.3%)
2021	6,791 (10%)	4,284 (6.3%)	1,717 (2.5%)
2041	7,996 (11%)	6,549 (9.0%)	3,247 (4.5%)

Source: Laing (2018), Table 1.7

For England and Wales, the 2011 census also showed that for those aged 65 and over:

- 57 per cent (5.3 million) were married or in a civil partnership;
- 29 per cent (2.7 million) were widowed or the surviving partner from a civil partnership;

- 8.7 per cent (798,000) were divorced or formerly in a civil partnership now dissolved;
- 5.5 per cent (509,000) were single (never married or in a civil partnership).

(Source: ONS, 2013)

More recent analysis shows that in 2019 marriage or civil partnership is the most common form of marital status for just over 50 per cent of all adults aged 16 and over in England and Wales. This is slowly declining over time for all ages except those aged 70 and over, where, particularly for older women, they are more likely to be married or divorced in 2019 than a decade earlier, and less likely to be widowed (ONS, 2020a).

While there is a greater incidence of older couples, ONS data also shows that in 2019 of an estimated 12.4 million people aged 65 and over living in England and Wales, 32 per cent were living alone, 65 per cent of whom were women (ONS, 2020b).

Living alone is more commonly the situation of the oldest old in the UK, where data also shows that nearly 15 per cent of those aged over 85 live in care home environments (Laing, 2018).

As noted for living in communal environments, these relationship changes may impact on living arrangements, as the current composition of the nuclear and extended family is fundamental to household formation. Tomassini et al (2004) and Stula (2012) provide comparative data for Europe and the US showing that since the Second World War there has been an increase in the number of older people, especially women, living in a one-person household where loneliness can be an issue (see Scharf and de Jong Gieveld, 2008; Dahlberg and McKee, 2014; Barreto et al, 2021).

Tomassini et al (2004) also consider the impact of family change on demography and culture within policy contexts that concern housing, health and social care. They indicate the degree to which childlessness varies between cohorts, impacting on intergenerational co-residence and the degree of social support across generations. In addition, financial resources and higher levels of education can lead to greater residential independence (Glaser and Tomassini, 2000). In making comparisons between (a) north-western Europe and the US and (b) central and southern Europe, they identify the individualistic culture of the former and the family culture of the latter, showing some association between on the one hand independent living and less frequent family contact, and on the other greater co-living and proximity to kin (Tomassini et al, 2004).

Informal family care, though diverse, is also a key part of enabling older people to age in place. In reporting on the EUROFAMCARE project, which drew on data from national surveys in five countries (Germany, Greece, Italy, Poland, Sweden, UK), Lowenstein and Katz (2010) state that the 'majority of family caregivers (over 80 per cent) felt caring was worthwhile and that they coped well even under difficult circumstances', adding that 'The positive value attached to family caregiving is probably the most critical element in ensuring good-quality care for older people with high levels of dependency.' (2010, p 193). There is, however, a balance between formal and informal care, and Lowenstein suggests that 'The specific mix is related to three factors: (1) family norms and care preferences; (2) family culture that guides the level of readiness to use public services; and (3) availability, accessibility, quality, and cost of services' (Lowenstein, 2005, p 407).

In contrast, Aboderin (2004, 2016), with particular focus on sub-Saharan Africa, comments both on diversity between nations and a lack of knowledge concerning ageing within the developing countries of the Global South. In considering variation in family support between generations, she shows how households are experiencing degrees of continuity and change (Aboderin, 2005). Family ties may still be strong, with many older people living with younger kin in two or more generation households, but levels of support – emotional, economic, personal – may vary. For younger generations, labour migration can result in living at a distance from the family home, and paid employment for women is becoming more common for those who are part of the same community. Consequently, family support, while common, is changing – leading to greater ambiguity regarding filial obligation at times of increasing economic austerity, while grandparents are providing more child support for grandchildren (Gangopadhyay, 2017). These changes are presenting similar patterns of intergenerational assistance to those seen in more developed nations.

Financial security

There is considerable diversity in people's material resources in older age, and this is central to where and how people live. As this quote from the WHO's report on ageing and health shows, inequality and levels of poverty exist in the developed world and for the oldest old: 'The prevalence of poverty among older people compared with that in the general population varies significantly across the world. In Europe, one in every five older persons has an income below the poverty line, with people older than 80 years being the most severely affected' (WHO, 2015a, p 162).

In later life, financial security draws on four main sources: earnings, pensions, social transfers/benefits and assets. Earnings are a major resource for many who either go on working or are encouraged to work beyond retirement age or to learn new skills and maintain an employment base. Pensions are of crucial importance to most, whether occupational, private or state, with non-contributory old age pensions long established in developed nations and being developed throughout the world (Walker, 1999, 2005). In addition, some may depend on social transfers for additional maintenance, while those at the other extreme will have assets based on owner-occupied property, inherited or organisational wealth, or intergenerational transfers (Walker, 1990).

Despite this diverse income base, the patriarchal employment infrastructure across nations means that certain groups, particularly women, are more at risk of financial insecurity. Inequalities are seen for

- women, who are more likely to be poorer than men;
- older women, with fewer pension rights gained through working life;
- older women, who are more likely to be poorer than men of the same age;
- older people living with grandchildren in developing countries; those who are living alone, often widowed older women, are at risk of poverty – rates exceed 40 per cent in Australia, Ireland, Japan, Mexico, Republic of Korea and the US (see WHO, 2015a, p 162).

Given this background to material resources, differences exist across the older population in the UK. Data from the Department of Work and Pensions (DWP) show that younger pensioners have higher incomes than those aged 75 and over (DWP, 2015; Independent Age, 2016). As of October 2021, the state pension age has risen to 66 for both men and women, and while people are receiving various levels of state pension, at the time of writing the weekly state pension was £179.60 per week for those who have paid 35 years of National Insurance contributions.

While pensioner couples are more likely to have other income sources, including private pensions and assets, 2.1 million or 18 per cent of pensioners in the UK live in poverty, having income 60 per cent lower than the median household income after housing costs (Francis-Devine, 2021). In relation to older people and living environments, this is said to particularly affect those from minority ethnic groups, private renters, social renters and those living in areas with higher levels of deprivation (Joseph Rowntree Foundation, 2021). These financial issues have a direct effect on housing tenure, living arrangements and accommodation, with an associated impact on accessibility. In the UK, the housing infrastructure is long established, complex and grounded in different forms of housing type. Issues of housing adequacy are discussed in Chapter 5.

The changing nature of intergenerational living, family support and care across generations, together with the continuing increase in the oldest old, are principal factors that can influence living arrangements in later life. Levels of inequality have been noted. In relation to particular environments of ageing, the growing incidence of cognitive impairment through dementia continues to impact on long-term care. We turn now to Environment.

Environment (E)

In the following sections, conceptual issues of space, place and materiality, critical themes for ageing, are discussed. They affect the relationship between person and environment. In Figure 1.4, the range of situations covered by the term 'environment' is indicated, and ageing in place, staying put, age segregation and age integration are important concepts.

Space and place

Andrews et al (2013) argue that many disciplines have contributed to what is seen as the 'spatial turn', highlighting how the early work of geographers Golant (1972) and Rowles (1978) introduced this perspective to social gerontology in order to better understand the daily lives of people in later life. Here a broader disciplinary base is used to discuss the spatial turn that contributes to environmental gerontology and geographical gerontology.

Space and place are often discussed alongside each other as key aspects of environment. Here, space is seen as an abstract concept that surrounds us with a depth and breadth that may be perceived and mapped as natural landscape in which human action expresses various forms of social

Figure 1.4: Facets of environment (E)

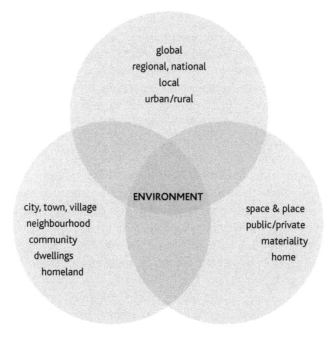

space. If social space is a dwelling, city, region or nation, then the social construction of place may lead to a location called home or homeland, within political territorial boundaries. Both spaces and places embody movement and meaning, and the concept of home is a central theme for understanding harmony and dissonance in later life. These views are not unique, and are influenced by humanistic geographers such as Relph (1976) and Buttimer (1980) as well as Yi-Fu Tuan, who commented in 1977:

> What begins as undifferentiated space becomes place as we get to know it better and endow it with value. Architects talk about the spatial qualities of place; they can equally well speak of the locational (place) qualities of space. The ideas of 'space' and 'place' require each other for definition. From the security and stability of place we are aware of the openness, freedom, and threat of space, and vice versa. Furthermore, if we think of space as that which allows movement, then place is pause; each pause in movement makes it possible for location to be transformed into place. (Tuan, 1977, p 6)

What is understood in the abstract may be transformed ideologically into something that displays different levels of power, with consequences for value and meaning. The work of Henri Lefebvre developed the idea of social space, in which urban and rural environments are discussed in terms of the context of everyday life, the social relations of production and lived space – which can be alienating. His early work pursued issues of social class rather than other issues of diversity (see 1991).

Urban sociologists and human geographers are pivotal in these debates. For example, both David Harvey and Doreen Massey have discussed the social construction of place. Harvey's view (1973, 1996) is concerned with the political economy of place under capitalism and issues of social justice (Harvey, 2000), where a threat to particular places (e.g. disappearance of employment) reinforces the personal need for a sense of place, drawing on Harvey's work on the importance of 'place-as-dwelling' (1973) and the value of the geographical imagination (Castree, 2007, 2011).

In contrast, Massey theorises space and place as an ongoing process (2005). While the global economy may be central to globalisation by introducing 'the power-geometry of it all' (1994, p 156) she reminds us that it is certain people in certain positions who drive how space is transformed and experienced as place. Within this social construction, she argues that issues of gender and ethnicity alongside social class can lead to very different experiences. She does not discuss ageing or later life as a defining variable, but her comment here on urban living for a pensioner demonstrates the impact of the global on consumerisation and social exclusion:

there are those who are simply on the receiving end of time-space compression. The pensioner in a bed-sit in any inner city in the country, eating British working-class style fish and chips from a Chinese take-away, watching a US film on a Japanese television, and not daring to go out after dark. And anyway the public transport's been cut…

There is in other words a highly complex differentiation. There are differences in the degree of movement and communication, but also in the degree of control and of initiation. The ways in which people are placed within 'time-space compression' are highly complicated and extremely varied. (Massey, 1993 in Cresswell, 2004, pp 65–6)

She goes on to rethink the terms 'sense of place', 'locality' and 'regionality', arguing for the importance of ubiquitous social relations that give places multiple identities and histories that are relational. She was a founding advocate of relationality, discussed in Chapter 2, providing a different response to a sense of place where globalisation may provoke anxiety or reactionary responses, is inward looking, nationalistic, has values boundaries and is defined predominantly through the global economy. There are parallels here to issues regarding the spatiality of ageing raised in later chapters (see Peace, 2015; Boccagni, 2017). In later work, Massey (2005) gives a comprehensive account of her understanding of space in relation to regionality, globalisation, identity and diversity, She develops the concept of time-spaces, indicating how they are inseparable from the establishment of ongoing power inequalities that influence the meaning of space at a specific time.

Power relations have been examined spatially in relation to gender differences and other aspects of diversity, showing how issues of control and human agency are central to experience and that the environment can present barriers to participation (Rose, 1993; Imrie, 1996; Bondi, 1998; McDowell, 1999). In the field of ageing and later life, Laws (1994, 1995) was an exception, with early conceptual work showing how space and place are central to the development of social identity in later life at both individual and collective levels. She argued that in relation to age there are 'several dimensions of spatiality – accessibility, mobility, motility, spatial scale and spatial segregation – which are involved in the mutual constitution of places and identities' (Laws, 1997, p 93). Each of these issues can be used to examine both the environmental and structural barriers that may prevent an older person from being integrated and connected with the wider community.

More recently, authors from health, social and cultural geography have addressed different levels of spatial scale in relation to the lives of older people (Andrews and Phillips, 2005; Andrews et al, 2013, 2018). At one extreme, population ageing can be defined through issues of health and well-being, with mortality rates being used to consider policy developments for health and social care across regions and nations (Warnes, 1999; WHO, 2002; Ford and Smith, 2008). Alternatively, concerns may lie with 'intimacy at a distance', where family dispersal prevents face-to-face informal care with a parent and leads to ongoing telephone, Skype or similar communications and partnership with formal home carers (Milligan et al, 2010). In health geography, the terms 'therapeutic landscapes' for issues of emotional healing and 'landscapes of care' have developed (Conradson, 2005; Milligan and Wiles, 2010; Williams, 2017) People have a sense of understanding place, and Wiles (2005a) conceptualises six different approaches to place when considering care in gerontology:

- place as a process – a part of social relations with family life or caring relationships;
- place as ongoing negotiation – moves, adaptations, changes made;
- contested places – between different people caring in different places;
- place expressing power relations – staff versus residents, gender issues in caring roles;
- places as simultaneously symbolic, social, physical – such as a care home;
- places as interrelated – home in neighbourhood, in town, in county, in nation.

These spatially defined issues embrace individual, social, economic and political processes (Blakemore, 1999), and Andrews et al (2013) comment that 'from a humanistic perspective, in many ways the idea of social space has brought abstract space "to life" in gerontology' (p 1344). This geographic literature contributes to the interdisciplinarity of understanding environments of ageing, which is returned to in Chapter 2.

Over time, different disciplines have considered human agency at similar or varied levels of spatial scale. In 1951, the psychologist Kurt Lewin discussed human interaction within a 'lifespace' that involved the 'psychological space' in which the P–E interaction takes place. Psychosocial aspects of personal behaviour in natural or built environments and social settings has been the concern of environmental psychology since the 1960s (see founders Proshanksy, 1976; 1978, Proshanksy et al, 1983; Canter, 1977, 2008, 2012; Scott and Canter, 1997). We return to place theory in Chapter 2. These are different perspectives for discussing what has been defined by some as the reduced life space of people as they grow older, with changes over the life course (Pastalan and Carson, 1970; Verbrugge et al, 1994; Johnson et al, 2020).

The meaning of 'place' in social gerontology takes us back to Tuan's quote, where it is defined as 'the locational (place) qualities of space'. Here, the definitions vary culturally from the nation in which one lives or moves to, from and within; to places that are specific and known to an individual or group, with an accepted function such as a hospital, community centre, retirement housing; to places known only through different forms of media; to places of personal attachment. These different forms of place lead to more abstract meanings of space within place, and we are reminded here that 'the meaning of space and place are not human universals, but depend on the larger cultural systems of which they are part' (Rubinstein and de Medeiros, 2004, p 62).

Public and private

Different aspects of space and place can be defined as public or private in terms of spatial action and agency. Elsewhere, this dichotomy has been defined:

> In terms of space – 'public' may be explained in the language of communal, civic, free, open and unrestricted but it can also be owned independently, a consumerized space such as in markets, shopping malls, […]; spaces that have become both regulated and open to surveillance (Madanipour, 1999, 2003). Public space may be known or unknown territory; somewhere that people find easy to travel through following familiar routes and 'short cuts'; or unfamiliar – which may be disorienting, leading to a sense of insecurity, or stimulating, leading to new experience. In contrast 'private' may be recognized in the language of individualized, familial, domestic, concealed, privileged, restricted, elite, intimate and may also be known or unknown; defined widely or only open to a limited group such as the domestic home or the consulting rooms of the doctor's surgery in contrast with the waiting rooms. Historically, this duality of public/private has been linked to social constructions of gender so that there are stereotypical associations of public with masculine and work, and private with feminine and home (Arendt, 1958; McDowell, 1999). In more recent decades changing lifestyles, particularly in relation to employment, have come to challenge these assumptions (Bondi, 1998). (Peace, 2013, p 30)

Various authors conceptualise space, behaviour and everyday living through different disciplines. For example, early research by British architectural scholars Hillier and Hanson (1984) demonstrates how space features, in the form and function of buildings, through spatial configuration, relates to issues of access, reach and depth that impacts on behaviour and the use of buildings. These issues are central to Percival's (2002) discussion of the use of domestic space across the daily lives of older people. This enables the concept of progressive privacy within settings that is seen to different degrees in all types of housing, whether ordinary or specialised. The environmental psychologist Robert Sommer's early work (1969) on the behavioural basis of design has been influential in showing how personal or intimate space centring on an invisible immediate distance around the body can be a crucial indicator of comfort and safety in interactions. This relates to how people personalise the spaces they live in, thereby presenting a form of ownership, an issue seen in the theoretical work of Rubinstein and de Mederios (2015), where an embodiment of space is linked to the private nature of place. In contrast, the architect and planner Oscar Newman (1972) discusses defensible space and territoriality, where the protection of space can lead to a sense of ownership. This may concern an individual or community, and can be seen as contested space – a physical space at the centre of conflicting interests between different social actors (Mitchell et al, 2003; Holland et al, 2007; Skinner and Winterton, 2018). It may be studied in both public and private spaces and places, as seen in empirical research referred to in Chapters 4 and 9.

The conceptual work of two eminent sociologists, Erving Goffman and Pierre Bourdieu, also contributes to this discussion. First, the so-called presentation of self foregrounds how a person's identity can be conveyed through different ways of being. Here, symbolic interactionist Erving Goffman's use of the dramatic analogy of performance in front and back regions relates to how public and private are recognised (Goffman, 1959). In a study of environment and identity in later life, the current author and colleagues referred to Goffman's work as follows:

> He makes this comment in relation to the 'front regions': 'The performance of an individual in the front regions may be seen as an effort to give the appearance that his activity in the region maintains and embodies certain standards' (1959, p. 110). ... In contrast 'back regions' allow the person to 'relax'; '... he can drop his front, forgo speaking his lines, and step out of character' (Goffman, 1959, p 115). (Peace et al, 2006, p 87)

This analogy was used to consider behavioural difference for older people living in various locations and housing types, for example when discussing how the liminal space from the front or back door to the street or garden enables semi-public or semi-private activity. Goffman's concern with how behaviour is contextualised continued in his seminal study of mental health facilities, *Asylums* (1961), where his analysis of institutionalisation paralleled that of Barton (1959) and Kleemeier (1961) – and contributed to a literature of dysfunction (Jack, 1998) discussed in Chapter 8.

More recently, the work of Bourdieu (1977, 1998) and the concept of habitus has become an important tool for research, providing an overarching framework for studying the relationship in later life between space, place and habitat in which the public and the private are embedded. Gopinath et al comment that 'habitus is a person's embodied, taken for granted way of thinking, being and acting, operating at a pre-conscious level' (2018, p 29). Bourdieu utilises the factors of fields (social spaces of engagement), capital (resources) and practice (action) to enable habitus (see Bourdieu and Wacquant, 1992). Various forms of capital – economic, social, cultural and symbolic – are part of the complexity of habitus that can be seen in the practice of the everyday demonstrated through individual routine and habit. While Bourdieu focuses on understanding issues of social class within capitalist societies, he provides a structure that has been used by many to consider ways of living (Hillier and Rooksby, 2002). In discussing the meaning of home across environments of ageing, we can consider the conceptual thinking of Wiles, Massey, Goffman and Bourdieu to aid our understanding.

Materiality

My interest in the meaning of home and the place in which people live introduces a third feature of environments of ageing – materiality. While Katz gives a broad definition, 'a term to identify the various places, technologies, things, rhythms, designs, mobilities and environments in which our experience of ageing is grounded and observable' (2019, p 1), we focus here on the relationship between personal identity and place attachment. Associations with place are not only social, but also embedded in Western developed countries through the consumption of material objects (Jones, et al, 2008) – furniture, equipment, artefacts, artworks, structures – that may convey particular significance and agency in later life (see Rubinstein, 1987; Rowles et al, 2004; Sherman and Dacher, 2005). In the spheres of art, craft and design, materiality may centre on the material itself across all mediums – from metals to media – with diverse skills incorporating the technological that produce artefacts with emotional, pleasurable and functional engagement.

In this text, there is a focus on materiality primarily through housing design, the importance of possessions and the development of equipment seen by some as assistive. The domestic dwelling has architecturally designed spaces for daily living activities – cooking, eating, sleeping and so on – labelled as kitchen, living room, bedroom or cultural equivalents. Yet people's use of space within the home adapts to meet their needs: it has multiple functions and meanings. We work at the kitchen table, yet if cooking is a pleasure then this space may have special meaning; access to technology enables media to stream in all rooms for all ages; the exercise bike sits in the living room and the sofa bed can change the room's function from gym to sleeping area; while a new type of gardening space may emerge through an added conservatory, balcony or window box. The 'smart' building or equipment may develop alongside, or within, an ageing housing stock, and there is a need to address both house adaptation and sustainability. How far someone becomes involved with the shape and design of their built environment very much depends on the facilitation of the expert as a spatial agent, and in Chapters 5 and 7 the co-design of alternative living environments, where individual expertise is brought together with the architectural or ergonomic specialist, is considered.

The dwelling accommodates objects and artefacts that make settings comfortable, enabling and meaningful. In this area of material culture, it is not surprising that 'new materialism' is more concerned with a philosophical approach to how humans engage or absorb materials so that they are socialised through them and they become symbols of ourselves (Csikszentmihalyi and Rochberg-Halton, 1981; Miller, 2008, 2010). For the anthropologist Miller (2005), materiality in terms of an artefact can be tangible and simply defined, yet mask the complex interaction with sense of self (Bachelard, 1958; Miller, 2001). In talking about 'objects' he says: 'The less we are aware of them, the more powerfully they can determine our expectations by setting the scene and ensuring normative behaviour, without being open to challenge. They determine what takes place to the extent that we are unconscious of their capacity to do so' (2005, p 5). There are echoes here of psychologists Lawton and Nahemow's (1973) environmental docility hypothesis regarding P–E fit and adaptation regarding comfort and proactivity, discussed further in Chapter 2. Both perspectives contribute to understanding the meaning of home.

Through this discussion of person and environment as separate entities, the way they meet is eluded to through meanings, attitudes to and behaviour within space and place. To conclude, I bring P–E together within the daily lives of older people through a health perspective.

The reality of the everyday

Health, behaviour and environment

The biopsychosocial interface between a person and their environment is the focus of this final section. The aim here is to consider how behavioural patterns that relate to biological ageing lead to a relationship with environment through a human ecology approach that sits alongside the social model of health. This approach is similar to that of Robert Kleemeier, a founder of environmental gerontology who provides an early account of how bodily change with age can relate to dwelling conditions concerning such issues as lighting, heating and noise (Kleemeier, 1959). This is part of the ongoing debate in gerontology that has been seen more recently in the cross-national

ENABLE-AGE research reported in Chapters 6 and 9, in which Iwarsson et al (2004) introduce the relationship between housing and health in very old age, commenting that 'the sharp rise in sensory impairment, mobility and gait problems, and dementia during the "fourth age" is a major threat to independent living in ordinary housing' (p 81).

Here, the association between housing and health could consider poor sleep or incontinence (Meadows et al, 2008; Venn and Arber, 2011; Bichard et al, 2012); instead, we focus briefly on dementia, which covers a range of cognitive impairment, sensory loss and mobility problems, conditions discussed in more detail later. While treatment or therapy may improve health conditions, prevention is not the focus of this section, although environmental adaptation both indoors and outdoors is considered in Chapters 5 and 9.

Cognitive change and dementia

Dementia is a global health concern (WHO, 2020a, 2015a, 2015b) that includes a number of conditions, with the most common being Alzheimer's disease and vascular dementia. It currently affects at least 50 million people across the world, with nearly 10 million new cases every year. There is currently no cure or modifying treatment. Over 800,500 people are living with dementia in the UK (NHS, 2020a; Public Health England, 2020), and while it is not an inevitable feature of ageing it is a leading cause of death in the UK. Women form a majority by almost 2:1 among this group.

Many people associate some memory loss, forgetfulness, misplacing things and 'absent-mindedness' as part of growing older, and some become anxious about developing a form of dementia (Whitbourne and Whitbourne, 2014, p 107), even if commonly this is not the case. Yet the experience of living with a form of dementia from early to late stage will see short-term memory loss gradually deepen, impacting on familiarity with people, place, time and space, which can alter personality and may be associated with wandering and agitation (Oruly, 2010). Depending on severity, a cognitive impairment may prevent people from carrying out normal daily activities or maintaining social relationships. However, while some comment that people with dementia may experience a 'shrinking world' (Duggan et al, 2008, p 191), more recent research is beginning to show the importance of person in place for maintaining social health as people with dementia engage with their local environment (Ward et al, 2018). This is discussed further in chapter 9.

The majority of people experiencing cognitive change and developing dementia live in the community in general needs housing, and access everyday services in buildings that are not specifically designed to meet their needs. This is an area that should be developed in terms of retrofitting current housing and providing more inclusive designs in relation to new builds. Over time, people with dementia will need greater support for the activities of daily living, and an enabling environment can be orientational, visually stimulating and facilitate security and safety, alongside changes in social/relational practice. People with forms of dementia are especially likely to attend healthcare buildings and live in care homes, and in Chapter 8 developments in design that do not lead to challenging behaviour, thereby increasing anxiety or agitation, are considered.

Sensory loss and mobility

In later life, sensory loss and changes to mobility can also combine to affect the ability to carry out activities at home or in the wider community. In the UK, approximately 2 million people are said to be living with sight loss, the majority of them older people, and there is a definite association with advanced age – older women and people from minority ethnic groups in particular having problems with certain conditions (RNIB, 2016), such as age-related macular degeneration, glaucoma, cataracts and diabetic retinopathy.

These conditions can have a particular impact when engaging with the wider community or carrying out activities within the home. Some people find going out without personal support a problem, and research shows how vision loss can lead to multiple disadvantages – including prevalence of falls, social isolation, depression and reduced emotional well-being (Wahl et al, 1999; Zimdars et al, 2012; Dhital et al, 2010; McManus and Lord, 2012; Peace et al, 2016, 2019). For a person with sensory loss, their circumstances may be compounded by, or compound, their mobility, and bringing these issues together indicates the importance of an environment that facilitates health-producing behaviour. In the home, adaptation through the use of stairlifts and walk-in showers may prevent falls, while walking outdoors in an environment where the danger of falling is at a minimum creates a feeling of security and safety. The inclusivity of initiatives to make the environment more age-friendly continues to be tested. For example, planning developments such as shared spaces where cars and pedestrians use the same road level leads to the loss of the pavement edge, which is of value to those who are vision impaired. Such planning should be labelled of ableist bias (Ward et al, 2018).

Person–environment interactions

In these two examples of the association of personal health and behaviour, it can be seen that the environmental context can be both enabling and disabling. We return to this form of interaction throughout the text, especially

Figure 1.5: Person–environment interaction

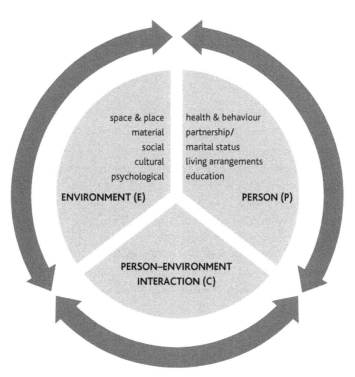

in relation to growing moves towards age-friendly and dementia-friendly cities and communities. How the environment actively helps to maintain well-being in later life is a central outcome for such initiatives, as seen in Chapters 4 and 10.

Conclusions

By ending this chapter with a discussion that focuses on biopsychosocial issues, the aim is to show that the relationship between person and environment is contextual. Figure 1.5 brings these three elements together, indicating how interactions are continuous, operating within different levels of spatial environment and personal experience. For everyone, individual circumstances affect behaviour, and where and how agency is developed and maintained impacts on feelings about self and association with others. Wider circumstances change over time, with environmental change being important for the consideration of ageing and later life. To develop this view, we need to revisit the theoretical perspectives that underpin environmental gerontology, to begin to judge whether the proposed spatial scales can be addressed through current thinking or need further development.

2

Theoretical development

Introduction

To establish the scope of this chapter, I return to two key factors. First, as outlined in Figure 0.1, environments of ageing can be seen on different but interrelating spatial scales. Second, the relationship between environments seen at these different levels relates to individual behaviour and quality of life, which is revealed through interactions. These factors are considered in the light of theoretical developments taken from two bodies of work, social gerontology (in particular environmental gerontology) and the developing theoretical literature in geographical gerontology that extends our understanding of ageing through the spatial turn, as seen in Chapter 1. In general, theoretical perspectives from social gerontology are centred on the individual based at the local- or micro-level, what can be called the near environment – the dwelling, neighbourhood or community, with some matters relating to city, town and village. The concern here is how ideas can be extended so that environments of ageing can be recognised at both meso- and macro-levels of analysis, involving individual and collective behaviour. Here, perspectives offered by geographical gerontology may be beneficial, as they extend interdisciplinarity and participatory methods and particular theoretical approaches.

Environmental gerontology: theoretical influences

As clinical, physiological and psychological aspects of gerontology were studied during the 20th century (Kontos, 2005a), a human ecological perspective developed in the US and in Europe, and this underpins many ideas in environmental gerontology (Kleemier, 1959, 1961; Bronfenbrenner, 1979; Bernard and Rowles, 2013; Rowles and Bernard, 2013). To discuss the historical and contemporary theory that has informed this field, literature concerned with the contextualisation of human ageing is drawn upon (see Peace et al, 2007; Oswald & Wahl, 2010; Scheidt and Schwarz, 2013). While this material originates across the social sciences, early theoretical development comes primarily from psychology and sociology. These disciplines capture the tension between individual and society that may be defined as person–environment (P–E) interaction.

Prior to the 1960s, early work in the US and Europe saw developmental psychologists identify the relationship between personal needs, motivating behaviour and what was called environmental press (Murray, 1938; Lewin, 1936, 1951), while urban sociologists reported the negative impact of environmental deprivation on health and well-being, with research into city living in Chicago developing the concept of urban ecology (Park and Burgess, 1925). This was not gerontological research focused on human ageing in context, and yet understanding of both perspectives was central to Kleemeier's analysis in 1959, which was seen as initiating environmental gerontology.

The late 20th century saw different approaches develop that would influence this growing interest in P–E interaction at both micro- and meso-levels. German psychologists Paul Baltes and colleagues were instrumental in developing a multidimensional and contextual lifespan perspective of human development utilising the Berlin ageing study (Baltes and Baltes, 1990; Baltes and Meyer, 1999); while the North American scholar Carstensen (1992) developed socioemotional selectivity theory to explain why the social exchange and networks of older people reduce over time, and Rudolf Moos (1974), later with Sonne Lemke (1996), developed a social ecological approach to evaluating treatment and residential environments for older people. This research has been influential, especially being noted by Wahl and Oswald (2010). In contrast, sociologists paid greater attention to the political economy and social construction of ageing, identifying underlying inequalities that led to the emergence of critical gerontology, oriented towards political action and concerned with the marginalisation of older people (Estes, 1979, 1993; Walker, 1981; Townsend, 1981; Minkler and Estes, 1991; Walker and Foster, 2014). Additionally, feminist theory's identification of the gendered nature of ageing both individually and structurally (Peace, 1986, 1993; Minkler, 1996; Arber et al, 2003; Calasanti, 2004) drew greater recognition to issues of diversity and human rights (Torres, 2019). Ageing, inequality and disadvantage in urban and rural environments features in Chapter 4.

Alongside critical gerontology, new humanistic and cultural approaches have emerged. These add subjective and emancipatory human goals to the ageing agenda (Moody, 1993, Katz, 2005, 2019). Twigg and Martin (2015a, 2015b), reflecting the cultural turn, examine how a multidisciplinary base incorporating arts, humanities and social sciences enables a greater deconstruction of meaning, including further understanding of issues relevant to environments of ageing – home, public place, and global and local locations to which older people are connected (Holland, 2015; Peace, 2015; Phillipson, 2015b).

This brief review shows how diverse perspectives can contribute to environmental gerontologists' viewpoints, and to the methods they use to research and interpret the interaction between person and environment. The work of ethnographers such as sociologist Jaber F. Gubrium (1975, 1986, 2005) and anthropologist Robert L. Rubinstein (1989, 1990; Rubinstein and de Medeiros, 2004, 2005), as well as geographers Graham D. Rowles (1978, 1983) and Stephen A. Golant (1984, 2018b) also need to be acknowledged. For example, Gubrium and Holstein have shown how the culture of local settings, offering particular levels of care, support and social engagement for older people, can generate a milieu that can reinforce both positive and negative meanings of ageing (1997). This detailed way of examining place is particularly important to understanding P–E interaction. The contribution made by Rubinstein and de Medeiros and Rowles and Golant is outlined later (see Chaudhury and Oswald, 2018).

Environmental gerontology: focus to date

While environmental gerontology research continues to engage with wider gerontological approaches, certain core themes that focus on the near or local environments of ageing have been central since the 1970s:

- P–E interaction
- place attachment
- relocation
- place theory – dementia

In the following sections, each of these areas is considered, including the seminal work of M. Powell Lawton (Lawton, 1980, 1989, 1998, 2001; Windley and Scheidt, 2003). They draw on the work of multidisciplinary researchers primarily from psychosocial disciplines, often collaborating with academic professionals from architecture, design, occupational therapy, nursing and social care – indicating the applied nature of outcomes. The literature discussed is dominated by scholars from the US and Germany, together with Scandinavian colleagues. Following this detailed dialogue, thinking about future directions for environmental gerontology that has taken place over the past decade is considered, before turning to geographical gerontologists who offer additional theoretical perspectives.

Person–environment interactions

How an individual achieves symbiosis with their environment or how an environment can be enabling or disabling is an ecological approach for which German psychologist Kurt Lewin developed an ecological equation, known as the Lewin hypothesis:

$$B = f(P,E)$$

This indicates that a person's behaviour (B) is a factor of the association between that person (P) and their environment (E), recognising the value of context in human development (overview in Lewin, 1951). This P–E experience can be appraised subjectively or objectively. Lewin's equation is still referred to in contemporary research (see Alonso, 2020), with the P–E relationship being explored through issues such as personal competence, embodiment, agency and comfort with outcomes, in terms of quality of life, morale and well-being.

Reflections on M. Powell Lawton

M. Powell Lawton was a ground-breaking academic in the area of environmental gerontology. A clinical psychologist, he became Director of Behavioural Research at the Philadelphia Geriatric Center and later Director of the Polisher Gerontological Research Institute within the Center (see Lawton, 1975a, 1989, 1990, 2000, 2001; Peace, 2017). In *Environment and Aging* (1980), his ideas concerning P–E fit were studied empirically at housing and community levels. Lawton commented that: 'the basic assertion underlying the study of the environment and behaviour is *that a person's behavioural and psychological state can be better understood with knowledge of the context in which the person behaves*' (p 2, author's italics).

In his early work, Lawton saw what he called P–E 'fit' through a competence approach, in which a person's behaviour related to how their competence matched the demands of their environment. Competence was defined in terms of 'biological health, sensory impairment, cognitive skill, and ego strength', researched through measurable behaviour such as no longer being able to cook a meal or finding climbing stairs makes you out of breath, which relate to activities of daily living (Lawton, 1980, p 9). It was in the 1960s that Lawton and Simon (1968), through research with older people living in institutional settings, considered how movement and the distance people travelled impacted on their opportunity to build social relationships. They developed the Environmental Docility Hypothesis, which reflected on how an older person with a particular level of competence was able to manage, control or be influenced by a particular environment.

A little later, Lawton and Nahemow's (1973) concern with housing quality led to the development of an ecological model that related environmental press (weak to strong) to personal competence (low to high), referring to the earlier work of the psychologists Murray and Lewin. This has been referred to as the 'Press-Competence (PC) model' or the Ecological Theory/Model of Aging (ET/MA): see Figure 2.1. The authors proposed that the lowered competence of a person experiencing high environmental press could affect behaviour and reduce well-being.

Figure 2.1: The Ecological Model of Ageing

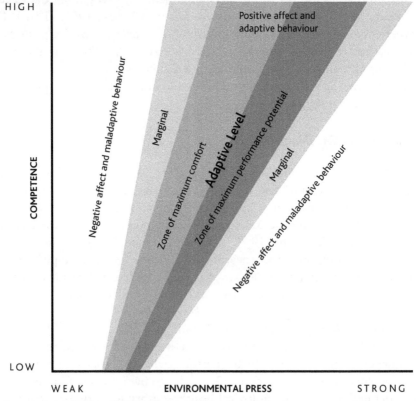

Source: Lawton (1980, p 12) (from Lawton and Nahamow, 1973)

Initially, Lawton and Nahemow were more concerned with objective rather than perceived competencies, with Lawton stating: 'although the study of aging people has shown clearly enough that most older people are far from "incompetent" in the usual meaning of the term, the fact remains that chronic disease and disability are more frequent as chronological age increases' (1980, p 15). Indeed, research has shown that when living with impaired mobility or vision loss, for example, there is a strong relationship between reduced environmental competence and the objective environment (Wahl et al, 1999), though such behaviours may be subject to change through home adaptation/modification and assistive technology – as noted earlier. Nevertheless, the concept of competence is still debated.

In Figure 2.1, an 'adaptation level' forms the central line, situating 'points at which environmental press is "average" for whatever level of competence the person in question has' (Lawton, 1980, p 12), and where press surpasses the level of competence so that people may experience stress impacting on behaviour (Lawton, 1982, 1983). Peace et al (2007) concluded that: 'The most central theoretical consequence of the PC model is that there exists for each ageing person an optimal combination of available competence and given environmental circumstances leading to the highest possible behavioural and emotional functioning for this person' (p 213). However, behaviour relating to both social and psychological characteristics may impact on P–E fit. Psychological concern may relate to personality, ego strength, well-being, positive and negative affect, while an understanding of lifestyle and behaviour relates to social circumstances, reflecting advantages and disadvantages in life that often impact the material and technological environment. When discussing health and behaviour at the level of the individual, other characteristics also affect well-being, as noted by Miller, quoted in Chapter 1, regarding the unconscious nature of 'objects' in underpinning self identity.

In the early years of its development, critics of the Press–Competence (PC) model raised concerns that older people could be seen as disempowered through environmental determinism and that they would actually be more engaged in this interaction. In their later work, Lawton and colleagues revisited issues of competence and environmental press, discussing how different levels of environmental stress could lead to positive or negative outcomes, and that the individual could be 'proactive' in producing 'environmental change' and 'environmental richness' (Lawton, 1982, 1983, 1985, 1998; Weisman, 2003). Their work also addressed the P–E relationship not only in institutional/dwelling settings but also in the community (Lawton, 1980; Lawton et al, 1984), defining the neighbourhood as a 'central ecological unit' and arguing that it could compete with home in importance (Newcomer et al, 1986). This was an interesting early advance – followed by Kahana et al (2003) (see the next section) – given the more recent global concern for the development of age-friendly cities/communities and housing (WHO, 2007) (see Chapters 4 and 5).

Since Lawton's death in 2001, much consideration has been given to his work (Wahl and Weismen, 2003; Scheidt and Windley, 2006; Chaudhury and Oswald, 2018), indicating the breadth of his contribution concerning the interface between environment and ageing – from housing design to multiple meanings of community, from home modifications to accommodation that supports changing physical competencies, to the development of objective measures such as the Philadelphia Geriatric Center Morale Scale (Lawton 1975b, 1979) and the Valuation of Life Scale (Lawton, et al, 2001), and to more understanding of the value of different research methodologies (Lawton et al, 1999). In his later years, Lawton was involved in environmental design for dementia care through the Weiss Institute, bringing issues relating to safety, orientation, social interaction, personalisation and negotiability to the fore (2001). This has been seen as offering a form of compensatory enablement. As Schwarz (2003) shows, Lawton's autobiographical work (1990) indicates that he spent time weighing up the balance between basic science and applied research, while always being conscious of the need for both. He explored how deductive and inductive frameworks relate to theoretical development, and how P–E synergy may be more important than their consideration as separate conceptions. In these first decades of the 21st century, some of this forward thinking is being studied in more detail.

Alternative views on person–environment fit

Alongside Lawton and his colleagues, other social scientists in the US were developing comparable perspectives through P–E congruence models, in which behaviour was related to how environment met the needs of the individual. The sociologist Eva Kahana (1982), working first with nursing home residents, considered the relationship between subjective personal preferences and the environment in relation to seven dimensions for congruence that occur within an individual's personal life space. They relate to a milieu, and were identified as:

- segregate – related to sameness or change for individual and environment;
- congregate – related to support for privacy, autonomy, individual expression if desired by individual;
- institutional control – individual need for support and control in relation to staff expectation of conformity and dependency;
- structure – individual or environmental need for order and ambiguity;
- stimulation/engagement – individual need for engagement and social and physical environmental input;
- affect – individual need for emotional display and ways of handling in social environment;
- impulse control – environmental rules versus individual control.

Later working with the psychologist Boaz Kahana, Kahana and colleagues extended their previous conceptualisation of P–E congruence to consider neighbourhood settings as a framework for future research. By exploring personal preferences and environmental characteristics through physical and social domains that were objective and subjective, such as opportunities for interaction versus solitude, they identified a new methodology to address the well-being of older people (Kahana et al, 2003).

   This conceptual development was related to Carp and Carp's congruence model (1984), which focused on P–E interaction in relation to needs for both life maintenance and higher order needs relating to self; this discussed issues of proactivity with the potential to improve cases of environmental press when it occurred in the community. The model embraced subjective understanding, and was influenced by Maslow's earlier work outlining the motivation of human needs (1964), a reference point for researchers concerned with the well-being of older people across a range of settings. The development of this model and Kahana's occurred in parallel.

Further reflections

More recently, Cvitkovich and Wister (2001, 2002) in Vancouver, Canada, have utilised Lawton and Nahemow's (1973) concepts of adaptation level and maximum zones of comfort and performance to compare four P–E fit models (after Lawton, Kahana and Carp et al) in order to address competence and congruence. They have developed a new life course perspective on P–E interaction that incorporates a temporal dimension; they call this the Multi-level Person–Environment Model or the Life Course Ecological Model of Aging. It builds on the three themes highlighted in Chapter 1 regarding space, person and time, and is quoted here:

- P–E interaction 'occurs within a life-space that is subjectively interpreted by the individual'; (after Lewin, 1935)
- 'individuals make subjective prioritization of P–E fit along a multitude of dimensions, such that some needs are more salient than others'; (after Kahana, 1982)
- 'temporal dimensions [...] coupled with life course principles, [...] demark specific changes in person–environment attributes, transactions, and thresholds that shape P–E fit'. (after Svensson, 1996)
        (Cvitkovich and Wister, 2002, p 20)

Their methodology is complex, drawing as it does on three major environmental domains at community level: structural resources – housing, neighbourhood, community; social support – family, friends, neighbours; and service support – homecare, community agencies, health services. In all these domains, priorities were unpacked, ranked, weighted and assessed through a new Likert P–E fit scale in relation to a person's life satisfaction. Personal characteristics were also collected. The model was tested with frail and non-frail participants, and was found to be more useful in predicting well-being than comparison with earlier competence and congruence models (see Cvitkovich and Wister, 2001).

Cvitkovich and Wister's attempt to project a life course perspective is imaginative. Utilising their own literature review, the authors outline expectations for changes in competence over time through variability of environmental demands and P–E interaction, commenting that 'frail older adults may lower their standards in order to maintain an independent living arrangement' (2002, p 19), indicating the importance of the psycho-social. However, they do not report their methodology for ascertaining life course data and retrospective/prospective accounts, while useful, cannot be validated. Nevertheless, their work is developmentally innovative, and they see it as a 'stepping stone for future revisions' (2002, p 27). They outline these reflections:

(1) That the subjective interpretation of the individual must be placed at the center of person–environment models;
(2) That person–environment transactions occur along multiple dimensions, but with different perceived levels of saliency; and
(3) That the timing, duration, and sequencing of person–environment transactions and thresholds vary across the life course of individuals.
(Cvitkovich and Wister, 2002, p 27)

Rubinstein and de Medeiros (2004), by examining 'the relationship of the self and the ecology of later life' (p 59), also provide a detailed critique of P–E fit models informed by an anthropological lens. They argue that theories of P–E fit have a 'nearly complete absence of sociocultural meanings in regard to the self, meaning, and the environment', and instead they are 'based around the many functional issues that elders may face' (p 60). In making this case they look in detail at three areas: the self, defined in a cultural space that may vary by place and within the subjective realm of the person, with the potential to change over time; cultural and personal meaning, where personal meaning is derived through cultural meaning that may or may not be shared to construct personal reality; and embodiment, which they see as referring 'to the complex set of meanings and physical realities associated with one's body' (p 63). They also note that reducing embodiment 'to a single, objectified variable would be to severely minimize the importance of the ongoing self–body–environment interaction' (p 63), which they discuss in relation to the cultural construct of old age and decline.

With these definitions in mind, Rubinstein and de Medeiros return to the theoretical positions outlined earlier, indicating how the visual model of the Ecological Model of Ageing has become a 'key theoretical cornerstone' with practice implications for the design of living settings (2004, p 64). However, they argue that P–E fit theories are based on what they see as 'thin description' – after Geertz (1993, 2000) – continuing: 'at best P-E theories clearly show the interaction of variables and measure press and competence, but they don't say much about the self, the person, or his or her life' (p 64).

To conclude, Rubinstein and de Medeiros discuss how everyday life is experienced phenomenologically, and explore how if we are to understand the P–E relationship people need to tell their story, to show how they live and how they see themselves, something that is culturally mediated. They argue that the older person lives through negotiating the body in relation to the environment, using strategies that can change across time: this becomes their personal ecology.

Finally, Keating and colleagues (Keating and Phillips, 2008; Keating et al, 2013) draw together research on rural ageing based predominantly at community level in order to develop a critical human ecology framework. Recognising human ecology as changing over a lifetime, they consider how human development interacts with the environment, with different contexts – which may be social, physical, economic or cultural – overlapping and impacting on each other. Keating (2008b) notes how, given varying personal capacity and resources, people achieve their best P–E fit in spite of environmental difficulties. This position is developed by Hennessy et al (2014) in relation to rural ageing and is discussed in Chapter 4.

Place attachment

The interest of some environmental gerontologists in the phenomenological issue of place attachment, which relates to self-identity, belonging and meaning, draws on the discipline of environmental psychology (Altman and Low, 1992; Manzo, 2005; Manzo and Devine-Wright, 2014). Place attachment considers how people develop environmental mastery or control; the way in which human attachment is central to the creation of social space, and how personal meaning enables a bonding with place that may be seen at both micro- and meso-levels from dwelling to location (see Relph, 1976; Cooper Marcus, 1992; Bronfenbrenner, 1999). While life course attachments to place may continue from childhood to adulthood, such associations can relate to certain events, prompting positive, negative or transitional meanings. This may also relate to association with particular people, which may change over time – making bonding stronger or weaker.

Here, key perspectives from social gerontologists Rubinstein and Rowles have emerged through different disciplines – anthropology and geography. In 1978, Graham Rowles published *Prisoners of Space?*, introducing ideas of importance to place attachment and self-identity in later life (Rowles, 1978). Early research was based on a detailed ethnographic study involving interview, observation and visual record with 15 long-term residents of a small Appalachian mountain community of 400 people. Initial analysis reported on behaviour that demonstrated the impact of environmental layers. One such layer Rowles calls a 'surveillance zone', space 'within the visual field of a residence' where people could 'watch' or 'be watched' (1981, p 304). He notes how this space could be used to enable people to be part of the community, engendering safety and security; where practical and social support was seen as mutual obligation between people. Long-term residents were seen to maintain a sense of identity through their ability to watch, communicate and participate.

Later analysis considered the *insideness* of place in old age, involving:

- *social insideness* shaped through everyday social exchanges;
- *physical insideness* enabled by the familiarity and routines that many may regard as the 'home' environment; and finally
- *autobiographical insideness* where 'place becomes a landscape of memories, providing a sense of identity'. (Rowles, 1983, p 114)

Here, an understanding of place embraces the geographic world experienced both physically and psychologically. This view has a generic value, drawing as it does on the wealth of material from detailed ethnographic studies. In later work, Rowles considers how people make ongoing adjustments within their home space as their capabilities change (2000). More recently, with Chaudhury, his consideration of home has explored the issues of recollection, imagination and self (Chaudhury and Rowles, 2005; Rowles and Chaudhury, 2005). These ideas are later developed with Bernard, reflecting on how home may be remade over time alongside relocation (Rowles and Bernard, 2013.).

In times of population ageing, it is important to explore the values and meanings that surround place attachment in later life. In many Western developed countries, the language of 'ageing in place' is common, and is used to support policy that enables people to stay in their own homes for as long as possible. The concept of home and the phrase 'as long as possible' are central here, and the essence of many comments that are made to researchers. Rowles's work tells us how attachment to place supports the ageing self. The complexity of this association is unpacked further by the conceptual model of place attachment that is developed by Rubinstein and Parmelee (1992). Utilising qualitative case study data, they consider how place attachment relates to three essential elements: geographic behaviour, identity and interdependence. The rationale for this model with regard to the individual builds on issues related to the development of life space through home; identity formed through personal experience, capturing life history; and how the individual creates both autonomous and relational ways of being – in this case within an American value base that foregrounds independence, reciprocity, autonomy and security.

Relocation

Place attachment also brings to mind what could be called place detachment. When testing their model, Rubinstein and Parmelee considered the centrality of place at both societal and individual levels in relation to three settings: the home and personal possessions; the residential neighbourhood; and residential care institutions for the aged, which they saw as public territory (1992, p 149). Analysis based on their research and reviewed literature indicates several key features. The authors indicate that people become 'home-centred' in later life, with this attachment seen as material, social, embodied and extended through long-term engagement. Through Rubinstein's (1989) psychosocial analysis of social-, person- and body-centred processes within the home, they indicate different aspects of self. These may be seen, for example, through the personalisation of culturally defined spatial layouts with interior design, furniture and decorative objects. Pressures experienced through poor housing design may or may not lead to adaptation or change. At neighbourhood level, the inclusion of all ages is noted as positive, and Rubinstein and Parmelee (1992) comment on the need for research at this level of engagement, a view they were expressing several years before the WHO developed the age-friendly cities and communities (AFCC) initiative in the early 21st century (see Rémillard-Boilard, 2018). They note that a lack of integration prevents the maintenance of a positive definition of self. Finally, their comments on age-related care environments view them as collective rather than individualised spaces. The authors regard these environments as depersonalising non-places that do not inspire affective attachment. While stressing positive features regarding the social environment, they note evidence of group exclusions. These findings show that people find ways of coping with their circumstances, and although the roles they had in the 'outside world' are not acknowledged, they maintain their individuality. Long-term care research involving nursing home residents reinforces the negativity of depersonalised living: while the setting has a purpose and may avoid isolation, it is not seen as home – an issue developed in Chapters 8 and 10.

This analysis of place attachment can be critiqued for being of its time in relation to work on neighbourhood and long-term care settings, but the essence of the findings contribute to ongoing discussion of relocation across the life course and especially in later life. In the US, gerontological research since the 1960s has considered the 'relocation trauma hypothesis', which suggests that moving into an institutional setting may impact on health and well-being, with some increase in mortality. This was questioned by Coffman (1983), and there has been ongoing critique (Castle, 2001). The research can be compared with Wiseman's (1980) and Heywood et al's (2002) discussion of push and pull factors that motivate changing accommodation – from issues of poor health to lifestyle attractions – and Litwak and Longino's (1987) view that moving may be seen in relation to chronological age, life events and motivation: the first around the age of retirement from employment; the second relating to returning to place of origin; and the last being to an institutional setting in very old age. While such moves will no doubt be undertaken for some, decision-making about relocation from a place that may or may not be seen as home is complex and unique in every case.

In recent years, important contributions to discussion of residential change have been made theoretically and methodologically by Golant (1984, 2011, 2012, 2015, 2018a, 2018b) in the US and by Peace et al (2005, 2006, 2011) in England. Stephen Golant, a geographical gerontologist with a long history of research in housing and residential alternatives, has sought to understand why people whose housing may not meet their needs choose to age in place. In discussing the theoretical perspective of 'residential normalcy', described as an 'emotion-based indicator of 'individual-environment fit' (2018a, p 193), he identifies two concepts central to decision-making over neighbourhood and care environment. The first is residential comfort experiences – which relates to the comfort, appeal and hassle-free nature of their residence (Golant, 2012) – and the second is residential mastery experiences – 'whether older people feel competent, empowered and in control of their lives and environment' (2018a, p 194; 2018b), judged through everyday experiences, both inside and outside the residential environment.

If both these concepts prove positive, then people will either not think of moving or if they do so it will be for reasons beyond their household. However, if their responses to these experiences conflict, or are negative, people may think of relocating – although it is not inevitable that they will move. Circumstances influence decisions: a person who is living alone will have very different considerations to a couple who have differing views but a commitment to each other. Moreover, the intervention of others may offer alternative ways to stay in place', or there may be opportunities to live in another location with family/friends or in other accommodation closer to family. Golant looks at a range of coping strategies that are either accommodative, where people may deny there is an issue to resolve, or assimilative, where they take action to make things manageable. It should be remembered here that moving home is also one of the most stressful things that people do (Lazarus and Launier, 1978; Hillcoat-Nallétamby and Sardani, 2019). In addition, older people often lack the information needed to make logical choices: they cannot access necessary resources, whether financial or social, and might lack the physical or psychological energy to cope with a transition of this nature. Again, the issues are both individual and societal, and Golant notes the difficulties around inequality that affect behaviour when living through times of financial austerity (2015). Yet not everyone views moving in a negative light. For Golant, residential normalcy reflects an expertise in researching options. His latest detailed discussion of this is to be found in *Aging in the Right Place*, in which comfort and mastery are viewed in a number of settings (2018b).

There are interesting similarities between the work of Golant and the key learning from Peace et al (2011). Influenced by Lawton's discussion of environmental pro-activity that leads to personal control and autonomy within the home, the latter reanalyses qualitative data from the British ethnographic study published as *Environment and Identity in Later Life* (Peace et al, 2006), which led to further reflection on the complexity of P–E interaction within housing and neighbourhood. The concept of 'option recognition' reflects situations where adaptive behaviour cannot rebalance environmental press that is impacting on an individual's independence and well-being. This tipping point leads to a range of strategic responses, including: modification of behaviour and environment, informal and formal support within the domestic home and relocation to alternative settings – all of which can influence how people feel about themselves. Further discussion of this is to be found in Chapter 6.

The research considered here focuses on the synergy between people and places who are grounded in communities and dwellings within Western developed countries. Many people live in the same place for several decades, gradually ageing in place as maturing selves. Continuity and change impact how they perceive their environment and see it as home, a continuing theme throughout this book. In this context, thoughts about relocation are guided by the work of specific environmental gerontologists. Not considered here are the implications for older people who relocate nationally or globally through migration; this is raised in Chapter 3.

Place theory and applied research in practice

The work of the US architectural authors Gerald D. Weisman, Keith Diaz Moore and Habib Chaudhury form a bridge between environmental gerontology and design. (Weisman, 1997, 2003; Diaz Moore, 1999, 2005, 2014; Weisman, et al, 2000; Chaudhury and Rowles, 2005; Chaudhury, 2008; Chaudhury and Cooke, 2014). Here we consider Diaz Moore's foundational theory of place and its application in relation to dementia-friendly environments.

The Ecological Framework of Place (Diaz Moore, 2014) is a complex abstract exploratory model. Working within gerontology, Diaz Moore draws on literature already considered in philosophical contexts such as Bourdieu's habitus, on geographical definitions of place (Tuan, 1977; Cresswell, 2004) and on developments regarding behaviour from environmental psychology (Canter, 2012). He states that the Ecological Framework of Place 'defines place as a socio-physical milieu involving people, the physical setting, and the program of the place, all catalysed by situated human activity and fully acknowledging that all four may change over time' (2012, p 183).

Human activity is based not only on the individual but also on the group. Organisational and cultural forms and interaction are defined as relating to behaviour and being dependent on motivation, cognition and affect as well as functional competence. He argues that people operate within what Diaz Moore calls the 'program' of a behaviour setting that has 'place rules' and 'place roles' (following Canter, 1977, 1991). He also defines place attributes as 'qualities we attribute to places on the basis of our own history, goals and identity' (Diaz Moore, et al, 2006, p 33), noting how the attributes of autonomy and identity (Oswald and Wahl, 2013), mastery and comfort (Golant, 2011) have been recently foregrounded in environmental gerontology. Finally, he acknowledges how cognitive affect relating to all aspects of the framework can change over time – diurnal, seasonal, annual and historical, with a life course perspective.

Diaz Moore tests his Ecological Framework of Place in relation to understandings from developmental psychology and environmental gerontology. From developmental psychology, he takes social embeddedness, temporality and in particular human agency, showing how place can impact different forms of agency – individual to institutional (Bronfenbrenner, 1999). With regard to environmental gerontology, Diaz Moore bases his discussion on Lawton's Ecological Model of Ageing (Lawton, 1980, 1989), which embraces environmental press and sees proactivity as related to pragmatic agency (Hitlin and Elder, 2007); the critique by Rubinstein and de Medeiros (2004); Golant's theory of residential normalcy (2011, 2015); and Wahl and Lang's discussion (2004), in which the social construction of place is seen as essential to understanding behaviour within the physical environment. Through this detailed analysis, Diaz Moore indicates how the Ecological Framework of Place addresses and includes issues raised by other constructs, models and theories, offering 'a heuristic framework to inform research, architectural design, and care interventions acknowledging the powerful role place plays throughout the life course and particularly later life' (2014, p 199).

Diaz Moore's work evolved in association with Weisman and the framework he proposes can be applied when considering environments for people living with forms of cognitive impairment. The impact of setting for people with dementia is discussed in more detail in Chapter 8, noting that unsupportive physical environments can present a form of environmental press that enhances challenging behaviours such as agitation and anxiety and leads to social withdrawal. Diaz Moore indicates that those who experience memory loss beyond forgetfulness may challenge the ability to live by routines, although he notes that routines may also be repetitive reminders of action in space (Diaz Moore, 2005). People with dementia may also suffer disorientation within inside and outside spaces, impacting on their perception of place (Chaudhury and Cooke, 2014), however, in Chapter 9 we see how exploration of outside place can be welcomed (Clark et al, 2020).

Understanding personal history and the knowledge of self may enable connection with place, and here the work of Tom Kitwood (1990, 1993) at the Bradford Dementia Centre, University of Bradford, outlines a theory of person-centred dementia care in which the subjectivity of the person aids communication in the present. Kitwood and colleagues developed the observational methodology of Dementia Care Mapping within formal settings such as residential/nursing homes (Kitwood and Bredin, 1992; Kitwood, 1997, Brooker, 2005), and this body of work has extended to consider the impact of the physical environment within the UK and other developed countries (see Chaudhury et al, 2013).

Gerald Weisman had particular expertise in the behaviour of people with dementia, undertaking work on wayfinding, signage and issues of architectural legibility from the 1970s onwards. Alongside Lawton, Calkins and other colleagues, he developed the Physical Environmental Assessment Protocol, which enables the measurement of environments for older people with cognitive impairment and facilitates a more therapeutic environment (see Lawton et al, 2000). By linking this work with the observational methods of Kitwood and colleagues, Weisman and his collaborators considered nine dimensions of the care environment: safety and security; personal control; awareness; orientation; privacy; support of functional abilities; regulation of stimulation; facilitation of social contact; and continuity of the self. This was regarded as a global quality assessment measure that could be used by trained professionals and developed for dementia care units within nursing homes; it provides an important example of applied research operating at a micro-level.

Forward thinking on person–environment in later life

In this chapter, key theoretical and conceptual positions that have contributed to environmental gerontology over more than 50 years have been outlined. When Bengtson et al were discussing theoretical development in this field in 2005, they did not mention the work of Lawton and others, considered here, regarding environments of ageing and the importance of context, rather, they were concerned with the problem-solving nature of research that leads to micro-level analysis focusing on issues such as agency. However, in concluding, they considered the possibility of 'theories *in* ageing' rather than '*of* ageing' opening 'a novel strategy for developing cross-disciplinary explanations and understanding' (Bengtson et al, 2005, p 17). In contrast, the later *Handbook of Theories of Aging* (Bengtson and Settersten Jr, 2016) includes a chapter by Wahl and Oswald (2016) that reviews the area of environmental gerontology, reinforcing the importance of space and place alongside time in understanding human ageing and the need for theoretical innovation instead of stagnation and ambiguity. In re-examining this literature here, we look initially at developments regarding the Ecological Model of Ageing, and then at future directions proposed by Scheidt and Schwarz (2013).

Developing the Ecological Model of Ageing

In 2010, German psychologist Hans-Werner Wahl gave the M. Powell Lawton lecture at the Gerontological Society of America Annual Conference, and his work was later developed for publication as Wahl et al (2012). The authors consider how the physical–spatial–technical environment that is now commonplace for people as they grow older, with personal pro-activity through housing adaptation/modification alongside the impact of assistive technology extends theoretical thinking. Bringing together issues from both ecology, ageing and lifespan development literature they focus on particular aspects of the P–E process: experience associated with belonging, and behaviour associated with agency being seen as fundamental to ageing well. A conceptual framework for future exploratory testing is outlined, aiming to move towards an integrative framework of aging well. Taking each element in turn, Hans-Werner Wahl, Susanne Iwarsson and Frank Oswald outline four propositions:

Proposition 1
It is useful to consider environment-related processes of *belonging* and *agency* in combination in order to better understand aging well.

Proposition 2
Processes of environment-related *belonging* gain in importance in the face of major age-associated functional impairment, whereas *agency* becomes less important.

Proposition 3
The interplay of *belonging* and *agency* can augment existing life span development models of aging well.

Proposition 4
The interplay of *belonging* and *agency* can augment the analysis of cultural frames and cohort dynamics regarding ageing well."
(Source: Table 1, Wahl et al, 2012, p 311)

The authors discuss each proposition in light of Lawton's ecology of ageing principles, indicating how the competence–press model may change over time as people experience different levels of functional ability. This relates to place attachment within all environments and to community-based embracing of ongoing technological development. The third proposition is linked to the 'selective optimization with compensation' model (Baltes and Baltes, 1990), in which factors such as home adaptation can be seen as creating compensatory strategies, and Cartensen's (2006) socioemotional selectivity theory. It is possible that further research could connect these lifespan developmental theories and the concepts of agency and belonging. Wahl et al make a case for using longitudinal studies to consider ageing in environment and also for developing new methodologies, including ways of measuring environment-related agency and establishing a new dataset that includes out of home and in-home spaces. They conclude by calling for a more sophisticated understanding both of residential decision-making and the future implications of technology in relation to ageing well.

This work is taken one stage further by Chaudhury and Oswald (2019), who developed an integrative conceptual framework of P–E exchange. Oswald, a long-time associate of Wahl who also worked alongside Iwarsson on the EU-funded ENABLE-AGE study (see Chapter 6), has taken the core focus of the model of belonging and agency and with Chaudhury has developed a more comprehensive framework (Figure 2.2).

> Building on a detailed understanding of the major components of P–E interaction based on individual characteristics, social factors, physical/ built environment and technological systems, the authors consider the processes of agency and belonging, and define outcomes centred on identity and autonomy following earlier conceptual research by Wahl and Oswald (2010, 2016), arguing that 'environment related outcomes echo fundamental developmental tasks in later life, namely, to remain independent for as long as possible, as well as to maintain one's integrity in identity'. (Chaudhury and Oswald, 2019, p 4)

Through discussion of three individual scenarios concerning people in advanced years living in both communal and residential settings, they indicate potential forms of association between identity and belonging, agency and autonomy. This is a framework for measurement development and innovative methodology, and an opportunity for multidisciplinary research – as called for by Wahl et al (2012). They conclude:

> conceptual contributions from post-structuralism, critical gerontology and practice-theoretical perspective on aging would argue that in a conceptualization of P–E exchange processes, it is useful to widen the scope of concepts and empirical analyses to dissolve the ostensive dualism of person and place for better understanding of the aging experience beyond a mere rational-choice perspective. (Chaudhury and Oswald, 2019, p 8)

Through reflecting on these comments, I agree that the apparent dualism of person and place may be limiting in terms of the spatial scale for research. It is important to extend this area of study by encompassing 'person' or

Figure. 2.2: An integrative conceptual framework of person–environment exchange

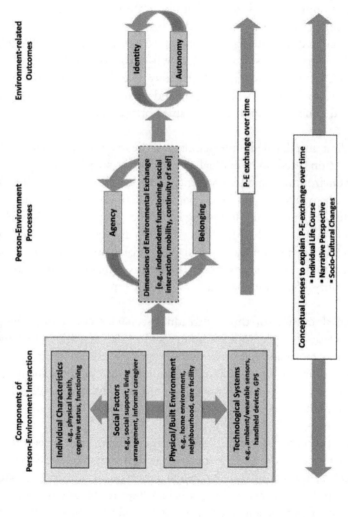

Source: Chaudhury and Oswald (2019), 1–9

'people', 'environment' or 'context', so the breadth of analysis can become more relational within and between people and place – from local to global. In addition, three areas need ongoing examination:

- First, recognition that the major components of P–E interaction provide an opportunity to refocus on aspects of the social that are intersectional, gendered, culturally diverse, internationally comparative and foreground inequalities.
- Second, through lifespan and life stage perspectives, there is the opportunity to analyse further individual/societal synergy or dissonance, exploring temporal change in relation to P–E within a critical gerontology that is also relational.
- Third, while autonomy is a central outcome in this framework, the concepts of authentic and delegated autonomy (Collopy, 1988; Leece and Peace, 2010) should be introduced in relation to interdependency, noting the variation in levels of precarity among older people.

These are issues raised in Chapters 4–8 which focus on later life in the UK across different forms of environmental living.

Future issues for environmental gerontology

With these thoughts in mind, we turn to issues discussed by Scheidt and Schwarz (2013) when concluding the edited collection *Environmental Gerontology: What Now?* They outline the importance of interdisciplinary academic and practice-led research to encompass all environments of ageing; the value of inclusive design and technology that facilitates the support of cognitive and physical impairment; a recognition that age-friendly communities are person-friendly, and must move beyond a need to justify the value of later life to promote a life course perspective; and for the recognition of inequalities that see certain older people ignored, stigmatised and excluded.

Researchers are already engaged with many of these issues. However, in reviewing the way forward, Scheidt and Schwartz also question whether theoretical development should be overarching or focused, whether global uncertainty should be addressed, and whether research needs to address variability in understanding issues of universality. Here, it is suggested that theoretical development should embrace both levels: that difference needs to be addressed at various spatial scales and that testing cultural specificity may indicate some themes are generalisable – an example being the importance of agency and belonging identified earlier.

The theoretical perspectives developed in this field are still centred on white middle-class patriarchal thinking, while women often in their fourth age from white and multi-ethnic groups still dominate the subject base. The recognition of diversity, including ethnicity, sexuality and disability, and the potential for further development of feminist theory has to be acknowledged. There is the potential for participatory thinking to develop research questions and undertake co-research. In future, research will be both multidisciplinary, when different disciplines work alongside each other, bringing separate expertise to the research question, and interdisciplinary, as researchers learn new methodological skills and integrate more fully. Scheidt and Schwartz see this as particularly true for work in environmental gerontology that has practical application. This topic is returned to in Chapter 9.

In the conclusion, we turn to theoretical approaches that have developed in social, cultural and human geography but have potential for environmental gerontology when considering different ways of engaging with personal affect and interaction across different spatial scales (Figure 0.1). As noted earlier, over the past 50 years, a group of social and health geographers have undertaken research on the geographies of ageing. A focus on space and place has been seen across diverse issues, whether community based or health and housing related, concerned with migration or with the global distribution of population ageing. Interest has grown particularly in the current century (see Harper and Laws, 1995; Andrews and Phillips, 2005; Andrews et al, 2007, 2018; Skinner et al, 2015 for the development of geographical gerontology).

Theoretical perspectives from geographical gerontologists

Geographical approaches were introduced in Chapter 1, and here I acknowledge the views of Massey et al who state: 'while we in a spatial discipline accepted that the spatial was always socially constructed so too, we argued, it had to be recognized that the social was necessarily also spatially constructed. What is more, we argued, the fact and nature of that spatial construction matter; they make a difference' (Massey et al, 1999b, p 6). To extend the understanding of spatial construction, two perspectives with universal application are considered here: non-representational theory and relational theory developed through realist geographical thinking (Lorrimer, 2005, Andrews et al, 2018).

Non-representational theory

Non-representational theory aids the understanding of meaning through issues of performativity. The language associated with this perspective may be less familiar in gerontological literature, yet the philosophical position is common in epistemological debate. The perspective is associated with the work of human geographer Nigel Thrift (see 1996, 2004, 2007) and others (see Dewsbury, 2000; Cadman, 2009; McCormack, 2017). This way of thinking has also been called 'more than representational' theory by Lorimer (2005, p 84), as it seeks to understand knowledge and performativity through embodied experience and practice that can appear psychoanalytic, rather than centring on social relationships.

Skinner et al (2015), when discussing non-representational approaches in relation to research on ageing, suggest that qualitative research has offered a social constructionist 'representational' paradigm, whereas non-representational theory 'bring(s) attention to the many unspoken and too often unacknowledged performances and practices involved in the reproduction of space, place and social life' (p 788). A range of themes linked to ageing, including participation in sports (Tulle, 2008, 2015) and experience of movement (Andrews and Grenier, 2015), use this form of thinking and develop innovative phenomenological methods. For example, Hetherington (2003) works with visually impaired people to understand how subjective understanding through touch may enable the co-construction of place – research that relates to the experience of home within retirement housing for Jo in Chapter 7.

In addition, Barron's (2019) research regarding sense of place demonstrates her methodological approach. By interacting with older people on photo-walks in Manchester neighbourhoods, she enables them 'to illuminate the often-fleeting factors that bind or buckle people's sense of place' (2019, p 8). Through these walking narratives, she demonstrates how people reveal 'performative pasts'; by conveying issues of continuity, change and emotions, they combine aspects of more-than-representational theory with aspects of their life course. When reflecting on her research, she comments: 'I highlight how moments of individual life-courses are brought to the fore and interwoven with narratives of place to preserve a continuity of identity in older age' (2019, p 10).

These ways of thinking extend the knowledge base and link theoretical development within geography (Lorimer, 2008). Reflecting on earlier qualitative work in environmental gerontology influenced by sociology, anthropology and geography, one could argue that this body of work has already taken into account issues of realism and non-representation, and it is perhaps more important to address the triangulation of mixed method approaches and analysis. Nevertheless, the merging disciplines introduce new methods that should be tested further (Peace, 2018).

Relational theory

It is essential to note the comment from Massey et al quoted earlier when understanding the relational turn that geographers discuss when considering space as a set of relations that are made and remade over time (Andrews et al, 2013; Skinner et al, 2015). Thrift defines a relational view of space as 'undergoing continual construction as a result of the agency of things encountering each other in more or less organised circulations' (2007, 86). Here, different phenomena come together whose association may not be expected, therefore being of importance when understanding human connections with environment that are informed by culture and require a reflexive approach. Hopkins and Pain (2007) look at how these relations can be explored through intergenerationality and intersectionality when researching engagement with space/place through diverse social constructions that relate to generation, life course events, gender, ethnicity, socio-economic status and so on. Variability and flexibility are key.

The synergy between diverse people and their environmental experience through both space and place has been central to the work of Golant, Rowles and the current author, all of whom were initially and are currently human/social geographers and gerontologists who have adopted humanistic (phenomenological) and mixed methods approaches to research, within the multidisciplinary community of environmental gerontology. In considering the value of relational dynamics within gerontology, the geographer Malcolm Cutchin identifies three cross-cutting themes, instabilities, transitions and negotiations (2018, p 217–22) which impact on agency in later life through ongoing reconstruction of spatial relations and relate to discussion of place attachment and relocation. He argues that instability may occur through change(s) over time related to the person or the environment, or both, while Wiles (2005a) deconstructs the process for health professionals when working with older people both in their own homes and long-term care settings. The value of different forms of longitudinal research in exploring process over time, though costly, needs reconsideration. For example, research by Thordardottir et al (2018) in a 'before and after' study of home adaptation demonstrates the need to understand the ongoing nature of change in both the health and well-being of the older person and their environment that creates instability.

Cutchin's next theme, transitions, is demonstrated in his own research. Through discussion of older people moving into assisted living residences, he considers place integration, illustrating how three older people cope with moving, readjusting and not settling. He suggests how engagement with habitual routines (see Rowles and Watkins, 2003) alongside the development of new activities and social engagement may create a positive association between person and place that is relational (Cutchin, 2013). Once again, the symbiosis seen in Bourdieu's habitus is noted here. These examples relate to moving between dwellings, and Cutchin (2018) considers downsizing housing as an under-researched area in which existing research shows the complexity of change to familial, social, spatial and cultural ways of being that are relational, and impact on re-engagement with place and sense of self (Luborsky et al, 2011).

His final relational dynamic is negotiations, this being to a degree reflective of adaptation within P–E fit and P–E congruence models that is able to include a range of transactional relationships where individuals continually renegotiate their sense of self within place. Here I consider negotiations at different levels, building on the example of older people with visual impairment discussed in Chapter 1. With regard to the navigation of local outdoor neighbourhood space, negotiations can involve individuals, local policy makers and national legislation for those with disabilities, resulting in an environment that aims to create synergy (Peace et al, 2016, 2019). These interactions may be viewed as relational.

The concept of relationality that is already embedded in the language of human, cultural, social and health geographies and also other disciplines is gradually becoming a part of social and cultural gerontology (Calasanti, 2004; Cummins et al, 2007; Jones, 2009; Burkitt, 2016). Indeed, Andrews et al, 2013 challenge gerontologists to consider a relational approach when rethinking space and place. In contrast, theoretical perspectives within environmental gerontology have developed through a focus on P–E interaction, at first addressing functionality as part of enabling competence and later embracing issues of human well-being and human development, with the gradual recognition of the importance of a life course perspective that encompasses time and context. Figure 2.3 demonstrates how these different approaches are both relational and contextual, and this association forms the basis of further theoretical thinking in Chapter 10.

Figure 2.3: Different ways of thinking

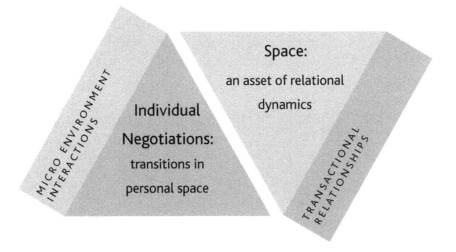

Conclusions

In the UK, the developing field of ageing and environment has seen support from the 1960s onwards for applied research relating to health, accommodation and care. There has been ongoing concern over quality of life in institutional long-term care and specialised housing, as well as in later general needs housing and community living. These are trends seen in many Western developed countries, leading to concerns regarding institutionalisation, person-centred care, ageing in place, P–E fit, meaning of home, age-related housing and age-friendly environments. The field has origins in psychology and sociology, yet is multidisciplinary across the social sciences and multi-professional – drawing as it has done more recently on architecture and design, technology, ergonomics, engineering and computer science. This diversity has led empirical research in environmental gerontology to be seen as strategic and applied, and the value of multi- or interdisciplinary research is only beginning to be fulfilled, with the development of methodological innovations and the consideration of new theoretical perspectives.

This chapter has been dominated by the work of North American and European gerontologists who focus on interactions in local or community environments on a micro- or meso-scale. For those whose interests lie beyond the near environment, where non-representative approaches are familiar, relational perspectives may offer new approaches. It can be argued that we should never centre our discussion of the lives of older people on a local or national level without understanding a much broader context; and the opposite is also true. Strategic developments and personal challenges at wider levels can affect the inclusion or exclusion of people at different stages of later life. As indicated in Figure 2.3, the coming together of different ways of thinking through the work of geographical gerontologists may allow a broader base for environmental gerontology, enabling the consideration of global issues that have an impact on population ageing – and this is the focus of Chapter 3.

3

The global context

Introduction

> … by 2050, one in six people in the world will be over age 65
> (16%), up from one in 11 in 2019 (9%). By 2050, one in four
> persons living in Europe and Northern America could be aged
> 65 or over. In 2018, for the first time in history, persons aged 65
> or above outnumbered children under five years of age globally.
> The number of persons aged 80 years or over is projected to triple,
> from 143 million in 2019 to 426 million in 2050. (UN, 2020)

In the preface to this book, it was noted that a key objective was to address
environments of ageing at different levels of spatial scale (Figure 0.1). This
chapter focuses on the global context. As this quote from the United
Nations (UN) shows, population ageing continues to advance, occurring
during a period of dynamic change when globalisation is producing time–
space compression through technological development, and when global
capitalism is resulting in consumerism becoming more universal (Sassen,
2004; Jones et al, 2008). The interface between major transformations in
global health, demography and household composition is changing during
a time of parallel challenges regarding urbanisation, migration, climate
change, the built environment and technological development. Neoliberalism has become the dominant political force, leading environments to
become more or less inclusive for different cohorts, generations and groups
(Walker, 2005; Phillips and Feng, 2018; IMF, 2020a, 2020b). The issues
addressed here are historic and ongoing, with authors such as Phillipson
(2003, 2007a, 2007b) alerting us to their breadth, diversity and impact
on the ageing individual (see Figure 3.1). Recognition of such changes is
discussed internationally and made local through social media (Hyde and
Higgs, 2016; Ortega, 2018).

These are factors at macro-level that provide the global context for
population ageing; where strategic interactions supported through
supranational institutions – the European Union (EU), the Organisation for
Economic Co-operation and Development (OECD), the UN, especially
the Department of Economic and Social Affairs (DESA) and the World
Health Organization (WHO) – influence policy development at all levels,

Figure 3.1: Global challenges

including the UN 17 Sustainable Development Goals (see the Glossary). Throughout this text, global population ageing using WHO and UN data is defined as including people both 60 or older and 65 and over. Where discussion focuses on the UK, 65 or older is commonly used. In addition countries will either be described as 'developed' or 'developing' unless specified as low, middle and high income, using the terms that are employed by the WHO (WHO, 2015a).

A brief consideration of population change and health concerns underpins a discussion of global ageing, utilising multidisciplinary sources from demography, health geography, urban sociology and global social policy (see Grundy, 1997; Wiles, 2018; Phillips and Feng, 2018).

Global ageing, global health

The relationship between global health and global population ageing initially appears clear, but the association is complex. While many authors provide detailed analysis of global data (see Lloyd-Sherlock, 2010; WHO, 2015a; Hyde and Higgs, 2016), the main trends are summarised in Research summary 3.1. This uses UN and WHO statistics to contextualise discussion of person and environment at macro-level.

Research summary 3.1: Trends in global population ageing

Declining fertility and decreasing mortality (an increase in life expectancy) are leading to population ageing in nearly every country in the world. International health interventions regarding maternal and child health, malnutrition and infectious diseases have expanded, and often target developing nations and low-income regions (Koplan et al, 2009); while in high-income countries the history of population ageing has a longer time frame.

In 2013, two thirds of older people lived in developed countries, but the older population is growing faster in less developed regions, where more than three quarters will live by 2050. Northern Africa and Western Asia, and then sub-Saharan Africa are the regions with the fastest increase in the number of older people (see regional data in UN DESA, 2015, 2019b, 2019c; Phillips and Feng, 2018)

At present, women have a longer life expectancy than men, and older women are prominent in ageing populations. In 2013, the sex ratio globally for those aged 60 and over was 85:100 (M:F) and for those aged 80 and over 61:100 (M:F). Globally, in 2015–20, women who reached the age of 65 were expected to live another 18 years, men an additional 16 years. The gender gap between men and women is narrowing especially for those aged 80 and over (UN DESA, 2013, 2019c)

WHO (2015a) reports that over the age of 60 people may experience more than one chronic health condition: these are not only age-related losses related to moving, seeing and hearing, but also non-communicable diseases such as cancer, stroke, heart disease, respiratory disorders and dementia. Living with co-morbidities is found among older people living in low, middle and higher-income countries, with varied outcomes relating to access to healthcare and the costs of long-term care.

In 2015, approximately 5 per cent of the world's older population was affected by dementia – 47 million people. It is expected that this will rise to 75 million in 2030 and 132 million by 2050. Nearly 60 per cent of people with dementia currently live in low- and middle-income countries, which is where a majority of new cases will occur (WHO, 2017a, p 2).

The population aged 80 and over will increase threefold between 2020 and 2050. In 2019, Europe and N. America had the highest number in this oldest age group (53.9 million) followed by Eastern and South East Asia (48.6 million). By 2050 more than half of this age group will live in Eastern and South East Asia (177 million) followed by Europe and North America (109 million) (UN DESA, 2019c, p 6).

Globally, 4 out of 10 older people live independently. In developed countries, nearly three quarters live either alone, with their spouse or with a partner, supporting themselves financially through their labour, assets or public transfers. This is much less common in developing countries (25 per cent), even though traditional multigenerational living arrangements are declining (WHO, 2015a).

Sources: Adapted from data from Kalache et al, 2005; Phillips and Feng, 2018; UN DESA, 2013, 2015, 2019a, 2019b, 2019c; WHO, 2002, 2015a, 2015b, 2017a, 2020a

As noted, changes in population ageing are being seen in developed and developing countries. The UN statistics referred to in Table 3.1. regarding ten countries or areas with populations aged 60 and over, show that while European nations were the oldest in 1980 with the UK being the fourth oldest, more recently Japan has been the oldest, with 33 per cent in 2017a; and the inclusion of more Eastern nations is projected by 2050 (UN DESA, 2013, 2017a).

Table 3.1: Ten countries or areas with the largest share of persons aged 60 or over, in 1980, 2017, 2050

	1980		2017		2050	
Rank	Country or area	Percentage aged 60 or over	Country or area	Percentage aged 60 or over	Country or area	Percentage aged 60 or over
1	Sweden	22.0	Japan	33.4	Japan	42.4
2	Norway	20.2	Italy	29.4	Spain	41.9
3	Channel Islands	20.1	Germany	28.0	Portugal	41.7
4	United Kingdom	20.0	Portugal	27.9	Greece	41.6
5	Denmark	19.5	Finland	27.8	Republic of Korea	41.6
6	Germany	19.3	Bulgaria	27.7	China, Taiwan Province of China	41.3
7	Austria	19.0	Croatia	26.8	China, Hong Kong SAR	40.6
8	Belgium	18.4	Greece	26.5	Italy	40.3
9	Switzerland	18.2	Slovenia	26.3	Singapore	40.1
10	Luxembourg	17.8	Latvia	26.2	Poland	39.5

Source: UN DESA (2017a), p 9. Data source: UN (2017), Table 2. Copyright © United Nations All rights reserved

https://www.un.org/en/development/desa/population/publications/pdf/ageing/WPA2017_Highlights.pdf

By the middle of the 21st century, population ageing will be truly global, with WHO data indicating that countries such as Iran and Vietnam will have much higher proportions of older people than is currently the case, and that other developed industrialised nations will have more than a quarter of their population aged 60 and over (WHO, 2015a, pp 43–5). The WHO reports that sub-Saharan Africa already has twice the number of older adults than northern Europe, being projected to reach 157 million by 2050, and that if people survive to the age of 60, life expectancy for men and women may be mid-70s (UN, 2019c).

Aboderin (2004, 2005) considers ageing in developing countries, looking at continuity and change in family relationships and the influence of labour market development and structural inequalities; while Lloyd-Sherlock (2010) guards against generalisation in terms of poverty and economic vulnerability in later life within developing nations, with three case studies from South Africa, Argentina and India that look at diversity in individual experience. He considers economic development and privatisation of services, pensions and healthcare, indicating similarities and differences, and the impact that the needs of the old and the young have on relationships. Aboderin and Beard (2014) focus specifically on the need for health resources for older people in sub-Saharan Africa. They show how older people in urban and rural areas provide care for grandchildren who have often been orphaned by HIV/Aids, while also maintaining smallholder agriculture at a time when younger people have moved to urban areas (Hoffman and Pype, 2018). In some cases, older people both give support and receive care themselves (see also Aboderin and Hoffman, 2012; Rishworth and Elliott, 2019).

Data in Research summary 3.1 indicates the prevalence of co-morbidity among older people, and the WHO constitution defines health as 'a state of complete physical, mental, and social wellbeing, and not merely the absence of disease or infirmity' (WHO, 2006, p 1). This holistic view indicates how increased life expectancy is linked to global profiles of health and well-being, while cultural difference demonstrates diverse biosocial trends, including variation in personal gene profiles, diet, accommodation, financial resources, access to healthcare and resulting lifestyle. Most recently, recognition has been given to chronic health conditions through non-communicable diseases, with WHO reporting that they account for 63 per cent of all deaths (WHO, 2015a, pp 58–75). Correlations are beginning to be seen between levels of economic development, urbanisation, food availability, obesity and physical activity and health conditions such as diabetes (see Butler, 2005; Crimmins and Zhang, 2019).

With regard to increased longevity in Western developed nations, a 'rectangularisation of survival curve' has been noted by many observers – meaning that the variability in age of death declines, with compression into the upper years of life. People are more likely to spend longer living with chronic conditions that may be disabling (see Bennett and Ibrahim, 1992; Ebeling et al, 2018). In the UK, the Office for National Statistics (ONS) (2018a, 2019b, 2020d) estimated that those aged 90 and over rose from 579,776 in 2017 to 584,024 in 2018, with 13,170 centenarians in 2018 and 13,330 in 2019. This longevity may affect where the oldest old live at the end of life. Environments of ageing in light of the COVID-19 pandemic are considered in Chapter 10.

When defining global health, Koplan et al (2009) comment that it 'is a synthesis of population based prevention with individual clinical care' (p 1995). This raises the question whether population ageing is a consequence of developments in global health that have enabled an increase in life expectancy. At one level, the answer must be yes, but political, social, biological and cultural factors will also impact on the characteristics of any national population; they are part of the environments of ageing. For example, although China has seen dramatic improvements in urban and rural healthcare provision since the late 20th century, the effects of the one-child policy initiated in 1979 led to a decrease in the birth rate and an increase in life expectancy. Despite some modifications to this policy in rural areas during the 1980s, it was not until October 2015 that reversion to a two-child limit took place, because of a predicted decline in the labour force and also the need for family care of an ageing population (Phillips and Feng, 2015; Feng et al, 2016). China is now ageing at one of the fastest rates in the world. While Japan is currently the oldest country globally, UN data indicate that while 12 per cent of China's population was aged 65 and over in 2019, by 2050 this is projected to be 27.5 per cent (Population Reference Bureau, 2019; China Power Project, 2020).

A further question may lie in person–environment (P–E) interaction, one aspect of the Koplan et al (2009) synthesis between prevention and care. In recognising the development of co-morbidity through chronic health conditions, the WHO discussion of global health and ageing takes into account the need for global long-term care, expressed simply as 'a means to ensure that older people with a significant loss of capacity can still experience Healthy Ageing' (WHO, 2015a, p 127), where the environment and technological change will be crucial (WHO, 2003, 2015a, 2015b). As this discussion shows, it is important to illustrate the diversity of demographic change across world regions.

The urban/rural continuum

The second global challenge in contextualising environments of ageing is ongoing urbanisation and change within the urban/rural continuum. In 2018, the UN made this comment on urban development: 'Globally, more people live in urban areas than in rural areas, with 55 per cent of the world's population residing in urban areas in 2018. […] by 2050, 68 per cent of the world's population is projected to be urban' (UN, 2019b, p xix).

Urbanisation varies significantly across geographical regions, with North America, Latin America and the Caribbean having more than 80 per cent of their population living in urban areas, followed closely by Europe (74 per cent) and Oceania (68 per cent). The level is approximately 50 per cent in Asia, while Africa 'remains mostly rural, with 43 per cent of its population living in urban areas' (UN, 2019b, p xix)

UN-Habitat advocates a new model of urbanisation given the diversity of city type (UN-HABITAT, 2016, p 37). Worldwide, there are a growing number of megacities, with the WorldAtlas reporting '37 each with a total population of more than 10 million people' (WorldAtlas, 2020), each of which has a potential density of at least 2,000 persons/square km, including merged urban areas. The UN suggests that this number may rise to 43 by 2030 (UN, 2018a, 2019). Currently, Tokyo is seen as the largest megacity alongside Shanghai, Beijing and Karachi, with variation dependent on whether metropolitan area or city boundaries are used (WorldAtlas, 2020).

Referring to the UN regions, the Americas and Asia have approximately 20 per cent of their populations living in cities of at least 5 million. Nevertheless, city size is diverse. In 2011, the OECD and the European Commission presented a new definition of a city as having a surrounding hinterland of 50,000 people, identifying 828 such cities in the EU, Switzerland, Croatia, Iceland and Norway (Brezzi et al, 2011). In regions such as Europe and Africa, at extremes of the development continuum, a majority live in relatively small cities with fewer than half a million inhabitants (UN, 2011, p 1), even though in developing countries urbanisation is happening much faster than historic growth in north-west Europe (Montgomery, 2008; Champion, 2011). Reflecting on these transitions, Phillipson considers the main elements of urbanisation to be driven by city size, the speed of development and urban complexity, referring to places of production and consumption that are interconnected globally (2010, p 597). Such change is reflected in informal settlement and slum dwellings, population mobility and changing family patterns, which contribute to growing inequality and exclusion (UN-HABITAT, 2016, p 17).

At a structural level, urbanisation raises many issues: city development, regeneration, urban sprawl and suburbanisation, gentrification, city decline, adequacy of housing infrastructure, homelessness, planning governance, transportation, sanitation, the changing location of facilities such as healthcare, and ongoing sustainability. These activities need to be addressed inclusively for all ages (Lofland, 2017) but many have specific implications in later life. The globalisation of economic resources, trade partnerships and industrial development means that while some cities continue to develop, others are experiencing a decline that impacts on the lives of the urban poor of all ages and contributes to levels of vulnerability; examples in the US are Detroit and Chicago (Sassen, 2001, 2004; UN-HABITAT, 2008; OECD, 2015). Research from the EU Urban Audit concerning quality of city life adds to this picture. A recent intergenerational survey from 2015, which covered 83 cities (the 28 EU countries, as well as the 'greater' cities of Paris, London, Athens and Manchester) indicated a diversity of satisfaction with urban living. The most common concerns related to health services, education and training, and unemployment, with housing fears being more important than unemployment in seven cities. Other concerns included safety, public transport, road infrastructure, air pollution, social services and noise (EU, 2016, pp 164–6).

Issues of urbanism are part of the experience of population ageing, and urban sociologists believe environmental gerontology should reconsider ageing in this light (Phillipson, 2004, 2010; Buffel and Phillipson, 2018). For example, although suburbanisation after the Second World War may be a common experience, long-term suburbanites may find gentrification that encourages younger working families to move into their neighbourhoods a challenge. Empirical research in the UK has shown how this experience affects the lives of older working-class residents, whose voices are too often unheard (Buffel and Phillipson, 2019).

While acknowledging the dominant urban population, although definitions vary, nation specificity must be noted when considering evidence concerning urban/rural living (Scharf et al, 2005a). In 2018, 45 per cent of the global population was living in rural areas (50 per cent in Asia and 57 per cent in Africa) (UN, 2019) and literature shows how population density, settlement and physical distance or drive/fly time between settlement(s) have been used to indicate levels of rurality (Hart et al, 2005; Keating and Phillips, 2008; Baylis and Sly, 2010, EU, 2019). Hennessy et al (2014) state that:

> In the majority of countries, it has been noted that rural areas continue to be disproportionately elderly (Kinsella, 2001) and the growth of the older segment of the population is occurring faster in rural than non-rural settings. Worldwide, 9.7% of rural population are aged 60 and over; in Europe, this figure is 22.9%, which is greater than the proportion of their counterparts (19.1%) living in urban areas (United Nations, 2009). (2014, pp 1–2)

The weighting towards an ageing rural population in parts of developed nations continues, is seen in Eurostat data for each of the EU-28 nations (EU, 2019, p 25). Analysis shows that in rural areas there were twice as many very old women to men, varying between 3:1 in Baltic states to 1.47:1 in Cyprus and Greece.

Figure 3.2: UK population distribution by percentage aged 65 and over, 2016 and 2039 (projected)

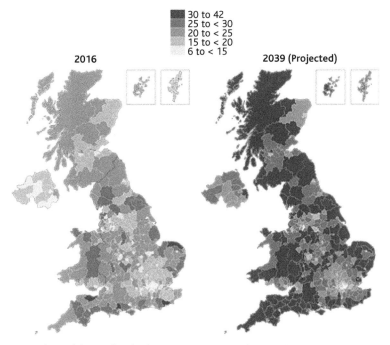

Source: ONS (2018a), licensed under the Open Government Licence. v.3.0
Source for Figure – 2016 mid-year population estimates for UK, Office for National Statistics, 2014-based subnational population projections for UK, Office for National Statistics, Welsh Government, National Records Scotland and Northern Ireland Statistics and Research Authority, contains OS data © Crown copyright 2018, London: ONS

A focus on the environments of ageing has to acknowledge these parallel trends. Figure 3.2 maps the distribution of population aged 65 and over for Britain in 2016, projected to 2039 (ONS, 2018a). In the UK, the official Rural–Urban Classification defines areas as rural if they are outside settlements with a resident population greater than 10,000 (DEFRA, 2016), and this projection indicates that coastal and many inland rural areas will gain a higher percentage of older people – through a combination of baseline population, ageing in place and post-retirement migration. Rural ageing is expected to grow particularly among post-retirement age groups, as seen in Figure 3.3 for 2016.

Further analysis has shown higher proportions of those aged 75 and over in particular locations – rural Wales, the South-West and South-East England (Bayliss and Sly, 2010). This is a European trend also seen in rural parts of Germany, Italy and Spain, where more than 35 per cent of the population is expected to be aged 60 and over by 2025 (Eurostat, 1999 in

Figure 3.3: Percentage of population within age bands by rural–urban classification (LSOA) in England, 2016

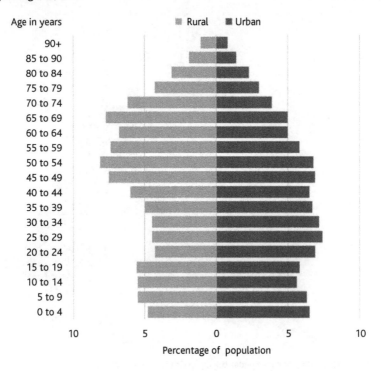

Source: Office of National Statistics licensed under the Open Government Licence .v.3.0. (2018a)
Living Longer: how our population is changing and why it matters. Figure 4. London: ONS
Note: LSOA stands for Lower Layer Super Output Area (see Glossary)

Phillipson and Scharf, 2005). At the other extreme, alongside London, lower percentages of older people (65 and over) are noted in urban centres such as Manchester, Oxford, Nottingham, Birmingham, Cardiff and Edinburgh, places of population change and diversity both cultural and intergenerational (Eurostat, 1999).

Definitions of rural and urban vary between nations depending on economic, social and cultural development (Requena, 2016). However, for those involved in rural studies, contemporary issues are often related to what is referred to as the 'mobilities turn', in essence the ways in which transportation, communication and technological development impact on the meaning of space and place for all ages (see Schwanen and Ziegler, 2011; Burholt and Dobbs, 2013; Shucksmith and Brown, 2016). Additionally Scharf, et al (2016), focusing on rural ageing in Ireland, highlight the heterogeneity of late life living and recognise the importance of inclusion and exclusion within defined communities. While some define rural living as related to 'everyday life in geographically bounded communities'

Shucksmith et al (2012, p 291), others argue that in Europe the divide between rural and urban is becoming blurred as personal mobility allows people to maintain their jobs and services while moving between localities (Champion, 2012, p 81). People have an urbanised lifestyle even though they may leave a city or town for periods of rural/semi-rural/suburban living on an occasional or regular basis (Soja and Kanai, 2008). Edmondson and Scharf (2015) comment that in later life transitions to different environmental experiences can afford opportunities for participation and agency – visiting family members, being second-home owners or becoming more permanent retirees. For some, establishing self in place may be periodic, while for others it is permanent.

This dichotomy of rural/urban living in later life is returned to in Chapter 4 as central to residential mobility both within and between nations. Here, though, it leads to the next major challenge – patterns of migration in relation to global population change.

Patterns of migration

Defined as the movement of population across national boundaries, migration is a constant global phenomenon (Urry, 2000; UNHCR, 2016, 2018; Dobie, 2019). The UN (DESA) Population Facts (2019d, 2019e) concerning international migrants distinguish between voluntary migration and forced migration (involving refugees and asylum seekers) and show that in recent years the latter has grown at a much faster rate that the former. They report that international migrants formed 3.5 per cent of the global population of 7.6 billion in 2019; almost 12 of every 100 inhabitants in the Global North compared with only 2 in 100 in the South (2, p 1).

With regard to the UN regions used in relation to the Sustainable Development Goals (see Glossary), Europe and North America have the largest number of international migrants, while migrant populations in Northern Africa, Western Asia and sub-Saharan Africa are growing more rapidly. Internal regional corridors of travel are common within Europe, Northern Africa, sub-Saharan Africa and Western Asia. Table 3.2 lists the top ten countries of origin for international migrants and the top ten countries that host most migrants in 2019; this accounts for a third of all international migrants.

Migration has particular implications for the ageing population, impacting on multicultural and intergenerational lifestyles and living arrangements whether as 'movers' or 'remainers' (Casado-Diaz et al, 2004; Warnes et al, 2004). Movement at different points of the life course can affect where and how people settle, and for older people where they may 'age in place'. Data from UN DESA (2019g) shows that adults of working age (20–64) form the growing proportion of migrants; between 1990 and 2019, this increased by 4

Table 3.2: International migration: top ten places of origin and destination in 2019

Places of Origin	Places of Destination
India	United States
Mexico	Germany
China	Saudi Arabia
Russian Federation	Russian Federation
Syrian Arab Republic	United Kingdom
Bangladesh	United Arab Emirates
Pakistan	France
Ukraine	Canada
The Philippines	Australia
Afghanistan	Italy

Source: United Nations, Department of Economic and Social Affairs, Population Division (2019f) International Migration, Population Facts, No 2019/4, p 3. September 2019. Copyright © United Nations All rights reserved.

per cent for women to 72 per cent, while men saw a 5 per cent increase to 76 per cent. The percentage of young migrants aged under 20 has declined to 14 per cent in 2019 from 19 per cent in 1990, while older migrants, aged 65 and older, has remained stable during this period at approximately 12 per cent, with more older women than men. A north–south split is seen across these statistics (UN DESA, 2019e, p 4). Commenting on the older migrant population in 2020, the Migration Data Portal notes:

> The estimated number of older migrants aged 65 or above in more developed regions increased by more than 12 million from 1990 to 2019, while in less developed regions, it only increased by a bit more than a million (ibid.). This is due to the fact that more developed countries in the northern hemisphere were the destination of the majority of international migrants who subsequently aged. In addition, the fact that migrants living in the southern hemisphere tend to return to their countries of origin as they age, explains why the estimated number of older migrants is only rising in developed regions. (Migration Data Portal, 2020)

UN DESA has also shown that 19 per cent of the foreign-born population live in urban areas, with a much higher percentage in major global cities (UN DESA, 2018c, p 3).

With this global profile, there is a need to unpack the distinction between voluntary and forced migration, and to relate this to population ageing. In 2006, Warnes and Williams, drawing on work by the European Science

Foundation Scientific Network concerning older migrants in Europe (Friedrich and Warnes, 2000; Warnes et al, 2004), began to develop a typology of migration and ageing that recognises the different needs of: labour migrants, return labour migrants, amenity-led migrants and family-oriented retirement migrants, so they can be considered globally (Warnes and Williams, 2006). Later, Warnes (2010) provided a detailed analysis of global migration history, the evolution of different forms of migration, including contemporary movements, and the position of ageing in relation to migrant types.

Older migrants in both the developed and developing world may include:

- **Labour migrants**, who moved for employment especially post-Second World War and throughout the 20th/21st centuries; they may now be experiencing old age as first- or second-generation migrants not in their native homeland (Blozman et al, 2004; Burholt, 2004).
- **Amenity-seeking pre-/post-retirees**, such as those 'snowbirds' moving from north/west Europe to southern Europe, or moving from the northern states of the US to the southern states (King et al, 2000). They are often affluent, less family oriented, own property in a different nation and are able to cope with cultural change and language differences. Their moves may be seasonal or they may decide to live out their lives beyond their original homeland; re-establishing the meaning of home (Huber and O'Reilly, 2004).
- **Return migrants**, who are older people who decide to return to their country or place of origin both within and between countries (Percival, 2013a, 2013b). They include both return labour migrants and return amenity-seeking migrants. Research shows the complexity of decision-making and the potential for relocation to happen or not (Blozman, 2013; Christou, 2013).
- **Family-joining migrants**, who move to be nearer family members for emotional attachment and social support outside their homeland.
- Those who are not migrants themselves but whose lives are influenced by the migration of family members and friends, and where **intimacy at a distance** often relies on communication through technology and travel. In these circumstances, older family members may also find themselves running 'skipped generation' households of grandparents and grandchildren that offer key care and support (UNPF/HelpAge International, 2012).
- **Refugees/conflict migrants**, who have fled their homeland owing to conflict, famine, natural disasters and may seek asylum. Older people in these emergency situations are faced with many disadvantages relating to health and welfare, poverty, housing and racism/ageism. (Dwyer and Papadimitriou, 2006; Phillips and Feng, 2018)

Many older migrants living in European countries face challenges through limited language skills, inadequate income and poor access to health services or acceptable housing (Boccagni, 2017). In Africa, migration between countries raises issues for those who move and those who remain (Hall, 2017). While the cause of population migration varies, another issue that affects residential mobility is the challenge of climate change. This global theme, which involves the sustainability of the built environment, impacts on the spatial environments of ageing.

Climate change

A focus on the environments of ageing has to acknowledge risk factors in relation to climate change. Whether you live in an inland urban area, a coastal zone or a rural village, no one escapes the growing experience of global warming and the potential unsustainability of the environment (Thunberg, 2019). Extreme weather events – cyclones, flooding, heatwaves, hurricanes and tornadoes – are leading to scientific understanding of climate change and the need to make the world more sustainable. 'Climate action' is the 13th UN Sustainable Development Goal (UN DESA, 2017; UN Development Programme, 2017), addressed globally by the Intergovernmental Panel on Climate Change (IPCC) (see the Glossary). The IPCC is currently working to the Paris Agreement on Climate Change (the Sixth Assessment Cycle) enforced in 2016 in relation to cutting greenhouse gas emissions (IPCC, 2018) (see Chapter 10).

At the annual UN Climate Change Conference (COP 25), held in Madrid in December 2019, the IPCC presented their most recent state of knowledge reports on:

- global warming of 1.5 °C
- climate change and land
- the ocean and cryosphere in a changing climate
(IPCC, 2018, 2019a, 2019b, 2019c)

The last of these relates to the unique role of the ocean, its frozen components including snow cover, glaciers and icecaps, and the impact of global warming on the shrinking cryosphere, ocean warming and the rise in sea levels. Consideration is given to the complex functions of all these factors with regard to the climate system and human behaviour – trade, transport, tourism. Commenting that approximately 10 per cent of the global population lives either in high mountain regions or low-lying coastal regions, the IPCC projects that figures will rise dramatically by 2050, with more than one billion people living in coastal areas (IPCC, 2019b, Ch. 2).

Approximately 2 per cent of global land area is in the low elevation coastal zone (LECZ), yet 10 per cent of the world's population and 13 per cent of the urban population live there (The Earth Institute, Columbia University, 2007). Earth scientists McGranahan et al (2007) bring together spatial geophysical and demographic data to show how the urban form can become 'a disaster waiting to happen' owing to development in coastal areas. Through analysis of material from 224 countries, they highlight particular vulnerability in the least developed countries, with 75 per cent of people in the LECZ living in Asia, contrasting with 11 per cent in OECD countries.

Population ageing forms a part of vital demographic data, yet it has taken dramatic climatic events leading to displacement and mortality to highlight the importance of spatial patterns and the diverse physiological, psychosocial and cultural impacts experienced by older generations (McCracken and Phillips, 2016). Following the Indian Ocean earthquake and tsunami in 2004 and the East Japan earthquake and tsunami in 2011, research with displaced older survivors living in temporary accommodation has highlighted how they were coping with the loss of family and friends, and showed that they needed professional help for health and social care. Even though encouraging people to leave their homes can be complex and demanding, planning in advance for such disasters should recognise the emotional and cultural needs of older people (Tomata et al, 2014; Okamoto et al, 2015; Soonthornchaiya et al, 2018; Harper, 2019).

In 2018, the WHO drew attention to the relationship between climate change and health, indicating the potential for 250,000 additional deaths per year through 'malnutrition, malaria, diarrhoea and heat stress' between 2030 and 2050 (WHO, 2018). There is developing evidence from public and environmental health research that older people are particularly vulnerable to temperature variation and heat mortality (Hajat et al, 2007, Watts et al, 2019). Both Klinenberg (2003) and Ogg (2005) have drawn attention to the impact of heatwaves in later life. During the summer of 1995, a heatwave caused an estimated 800 fatalities in Chicago that were substantially higher among the 'poorest and most vulnerable members of the elderly black population' (Ogg, 2005, p 5). Older Black men suffered more highly than older women, as did those living in underpopulated neighbourhoods with a higher crime rate and experiencing greater social isolation. In contrast, mortality was lower among more close-knit Hispanic communities.

A slightly different picture emerged in France during an unprecedented heatwave in August 2003 (Lagadec, 2004; Ogg, 2005, p 6), Over a two week period, an estimated 15,000 additional deaths were recorded across France, the majority of whom were older people. While many details concerning those who died are still unknown, certain characteristics have been established. Being an urban dweller was common, yet while some were socially isolated this was not a general characteristic. The greatest number of fatalities occurring in Paris were among people living in their own homes, retirement homes and hospitals, more likely to be aged 75 and older, and women. Of those who died, 70 per cent were women and 30 per cent men, in contrast to the Chicago data. However, Ogg states: 'In total, 42% of the 15,000 excess deaths registered during the heat wave occurred in hospitals, 35% at home, 19% in retirement homes and 3% in private clinics' (2005, p 17). This pattern may not be surprising given the gender longevity advantage for women and the fact that hospitals and retirement homes may accommodate some of the oldest old, with women more likely to suffer problems of thermoregulation than men (Ogg, 2005, p 17). At the same time, many younger people were away from the cities taking annual holidays, and were not able to offer support to family members; this led to a major public and political discussion concerning care and the ageing population. Through his analysis, Ogg begins to show how the themes outlined in this chapter are interrelated. First, he notes that 'urbanity can be directly related to the climatic conditions of heatwaves' (p 26) through the 'urban heat island effect', with inner cities retaining higher heat levels than suburbs and rural areas; and second, that for those living in retirement homes and other institutions the lack of air conditioning may have caused higher than average death rates – a design issue that needs further examination.

Energy and transportation are two areas where emissions of pollutants into the air can result in global warming. Traffic pollution can cause mortality (Atkinson et al, 2016) across all ages, and yet transportation and mobility become crucial factors in later life. Chronic health conditions can increase vulnerability to the impact of atmospheric conditions, and vice versa. In London, the current mayor, Sadiq Khan, is aiming to develop the Ultra Low Emission Zone, which was created in 2019 following legal recognition of poor air quality.

Nevertheless, older people are just as likely to hold materialist values that relate to consumption patterns and driving habits as other generations. They too are therefore contributors to pollution as well as victims of climate change.

Over past centuries, energy consumption in industrialised nations has been dominated by the use of fossil fuels, with alternatives such as nuclear energy being experienced as dangerous and problematic (Dittmor, 2012). Even though there needs to be further mainstream acceptance and investment in wave, wind and solar energy in the UK, it is one of the 21 countries seen by Nhede (2020) to be developing renewable energy effectively, now generating more electricity from wind farms than from coal power plants (Nhede, 2020). Further discussion of global concern over climate change is developed in Chapter 10 as the UK with Italy host the UN COP26 Climate Change Conference in Glasgow in November 2021.

The built environment

The combination of locality and dwelling providing levels of shelter, security, familiarity and meaning (Peace, 2015) is central to environments of ageing and requires sustainability. While not denying the traumatic experience of homelessness (Crane et al, 2005; Crane and Joly, 2014; Grenier et al, 2016), the restricted living of older and disabled prisoners (Glover, 2012) or the transience and lack of rootedness that exists for many, the desire to find affordable housing is argued to be a basic aspiration, and a reason why the built environment is to be found in a discussion of global population ageing.

The WHO raises these concerns in its report on ageing and health, noting issues of housing adequacy within both economically developed and less economically developed nations. It states:

> The right to adequate housing encompasses a range of concepts relevant to older people, such as:
>
> - guaranteeing legal protection of tenure against forced evictions, harassment and other threats;
> - being sufficiently affordable such that the costs do not threaten or compromise the occupants' enjoyment of other basic needs;
> - ensuring access to safe drinking water, adequate sanitation, energy for cooking, heating, lighting, food storage and refuse disposal;
> - ensuring habitability – that is, guaranteeing physical safety, providing adequate space, protecting against threats to health and against structural hazards, and not being located in polluted or dangerous areas;
> - ensuring accessibility and usability, for example by taking into consideration declines in capacity;
> - facilitating access to transportation, shopping, employment opportunities, health-care services and other social facilities;
> - respecting the expression of cultural identity. (WHO, 2015a, p 162)

The form and function of housing and surrounding areas provide the context for daily living. The built environment is central to our understanding of materiality in this text, while not ignoring the importance of the natural physical environment in situating and developing personal well-being. The basic infrastructure of villages, towns and cities includes sites for education, employment, health and welfare as well as residential housing and transportation. Through historic development, housing type and form will vary enormously according to landownership and economic investment, both public and private. Variation is seen from high-rise apartments to duplexes, bungalows to terraces, maisonettes to chawls, favelas to shanti,

Figure 3.4: Housing – so much diversity

pueblo to hogan, as noted in Figure 3.4 (see Rapoport, 1969, 1985, 2005). Issues of climate change in relation to sustainable housing have already been noted, and ongoing research and future practice regarding resistant building materials, together with sustainable heating and lighting energy alongside inclusive design, are essential.

In addition, communality of function relates to activities of daily living where cultural and financial differences determine the spatial layout of dwellings. Defined internal spaces such as kitchen, toilet, bedroom and living room alongside external corridors, balconies, gardens or garages may have more or less importance culturally and financially (Kent, 1993; Ozaki, 2002).

The term 'home' is a commonly used multidimensional concept that may relate to a family dwelling as the basic social group or to another intentional group, including those living in intergenerational or age-specific co-housing. As people age, we see that in different circumstances, cultures and nations living arrangements will vary from extended to nuclear families, to forms of coupledom or living alone (Blunt and Varley, 2004). There will be differences in the degree to which people continue to live in their own home as they age or move to what they may see as more appropriate housing (Peace et al, 2011). Residential housing may be owned or rented, and this will vary depending on the nation and its housing history and policy. Unpacking the meanings of home is a running theme in this book.

Architectural design, housing type and building construction evolve over time and are directed by housing policy. Across the 20th century, attention has been given to home ownership by young mobile nuclear families alongside more or less development of public/social housing and rather less concern for lone person households (Matrix, 1984; Colquhoun, 1999; Jabareen 2005). Currently, there is a call for housing reform in many countries owing to housing shortages, high rental costs, increasing house prices and declining ownership, where national and local policy is directing housing quality (Adler, 2017). Across the century, the gradual emergence of 'social architecture' has been noted, where design practice seeks to enhance well-being with co-design being valued (Mumford, 1928, 1938; Goldsmith, 1963, 2001; Clarkson et al, 2003; Coleman et al, 2003; Keates and Clarkson, 2003a, 2003b).

Nevertheless, change to more inclusive design has been slow to emerge for many, including those whose needs are physically embodied either across life or in later life and those who are denied recognition through gender and culture (Matrix, 1984; Huppert, 2003; Peace, 2016). Boys (2014, p 2) challenges all involved in design to see working with disability as a starting point, and in many countries legislation and building regulations have begun to take account of more inclusive design not only for housing standards but also for accessibility to transportation (see Construction Industry Council, 2017). Inclusive or universal design are terms used by architects, designers, engineers and ergonomists particularly in the developed world when they are attempting to meet the needs of a wide range of people for particular types of housing, environment or product (Preiser and Ostroff, 2001; Coleman et al, 2003). For older people, some age-friendly design initiatives are evolving more commonly in specialised settings than in ordinary housing, and are beginning to be addressed for those working beyond state retirement age (Clarkson et al, 2003; American Institute of Architects, 2014, Thomson, 2018, Centre for Ageing Better, 2020). Marion Bieber, aged 81 and leading a study group on 'design for all ages' in the University of Third Age says: '[I] believe that understanding the needs of the consumer of all ages is vital. What I call good design is appropriate design for all to enjoy and that can only be achieved by changing attitudes to ageing, and constant consultation in the early stages of idea development' (2003, p 57).

This focus on inclusive design in the built environment sits alongside the WHO supranational initiative to encourage the creation of age-friendly cities and communities (AFCC) (Plouffe and Kalache, 2010). Originating in the WHO Healthy Cities Movement in the 1980s (WHO, 1986, 2003), since 2005 the global WHO AFCC initiative has aimed to promote active ageing 'by optimizing opportunities for health, participation, and security in order to enhance quality of life as people age' (WHO 2002, 2007, p 1). Initial development took place across 33 cities – from Mexico City to Istanbul, from New Delhi to New York – where focus groups heard the views of a diverse group of people aged 60 and over. One hundred and fifty eight groups with 1,485 older participants were involved, as well as 250 caregivers and 515 service providers (WHO, 2007), resulting in the definition of eight key age-friendly topic areas (see Figure 4.2) (see Rémillard-Boilard, 2019).

AFCC is now a worldwide programme with major advocates, and as of 2020, there are over 1,000 communities and cities within the Global Network of Age-friendly Cities and Communities, which began in 2010 with 11 cities (WHO, 2020b). This initiative offers an approach to developing a more socially inclusive way of living for people in later life. Here an initiative at supranational level promotes environment as key to health development and central to active enablement, while recognising the diversity of needs within varied contexts (Beard and Petitot, 2011). The built environment is only one aspect of this policy development, which seeks to encourage civic and social participation among people in later life. In Chapter 4, this initiative and the construct of 'age-friendly' (see Rémillard-Boilard, 2019) is explored in more detail.

Technological development

The last global theme considered here is technology, which became a part of most people's lives beginning in the post-war period and more widely in the 21st century. In 2010, McCreadie highlighted that 'technology is now an essential part of everyday life in all countries, to varying degrees, of the world. The wealthier a country is, the more likely its citizens are to depend on a huge and constantly changing range of technology in their day-to-day activities' (p 607).

How information and communications technology (ICT) is reported sometimes fails to recognise its potential breadth. In Table 3.3, the mobile phone, television, computer and tablet are shown to be the most commonly used forms for all adults in the UK in 2017. These widespread forms of global technology exist alongside a range of assistive technologies particularly in developed countries, with the microwave sitting alongside the dishwasher within domestic homes, for example (Saville Rossiter-Base, 2019).

Interestingly, for the population aged 55 and over, the TV, mobile phone and radio are the most commonly accessed and used forms of technology, whereas for younger people the TV and mobile phone compete. For many, technology means the use of a computer and being online. Data from the Office of National Statistics (ONS, 2018b) shows that 89 per cent of British adults of all ages used the internet on a weekly basis in 2018, which was 38 per cent higher than in 2006. For those aged 65 and over, 48 per cent used the internet for online shopping in 2018, rising from 16 per cent in 2010 (ONS, 2018b, reported by Marston et al, 2019). In contrast, access to the internet was much lower for people aged 75 and over, less than 50 per cent across the UK (ONS, 2019a).

Table 3.3: Adults' access to and use of media/devices, UK 2017

	55–64		65–74		75+		All Adults	
				%				
	Access	Use	Access	Use	Access	Use	Access	Use
Mobile phone	93	84	90	78	86	72	94	89
Computer	70	62	65	57	51	45	73	67
Tablet	63	57	54	48	34	28	65	58
Standard TV	68	62	81	77	88	85	67	58
DVR	57	49	45	36	41	37	52	44
Radio	73	61	66	59	75	66	58	47
Smart TV set	45	42	32	30	18	16	46	44
Games console	17	5	6	2	1	0	38	21
Wearable tech.	10	6	3	1	2	1	13	9
Streaming media player	17	13	9	6	3	2	21	17
Any TV	99	93	99	97	99	96	97	91

N=1,875 adults 16+.

Source: Adapted from Fig. 1, Ofcom (2018), p 23.

With regard to the environments of ageing, both community and dwelling based, technology can assist communication, activate mobility, aid navigation, provide entertainment and education, enhancing leisure, monitor health and social care, and enable and motivate behaviour through human–robotic interaction (Paterson, 2010; Schillmeier and Domenech, 2010; Jones, 2015). Focusing on personal communication, consumer capture varies, and the mobile phone remains dominant in terms of availability, followed by the computer (particularly laptops/tablets) facilitating contact with others and wider internet use. Those concerned with the distribution of mobile phones indicate different degrees of technological impact. Data relating to people of all ages may indicate greater use in developed nations such as Saudi Arabia or Russia and less use in a majority of developing African countries (Bates, 2016); while variation in terms of socio-economic status, education, occupation, gender, ethnicity and age influences the pattern of use. The impact of the mobile phone is noted among young people in some developing nations. In Nigeria, where the median age in 2018 was just under 18, it was reported that there were 146 million active mobile phone users and 92 million internet users in a population of just over 195 million, or 74 per cent and 47 per cent respectively, reflecting a rapid rise in use (Johnson, 2020).

The creation of the virtual environment is central to networked societies, impacting on how time and space are perceived (Castells, 1996, 2009; Jones, 2015). More older people across the world are communicating with their family and friends using social media platforms such as Skype, Instagram, Facebook and Zoom on laptop computers to maintain intimacy at a distance (see Turner et al, 2007; Porter, 2016; Ahlin, 2017; Liu, et al, 2018) with a slightly greater number of Facebook users being older women than men (Loe, 2010; ONS, 2019a; Johnson, 2020).

A series of issues are raised here regarding access to technology for the older population, including financial resources, personal motivation, availability of suitably designed products for people with special needs, the ability to learn new skills with access to tuition, which may be informal and within the family or more formal and communal, and the influence on care between generations (Selwyn et al, 2003; Freeman et al, 2020). Older people have experienced different forms of exclusion from technology, particularly the need for skills development (Holland, 2014; Jones, 2015). Yet while these issues regarding the 'digital divide' will be true for some, particularly members of the oldest old where poorer health and living with dementia is more common, the stereotypical view that older people are just not involved in using technology is changing. In 2012, Holland noted this contradictory view:

> According to Ofcom, the UK's independent communication industries regulator, in 2009 the growth in internet take-up that year [...] appeared for the first time to have been driven by those aged over 55, for whom the use of email was particularly important (Ofcom, 2010). [...] and in 2010 it was still the case that 64 per cent of those individuals who had never accessed the internet were aged over 65 (ONS, 2010). (2012, pp 156–7)

Yet as Table 3.2 indicates, statistics from Ofcom ten years later shows that mobile phone use has risen dramatically, while computer use for the 55–74 year olds lies between just over half to two thirds.

While these forms of technology have a personal and general value for many living in all forms of accommodation, other forms of technology known as Telecare and Telehealth/medicine may have specific value for those living alone as vulnerable adults in any setting and have potential for more integrated care (Goodwin, 2010; Bowes and McColgan, 2013). In the UK, Telecare alarm systems are more common in specialised housing and focus on safety and security. They commonly involve an older person wearing a pendant alarm or pulling a cord that enables personal contact through a call centre should the user feel at risk or experience an emergency such as a fall. These alarms are sometimes used alongside safety sensors for gas leaks or bath floods. Telehealth/medicine refers to a more clinical service and may target an acute or chronic healthcare need; for example, through follow-up or specialist consultations through telephone, video communication or two way messaging; prompting medication management at certain times; or providing electronic surveillance and monitoring to record movement and location (through GPS systems). All of these may be of value to individuals and/or formal/informal carers of people with cognitive impairment. The use of technological solutions such as these may lead to less human contact (Poole, 2006), and while technologies can enable independent living, the ethics of these forms of monitoring and surveillance continue to be discussed (Mortenson et al, 2015).

Research focusing on the value of one product or technological development is a complex issue. It encompasses diverse fields – from assistive technology to human–computer interaction, from ergonomics to gerontechnology, from telecare to robotics, from sensor-related door opening to social networking (see McCreadie, 2010; Sixsmith and Guttman, 2013; Holland, 2014). These areas are more or less applied or product driven, and consideration of such interactions is a relatively recent addition to the discussion around personal interaction with the material environment and the environments of ageing. A gradual increase in the use of assistive technology can clearly be seen, and how enabling this can be is discussed further in Chapters 5 and 10. Solutions that make life sustainable through ongoing technological development are key to issues raised regarding living with climate change and developing an inclusive built environment.

Social exclusion in later life

Having considered this wide range of global issues where population ageing is an important parallel trend, we turn to issues of social exclusion and inequality that influence the effects of global trends on individual lives. Scharf and Keating (2012) define the concept of social exclusion for individuals and groups in later life by discussing its multidimensional nature, which is seen as dynamic, agentic and relative to the general (normative) context within society. They indicate three interrelated 'drivers' that contribute to exclusion: structural drivers that operate at national or supernational levels such as age discrimination, changing values and behaviours that marginalise older people, and the impact of social and economic policies; individual drivers related to personal, social, economic and health circumstances; and environmental drivers that relate to living environments in later life (2012, p 8).

To further deconstruct their understanding of old-age exclusion, Scharf and Keating present with Walsh the findings of a detailed international scoping review and knowledge synthesis (Walsh et al, 2017). Frameworks for conceptual development are varied, and include issues such as economic deprivation and austerity, cumulative disadvantage, institutional disengagement, the impact of critical life events and spatial segregation. Across these issues certain domains appear, and through further analysis the authors define an 'old age exclusion framework' as a basis for targeted research. They propose this definition:

> Old-age exclusion involves interchanges between multi-level risk factors, processes and outcome. Varying in form and degree across the older adult life course, its complexity, impact and prevalence are amplified by old-age vulnerabilities, accumulated disadvantage for some groups, and constrained opportunities to ameliorate exclusion. Old-age exclusion leads to inequalities in choice and control, resources and relationships, and power and rights in key domains of neighbourhood and community; services, amenities and mobility; material and financial resources; social relations; socio-cultural aspects of society; and civic participation. Old-age exclusion implicates states, societies, communities and individuals. (Walsh et al, 2017, p 93)

The global themes introduced here, regarding the urban/rural divide, migration, climate change, the material environment and technology, have begun to show how certain factors impact on the inclusion of people in later life. A particular aim of this text is to test this framework, and to observe how issues at a global level relate to advantage and disadvantage in later life as they are experienced at national and local levels.

Conclusions

The macro-level provides the widest context for exploring the P–E interface in later life. These first three chapters are a foundation for understanding issues relating to person and environment, the current theoretical development underpinning environmental gerontology and the major related global challenges. It is possible to capture different levels of the spatiality of ageing and begin to see the interchange between them. This analysis draws upon strategic developments and personal challenges at meso- and micro-levels that affect social inclusion in later life; while the following five chapters focus on environments of ageing within England and the UK.

4

Environmental living

Introduction

While different dimensions of environment – physical, social, cultural, political – can be considered separately, together they form the environmental context of place that is central to an ecological perspective. Throughout their lives, people live in dynamic interaction with this context, developing psychological understanding of it (Wahl and Lang, 2004; Keating et al, 2013), a view referred to here as 'environmental living'. Environmental living in later life is the focus of the following five chapters. We move to national (meso-) and local (micro-) scales of reference, using the UK and England as an example, in which locations, settings and situations can be examined. As these scenarios are central to research undertaken by the author and colleagues over the past decades, Chapter 6 forms a bridge to empirical research connecting issues relating to intergenerational and age-related environments. The concept of 'home' alongside associated issues of 'homeland' is pivotal in this discussion; it is introduced here and is a running theme throughout.

Home and homeland

The word 'home' has diverse cultural definitions and is at the heart of a breadth of literature. For many it is a locational term, which is focused on specific housing yet often has a broader base regarding neighbourhood, community, city and nation – connecting with the concept of homeland. This extended definition includes layers of attachment that help to define a person's identity within a particular place. Space and place merge in a meaning of home that is associated with the personal through positive concepts of belonging, security, familiarity and privacy, while sometimes guarding negative concerns regarding gendered domestic activity, non-decent housing, isolation, loneliness and a life of fear or abuse (Peace, 2015).

Consideration of the meaning of home is essential to discussion of the environments of ageing as part of the person–environment (P–E) dynamic, place attachment and the understanding of ageing in place. Chapters 4, 6, 7, 8 reflect on its meaning through physical/built, social, locational and personal aspects to understand how a sense of home embodies the older person through times of continuity, relocation and change. A question raised by the author elsewhere will continue to be considered: 'Can the ideology of home be re-created throughout later life in any place including non-domestic and age-segregated communal settings?' (Peace, 2015, p 450).

The older population is truly heterogeneous and has diverse social capital. Differences can exist between home as place and home as dwelling, with ambiguity between positive and negative meanings. For environments of ageing, this poses a question about whether the meaning of home can embrace a sense of social inclusion or exclusion, or both. Issues of gender within a patriarchal society have impacted the design of dwellings over centuries, with women designers making a case since the later 20th century for more inclusive design that will assist everyday living for women across the life course, thus raising issues of family care (Boys et al, 1984; Foo, 1984).

Design may also impede older people: if they are unable to negotiate their immediate neighbourhood or participate in their community, they may experience social exclusion. Yet at the same time they may feel at home in their own dwelling, where boundaries define privacy and allow autonomy, and social relations enable an inclusion that is uniquely personal. How does the definition of homeland impact on issues of social inclusion? Do complex aspects of environmental living affect the individual in different ways? These questions are addressed in the following chapters and in a discussion in Chapter 10.

Home as place

In this chapter, the focus is location, primarily in Britain, and the impact of location on rural/urban lifestyles. This leads to deliberation on whether or not this is an age-friendly place and the chapter ends with reflections on place as home. To begin a focus on rural/urban living demands, that consideration is given to population diversity.

Population distribution in the UK

In mid-2019, the UK population was estimated to be 66.8 million with 12.4 million (18.5 per cent) aged 65 and over, projected to be 25 per cent by 2050 (ONS, 2020a). The oldest age group, 85 and over, currently 1.6 million (2.5 per cent), is predicted to double to 3.2 million by mid-2041 and treble by 2066 to 5.1 million (7 per cent of the population) (ONS, 2018a, 2020a). Both fertility and mortality rates are declining and there are changes in migration, leading to a rebalancing of the population towards older age groups. Variations in the ratio between working and non-working populations are resulting in slightly higher old age dependency ratios. Life expectancy at birth is slowing down, remaining constant between 2015 and

Table 4.1: Population estimates for the nations of the UK, 2019

	Population 2019	Population aged 65 and over (2018/2019)
England	56,286,961	18.5% (mid-2019)
Wales	3,152,879	16.2% (mid-2019)
Scotland	5,463,300	19% (mid-2018)
Northern Ireland	1,893,667	15% (mid-2019)
Total	66,796,807	18.5% (mid-2019)

Source: ONS, 2020a, licensed under the Open Government Licence v.3.0

2017 at 79.2 for males and 82.9 for females (ONS, 2020b), continuing to indicate slightly more older women than men.

Table 4.1 indicates the difference in population size in the four UK nations, the dominance of England and estimates for the percentage of population aged 65 and over. Information described as Great Britain, Britain or British relates to England, Scotland and Wales.

As noted in Chapter 3, rural ageing varies across the UK, and the distribution is far from uniform (See Figures 3.2, 3.3). Although approximately 90 per cent of all ages in the UK live in urban areas – cities, towns and suburbs (Champion, 2008; Phillipson, 2010) – there are contrasting urban–rural geographic differences across the four nations. In England in mid-2014, 83 per cent were living across urban communities from town to city to conurbations, even though the older population was more likely to be rural/semi-rural (DEFRA, 2016) especially in South-West and South-East England. More than two thirds of the population in Wales and Northern Ireland live in urban/semi-urban areas, with a greater proportion living in rural and semi-rural locations across both countries. In Scotland, 83 per cent of the population is reported as living in 2 per cent of land that is not seen as either accessible rural (28 per cent) or remote rural (70 per cent) (National Records Scotland, 2018; NISRA, 2020; Welsh Government, 2020)

An extreme comparison is given in Table 4.2 between the population distribution of London, the metropolitan capital with 33 local authority districts including inner and outer London boroughs plus the City of London, and the rural county of Cornwall, in South-West England. While each London borough is distinct, this profile shows that metropolitan London has a lower percentage of older people, is multicultural and has a very much higher population density than rural Cornwall. While life expectancy has been relatively slow to increase in the past decade, there is a four to five year variation for women and men living in different London boroughs, where diverse socio-economic factors relate to health inequalities (Greater London Authority, 2018).

Table 4.2: Characteristics of metropolitan London and the county of Cornwall, 2019

	London	Cornwall
Population estimates 2019	8.962 million	569,578
% population 65 and over	12.2%	25%
population density	5,701/km2	160/km2
life expectancy?	79.6 M/83.8 F	79.8M/83.3 F
ethnicity white British	45%	95.7%

Sources: Lumby, 2019. Adapted from data from ONS (2020a, 2020c, 2020d, 2020e), licensed under the Open Government Licence v.3.0

Those aged 20–40 form the largest age group in London. In contrast, recent data for London boroughs show very low populations aged 65 and over particularly in Tower Hamlets (7 per cent), Lambeth (8 per cent) and Newham (8 per cent) (Wills and Belcher, 2020). Although some of the younger age cohorts may age in place, it has been more common for middle-aged residents to move out of the central London boroughs to suburbs in outer boroughs or beyond. The implications of very high house prices, increased private renting and the desire to be family homeowners will have a marked effect on age patterns within the capital city in coming years (McKee, 2012; Druta and Ronald, 2016; Minton, 2017a).

Such locational differences reflect generational variation in the pull and push of employment, suburbanisation, retirement patterns, residential staying put, relocation and attachment to place. Explanation for patterns of movement include internal migration, external immigration, the dominance of a younger working population living in metropolitan London and an older population that has either aged in place, benefited from having had a second home or moved to coastal retirement areas. The Cornish population distribution showed a slightly greater proportion of older women in the 75 and over age groups in the 2011 census.

A multicultural population

As seen in Table 4.2, the multicultural nature of the capital provides an extreme contrast to Cornwall. Consequently, as internal migration and external immigration are added to this rural/urban profile, a more complex picture emerges (Davies, 1999). The diverse population in the UK emerges from a history of empire – through colonisation, industrial development, world trade, labour force shortages, leisure consumption, humanitarian response to conflict, membership of the European Union (EU) and departure at the end of 2020, all of which influence the distribution of the ageing population, with variation across the four nations. As a colonial country, patterns of migration reflect this past history, and here as an example in-migration from the mid-19th century, with Irish immigrants to Britain escaping poverty and famine in Ireland through potato crop failures and English land ownership, is considered. There are said to be as many as 6 million people with Irish heritage or 10 per cent of the UK population and the Office of National Statistics (ONS) reports that between 2013 and 2015 one in three Irish-born people were living in London, the south-east and north-west (ONS, 2018a)

A subsequent period of substantial labour migration was encouraged after the Second World War, from the late 1940s to the 1970s. This was primarily to urban areas, with immigration from Commonwealth countries including the Caribbean and West Indies, India, Pakistan and Bangladesh leading to particular concentrations of migrant communities in London, the cities of the West Midlands (Birmingham, Wolverhampton, Coventry), Manchester, Bradford, Leicester, Liverpool, Luton and Cardiff. Those coming later to join family members or for education have found themselves living predominantly in towns and cities. Migrants from Canada, Australia and New Zealand have also settled particularly in London.

The other major development leading to population diversity and multiculturalism has been through the UK's membership of the EU (and its predecessors) since 1973 and the open borders for trade and labour movement between EU nations. In the late 20th and 21st centuries, labour migration especially from East European EU countries such as Poland, Romania, Serbia, Ukraine and Bulgaria has seen place-specific communities develop, an example being a Polish community in Crewe. Such diversity has contributed to public discussion and political debate regarding continuing migration, a factor contributing to Brexit, which was finalised at the end of December 2020 (see the Glossary). Owing to this change, it is difficult to predict migration flows as the UK begins to realise a new set of relationships with other countries/regions.

Recent data concerning the multicultural nature of the population relate to England and Wales and come from the national census in 2011, in which 18 ethnic categories were recorded under five overarching groups: white (4), mixed/multiple ethnic groups (4), Asian/Asian British (5), Black/African/Caribbean/Black British (3), other ethnic group (2) (ONS, 2018c). White was the major ethnic group in 2011 for 86.0 per cent of those recorded; with White British being the largest category with a population of 45.1 million (80.5 per cent). The sub-category White Other includes migrants from countries such as Australia or Poland. People from Asian ethnic groups formed 7.5 per cent of the population, followed by 3.3 per cent from Black ethnic groups.

Urban/rural difference embodies the varied distribution of minority ethnic groups across regional areas of England and Wales, with London

Table 4.3: Ethnic population of England and Wales by age cohort, 2011

Ethnic group ('000s)	50–59	60–69	70–79	80 and over
White British	2,958 (13%)	2,811 (12%)	1,931 (8%)	1,536 (7%)
BME	308 (8%)	172 (5%)	114 (3%)	57 (2%)
White other	104 (8%)	64 (5%)	38 (3%)	29 (2%)
Indian	79 (11%)	48 (7%)	29 (4%)	12 (2%)
Pakistani	37 (7%)	18 (3%)	12 (2%)	4 (1%)
Bangladeshi	11 (5%)	7 (3%)	4 (2%)	1 (0%)
Black African	33 (6%)	13 (3%)	6 (1%)	1 (0%)
Black Caribbean	44 (14%)	22 (7%)	24 (7%)	9 (3%)

Source: Standard table DC2101EW, 2011 census from de Noronha (2019), p 10

a uniquely multicultural metropolis, as seen in Figure 4.1. with 44.9 per cent White British and 40.2 per cent of residents identified as belonging to Asian, Black, Mixed or Other ethnicities. The West Midlands region follows London in terms of diversity, especially in relation to the Asian and Asian British communities.

This intergenerational data provides a national locational context for discussing environments of ageing for multicultural communities, and further analysis unpacks the age range. As many minority ethnic groups have a lower life expectancy than the White British, population distributions for Black and minority ethnic groups are often given for those aged 50 and over. Table 4.3 gives comparison with the White British older population at the last census, and reflects both historical migration patterns of the older generations and the growing similarities of the younger groups, particularly for Indian and Black Caribbeans. Multiculturalism has a predominantly urban trend, with each town/city witnessing a gradual development of an even more diverse ageing population in terms of language, diet, religion and culture.

Key issues

This UK profile raises a number of issues. First, there is the contrast between the growing ageing population in rural and coastal areas (in all four nations) and the intergenerational and multicultural population within urban areas. This demographic difference needs to be acknowledged particularly in strategic discussion and policy decisions relating to housing, service provision and transportation, as well as wider issues such as urbanisation and the impact of climate change, particularly in rural and coastal areas.

Figure 4.1: Areas of England and Wales by ethnicity, 2011

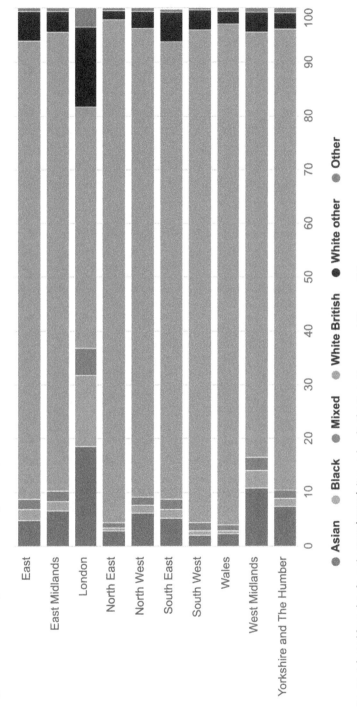

● Asian   ● Black   ● Mixed   ● White British   ● White other   ● Other

Source: Adapted from data from the ONS (2020e), licensed under the Open Government Licence v.3.0

Second, the gradual ageing of first- and second-generation migrant groups will increase within urban areas especially in the West Midlands, the North and parts of London. Multiculturalism will have different effects, perhaps most crucially in relation to living arrangements, housing tenure, overcrowding, intergenerational support and informal care, and knowledge regarding service provision. Issues relating to language, diet, health, religion and culture are being recognised (Lievesley, 2010; Phillipson, 2015a, Shankley and Finney, 2020). The formal caring workforce also draws heavily on migrant groups, an issue brought to the fore most recently by the COVID-19 pandemic, which has had particular impact on minority ethnic groups, as further discussed in Chapter 10. The impact of this diversity is not as prevalent in rural areas.

Nevertheless, periods of austerity and economic insecurity influence ageing in place in all locations, and the dichotomy between the 'haves' and 'have nots' can be pronounced. Inequalities exist where housing costs, income stagnation and intergenerational inequities are prevalent. There is a need for an intergenerational discussion over housing assets, financial transfers and ongoing support (Alexander, 2018). This profile of diverse population ageing provides a national backdrop for turning to urban and rural communities as places to live in later life.

Living in urban and rural communities

The following discussion picks up the urban/rural challenge from Chapter 3 and considers environments of ageing within intergenerational communities, where people are familiar with a particular physical and socio-cultural environment that many will have chosen through family or personal history, connections or employment opportunities. While length of residence will vary, many older people may be long-term residents who have developed an attachment to place over time (Rowles, 1983, 2018; Smith, 2009).

Are our views of urban and rural living stereotypical? In the UK, it is often thought that the 'rural idyll' is one where well-being is found through attitudes, values and tranquillity that come from being more closely in touch with nature (Halfacree, 1993, 2006; Giarchi, 2006). The pace of life may be thought to be slower and more relaxed, even though ageing in rural areas has been challenged by structural issues – limited public transport and greater distance to services, with loneliness and social isolation increasing as a consequence (Wenger, 1995, 2001; Scharf and Bartlam, 2006; Walsh et al, 2012; Walsh et al, 2015). In contrast, stereotypes regarding urban living comment on a hurried and impersonal yet stimulating and progressive lifestyle, focused perhaps on younger generations. Wenger (2001) argues that rural living in later life is neither better nor worse than living in urban areas (p 126).

While the rurality of ageing was noted in Chapter 3, the English Housing Survey (2014–15) shows that older households (55 and older) are predominantly urban dwellers (77 per cent), slightly lower than younger households (84 per cent), even though in comparison a greater number of older households are found living in villages, hamlets and isolated dwellings (DCLG, 2016). This duality of presence in different types of environment is important (see Figure 3.2) relating to the rural–urban classification system (see p 99). While certain characteristics are generic across place, for example the natural environment is valued, engagement with media and technology is universal even if internet systems may not be as efficient in rural areas (Bhatti, 2006; Peace et al, 2006, Townsend et al, 2015)

As noted when commenting on rural/urban difference population size, density as well as distance to other settlements are important and nation-specific. For example, while a population of fewer than 10,000 may be seen as rural in the UK, this can be fewer than 1,000 in Canada, even though variation in landscape, transportation and services can affect life in both environments (Chapman and Peace, 2008; Keating and Phillips, 2008). If there are similarities between the lives of older people living in very different types of rural community, then is the difference between rural and urban living that dissimilar? Edmondson and Scharf, in agreement with Wenger, comment that 'as far as the impacts of ageing are concerned, urban and rural environments may not always be as different as is popularly assumed' (2015, p 412).

To further reflect on these lifestyles, we turn to four major British studies. Research summary 4.1. outlines the aims, locations and methodology for each study.

Research summary 4.1: Urban/rural research

A. *The Family and Community Life of Older People* Phillipson et al (1998, 2001)

Aims: to revisit earlier research (Sheldon, 1948, Townsend, 1957, Young and Willmott, 1957, Willmott and Young, 1960), with data forming a baseline for research regarding family and community in the late 20th century.

Location: three urban areas: Bethnal Green, in the London boroughs of Newham and Tower Hamlets, the city of Wolverhampton in the West Midlands (working-class communities), Woodford (a more middle-class suburb), outskirts of London in Essex.

Methods: a two-stage study: (a) questionnaire survey with 627 people of pensionable age concerning household structure, social networks, support, social context; (b) qualitative interviews with 62 people over the age of 75 drawn from the first survey to consider the views of vulnerable adults; 19 members of individual networks, mainly sons and daughters, and 35 qualitative interviews with people from Indian and Bangladeshi communities also interviewed in the main survey.

Funded by: ESRC 1996–99, Keele University.

B. Social Exclusion of Older People in Deprived Urban Communities of England Scharf et al (2002), Scharf, Phillipson and Smith (2005a, 2005 b), Smith (2009)

Aim: to identify social exclusion for older people in deprived urban communities.

Location: undertaken in the most deprived locations in the 1998 Index of Local Deprivation in the cities of Manchester, Liverpool and the London Borough of Newham.

Methods: nine areas at ward level were selected to carry out survey research aiming to reach 600 people aged 60 and over. Two groups were considered, one gained randomly through the electoral register and a further sample of minority ethnic groups gained through snowball techniques.

Funded by: ESRC, Growing Older programme 1999–2004. Keele University

C. Rural Disadvantage: Quality of Life and Disadvantage amongst Older People: a Pilot Study Scharf and Bartlam (2006)

Aim: to consider disadvantage in a rural location.

Location: a pilot study in three counties in the Midlands and North-West of England.

Methods: Qualitative research. Two stages: (a) screening questionnaire to identify people experiencing one or more forms of disadvantage, vulnerability and quality of life (building on work undertaken in urban communities Study B), non-probability sample of 91; (b) sub-sample of 21: (i) interview guide for semi-structured in-depth interviews – including daily experiences, perceptions of rural life, household finances, social relationships, access to services and amenities plus biographical context to enable life course perspective; (ii) eight case studies of multiple disadvantage.

Funded by: Commission for Rural Communities, 2006, Keele University.

D. Grey and Pleasant Land: An Interdisciplinary Study of the Connectivity of Older People in Rural Civic Society(GaPL) Hennessy et al (2014a), Hennessy and Means (2018).

Aims: to consider how older people are connected to rural civic society; the impact of connectivity on quality of life; the diversity of experience by person and place. **Location**: six rural locations varying in type from 'remote and deprived' to 'relatively affluent and accessible' in South-West England and Wales (Hennessy et al, 2014b, p 14–20).

Methods: an interdisciplinary study with six work packages exploring particular 'connectivities' (Henessy et al, 2014b , p 11–14). Utilising quantitative, qualitative, arts-based techniques/methods including a quantitative survey of 920 participants, aged 60 and over, regarding the local community, participation in activities, social networks, available support, transport, service availability, use of media and telecommunications.

Funded by: UKRI/ESRC, New Dynamics of Ageing Programme. 2009–12. Universities of Plymouth, West of England, Swansea.

Study A

Although these studies have different aims and objectives, they identify trends that interrelate. Through comparison with research from the post-war period (see Research summary 4.1), the first study from the end of the 20th century focuses on family and community living for older people, including members of Indian and Bangladeshi families in urban environments (Phillipson et al, 2001, pp 20–34). While examination of social networks and support indicates the continuing importance of the family with kinship bonds as fundamental as those in rural areas (Wenger, 1995, 2001), difference is seen over time. A majority of the white British population live as nuclear rather than extended families, with older generations leading separate lives both as couples or on their own. In contrast, multigeneration households remained central to those from minority ethnic groups in all locations. Interestingly, while proximity of kin remained in more working-class areas, in the suburb of Woodford, older people commented on moving nearer to children after bereavement.

By studying social networks, the study shows that 'four out of five [live] in a one or two generation network' (Phillipson et al, 1998, p 285), with respondents in Woodford having the highest same generation networks, highlighting the significance of friends. Fewer than one in five placed themselves in a network with more than two generations, showing that grandchildren were seen but were not as central to the older network as children or friends. The researchers argue that 'relationships in old age are more focused than in the past' (Phillipson et al, 1998, p 286). The research confirms the important role of friends (non-kin) in the social network of older people, especially to those who are childless, and that they may be a substitute for family in situations where other relatives are not available. However, they also show that neighbours are much less prominent in the personal networks of these respondents; this was not seen in other studies at the time (Knipscheer et al, 1995).

At the time, Phillipson et al (1998, 2001) raised contemporary policy issues concerning community care for older people, demonstrating that there was no indication that the family would leave the social care of their older family members solely to the state; a position that remains crucial to contemporary lives more than 20 years later. While the significance of non-kin within social networks is illustrated, in terms of social support, both kin and non-kin are seen as becoming more important, which may relate to the number of very old people with health issues in this sample. Currently, the position of informal (family) and formal carers underpins the experience of social home care in all locations, impacting on staying put in later life (see Chapter 5). In addition, the grandparenting role of older people has developed as support for working parents (Glaser et al, 2013).

Study B

In contrast, the second study, also from Keele University, addresses issues of exclusion for urban elders (Scharf et al 2002, 2005a, 2005b). Social exclusion in old age is defined as 'a multi-dimensional phenomenon', including exclusion from material resources, social relations, civic activities, basic services and neighbourhoods (Scharf et al, 2005b, p 76), and focuses on 'measures of exclusion' to consider whether they can distinguish between older people in terms of more or less deprivation and consequently levels of social exclusion.

Research by Scharf et al (2005a) was undertaken in three deprived urban areas. Data analysis for 581 respondents, including those from minority ethnic groups, considered multiple disadvantage that distinguished different groups of older people. Just over a third were seen as 'vulnerable to the cumulative impact of multiple forms of exclusion' (2005b, p 76). The complexity of this analysis indicates associations between material poverty, social isolation and loneliness (as exclusion from social relations), which impacts on attitudes to the neighbourhood. Certain sub-groups emerged as more vulnerable, including:

- those within a deprived community with higher rates of chronic ill-health that affected quality of life;

- the oldest old, 75 and over, highlighted the link between a lack of access to basic services and feelings of neighbourhood safety;
- women more than men demonstrated greater exclusion from civic activities.

Important variation between both minority and majority ethnic groups indicated the need to recognise the complexity of diversity. Indian and Black Caribbean older people were 'less vulnerable to the different forms of exclusion than were each of the other ethnic groups' (Scharf et al, 2005b, p 81), and their involvement in religious and community groups may be important here. In contrast, Somali and Pakistani older people who were less well established were most excluded in domains relating to material resources, social relations and basic services. Alongside these findings, the white British respondents were at greater risk of exclusion owing to how they felt about their neighbourhood and involvement in civic activities.

  Despite some concerns over the methodological approach and response rates, these are important findings that contribute to the understanding of ageing in place. In their conclusions, the research draws attention to how issues of social exclusion need constant examination, as seen at the end of Chapter 3. This research, alongside Phillipson et al (2001), outlines the following issues as central to the lives of urban elders by the beginning of the 21st century:

- change in family connections;
- an increase in non-kin alongside kin within social networks;
- the complex impact of deprivation for diverse groups.

These issues form part of a baseline from which to explore how age-friendly places can be developed, as well as a contrasting comparative platform in relation to following rural-based research.

Study C

In 2006, the Commission for Rural Communities funded a pilot study of rural disadvantage for older people by Scharf and Bartlam, building on work regarding urban deprivation. This research sought to capture the diversity of forms of deprivation within rural ageing, thereby providing a platform for future research. The voices of older people captured four types of disadvantage:

- lack of access to material resource;
- inadequate or poor quality social relations;
- lack of access to services and amenities;
- disadvantage linked to rural change.

(See Scharf and Bartlam, 2006, pp 26–44)

In particular, the research showed how people with limited resources, financial or otherwise, had modest expectations over their activities. They were proud and did not want to rely on state support; rather they got by through the help of family members and others. Only critical financial or health matters brought them in direct contact with services, and they suffered from limited local resources, lack of a car or infrequent public transport, and environmental issues that hindered poor mobility. While they saw rural living as isolated in many ways, most wished to stay in the countryside and to maintain their independence, even though they witnessed different ways of living among younger generations and felt they had little in common with newcomers. Seeing their surroundings and opportunities for social relations change caused some to become emotionally lonely, yet attachment to place was strong – as was a need to be resourceful. Finally, the researchers considered community outreach work, which some may find enabling.

Study D

This focus on social exclusion provides an important counterpoint to the detailed GaPL study of connectivity and rural ageing by Hennessy et al (2014), in which older people are part of community capital rather than seen as problematised through concentration on health and social support. Connectivity, defined as 'the link between individuals, groups or objects through some pattern, process or structure' (p 10), is a common construct across the research. Based in six rural locations, diverse methodologies (see Research summary 4.1) included a quantitative survey with 920 participants concerning 'the types of and levels of and influences on older people's connections to participation in rural community' and 70 oral histories (Hennessy and Means, 2018, p 149). Further sub-studies explored the nature and extent of connectivities that were spatial, social, cultural, technological and economic, leading to an overarching analysis through which the following dimensions of connectivity emerged:

- civic engagement
- social participation
- intergenerational relations
- connecting to the landscape
- connectivity and group identity
- virtual connectivity
- imaginative connectivity

(Means et al, 2014, pp 250–2)

The researchers highlight different aspects of connectivity through detailed findings – from actual involvement in civic engagement where 47 per cent reported that they were providing assistance to others and 38 per cent were undertaking some form of voluntary work (Curry et al, 2014, pp 31–62), to how intergenerational contact is maintained even in quite remote areas, to how connection to place can be seen through landscape (Bailey et al, 2014, pp 159–92), to how connectivity may be more common within communities of interest rather than being place-based (through research with Gypsy Travellers and lesbian and gay rural elders) (Means et al, 2014, pp 254–76).

The average age of respondents was 71.5 with little variation across the six sites, and health was reported as 'good'; this was a sample of an active ageing population, predominantly white British. Barriers to levels of connectivity may relate to variation in material resources, where, for example, those with lower incomes may have less access to a car or other forms of transport. The research comments that:

> … all seven of our connectivities are dynamic and constantly in flux […] Moving into later life in a rural area may predispose a person to certain types of connectivity over others, but the balance and spread of connectivity engagement is likely to continue to change for the rest of that person's life. (Means et al, 2014, p 252)

To make their case for the importance of connectivity in rural life, the researchers discuss theoretical underpinnings concerning social capital and critical human ecology. They consider how exchanges of capital – cultural, social, economic and symbolic, drawing on education, roles, skills, customs, financial resources, and attachments – can be experienced in combination (Means et al, 2014, p 257). Yet, they also explain that capital theory (Putnam, 2000) typically does not explore the socio-environmental context in which lived experience takes place. To do this, they develop a critical human ecology framework, grouping aspects of connectivity into:

- the *sociocultural* (civic participation, leisure activities, intergenerational relationships, social attachment to place);
- the *environmental* (amenity/environment-oriented physical attachment, corporal and virtual mobility, the taskscape, relating to employment); and
- the *creative* (aesthetic attachment to place, production of artefacts through leisure activities, imaginative mobility).

This demonstrates how each area of connectivity may change or adapt over time in relation to individual resources, the social resources of family, friends and community, and the impact of the national policy environment. Time is seen as a crucial component, and it enables a life course perspective that may be life long, or recent, in terms of social attachment to space and place that contributes to the development of self-identity.

The GaPL research considered the similarities of its approach to Bourdieu's concept of habitus, but ends by arguing in favour of the critical ecology model, building on Keating and Phillips's work as discussed in Chapter 2 (Curry et al, 2014). While they recognise that the lives of rural elders are influenced by strategic initiatives (impacted in times of austerity) that affect the maintenance of public services, transportation, access to new technology for those with limited financial resources and the capacity to support the community through civic participation and volunteering, they celebrate the actions of rural elders in terms of connectivity, and outline ways in which localism can be nurtured through community development (see Le Mesurier, 2011; Walsh et al, 2012; Burtholt et al, 2014; Hennessy and Means, 2018).

While findings from urban and rural communities are not directly comparable, these studies are iterative in terms of presenting a holistic scenario, despite their varied number of participants. They reflect changes in living arrangements and social networks; the value of intergenerational relations and communication; aspects of multiculturalism; the interface between diversity and deprivation; media and technological presence; the impact of austerity; and issues regarding connectivity. There is a call for community action to enable connectivity to be more comprehensive, embracing disadvantage, something that is also seen in the call for community outreach. The studies indicate similarities and differences in urban and rural ageing, recognising the importance given to personal safety and security, accessibility to continuing service infrastructure and the value of connectivity. This provides the framework against which to consider place as age-friendly whatever the location.

'Age-friendly' places

Such reflections lead to further consideration of the World Health Organization (WHO) Age-Friendly City and Community (AFCC) initiative introduced in Chapter 3 (WHO, 2007). Figure 4.2 outlines the eight domains that should be addressed if a place is to become age-friendly; these were raised globally through discussion with older people (Rémillard-Bollard, 2019).

As a preface to consideration of particular domains, it is important to note that parallel policy development within the UK recognised the need for a strategy that brought housing, neighbourhood and population ageing together.

Planning a lifetime neighbourhood

In 2008, the Labour government produced a key policy document, 'Lifetime Homes, Lifetime Neighbourhoods' (DCLG, DH, DWP, 2008), in which the section on neighbourhood referred to the WHO AFCC Guide checklist (p 98) and went on to report these views from a joint paper with the

Figure 4.2: Themes explored in the WHO's 'Global age-friendly cities: a guide' (2007)

Source: Handler (2014), p 15, based on WHO (2007)

International Longevity Centre UK. It is important to note that lifetime neighbourhoods should be viewed as:

sustainable communities that offer a good quality of life to all generations. More specifically, they should aim to be:

• Accessible and inclusive
• Aesthetically pleasing and safe (in terms of both traffic and crime), and easy and pleasant to access; and
• A community that offers plenty of services, facilities and open space.

Furthermore, we can add that lifetime neighbourhoods are likely to foster:

• A strong social and civic fabric, including volunteering, informal networks, and

- a culture of consultation and user empowerment amongst decision-makers; and
- A strong local identity and sense of place. (DCLG, DH, DWP, 2008, p 99)

Government support led to a commissioned report on Lifetime Neighbourhoods (Bevan and Croucher, 2011), advocating issues such as accessibility; diverse services and amenities; affordable housing. The 2000s saw professional bodies such as the Royal Town Planning Institute (RTPI, 2007) encouraging planners at national, regional and local levels to consider ageing as part of their brief, leading to innovative discussion over land use planning and accessibility in town centres to create healthy communities. In more recent years, new planning guidance has been developed in relation to people with dementia (RTPI, 2017), recognising that two thirds of the 850,000 people living with dementia do so within their own homes in the community.

Such initiatives have encouraged integration of the needs of the ageing population into national planning policy and also at local authority level – into Local Plans and more recently Neighbourhood Plans alongside community strategies. However, the 'Lifetime Homes, Lifetime Neighbourhoods' strategy, while remaining a much quoted document, no longer has the support of central government, even though the All Party Parliamentary Group on Housing and Care has been party to moving forward the recommendations (see Chapters 5 and 7).

Nevertheless, in Autumn 2021 over 40 UK cities, towns, boroughs, districts, counties and city regions have taken up the call to consider the meaning of being age-friendly. They are part of the UK Network of Age-Friendly Communities, which is affiliated to the WHO Global Network for Age-Friendly Cities and Communities and is supported by the London based Centre for Ageing Better (2021). To different degrees, the WHO domains interrelate. Here, we consider issues regarding transportation, communication and outdoor spaces before reflecting on what it means to be age-friendly.

Decentralised services, mobility and communication

As noted in Figure 4.2, while transportation was seen by older people as important in all locations, transport and mobility were seen as particularly problematic for those living in rural communities. Research by Walsh et al (2012) provides a useful example of this from Ireland and Northern Ireland, where 44 per cent and 35 per cent respectively of those aged 65 and over live in rural areas (p 347). Through case studies in both nations and the cross-border region, the authors show how changing economic and employment infrastructure has led dispersed older populations to have to cope with the centralisation of service provision, especially health services, in distant towns and cities. Availability of, and access to, transport can be crucial for rural elders who may face 'isolation and disconnection from the immediate and wider community" (Walsh et al, 2012, p 352). Additionally, personal well-being may be affected when someone cannot walk far and yet has to travel a distance from their locality.

This example parallels those highlighted in the GaPL study, where researchers also argued that maintaining connections could deter social exclusion (Shergold and Parkhurst, 2012). They explored the complexity of older participants' experience of travel and mobility (Parkhurst et al, 2014, p 126), showing how even though the car was an important form of transport, '62% of respondents had used 3–6 different modes in the year prior to survey, including buses, taxis, cycles and, notably for rural areas, mobility scooters' (2014, p 142). While the older GaPL respondents (aged 80 and over) reported most difficulty in accessing services, this was not true for all participants, and in many cases local facilities were in short walking distance. In the UK, free bus use by older people has been a key policy, while the health advantages of walking are publicised to encourage well-being.

Technology is clearly changing how people gain access to goods, services and communication. Here, the GaPL researchers' moved beyond the direct physicality of movement and considered Urry's (2000, 2007) mobility options, summarised here as:

- *utility travel* where a person needs to get from 'a to b' and transport planning is central;
- *virtual mobility* where technology enables communication through social media (email, Skype, Zoom) or where goods purchased on-line are delivered by others;
- *potential mobility* where people have access to a vehicle 'just in case' travel is needed;
- *imaginative mobility* where personal reflection can open up avenues to other places through past experience or media. (based on Parkhurst et al, 2014, pp 131–2)

Utilising this range of options could diversify connectivity. Rural elders are more constrained in their access to public transport than urban elders (RTPI, 2007, p 4; Parkhurst et al, 2014, p 147), and unsurprisingly, those with a car and internet access felt more satisfied and able to maintain their level of community engagement and gain information. While valuing the development of virtual mobility, and some using the internet daily for communication through emails, the need for maintenance and extension of information and communications technology (ICT) systems was noted, with research showing that across the UK three out of four people living in rural areas have access to very slow broadband coverage (see Evans et al, 2014b) and that ICT 'should not be seen as a replacement for corporal mobility for local social connectivity' (Parkhurst et al, 2014, p 131). Being aware of cohort differences, Parkhurst et al comment on maintaining the local infrastructure through 'enhanced pavements, lighting and off-road tracks' rather than 'lifeline' bus services to the nearest market town' (2014, p 152). Finally, their recognition of imaginative mobility links this research to earlier consideration of how attachment to place can be maintained through autobiographical insideness (see Rowles, 1978, 1983).

This discussion, though rurally based, raises issues of maintaining mobile lives: varied transport, access, frequency, street illumination and furniture, and technological infrastructure that makes a place more age-friendly. This is equally important to urban locations, and is returned to in Chapter 10. It also extends the topic from just transportation and communication to facilitating social and civic participation, and access to goods and services – all of which impacts on social inclusion. However, the reality of access to and skills regarding technology usage, including social networking, needs to be taken into account and may display cohort, ethnicity and social class differences (McCreadie, 2010; Jones, 2015), as discussed in Chapter 3.

Outdoor spaces

The AFCC domain 'outdoor spaces and buildings' draws attention to developing enabling environments through more inclusive design. Here we focus on outdoor spaces, with building design featured in Chapter 5. Holland (2015) comments: 'It is essential for social cohesion and democracy that older people are included in the public life of communities taking place in public spaces' (p 460). Public outdoor spaces are intergenerational environments where people vary their usage not only temporally and seasonally, but also in terms of their everyday routines (see Hauderowicz and Ly Serena, 2020 for detailed international discussion).

People's mobility and agility when navigating public spaces can influence attitudes and presence. Spaces may be seen as *contested* if people fit themselves alongside others, *avoided* if causing insecurity or fear that may also relate to speed of movement, or *unfamiliar* if there is little recognition or orientation within a new or old locale (Phillips et al, 2011; Peace, 2013). Here, we draw on findings from a case study of the town of Aylesbury, Buckinghamshire, that the author carried out with colleagues and participatory co-researchers in 2004–05 (Research summary 4.2). By observing public locations over a 12-month period, appreciation can be given to how the general public can, at different points in their lives, with varied roles (schoolchildren, parents, carers, grandparents) be seen as more or less comfortable and confident in different situations; this is supported by street survey data. Here, in terms of the material environment, older people mentioned the need for street furniture – seats with backs and armrests – as well as the ever-common request for supervised public toilets. Reliance on toilet provision within department stores in shopping malls was favoured over the café culture model, in which individuals ask if they can use the facilities of private cafes – as suggested by local policy makers (Holland et al, 2007, p 65).

Research summary 4.2: Social interaction in urban public places

Holland et al, 2007; Clark et al, 2009

Aims: to examine how different people use public spaces and to analyse how social interactions vary by age, gender and place. A case study of the town of Aylesbury.

Location: Aylesbury, Buckinghamshire, a market town in South-East England with a population of around 69,000 at the time of the research.

Methods: a form of participatory action research was used involving 46 members of the general public who volunteered to observe the town at nine public locations, including town squares, shopping mall, public park, canal banks and residential exterior spaces. Observations were undertaken in pairs and took place every day at 30-minute intervals over a 12-month period, thereby gaining seasonal and diurnal data. Training at The Open University and daily support was given by the central research team who also undertook street surveys and interviews with key stakeholders.

Funded by: Joseph Rowntree Foundation. Public Spaces Programme. 2005–07, Open University.

The study allowed greater understanding of daily and annual routines, patterns and flows, and also the impact of seasonal weather in both town centre locations and residential areas. For example, older bus users who came into the centre from surrounding locations arrived after 9.30 am when bus passes could be used, tended to arrive alone or with a friend during the week and only visited with other family members at the weekend. Research observing intergenerational interactions in public spaces offered a more complex scenario, in terms of types of group, speed of movement, contested spaces, the impact of diurnal and seasonal differences, transportation and the infrastructure of public toilets and seating arrangements, all of which impacts on the individual.

The picture captured here is partial, and it was through the street survey that issues regarding the need for street furniture and public toilets were raised in conversation. What was important, though, was to see how local policy regarding the closure of a public square through the national planning policy of regeneration could lead to behavioural change. Observations showed the movement of street drinkers to a central public park, where their decision to sit in a formal garden area had knock-on effects on the area as a sitting place for older people, and where their presence near a bandstand used by teenagers after school led to behaviour that indicated security of numbers. The findings from this research and the wider programme indicated, as Worpole and Knox comment, that 'The success of a particular public space is not solely in the hands of the architect, urban designer or town planner; it relies also on people adopting, using and managing the space – people make places, more than places make people' (Worpole and Knox, 2007, p 2). We return to this research in Chapter 9 when discussing Participatory Action Research.

A more intimate understanding of behaviour and the impact of particular health concerns on quality of life is fundamental to how a place can become age-friendly. The OpenSpace group at Edinburgh and Heriot-Watt universities have been central, alongside colleagues from Salford, Oxford-Brookes and Warwick universities, in research concerning Inclusive Design for Getting Outdoors (I'DGO, n.d.), a ten-year programme exploring the ability of older people to get out and about, barriers to accessibility and impact on quality of life (Sugiyama et al, 2009; Curl et al, 2015; OpenSpace, 2021). While a focus on cycling in later life has also promoted wellbeing (see Jones et al, 2017; Leyland et al, 2019).

Concern for dementia-friendly environments has become more apparent. Dementia-friendly design outdoors is an under-researched area, and yet short-term memory problems and spatial disorientation may displace people. In the UK, guidance by Mitchell et al (2004) for The Housing Corporation was central to recognising that when aspects of life may be changing the familiarity of place and settings is crucial. Through detailed qualitative research with older people with and without dementia, involving interviews, accompanied walks and environmental analysis, they capture the following issues as essential:

- the importance of legibility (e.g. street layouts);
- signage;
- environmental cues (gardens, civic buildings, historic buildings, places of activity, personal places).

They identify the characteristics of a neighbourhood for life that is inclusive for all (Mitchell and Burton, 2006), one aspect of a dementia-friendly community (see Mitchell, 2012). We return to design and research issues involving people with dementia in Chapters 8 and 9.

Ideas around dementia-friendly schemes sit alongside vision-friendly settings, introduced earlier and extended here through research by the author and colleagues (Research summary 4.3). In using this research to test the AFCC guidance, Peace et al (2019) comment that the most important concerns of participants were: 'the familiarity of a local neighbourhood alongside adapted housing, accessibility, and the importance of maintaining social relationships' (p 267). Even though, since 1995, national disability discrimination and equality legislation in the UK has led to greater accessibility in public open spaces through dropped kerbs, tactile paving and audible/tactile signals at pelican crossings, these initiatives need constant maintenance:

> Local journeys on foot posed considerable challenges with narrow pedestrian walkways sometimes particularly difficult. Pavements may not exist on some stretches of road, or be wide enough for easy passing. Indeed, for many the state of local pavements was a cause for considerable alarm as noted here:
>
> 'It can be a little bit frightening. And pavements I find a great problem because they are uneven and I fall if I'm not careful.' (Shirley from Herts). (Peace et al, 2019, p 265)

Research summary 4.3: Needs and Aspirations of Vision Impaired Older People

Katz et al (2012)

Aims: to consider the needs and aspirations of older people living with visual impairment both within the home and outside

Location: purposive sampling through groups and contacts with people who were visually impaired enabled the inclusion of both people from minority ethnic groups as well as people in late old age living in urban/semi-rural and rural locations from East Suffolk to Liverpool, Buckinghamshire to Coventry.

Methods: recorded in-depth interviews were carried out with 50 older people concerning everyday activities; home adaptation; relationships with family and friends; use of technology; activities outside locally and elsewhere; transportation; accessibility. The researchers used topics from the 'Facets of Life wheel' developed in the Environment and Identity study (see Research summary 6.1). Participants were aged 54–99: 36

women and 14 men; 32 white British, 18 from a range of Black Asian Minority Ethnic groups; over 50 per cent living alone; over two thirds owner-occupiers living in a range of housing types from detached houses to one-bedroomed flats (see Peace et al, 2016; Peace et al, 2019).

Funded by: Thomas Pocklington Trust, 2014–16, The Open University.

Some older people with vision impairment remain completely engaged with their local community, reporting their daily/weekly trips to local shops, church and gym, travelling by bus. For others, the social environment was more important; key people often assisted, such as a local shopkeeper who found goods that were required. Meetings of local groups for vision impaired people were essential, and access to them could involve bus journeys, lifts from others or the use of a taxi. Lack of confidence in transportation could prevent some respondents from going out without support, which could lead to loneliness and isolation. For many, the familiarity of people in place was essential to living a good life. Interestingly, when disseminating this research to members of the Kilburn Older Voices Exchange in London, one particular difficulty mentioned by vision impaired older people was local traders extending their shop front across the pavement, which constricted the section for walking, particularly when using a stick (KOVE, 2012). This was not reported by participants living in less densely urban environments.

For some, then, the environment can be unfamiliar. Phillips et al (2010, 2011) conducted innovative qualitative research with 44 older people to consider older people's use of unfamiliar space (OPUS) – how people cope with an environment not familiar to them as pedestrians, drivers or users of public transport. This mixed methods study involved response to virtual cave environments that were familiar/unfamiliar, interviews, qualitative records, for one group a trip to a 'real' unfamiliar place, and discussion with locals, participants and planners to add potential impact (see Phillips et al, 2010; Phillips et al, 2011). Findings indicate varied behaviour, with the use of landmarks, signage and personal experience when navigating unfamiliar towns, with some directional aids being more beneficial for walkers than drivers. Others were not so confident about finding their way and an unfamiliar place could cause anxiety that could result in a loss of independence and increased isolation. This novel research showed planners how barriers to navigation exist, and the importance of planning walking routes and areas. The research team embarked on the development of an OPUS walker tool.

Such varied research on outdoor spaces demonstrates a vital knowledge base for AFCC development.

The meaning of being age-friendly

Early reviews of the AFCC programme indicated how environmental change could enhance independence, interdependence and quality of life (Lui et al, 2009, reviewing literature since 2005). Initiatives ranged from those focused predominantly on the physical/material environment to those targeting the social environment, where the involvement of older people could be seen as essential to both central and local decision making. Three areas were underdeveloped: lack of attention to rural communities; lack of recognition regarding diversity and complexity when considering intergenerational solidarity; and lack of ongoing evaluation when consciously developing age-friendly communities through aspects of the physical/material and social environment (Lui et al, 2009, p 119).

The research on ageing in urban and rural communities discussed here did not focus directly on being age-friendly, yet outlined the relative importance of similar domains, foregrounding social exclusion and the value of connectivity in rural areas. When discussing Canadian age-friendly rural communities, Eales et al (2008) and Keating et al, (2013) define these as involving natural, human-built and social environments that offer different combinations of best fit for those with diverse lifestyles and identities. Consequently, the meaning of being age-friendly is complex. It is a process rather than a strategy, which has to mould to unique places yet draw strength from global partnerships.

Urbanisation, population ageing and the AFCC strategy provide a useful interface for discussing P–E congruence. For example, London, one of 33 world cities in initial WHO consultations, held focus groups with older people in the multicultural London boroughs of Newham and Waltham Forest during 2005. This detailed research was supported by Help the Aged, and carried out by the Institute of Gerontology at Kings College and Ipsos MORI Social Research Institute (Biggs and Tinker, 2007; Age Concern and Help the Aged, 2009). Participants commented on the importance of engagement with others, including family, friends and those met at community centres; a facility to be maintained and promoted. Accessible and good public transport, sometimes door-to-door, was essential, and free travel for older people in London through the Freedom Pass was valued enormously (see Glossary, London Councils (n.d.) and update in Chapter 10 during the COVID-19 pandemic). The wider material infrastructure – clean streets, adequate lighting, street furniture, wheelchair accessibility through ramps and parking facilities – was already considered age-friendly, with the exception of the common request for clean public toilets. In these London boroughs, specialised (public sector) social housing was seen as an asset, and the researchers raised the issue of good housing in their recommendations.

However, not every response was so positive. Participants commented on personal attitudes towards older people, showing how rowdy behaviour and inconsideration by the general public could affect how they lived their lives. It was reported that 'there is a general view that ageism is endemic and institutionalised' (Biggs and Tinker, 2007, pp 15–16). A fear of crime and feelings of vulnerability could result in staying indoors at night especially during the winter months, leading some to feel housebound. Respondents recommended more visible community police. The age-friendly community needed to be one where adequate support – ranging from help with home adaptation to a wider range of household tasks – could enable people to age in place. Being active in the community enabled you to gain the information you needed to stay engaged, but some felt isolated and disengaged from the wider community (Minton, 2017a).

The researchers contextualised concerns over being age-friendly in a world city stating that 'fast moving international populations, differences in wealth and in embeddedness in local neighbourhoods – are balanced by progressive policies toward social inclusion of older people and people with disabilities, which have radically influenced the all-important detail of everyday life' (Biggs and Tinker, 2007, p 6).

Further findings have come from the follow-up study (Tinker and Ginn, 2015) commissioned by the Greater London Authority (GLA). This reassessed the WHO domains, developing a model for London. Flexibility surrounding direct adherence to the framework was noted across the global network (see Menec et al, 2011, Caro and Fitzgerald, 2016; Warth, 2016). Employment, skills and income were seen as crucial to understanding the everyday lives of people aged more than 65 living in the metropolis, where inequalities between 33 local authorities in terms of health, life expectancy and housing experiences are considerable – relating to social class, poverty levels and the diversity of the older population in terms of gender, age and ethnicity (Marmot et al, 2010; Tinker and Ginn, 2015, p 32).

This evaluation outlines the challenges faced in developing an age-friendly strategy within a metropolitan context, taking into account economic austerity and service cuts, alongside partnership working that involves stakeholders at all levels facilitating access to degrees of power and control, while centralising the voice of all older people, both active and vulnerable. The 2015 study highlighted some London-wide strategies that benefited all ages. For example, hosting the Olympic and Paralympic Games in 2012 enabled improvement in accessible transport; and the GLA adopted 'Lifetime Neighbourhoods' for outdoor spaces, also developing a Green Grid (GLA, 2020) that will create a 'green infrastructure' across London for the benefit of people and wildlife (e.g. cooling the urban environment; encouraging walking and cycling). However, such overarching policies must be embedded in the local, and the individual boroughs face difficult decisions. The researchers identify aspects of all AFCC domains in which further work is needed to enhance the well-being of older people (Tinker and Ginn, 2015, pp 7–8).

These findings underpin issues that have been raised by authors critiquing age-friendly policies, particularly in urban environments experiencing social and economic change. Buffel et al (2012) comment on both the constraints and opportunities for older people experiencing city living. To their disadvantage, poverty, deprivation and poor housing can be more common, especially for migrant groups that are frequently city dwellers. Fear of crime, lack of engagement and loneliness may be experienced and a traditional neighbourhood may feel gentrified by outsiders and cause people of different generations to need to re-engage. While the infrastructure of public spaces can be problematic, and traffic congestion can impact on health, lead to accidents and influence pedestrian safety. In contrast, to their advantage, there are social and cultural resources, parks and open spaces, shops and community services, and researchers comment on attachment to place especially for migrant groups, where proximity to family and friends provides an important social network that gives a sense of greater inclusion within their specific community than indigenous elders may sense in the wider community (Pain et al, 2000; Pain, 2001; Scharf et al, 2002; Buffel and Phillipson, 2011). It has also been noted that sustainable development in cities has to acknowledge social justice (Buffel et al, 2012; Buffel and Phillipson, 2016, 2019).

Thomese et al (2019) draw attention to issues where industrial change, global migration and a lack of local resources can influence the meaning of community and neighbourhood change, affecting the understanding of age-friendly. Spatial segregation can divide those seen as privileged from those seen as unequal (Phillipson, 2007a). This approach relates to that of Kelley et al (2018), advocating how environmental gerontologists and those researching AFCC need to address macro-level issues alongside their focus on the near environment if they are going to combat the way in which age is seen as an invisible issue. Older people's involvement in decision making and consultation on the meaning of age-friendly across all communities needs to be central. Change needs to be recognised as necessary and owned collectively and intergenerationally. The age-friendly community should be based on a definition of age that is based on greater solidarity. Without this, greater segregation between ages will continue – as will the potential for greater social exclusion.

Reflecting on place as home: the urban/rural lens

While recognising concerns around the concept of age-friendly and the inequalities that exist, we now hold an urban/rural lens to the earlier discussion about the meaning of home. Research indicates that attachment to place for older people is often neighbourhood-centred, with social relations and well-being having developed through networks within and beyond family, including virtual ties with others at a distance; evidence also shows cultural connectivity among migrant communities. As a result, it is argued here that perceptions of the importance of the local micro-space of neighbourhood within a wider community can contribute to the other, more personal, understanding of dwelling as home.

Quotes have been chosen from three of the urban/rural studies discussed earlier to illustrate both positive and negative perspectives on place and experience of change:

'I like the position of it. It is very friendly, helpful neighbourhood.' (Woodford, 81-year-old woman, widowed, Study A)

'It's my home, my roots are here. It's what I'm used to living here and working here for so many years.' (Bethnal Green, 76-year-old woman, widowed, Study A)

'It has 'gone down'. There were elderly people about our age but they are all young now.' (Wolverhampton, 83-year-old man, married, Study A)

'The only thing now about Bethnal Green is that the ethnics are taking over ... This bit of Bethnal Green is losing its identity.' (Bethnal Green, 77-year-old man, married, Study A)

'I am living surrounded by racist people, can't go out because of them. I don't feel safe. They don't like me to live here.' (Bethnal Green, 69-year-old man, married, Study A)

'Well my mother died three years ago and I'm not interested in this house at all now.' (68-year-old man, Study B)

'We have a lot of new people come into our village through the new houses. Some are very nice, but others really don't want to know you, and a lot of them are not country people. And we are down to earth, country people.' (Miss Richards, aged 79, Study C)

'Well people looked after one another more didn't they? You know the families. Somebody was there from the family, they looked after them. Well they don't now, do they? No, it's much different.' (Mr Hughes, aged 74, Study C)

'Everybody is fairly friendly, look after each other's interests. We have a neighbourhood watch going.' (Wolverhampton, 70-year-old man, married, Study A)

Sources: Study A Phillipson et al, 2001, pp 90–9;
Study B Scharf, Phillipson and Smith, 2004 and 2005a, p 34;
Study C Scharf and Bartlam, 2006, pp 60 and 73

These comments give some sense of the meaning of home in terms of place, addressing attachment through: friendship, community support and feelings of rootedness, alongside a sense of detachment through hostility, urban deprivation, racism, personal loss and intergenerational change through housing regeneration, and attitudinal difference. Access to qualitative data from the final study was not available.

In Study D, Burholt, Curry and their Canadian colleagues (Burholt, 2012, Burholt et al, 2014) consider forms of place attachment and belonging in rural locations through quantitative analysis of data from the GaPL study. They show how length of residence is associated with social place attachment (activities, actions, involvement), with this being stronger for women than men; physical place attachment (aesthetic attachment, bonding with nature), which relates to location and has greater association for those living in remote rural areas; and amenity/ environment oriented attachment (quality and access to services), which has a particular association with health. These associations relate to meanings of self-identity and well-being.

Figure 4.3 identifies both positive and negative issues that relate to place as home in rural/urban communities. While the views presented here draw upon specific studies, they are used to illustrate variation in understanding the meaning of place. The diversity of the older population has to be addressed alongside issues such as the decline of some inner city retail services, the remote nature of rural village life and issues of safety and security. Multicultural living needs to be acknowledged in community development in all locations, as it will impact on segregation and integration. Here are issues regarding the green environment, urban deprivation and regeneration; service infrastructure including slow internet connection; social networking; concerns over rural transport; multicultural and intergenerational living; isolation and connectivity. All these factors build the picture of place as home being experienced through levels of inclusion and inequality. Some urban dwellers may see themselves as 'urban villagers', combining the best of both worlds and valuing their association with a multigenerational place that has local services and where they know their neighbours (Scanlon et al, 2016). Others, such as LGBT+ members, may feel a greater attachment to their communities of interest than of place, as Willis et al (2018) discuss for LGB elders in terms of home and rurality.

Figure 4.3: Reflecting on meaning of home as place: the rural/urban lens

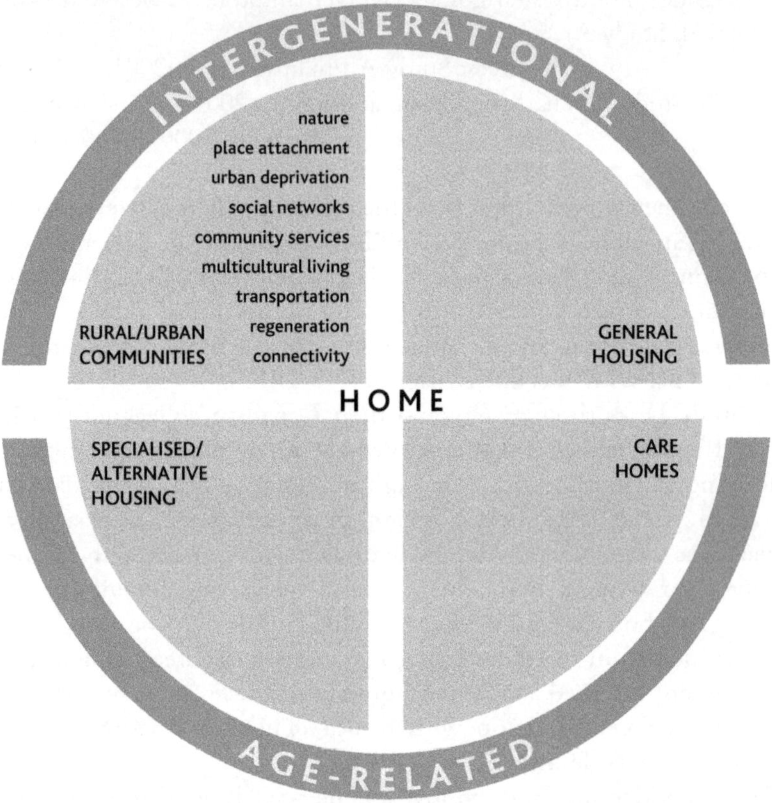

This figure will develop across the following chapters, building the complexity that underpins the meaning of home in different ageing environments.

Conclusions

This chapter has considered home as place, focusing on urban/rural environments through recent research that concerns the lives of older people. By maintaining a community focus, it has come back to the global AFCC strategy, and has begun to reflect on the meaning of being age-friendly, considering issues of inclusion in the outdoor environment, the importance of transportation and communication. This has led to a reflection on the relationship of place to the meaning of home. Chapter 5 moves from location to the environments of ageing found across general needs housing.

5

Housing in later life

Introduction

More than 90 per cent of older people in the UK live in general needs housing, forming the major component when discussing environments of ageing. Table 5.1 outlines the range of housing forms in later life. Approximately 5–6 per cent of the older population live in age-related communal housing, discussed in Chapter 7 along with co-housing, intentional housing that can be intergenerational or age-related. Additionally, 4–5 per cent live in care homes (residential and nursing care), which includes 15 per cent of the population aged 85 and over (Laing, 2018) and forms the focus of Chapter 8 (comparable typologies are seen in the Housing our Ageing Population: Panel for Innovation (HAPPI) report, written by Barac and Park, 2009, p 2 (see Glossary) and Park and Porteus, 2018, p 131).

This chapter focuses on mainstream housing, where housing type, tenure, standards and markets embed individual housing histories. It begins with a reflection on housing development during the 20th century to contextualise environments of ageing identified through the English Housing Survey. Then it moves to the built environment and housing policy, reflecting on how building regulations affect housing design. Issues regarding inclusive design and how dwellings seen as non-ableing could be retrofitted or adapted are discussed alongside the growing development of assistive technology. The chapter ends with further reflections on housing as home, the impact of receiving care in current housing and how older people are becoming involved in co-designing future housing. This sets the scene for the empirical research that is featured in Chapter 6, where general housing is considered with regard to the meaning of home.

Housing development in the UK: 20th century onwards

At the turn of the 20th century, the UK (as home to the industrial revolution) faced a need for housing reform, particularly 'slum clearance' for the working poor who were living in the worst conditions. In this brief history, we focus primarily on developments in England. In the late 19th century, housing reform was an endeavour noted in the efforts of bodies such as the Peabody Trust in London, industrial proprietors such as George Cadbury and William Hesketh Lever working to house their employees in Bournville and Port

Table 5.1: Housing in later life in the UK

General housing – general needs, lifetime homes, adapted homes. Diverse living arrangements for families with or without children, couples/partners, friends or singles of all ages.
Specialised/alternative housing – sheltered housing, retirement housing, very sheltered housing/assisted living, extra-care housing, close care housing, retirement villages (continuing care communities), co-housing. Co-housing may offer both intergenerational and age-related living.
Care homes – residential care homes, nursing homes, specialised care homes for people with dementia – predominantly people living alone within a communal setting.
Other forms of housing – prisons, bed and breakfast accommodation (for low-income people living on welfare benefits), hostels/refuges for homeless people, people suffering domestic abuse.

Sunlight in the Midlands and North-West England respectively. These were precursors to the developing garden city movement, with initiatives including Letchworth Garden City in South-East England following the vision of Ebenezer Howard in *Tomorrow: A Peaceful Path to Real Reform*, originally published in 1898 and later reissued (1902). Here, the philosophical approach was to see cities beyond the built environment as political, social and economic bodies 'self-sufficient "social cities" of 250,000 people, set with their own commerce and industry in the countryside' (Colquhoun, 1999, p 5). Sustainability was central and space was key to residential design, with architects Raymond Unwin and Barry Parker working to a density of 12 houses per acre (Park, 2017), each home including a garden, an ideal *rus in urbe* stereotype still noted in the UK today, and a direct contrast to the remaining terraced housing of industrial towns from Victorian and Edwardian times.

Such developments were not common, and following the Housing of the Working Classes Acts of 1890 and 1900, the state was to intervene directly in housing. For the first time, local authorities were able to buy and develop houses for rent; the beginning of council and later social housing. Perhaps unsurprisingly, it was the experience of the First and Second World Wars that gave further impetus to town planning and housing development with the Tudor Walters Report, 1918 (Park, 2017), which set out design criteria that promoted semi-detached houses with short corridors and generous space standards. The Housing Manual of 1920 from the Ministry of Health illustrated 'cottage' designs. However, tensions began to be seen between housing costs and housing quality. Colquhoun states:

The Tudor Walters Report recommended separate parlours, but the Health Ministry preferred non-parlour types because these were considerably cheaper to build. Kitchens were merely 'sculleries' and the bathroom was on the ground floor with the coal store nearby. These houses lacked many of the facilities that are now taken for granted but, at the time, they were major improvements on previous housing. (1999, p 7)

The Women's Design Group has considered housing design from the late 19th century, and has commented on housework and housing design (Boys et al, 1984; Matrix, 1984). Throughout this discussion, it is important to note the relationship between political bodies for housing, public health, health and social care, as it remains crucial to the current development of accommodation and care, as well as the personal housing histories of older people.

The vision of the garden city movement changed as patterns of economic recession and growth saw the rationalisation of public housing, with the private sector building three quarters of the 4 million dwellings built between 1919 and 1939; while the post-war years saw more immediate

Figure 5.1: Terraced housing – early 20th century

municipal housing construction, creation of prefabricated housing and the building of high-rise flats in urban centres (Ministry of Health/ Ministry of Works, 1944). Gradually, mixed housing developments and 'neighbourhood units' for 5,000–10,000 inhabitants, with a basic infrastructure of shops, school and community facilities, became part of housing policy. Additionally, building construction was influenced by developments in other European cities, such as Amsterdam, Vienna and Berlin, through designers such as Le Corbusier and those trained at the Bauhaus, and the use of concrete, wood and steel building materials (Colquhoun, 1999, p 8). Throughout the 20th century, ideas about ideal city housing density fluctuated, and transportation systems were integrated with housing as the car became commonplace.

Urban development led to the creation of overspill housing for the bigger cities, particularly London and Glasgow, with a number of new towns, for example Stevenage, East Kilbride in Scotland and later, in the 1960s and 1970s, Warrington and Milton Keynes each seeing a range of mixed housing developments.

The 1970s also saw the development of suitable space standards for public housing. The Parker Morris report *Homes for Today and Tomorrow* (1962) set out overall dwelling sizes for the number of occupants, and these standards were mandatory for public sector housing between 1969 and 1981 (MoHLG, 1962), becoming a benchmark for good practice. It had been hoped that the private sector would also work to these standards, but this was not always the case – the focus being on more 'low-cost' starter homes with lower floor space standards (Milner and Madigan, 2001). The election in 1979 of a Conservative government, led by Margaret Thatcher, saw a number of changes in this field, including the removal of statutory building guidance for settings such as care homes and the abolition of the Parker Morris space standards. The 'right to buy' initiative in England and Wales introduced in the Housing Act (1980) continued a strong ideology of home ownership, enabling thousands of council tenants to buy their housing at discounted prices. By 1999, 2.2 million properties had been sold by local authorities, new town corporations and housing associations (Parry, 1996; Town and Country Planning Associates, 2015).

During the past 40 years, central government in the UK has remained essentially centrist, moving between more or less conservative or social ideologies. While housing trends are what McKee et al (2017) call spatially nuanced, with important differences across the four UK nations, in England, governance has remained the responsibility of the UK government at Westminster, even though the development of a mayoral role with particular responsibilities is seen in major cities, such as London and Manchester, alongside some decentralisation to regional offices of government

(Maclennan and O'Sullivan, 2013). Consequently, differences in power, responsibility and fiscal autonomy remain, and commitment to central government housing policy is not a prerequisite for the devolved nations (Mooney and Scott, 2011).

Figure 5.2: High rise mid-20th-century housing

Figure 5.3: Estate housing – Milton Keynes New Town

Here, the focus is primarily on England. A number of recent policy changes have affected housing experience across all ages:

- Since 1980, English local authority landlords have been able to provide secure or lifetime tenancies in social housing. However, this changed with the Housing and Planning Act 2016, which introduced fixed term tenancies of between two and five years, renewable following a housing review to determine the need for such housing. While landlords have discretion over this practice, it is seen as devaluing the legitimacy of social housing as a permanent housing function for those with limited financial resources (Bevan and Laurie, 2017).

- The Local Government and Housing Act 1989 (part viii) saw the introduction of the Disabled Facilities Grant for the provision of facilities for a disabled person. It is a means-tested grant to help people on low incomes access adaptations to their homes (see adaptation/ modification section).

- From 2011 onwards, local authorities were encouraged to pass social housing development to housing associations (HAs**)** – non-governmental organisations with a long history of providing specialised housing for older people, community development and home improvement agencies (McKee, 2015b). The right to buy was extended to housing rented through HAs from May 2016 through the Housing and Planning Act 2016 (see Bevan and Laurie, 2017).

- The National Planning Policy Framework (NPPF), which was developed in 2012, provides the structure for producing Local Plans for housing and other developments, which are produced by local planning authorities (LPAs). The updated NPPF was published with amendments in February 2019 (see Barton et al, 2019).

- In 2013, the Conservative government introduced a spare room subsidy known as the 'bedroom tax', reducing housing benefits for people living in social or HA property with extra space. This tax did not affect those receiving a state pension, yet impacted on views regarding having a 'home for life' for people living in social housing (Morgan and Cruickshank, 2014) (see Glossary).

- The Neighbourhood Planning Act 2017 gives communities power to develop a shared vision. Neighbourhood plans introduced under the Localism Act 2011 are approved by LPAs and take precedence over Local Plans, which are seen as non-strategic (Local Government Association, 2017a, 2017b).

- Most recently, the safety of tenants living in high-rise social housing has been central to discussion of housing policy in response to the death of 72 people of all ages following a fire at Grenfell, a tower block in north Kensington, west London, on 14 June 2017, with issues regarding materials used in the cladding of buildings, procedures for evacuation and resourcing of maintenance issues (Minton, 2017b).

Moving into the 21st century, housing policy embracing life course needs has remained central, with individual architects and architectural groups producing innovative housing schemes and development plans that aim to build low-rise but high-density buildings as high-rise flats have become less popular (Colquhoun, 1999). The involvement of users in participatory design and community architecture has grown (Scott, 2017; Luck, 2018), and yet there is still a housing crisis in terms of new build. Nevertheless, the position is contradictory, as the UK still has the oldest housing stock in the EU, with 38 per cent dating from before 1946 (Piddington et al, 2017). The poor conditions and environmental hazards that are to be found in non-decent housing impact on personal health, and 26 hazards have been identified – including excess cold, the potential for falls on stairs and in level areas, fire, pests, dampness and overcrowding. Nicol et al state:

> if we could find £10 billion now to improve all of the 3.5 million 'poor' homes in England, this would save the NHS £1.4 billion in first year treatment costs alone. It is estimated that such an investment would pay for itself in just over seven years and then continue to accrue benefits into the future. (2016, p 6)

Housing characteristics in later life

With this in mind, what are the characteristics of older people's housing and their living arrangements? The focus here is on England, using data from the annual English Housing Survey (EHS), beginning with the latest annual survey for 2019–20 (MHCLG, 2021a) with additional comparative data from EHS 2014–15 (DCLG, 2016) and EHS 2018–19 (MHCLG, 2020a) where additional analysis was undertaken by age. See Glossary for discussion of age classification and methods. The latest dataset for EHS 2019–20 provides data for households and dwellings concerning the physical environment and forms of tenure published during 2021.

Tenure and age

Owner occupation reflects an ideological position in a free market economy that encourages housing consumption, a financial asset to be inherited by the next generation (Saunders, 1990) and currently associated with a call for older people to consider 'downsizing' family housing and releasing property equity through 'rightsizing' (Hammond et al, 2018). During the second half of the 20th century, home ownership has been prized in the UK, as seen in the response to the 'right to buy' policy, developed under the Thatcher government in 1980, enabling council tenants to buy their housing at a reduced cost (see Glossary). It has become a welfare asset (Fox O'Mahony and Overton, 2015). Over the past 40 years, this housing asset has become a liability for some in terms of the need for maintenance and adaptation, and has become central to financing different forms of alternative accommodation and care in later life, something that can affect intergenerational relations (McKee et al, 2017; Preece et al, 2020).

Data from EHS 2019–20 reports that 65 per cent of all households (estimated as 23.8 million) were owner occupied; 19 per cent were private rented and 17 per cent were social rented – with 10 per cent rented from housing associations (HAs) and 7 per cent through local authorities (MHCLG, 2020e). There has been only a gradual decline in owner occupation since a peak of 71 per cent of households, reported in 2003 (MHCLG, 2020e). In the latest survey, London has a very similar profile to the nation, but a higher percentage of private renters (28 per cent) and a lower percentage of owner occupiers (49 per cent) – reflecting the younger population, even though the percentage of those owning with a mortgage is rising. Further analysis of data for households across England shows that two thirds of private renters are aged under 45 alongside a growing number of younger owner-occupiers aged 25–34. The growth of HAs as providers of social rented housing is also seen, while in London local authorities remain important providers.

Discussion of tenure and living arrangements draws on EHS 2018–19 life course analysis (MHCLG, 2020a) and EHS 2019–20 data (MHCLG, 2021a, 2021b, 2021c). There is an increasing proportion of outright owner occupiers with age – particularly those born in the post-Second World War period. However, in terms of type of tenure, variation exists around retirement age. Although owner occupation is dominant among those aged 55–64 (74 per cent), with a greater number still in employment, a greater number also own with a mortgage. This contrasts with those aged 65 years and over where, by 2019–20, data shows 80 per cent were owner occupiers and 74 per cent were outright owners. A smaller percentage in both age ranges are renters, although comparison across EHSs during the previous decade shows an increase in older renters aged 50–64 in both private and social rented sectors, as well as a slight decline in owner occupation. Additional analysis also shows a higher proportion of social renters for households headed by someone aged 80 or over (MHCLG, 2020a), with the EHS 2019–20 reporting that: 'The most prevalent group in the social rented sector were households with an HRP aged 65 years and over (26%)' (MHCLG, 2020e, p 9, 2021c; see Household Reference Person in the Glossary).

Despite this variation in housing assets, marginal changes in tenure patterns in the UK show a slight decline overall in owner occupation and an increase in private renting particularly for people aged 25–35, trends noted at a similar rate in other European countries (Scanlon et al, 2004a). However, the dominance of self-owned housing also facilitates the potential use of housing equity. Even though the UK is said to have the most advanced equity release schemes in Europe, research from 2012 shows limited use of this resource either for home improvement or non-housing consumption (Jones et al, 2012). More recently, this appears to be changing, with £3.4 billion worth of equity being released by seniors in the UK in 2019 to pay off mortgages and debts through life-time mortgages or home reversion (Jones, 2020).

These either involve money being borrowed against the value of the home and repaid when the house is sold or the house being sold while people remain as occupants until they die or move to a long-term care facility. The UK is currently seen as an asset-based welfare system, as house value is assessed when paying for social and long-term care (see Wood, et al, 2020).

The situation and well-being of older households

Living arrangements identified in the 2019–20 EHS indicate expected patterns: that a higher proportion of the oldest age group are living alone, or as part of a couple with no children, while the late middle-aged are also likely to live as a couple or in some cases as lone parents with non-dependent children (MHCLG, 2020e, p 9). These are generational changes supported by earlier survey data, in which lone households accounted for nearly half (47 per cent) of those aged 75–84 and 61 per cent of those aged 85 or older, a majority being older women (ONS, 2018a). There is also a growing incidence of people living with long-term illness and disability as they get older, particularly among those aged 80 and over (MHCLG, 2020a) with greater prevalence among households (54 per cent) in the social rented sector as opposed to owner-occupiers who owned outright (39 per cent), reflecting their older age profile (MHCLG, 2020e, p 11).

Such patterns have a bearing on everyday living in housing seen as over- or under-occupied. Few older people as owner occupiers or renters live in overcrowded housing. They live in more spacious and/or accessible properties than younger households, in detached and semi-detached houses and bungalows, as shown in Table 5.2. At this time, a higher percentage of those aged 75 and over lived in bungalows (25 per cent) than those aged 65–74 (18 per cent) or 55–64 (7 per cent). The age of the UK housing stock was noted earlier, and among the oldest survey households, a quarter of 75–84 year olds and a third aged 85 and over lived in homes built before 1945 (DCLG, 2016, p 19).

Table 5.2: Households by housing type: English Housing Survey 2014–15

	Older households	Younger households
	Oldest 55 and over	Oldest under 55
Detached houses	22%	14%
Bungalows	16%	3%
Semi-detached houses	24%	26%
Terraced houses	23%	34%
Flats	15%	24%

Source: DCLG (2016). © Crown copyright, 2016

Even so, though dependent on housing type and location, these older households had greater average internal floor space – 95m^2 – than younger households – 85m^2. The increased space was especially true for those aged 55–64, particularly owner occupiers, and all older households were more satisfied with their housing situation than their younger counterparts. Data from the later EHS 2018–19 (MHCLG, 2020a, pp 20–1) report 55 per cent of households aged 65 and over were classed as 'under-occupiers' based on the 'bedroom standard' (commonly known as the bedroom tax, as noted earlier) for social and housing association homes introduced in 2013. This is an indicator of occupation density: having two or more spare bedrooms can lead to a reduction in housing benefit. It is defined as 'A standard number of bedrooms […] calculated for each household in accordance with its age/sex/marital status composition and the relationship of the members to one another' (MHCLG, 2020a, p 35) (see the Glossary). Unsurprisingly, greater space is higher among owner occupiers (65 per cent) than private renters (27 per cent) and social renters (14 per cent).

The value of housing space is raised by many older people in empirical research when they discuss how they reorganise their living environments (Kellaher, 2002), and comment is sometimes made concerning the use of separate bedrooms owing to sleeping difficulties between partners, as noted here:

> Three nice bedrooms, well two are quite large […] The other one … The main … I sleep in one, my wife sleeps in the other because once I had this trouble with this thing, I used to have to get up three or four times a night and disturbed her. So I've got used to now sleeping in me own double-bed, she sleeps in her own double-bed and that's it, we're quite happy you know. We have a cup of coffee in bed together in the morning and that's it. No problem. (Peace, 2002a, p 64)

While this couple now have one spare bedroom, if they were a younger married couple living in social housing they would only be seen to need one of their three bedrooms in relation to the bedroom standard. Owner occupiers and people over state retirement age are not affected by this policy, yet this inequality has raised some animosity between age groups.

In contrast to this spatial diversity, the 2019–20 EHS report also highlights that overcrowding has increased in both private and social rented sectors. Additionally, as reported widely, more than one in five of those households headed by someone aged 75 years or over (CfAB/CARE, 2016) live in non-decent housing that does not meet conditions relating to health and safety, state of repair, reasonably modern facilities and services, and thermal comfort (DCLG, 2006, 2016; MHCLG, 2020a, pp 32–6, 2020d). Although the number of non-decent dwellings declined between 1996 and 2014, from 44 per cent to 19 per cent of all households (DCLG, 2016, p 23), the oldest lived in housing with high levels of disrepair, and 65 per cent had at least one household member with long-term health conditions (DCLG, 2016, p 14). Perhaps unsurprisingly, while many older households had income that could meet repairs, including through housing equity release, the oldest group were some of the poorer households. Poor housing quality is directly related to health through extreme cold and falls, as reported by the government in *Housing for Older People* in 2018 (House of Commons 370, 2018), citing the work of the Building Research Establishment (Nicol et al, 2016) noted earlier.

Cultural diversity

This overview describes the housing experienced by older people, using England as a UK example. However, what is missing is any sense of the impact of cultural diversity (MCHLG, 2020b, 2020c, 2020f, 2021b, 2021c). Chapter 4 considered the multicultural nature of UK society, particularly in urban areas. This is reflected in inequalities between groups regarding housing tenure, especially variation in owner occupation and social renting noted in Table 5.3.

Differences in housing tenure for different ethnic groups are linked to a number of issues: the socio-economic status of households, cultural values and racial discrimination regarding housing access. These are compounded when age is taken into account. In particular, home ownership and the prevalence of social renting relate to former and current employment status. For example, from the age of 45 and over, more other than white British households are social renters than white British; for those households aged

Table 5.3: Home ownership, social and private rented housing, 2018

Households all ages by ethnicity, England (%)			
	home ownership	social rented	private rented
All households	63	17	20
White British	68	16	16
Indian	70	7	19
Black Caribbean	40	40	20
Black African	20	44	36
Bangladeshi	46	33	21
Pakistani	58	13	29
Chinese	45	10	45

Note: Adapted from combined data from MHCLG (2020b, 2020c, 2020f), © Crown copyright, 2020

Source: 'All households' relates to all 18 categories of ethnicity – see Glossary

65 and over, the figures are 25 per cent and 15 per cent respectively (see MHCLG, 2020c, 2021c).

Additionally, while concern over all older respondents in non-decent housing was mentioned earlier, by ethnic group this accounts for 33 per cent of mixed white and Black African households and 24 per cent of Bangladeshi households (MHCLG, 2020d). As Nigel de Noronha (2019) notes, housing deprivation across older Black, Asian, Minority Ethnic (BAME) groups is common particularly for Bangladeshi, Black African and Pakistani households living in flats and terraced houses. They are more commonly part of 'other' households, both extended families and in other sharing arrangements, subject to overcrowding and housing disadvantage through a lack of central heating and shared kitchens and bathrooms. While noting the higher percentage of social renters, growing numbers from minority ethnic groups are living in the private rented sector (Finney and Harries, 2013). De Noronha mentions stories of 'racial exclusion by local authority housing authorities, private landlords and neighbours, as well as more recent experiences of stigmatisation, gentrification and displacement. The unequal distribution of property types between ethnic groups reflects patterns of cumulative disadvantage' (de Noronha, 2019, p 2).

Marital status and living arrangements among different cultural groups require further investigation. While support and security may be seen for some, through being a part of an extended family, this is not always the case. Support does not necessarily mean living in the same accommodation, but might be indicated by being part of a shared community. For those aged 65 and over, while living with a partner is common and census data shows more Indian, Pakistani and Bangladeshi respondents living as a couple than white British, living alone can lead to social isolation. Data analysis shows a higher percentage of Bangladeshis were widowed and Black African and Caribbean ethnic groups separated or single compared with other groups (de Noronha, 2019, pp 20–1).

Personal health and well-being needs to be considered in relation to housing experiences. In particular, older Pakistani and Bangladeshi people report higher levels of limiting long-term illness or disability compared with other ethnic groups (de Noranha, 2019), and there are similar issues regarding a lack of home adaptation and access to health and social care services across all groups. The housing circumstances of older people from BAME groups is an under-researched area, and as discussed in Chapter 7, alternative housing arrangements also need consideration (see De Noronha, 2017). Similarly, knowledge concerning older lesbian, gay, bisexual and transgender (LGBT+) people is limited, with a major review by Addis et al (2009) in Wales indicating the impact of discrimination in the areas of health, housing and social care.

Liminal spaces – gardens and balconies

The diversity of population sits alongside the diversity of housing location. Landscape and surroundings were central to the vision of the garden city movement, passing down a love of gardens, a plot of land – or if not gardens, then access from the home to liminal space between housing and street that can be more or less public, dependent on ownership. There are also inequalities, and while 80 per cent of English households have access to a private or shared garden, findings from the EHS (2019–20) indicate that exterior space varies from the largesse of detached houses to smaller spaces surrounding social rented homes to the balconies and communal spaces attached to purpose-built flats (MHCLG, 2020a, 2020e). One in eight households have no garden, and those without are higher among minority ethnic groups – with the Black population nearly four times more likely than the white population to have no outdoor space (ONS, 2020f).

In the 'Environment and Identity' study (see Research summary 6.1), two forms of public/private space that are liminal to housing were defined (Peace et al, 2006, pp 76–7). First, there is enclosed external space – garden, yard, balcony – that is entered either through the private space of the home or via a public approach, from street or drive. This can be so-called defensible space, with the occupants having different levels of control over it and participation in its creation. The second type, referred to in the study as 'tended and watchful space', is internal space that brings the natural environment into the home – window box, balcony or conservatory. Some respondents in the study reported gardening as an ongoing hobby; others developed skills through having more time in retirement; while for others the liminal space was therapeutic – a place to sit and relax.

Bhatti (2006) considers the psychosocial significance of the garden and its extension of the meaning of home. Analysing a directive on gardening through the Mass Observation Data Archive, he recognises the gendered nature of gardening, with women perhaps spending more time in the garden reflecting about nature and plants, and men seeing it more as a 'doing' space. Scott et al (2014), in Australian research, recognise personal attachment through the aesthetics of place, commenting on the benefits of gardening for physical activity and exercise, mental health and achievements. As many researchers show, the natural world and, at its micro-level, the garden can be valued across the life course. People will remember others in a particular place, a grandparent, aunt or partner who loved to garden, or will remember a place where they enjoyed playing with siblings or on their own, exploring, thinking, finding their own personal space. Milligan and Bingley (2015) see this as a relational process that can change with the passage of time. All researchers comment on people's changing physicality, and how the garden may form an aspect of environmental press where having to adapt or modify your gardening is taken into account; for some this forces a move. People may seek help, while others set limits on what they can achieve, modify their tools and use raised beds. More research is needed on this topic – with those who do not garden and those who use settings such as allotments or communal gardens in retirement housing. Nevertheless, to date gardening is seen as social, practical, sensory and restorative, and as adding to the understanding of the creation and recreation of the meaning of home.

Future housing decisions and developments

In the EHS 2014–15, only 9 per cent of older households had moved in the last three years, preferring to stay put; while moving was true for over a third of younger households. The minority of older movers included many who moved within 10 miles of their previous housing (64 per cent) and a smaller number who travelled more than 10 miles, commenting that family and personal issues, wanting a smaller property and a better neighbourhood were their main reasons for moving (DCLG, 2016, pp 14–16). While most movers maintained the same property tenure, those who rented were more likely to have been previous home owners, reflecting the slight transfer of tenure noted earlier (Best and Martin, 2019). To add to this picture, the EHS 2018–19 report considered satisfaction with aspects of housing (Table 5.4): although this was high for all ages, older people were most likely to report greater satisfaction with their accommodation, tenure and surroundings, which supports views concerning ageing in place.

The 2019–20 EHS also considers levels of well-being across different tenures such as satisfaction, life being worthwhile, happiness and feelings of anxiety (MHCLG, 2020e, 2021a, 2021c). Here, the views of HRPs from outright owner-occupiers revealed the highest positive scores and lowest for anxiety; these were followed by owner-occupied mortgagers, private renters and social renters who showed the highest levels of anxiety. Discussion begins to indicate the complexity of people's lives, raising issues such as

Table 5.4: Housing satisfaction in England by age, 2018–19

	Age of HRP (Household Reference Person)				
	16–34	35–64	65 and over	65–79	80 and over
Satisfaction with: Accommodation	87	89	95	94	97
Tenure	81	89	96	*	*
Area	84	87	90	*	*

Source: MHCLG (2020a). © Crown copyright, 2020
(* data not given)

housing costs, dissatisfaction with housing management and satisfaction with the wider community.

Researchers have shown that as people get older they spend more and more time within their home and its immediate surroundings (Baltes et al, 1999). Some may enjoy having access to greater space and many appear satisfied living in their current location. The EHS data reveals some of the issues that prompt a move, yet also shows that some of the oldest old are living in non-decent housing – which may include accommodation that has generally been built for people who:

- don't have trouble climbing stairs;
- don't need to use a wheelchair;
- can see and hear perfectly well;
- don't feel the cold;
- can stand for periods of time;
- don't accumulate too many possessions;
- don't need space for their hobbies;
- are able to bend and stretch; and
- never ever have any difficulty ...

Does this make a difference? To consider these issues, comment begins by considering more inclusive design, the work of the Housing our Ageing Population: Panel for Innovation (HAPPI) team, housing adaptation, smart homes and technological development, before consideration of how the perception of home within general housing may be changing.

Inclusive design for all?

Over more than half a century, researchers from many disciplines have considered how housing and health needs have been held as discordant, stressing the importance of their compatibility (Nicol et al, 2016) and the value of more inclusive design (Matrix, 1984; Goldsmith, 2001; Clarkson et al, 2003; Boys, 2014). While the importance of gendered activities and design has already been mentioned, here the environmental paths of disability and ageing studies come together. Knowledge surrounding the experience of disability has led to different ways of thinking, and the development of social models challenging pathways of discrimination are now being applied to discussion of dementia (Thomas and Milligan, 2018; Shakespeare et al, 2019). How people perceive themselves as getting older with what is recognised as a disability or a long-term condition (Wahl et al, 2009; Verbrugge et al, 2017) has led in recent years to greater partnerships between those concerned with independent living and housing for all. The HA Habinteg defines impairment as 'an injury, illness, or congenital condition that causes or is likely to cause a loss or difference of physiological or psychological function' (Habinteg, 2015, p 1). Where such a condition leads to issues with mobility, to using a wheelchair or other mobility aid, or a sensory impairment, living in 'general needs' housing can present problems owing to housing design.

Following the Disability Discrimination Act 1995 (DDA), it became unlawful to refuse to provide services, or provide services of a lower standard or on a less favourable basis, to disabled people on the basis of their impairments. The DDA has been used to challenge policies and practices regarding attitudes, organisational practices and the environmental issues arguably given greater mandate by the merging of areas of discrimination regarding race, ethnicity, gender, disability and age under the Equality Act 2010. Here, attention is paid to the micro-environment of new build housing using the four concepts central to spatial behaviour across the life course: habitability, accessibility, visitability, usability. The phased implementation of the DDA led to the extension of building regulations in 1999 (Approved Document Part M in England and Part T in Scotland) (Milner and Madigan, 2001), which required that all new housing should be accessible as defined by principles of visitability, where anyone using a wheelchair or other mobility aid should be able to visit. The Centre for Accessible Environments set out the following minimal criteria:

- level entry to the principal, or suitable alternative entrance;
- an entrance door wide enough to allow wheelchair access;
- WC provision on the entrance or first habitable storey;
- adequate circulation and wider doors within the entrance storey;
- switches and socket outlets at appropriate heights from floor level;
- levels of gently sloping approach from car-parking space to the dwelling or, where this is not possible, easy-going steps, but not a stepped ramp;
- where a lift is provided in flats, a minimum lift capacity and dimensions will be recommended;
- where a lift is not provided, the common stair to be designed to suit the needs of ambulant disabled people.

(Langton-Lockton, 1998, 72)

Historically, a lack of communication between parties concerned with population ageing and issues of disability led to separate pathways delaying the development of enabling environments for all.

Lifetime homes, lifetime neighbourhoods

Ongoing discussion at the turn of the millennium recognised the need for a strategic approach to housing and ageing, and welcomed the Labour government's social reform through the consultation document 'Lifetime Homes, Lifetime Neighbourhoods' (LTH, LTN) in 2008 (DCLG, DH, DWP, 2008) (introduced in Chapter 4 in the context of lifetime neighbourhoods). In terms of homes, the strategy covered more inclusive design, building on earlier work from the Helen Hamlyn Foundation (Kelly, 2001) and the Joseph Rowntree Foundation (1997); provision of housing advice; funding and promotion of handyperson services; future development of home improvement agencies (HIAs) under Foundations (see DCLG, 2009); and changes to the disabled facilities grant (DFG) (see adaptation/ modification section).

Owing to the change of government in 2010, the LTH, LTN strategy did not lead to legislation. Nevertheless, it has become an influential reference tool for people concerned with the development of more inclusive design and age-friendly environments. The following action points were proposed for development by 2013:

- new housing advice and information service;
- developments in equity release;
- new national rapid repairs, adaptation service and Warm Front (see Glossary);
- DCLG to implement a number of recommendations concerning the DFG;
- lifetime homes – to make LTH standards the norms for new housing;
- planning – development of Planning Policy Statement 3;
- to improve specialised housing. An innovation panel to be commissioned by DCLG/Department of Health to report to an interministerial group;
- recognition of the interrelationship between health, housing and social care.

(Source: DCLG, DH, DWP, 2008, pp 147–54)

While change is still ongoing, up until 2021 there have been various initiatives which are seen by many stakeholders as encouraging. The LTH, LTN strategy saw housing advice and information as crucial for developing environments where older people wish to live. The Housing Learning and Improving Network (Housing LIN) and the Elderly Accommodation Council (EAC) now provide this function as separate not-for-profit enterprises. The originator and director of Housing LIN, Jeremy Porteus, describes the organisation in his welcome online as a 'professional network […] to provide the latest policy, practice, research and innovation in housing with care for older and vulnerable people' (Porteus, 2011), and has held a particular remit for extra-care housing. The EAC originated in 1985 and runs FirstStop, the only nationwide advice service.

Figure 5.4: Lifetime Homes model

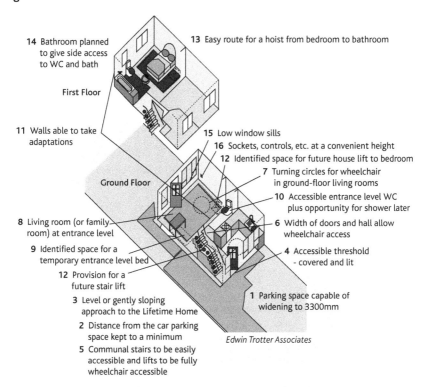

14 Bathroom planned to give side access to WC and bath

First Floor

13 Easy route for a hoist from bedroom to bathroom

11 Walls able to take adaptations

15 Low window sills

16 Sockets, controls, etc. at a convenient height

12 Identified space for future house lift to bedroom

7 Turning circles for wheelchair in ground-floor living rooms

Ground Floor

10 Accessible entrance level WC plus opportunity for shower later

8 Living room (or family room) at entrance level

6 Width of doors and hall allow wheelchair access

9 Identified space for a temporary entrance level bed

4 Accessible threshold - covered and lit

12 Provision for a future stair lift

3 Level or gently sloping approach to the Lifetime Home

1 Parking space capable of widening to 3300mm

2 Distance from the car parking space kept to a minimum

Edwin Trotter Associates

5 Communal stairs to be easily accessible and lifts to be fully wheelchair accessible

Note: Standard 5 on lifts and communal stairs applies only to flats

Source: Joseph Rowntree Foundation (1997); redrawn by The Open University for Peace, 1998 (see also Sopp and Wood, 2001). © Joseph Rowntree Foundation

Figure 5.4 provides a floor plan of the Lifetime Home model, demonstrating visitability, where circulation space is used to enable easier access for people who may be wheelchair users, have mobility issues or sensory impairments, or those who need a range of accommodation on one level; access for all to energy sources; walls that enable adaptation; and access to a car or other vehicle. Initial ideas came through the work of the Joseph Rowntree Foundation (1997) and these were picked up by the HAPPI panel.

A HAPPI future

A further action point from LTH, LTN involved establishing an innovation panel (HAPPI) to consider specialised housing in later life. The All Party Parliamentary Group (APPG) on Housing and Care for Older People and the Housing LIN were central to the development of HAPPI, named after the title of the first report (Barac and Best, 2009) that was chaired by Lord Richard Best (see Glossary). While comments are made here on work that impacts on the future of general needs housing, more detailed discussion concerning the work of HAPPI is found earlier in this chapter regarding older renters and in Chapters 7 and 10 (relating to specialised housing and rural housing). In 2009, HAPPI reviewed settings of good practice, identifying ten key points regarding design that cover all types of future new build housing for older people:

- Generous internal space standards with potential for three habitable rooms and designed for flexible layouts
- Plenty of natural light in the home and circulation spaces
- Balconies and outdoor space, avoiding internal corridors and single-aspect flats
- Adaptability and 'care aware' design which is ready for emerging telecare and telehealthcare technologies
- Circulation spaces that encourage interaction and avoid an 'institutional feel'
- Shared facilities and community 'hubs' where these are lacking in the neighbourhood
- Plants, trees, and the natural environment
- High levels of energy efficiency, with good ventilation to avoid overheating
- Extra storage for belongings and bicycles
- Shared external areas such as 'home zones' that give priority to pedestrians

(Twyford and Porteus, 2021, pp 48–9)

Ways forward for accessible housing

Following discussion of spatial access and further consultation, the Conservative government introduced national technical housing standards in 2015 (Habinteg, 2016; DCLG, 2015), outlining three categories of accessibility for new build housing aimed at ensuring an adequate supply of accessible homes (Table 5.5). These changes, offering limited support for accessibility standards with only visitability issues mandatory in new builds, were critiqued by organisations involved in housing for older people and people with disabilities (Habinteg, 2015). Category 2 still defined special needs at a time when many hoped for greater general inclusion. Nevertheless, some governance bodies, such as the Greater London Authority (The London Plan, 2021), have retained the requirement that all new housing should be built to the higher standards of accessibility (Mayor of London, 2015), although few London boroughs meet the agreed levels of compliance (Mayor of London, 2018).

Table 5.5: Standards for accessible housing

Category	Description	Status	Previous Standard
Category 1/M4(1)	'Visitable' dwellings	Mandatory for all new build dwellings	Unchanged since 2004
Category 2/M4(2)	Accessible	Optional	Lifetime Homes standard (or a local variation)
Category 3/M4(3)	Wheelchair user dwellings	Optional	Wheelchair housing design guide (or a local variation)

Source: MHCLG (2015, 2020f)

In 2018, a Housing White Paper 'Fixing Our Broken Housing Markets' (MHCLG, 2017) that presented policy preferences drew attention to the desperate shortage of new build homes, and a cross-party House of Commons Select Committee for Communities and Local Government, now the Ministry of Housing, Community and Local Government (MHCLG), published 'Housing for Older People', paradoxically reporting the need for a national strategy (MHCLG, 2019b). Emphasising the diversity of older people in terms of 'age, tenure, geographical location, income, equity and individual preference' (p 3), issues from LTH, LTN are developed, and there is a focus on those who wish to stay put or consider a move. The following recommendations are made:

- additional operational funding for HIAs including a handyperson service for older people in each local area;
- refunding by the government of the existing FirstStop Advice Service to provide an expanded national telephone advice service that provides holistic housing advice to older people and signposts them to local services;
- ongoing consideration of fuel poverty to deal with heating issues, acknowledging that those in advanced old age spend more time within their home than other age groups;
- measures to help older people overcome the barriers to moving home, including accreditation for companies providing tailored services for older people who are moving and better customer service from lenders applying for a mortgage;
- encouraging national and local planning policies that support the building of varied housing for older people – extra care, retirement, sheltered and accessible housing across the social and private sectors;
- building of all new homes to accessible and adaptable standards so they are 'age proofed' and can meet the current and future needs of older people;
- recognition that both established and new housing occupied by older people needs to be close to local services, amenities and public transport.

Most recently, a consultation from the MHCLG (2019a) has sought views regarding raising accessibility standards for new homes by December 2020, recognising the importance of suitable homes for older and disabled people.

The White Paper of 2018 recognised the association between housing, health and social care, with integrated working often being essential. Noting that the majority of older people live in general housing, and often alone, attention is drawn again to the concept of under-occupied housing. Issues of downsizing or right-sizing are discussed alongside maintenance of the current housing stock and innovations in new builds. The need for varied housing types directs attention to local and regional planning.

It is noted that if local government wishes to encourage right-sizing, innovative local plans for housing that attract older movers need to continue to be developed (see Local Government Association, 2017a, 2017b, 2021). Consequently, design issues for new builds need to incorporate design features that have intergenerational acceptance. Park and Porteus reflect on the work of HAPPI, accepting and promoting their ten design principles, and they make this point about current new build housing: 'it is inevitable that the vast majority will, at some point, be occupied by someone aged 75 or above. Age-friendly housing should therefore become the norm rather than the exception; acknowledged as an important step towards universal design but still not…' (2018, pp 18–19).

More recently, in August 2020, a planning white paper 'Planning for the Future' has been released focusing on change in planning strategies for future housing development following the challenging times caused by the COVID-19 health pandemic (MHCLG, 2020). The RTPI (2021) response in a recent paper 'Planning for a Better Future' raises challenging issues including: providing affordable housing; tackling place inequality; establishing a green industrial revolution; providing sustainable modes of transport; working towards a zero-carbon infrastructure; and maintaining local community involvement in the planning process. These debates sit alongside the Health and Care Bill (House of Commons Bill 2021–22) where housing, health and social care interact (The King's Fund, 2021b).

Changing the nature of home?

This update on policy development and current thinking reveals the dichotomy between developing new forms of specialised housing with more inclusive design and the needs of many who wish to stay in their own homes, which may benefit from not only new builds but also adaptation (Heywood, 2005). The wider issue of retrofitting takes into account issues such as energy efficiency that relate to legally binding climate change targets (Hamilton et al, 2013). Here the question becomes how general housing, both current and new build, can embrace support systems that are structural, technical, social and sustainable; new forms of general housing that people of all ages might prefer in the future.

Housing adaptation/modification

Internationally, those concerned with housing adaptation or modification describe environmental barriers in houses and apartment buildings as including outdoor steps, narrow entrances and hallways, lack of elevators, inaccessible toilets and bathrooms, small room sizes, baths rather than showers, steep internal stairs, inaccessible showers with stepped entries, and poor design regarding insulation, access to power and water supplies (Powell et al, 2017; Adams and Hodges, 2018; Peace and Darton, 2020b). In 2018, 9 per cent of homes in England had accessibility features that deemed them 'visitable', a rise from 5 per cent in 2005 (the most common feature being an entrance-level toilet) (MHCLG, 2020a). This is limited progress, and it is perhaps unsurprising that for those in their late 80s 'more than one in three … have difficulty undertaking five or more activities of daily living (Marmot et al, 2016)' (Centre for Ageing Better (CfAB), 2017, p 2). The EHS (2019–20) has issued a report focusing on the 1.9 million (8 per cent) households where at least one person has a long-standing health condition and requires adaptations either inside or outside their home. Of this group, 81 per cent felt their housing was suitable for their needs, yet the 374,000 who felt their circumstances were unsuitable make up 2 per cent of all households in England, including 13 per cent who were 75 years or over. While tenants were more likely to enquire about making changes, owner-occupiers and middle-income households were less likely to make those changes. Interestingly, those under 55 years of age were more likely to say their accommodation was unsuitable and move to somewhere more suitable than those who were older. Various adaptations were mentioned and, for 42 per cent (819,000) of people in need of an adaptation, the most important adaptation was a hand or grab rail in the kitchen or bathroom (see MHCLG, 2021d).

These findings build on the earlier discussion of non-decent housing, and the question becomes whether life could be made easier through home adaptation, saving money for the NHS, and whether is this feasible. Older homeowners and renters, living alone or as a couple, may or may not have access to financial resources and/or the understanding to make informed decisions about housing adaptation. Many homeowners may need to be self-funders (Alonso-Lopez, 2020) if they wish to further age-proof their home, possibly by drawing on housing equity, while those with low incomes may be able to apply for the DFG (Mackintosh, 2020). As noted, DFGs have become the major source of statutory support for disabled people seeking adaptation in both private and public sector housing in the UK, with 65 per cent currently going to people aged 60 and over. Funded through the Better Care Fund, it is still a poorly resourced area. The level of grant awarded is dependent on a test of resources that is designed to ensure funding is granted to those in greatest need within set limits. A difference is seen between:

Minor home adaptations – commonly adaptations costing under £1,000, including hand rails, grab rails, ramps, steps, lighting improvements, lever taps, heating controls, a key safe, door/window/curtain opening closing equipment and monitoring equipment for specific conditions (CfAB, 2017, p 3). They are seen as 'cost effective interventions for preventing falls and injuries, improving performance of everyday activities and mental health' (Powell et al, 2017, p 16), and financial resources may come through occupational therapy teams.

Major home adaptations – may cost £1,000–£10,000 and include bathroom adaptations, level access showers and wet-rooms, toilet installation/ replacement, door widening, alterations to room layouts, kitchen adaptations and stairlifts. More extensive adaptations may include the provision of an extra bedroom or bathroom (CfAB, 2017, p 3).

As noted earlier, increased investment in the DFG is ongoing, and in 2008 the independent charitable organisation Care & Repair England developed the Home Adaptations Consortium, which continues to lobby government bodies (Local Government Association, 2017a).

A gradual recognition of the value of housing adaptation/modification is growing, particularly in developed nations. Research is beginning to show how home improvement can provide a return on building investment that improves personal well-being and reduces the frequency of falls, subsequently deferring costs to health and social care services (Fänge and Iwarsson, 2005; Heywood, 2005; Adams, 2016; Petersson et al, 2017; Aplin et al, 2020; Keglovits and Stark, 2020; Peace and Darton, 2020b). The role of the professional occupational therapist (OT) is becoming increasingly recognised, and in the UK, the Royal College of Occupational Therapy has promoted an international network, seeking to establish a code of practice for work with older people (Royal College of Occuational Therapists, 2019) and joining with the Housing LIN to publish good practice.

A recent special issue of the *Journal of Aging and Environment* (Peace and Darton, 2020a) focuses on adaptation, offering perspectives from across Western developed countries – Sweden, Spain, Australia, US and England (Slaug et al, 2020; Thordardottir et al, 2018, 2020; Alonso-Lopez, 2020; Aplin et al, 2020, Keglovits and Stark, 2020; Mackintosh, 2020). Editors Peace and Darton discuss cross-cutting issues for countries where adaptation is seen as a relatively modest structural development that can modify national housing stocks. Systems focus on the needs of the most vulnerable older and disabled people, who are often living alone and with low incomes and are referred for assistance through health and social care services. Home adaptation for people with dementia living in the community needs further consideration. Accommodation is commonly assessed by OTs to consider the potential for adaptation, resulting in what may be seen as standard interventions such as converting bathrooms to shower rooms. Often people do not have the information they need to know that home adaptation/modification may be available through financial support rather than self-funding (Alonso-Lopez, 2020).

For the countries reporting here, only Sweden has a tax-funded service that provides housing adaptations tailored to the individual and based on functional needs rather than age. Data from 2016 reported by Slaug et al (2020) indicates that 74,000 housing adaptations are commonly granted each year, and while this aims to make the environment more accessible, in times of austerity adaptations have been reduced alongside requirements for accessible housing in new builds. Research by Thordardottir et al (2018, 2020) and Aplin et al (2020) on the experience of home adaptation shows how personal need and environmental change may be ongoing and that longitudinal evaluation is required. This body of research shows how housing adaptation can be a public health issue, especially for those who wish to stay put in their own homes for as long as possible. The experience of housing adaptation is commented on by two older people in Chapter 6.

Finally, the impact of the COVID-19 pandemic has led many to reconsider remote working, and for OTs this may affect assessment for housing adaptation. Read et al (2020), researchers at Sheffield and Sheffield Hallam universities, have explored remote pre-discharge OT assessments of a patient's home using 'secure digital videoconferencing' instead of being on site. This multidisciplinary study involved computer scientists, OTs and health service researchers, who developed digital ways of working. The equipment enabled a hospital-based OT 'to communicate and capture images via a hyperlink that is texted or emailed to a smartphone controlled by a trusted visitor (such as a relative or member of a third sector organisation)' (Read et al, 2020, p 3). The trials appeared successful, given the need to ensure the safety, training and induction of the visitor through standardised practice. This procedure could save resources, but may also change the nature of the OT role with some older people – especially the very old. However, if it takes place in advance of hospital discharge, it might release time for a different level of support. This example highlights how technological development has the potential to change lives, as seen in smart homes.

Smart homes

Alongside housing adaptation, technological development has the potential to change lives by supporting personal health and changing the housing and care environment. Since the turn of the century, research programmes in the UK that engage the business community, multidisciplinary researchers and local government, funding both preventative and assistive technology, aim to deliver systems that enable people to stay in their own homes or live in sustainable housing and neighbourhoods, thereby prolonging health (Audit Commission, 2004; DCLG, DH, DWP, 2008; UKRI, 2021. The Preventative Technology Grant (2006–08; ODPM, DH, 2006) aimed to support local councils' investment in telecare to support more older people living at home.

Early British research regarding smart home technology for affordable social housing markets (Gann, et al, 1999) involved the development of two demonstration dwellings in York and Edinburgh that were fitted with intelligent ceiling roses, infra-red sensor receivers, window, door and curtain openers, moveable cupboards or kitchen sink, smoke/heat detectors, radiator controls and movement detectors to research possibilities and response. At that time, the market for technologies was immature (1999, p xv), and consumers were unconvinced or ill-informed about potential benefits or sources of supply. Still under-developed was the infrastructure that facilitated installation systems, and with little governance at national level, such developments could not be reached by particular housing markets.

Nevertheless, ongoing developments continue, and in 2006, 1.5 million older people were said to use some form of telecare (Poole, 2006). The UK's largest ongoing telecare pilot study in West Lothian, Scotland, began in 1999, aiming to mainstream technology in general housing and housing with care for everyone aged 60 and over through its Home Safety Service – alongside a radical change in care culture that provided ongoing support through enablement. There is an ongoing evaluation that indicates how technology becomes taken for granted over time. Older people comment that it enhances their safety and security, helping them to sustain independent living and a better quality of life, while informal carers report on the reassurance it has given them, and the majority of professional staff support the positive benefits it brings to their work (Bowes and McColgan, 2006, 2013). Currently, private developers are seeking to increase the development of smart housing (Wondrwall, 2020).

As Park and Porteus (2018, pp 98–9) stress, connectivity that enhances health and well-being in later life is facilitated through technology that enables communication, easier travel and greater personal control within the home. Yet a genuine ambivalence regarding the ethics of personal versus technical contact when caring for people with support needs continues to be heard (Percival and Hanson, 2006; Fisk, 2015; Jones, 2015; European Parliament 2020). Changes to the built environment may enhance levels of comfort, security and autonomy, thereby maintaining place attachment or making the home space open to revealing personal frailty and becoming more institutionalised. Milligan et al (2010), through an EU Ethical Frameworks for Telecare Technologies for Older People at Home study, identify how surveillance and monitoring can be intrusive for some, destroying the possibility of independence and personal control, while enabling others access to very basic data about the self in an aim to keep users alive. But for other users the safety and security of being able to gain access to others through personal communication, however remote, is valued, and they do not have a problem with wearing a pendant alarm and using it. These views are supported by a range of research that indicates the value of both personal and technological care and support (Barlow et al, 2007; Schillmeier, 2008; Schillmeier and Domenech, 2010).

Home care, home share: part of the environments of ageing

With this technological development in mind, we return to personal interaction, home sharing and home care – essential parts of the everyday for many older people living in community-based housing. New ideas about housing types acknowledge that as people grow older their health, both physical and mental, changes, and their need for support and care services may increase. While this is not a book that centres on care, ordinary housing is a care environment, sometimes defined by health geographers as part of the landscape of care (Milligan, 2009). In the main, those in need of care will be living alone or as a couple, and the experience of home care can be seen as informal, formal or both. Informal care is provided primarily through a partner, family, friends, neighbours, parent or friend. While this is more commonly gendered work, often a daughter or daughter in law's role, the growth in coupledom places the role evenly on spouses/partners (Gopinath et al, forthcoming).

The charity Carers UK estimates the number of adult carers as 6.5 million, or 1 in 8 adults for all caring relationships, with the Alzheimer's Society indicating hundreds of thousands of people caring for people with dementia (2018). Some carers try to maintain their working lives while caring, but others will have given up employment; and for some the role may become overwhelming (Carers UK, 2019; ONS, 2019b).

The task of caring can be a 24/7 occupation, from the practical such as shopping or laundry to the personal – aid with rising, feeding, washing, toileting, giving medication, putting to bed, watching and the 'being there' of companionship. For many older people, a combination of family members and home carers provides this support, while others rely solely on the service of paid home carers. The route to obtaining home care services is complex. People with financial resources may directly purchase assistance from a home care agency, while others will go through their local authority to seek means-tested support through personal need and detailed financial assessment (Age UK, 2019). Assessing the quality of home care agencies is part of the work of the Care Quality Commission. Research by Giebel et al (2020) indicates how, during the COVID-19 pandemic, there was a withdrawal of social services and support for people with dementia living at home, leading to increased dependency, pressure on unpaid carers, and concern over continuing support (see IDEAL, n.d.).

The home environment embraces privacy, familiarity, personal possessions and routines; personal identity is displayed and the individual maintains levels of control. The informal carer as partner will have the most intimate knowledge of the value attached to home in contributing to the personal identity of the other. Yet as a place of formal care for the visiting home carer, this home temporarily becomes a workplace, where they may engage with the cared-for on a very intimate level through bathing or toileting alongside meal preparation and giving medication. Privacy levels within the home will change across time and space (Twigg, 2000). In Canadian research, Angus et al (2005) undertook detailed ethnographic work with 16 people in receipt of formal home care, utilising Bourdieu's concept of habitus to discuss the shifting fields of practice when relating domestic and social/healthcare experiences. As Twigg (2006) indicates persuasively, there can be striking spatio-temporal differences in routines between body times, domestic times and service times, with the formal home carer perhaps having 15 or 30 minutes to carry out essential tasks. This juxtaposition needs to be recognised when thinking through everyday experiences, the impact on a changing meaning of home and how autonomy can be maintained within this interdependent lifestyle. How the structural and technical can support the social is fundamental to the way forward.

Finally, the different arrangement provided by intergenerational home sharing should be added to this discussion. This is not a form of care but companionship and company. Home sharing involves people with spare rooms offering affordable secure accommodation in return for someone who can lend a hand. Rather than being the informal care mentioned here, it is an arrangement that offers companionship and often reduces loneliness. Homeshare UK is a network of more than 20 organisations across the UK and Republic of Ireland that vet, match and oversee interactions between givers and sharers. The concept is global, though exists primarily in English-speaking developed nations, and it provides a different form of ageing in place (see Homeshare UK, 2021; Homeshare International, 2021). Although an under-researched area, evaluations indicate unique benefits through social exchange, the enhanced agency of the older person and functional support, with older homeowners gaining greater companionship and assistance (see Altus and Mathews, 2000; Mirza et al, 2019; Bagnall, 2020). While these older people are sharing their space, others are involved in new design.

Co-designing housing alternatives

Research by architects and anthropologists – Hanson et al, (2001) has confirmed the importance of flexibility for managing internal spatial arrangements in later life. Through detailed analysis of floor plans for 240 dwellings occupied by older people and 60 case studies, they demonstrated how space decreases with dwelling type from semi-detached housing to nursing home (see Kellaher, 2002, pp 48–9). Focusing on ordinary housing, Kellaher considers the adaptation of domestic space:

> People attempt, and frequently succeed, in re-configuring their space to be more appropriate – to be a better fit, not just with the past and the present, but in anticipation of a future that may hold unknown incapacities and adjustments. Older people recognise that even where individuals and couples do not live within close kinship contexts, domestic space still needs to reflect the relationships between inhabitants and visitors [...]. This may entail more complex morphology than many providers are accustomed to make available in purpose-built housing for older people... (Kellaher, 2002, p 54)

These views align with earlier discussion of the use of space in general housing, and also in the DWELL study (Designing for Wellbeing in Environments in Later Life) (Barnes et al, 2015; Park et al 2016), which was based on the aspirations of older people wishing to live in intergenerational communities. This co-design project based in Sheffield was guided by third agers (aged 55 and over) as potential 'right-sizers' looking for 'easily accessible, conveniently located, energy efficient, easier to maintain' (Park et al, 2016, p 7) housing; not necessarily smaller but manageable. They aimed to develop prototypes for age-friendly housing and neighbourhoods that demonstrated affordances for all, alongside guidance for housing in later life to enable integration between professional and local authority directives.

The research involved 150 Sheffield residents who took part in visits to different settings, focus groups, interviews with stakeholders and consideration of plans. In developing a brief, they wished for a home that was connected, pleasurable, spacious, manageable, accessible, sociable, adaptable and green. Discussion indicated support for the bungalow housing type, yet willingness to consider apartment living if spacious and secure, where a good location would see shared space that could include allotments; fewer bedrooms, but space to accommodate separate living for partners and guest; and parking. In the main, they were owner occupiers who recognised the need for accommodating diversity and that health needs could impact well-being and change their circumstances. Incorporating these views, the research team developed housing plans that were low rise, using the bungalow as a model; mid-rise and high rise, including what is they termed co-housing lite, where internal communal event spaces are planned alongside apartments of varied sizes; management could include collective decision making (Park et al, 2016, pp 50–77).

In reflecting on their participatory research, Park et al (2016) discuss the ways in which downsizing is often presented to older people as a way of bypassing housing maintenance and environmental press at a time of housing shortages for first-time buyers. They argue that housing options in later life should move beyond specialised housing, and understand the 'need to reframe housing from a life course perspective and recognise that older people are active citizens with community rights' (2016, p 1). When considering the LTH model, they recognise the need to go beyond a focus on physical accessibility and utilise the HAPPI design recommendations in new ideas. They recognise that new general needs housing has to be seen as viable and developed by the local authority in a local plan. In this way, people may accept that they are not downsizing but right-sizing.

Finally, during 2021, the All Party Parliamentary Group for Housing and Care of Older People has been considering housing for people with dementia. Looking again at their principles, they have developed new 'dementia-ready' HAPPI features (Twyford and Porteus, 2021), including greater concern for space standards, natural light and access – both visually and to outdoor spaces (p 48).

Conclusions

This chapter has aimed to provide a comprehensive picture of issues surrounding general needs housing, where the majority of older people live either as a couple or on their own. This is a picture seen during years of growing concern over the shortage of new build housing, and calls for incentives for older home owners to downsize and release housing for younger families (Royal Institution of Chartered Surveyors, 2016). Yet a way of life that maintains community living is favoured. How does this relate to the synergy between person and environment in later life? At the end of Chapter 4, we reflected on the meaning of home through a rural/urban lens. Such reflection returns in relation to general housing at the end of Chapter 6, after we have heard from people for whom this is home and who may, or may not, be thinking about alternative ways of living.

6

Housing histories, housing options

Introduction

When asked if they might move after retiring from paid employment, and whether this might be to special housing geared towards older people, many research respondents will say they haven't really thought about it and wish to stay in their own home for 'as long as possible'. This is despite the fact that their stories show they have thought about it even if it has not been widely discussed, and some have been used to moving throughout their lives (Holland, 2001; Wiles, 2005b; Peace et al, 2006). Attachment to place involves the coming together of levels of environmental understanding, and it has been noted 'that individual experience of place is layered and that knowledge of personal biography and experience in time and space leads to greater clarification of the complexity of person–environment interaction' (Peace et al, 2011, p 754).

Here, vignettes from anonymised and real name participants who wished to be named in research are introduced and they have all given consent for their stories to be told. They have been drawn from three British research studies that consider the detail of environment and ageing. The concept of 'option recognition', which captures the extent of environmental impact on decision making in later life, is then introduced. Consideration is given to how this theoretical development relates to research within other developed countries, especially the ENABLE-AGE researchers who similarly take into account the normality of environmental continuity and change in very old age. To conclude, the lens of general housing is used to reflect on the meaning of home.

Staying put?

The first vignette for Teresa and Sidney comes from the Transitions in Kitchen Living study (2009–11) (Peace et al, 2018), discussed in Research summary 9.1 as an example of interdisciplinary research methodology. Quotes from the original interview scripts have been anonymised. Focusing on the domestic kitchen in later life, housing histories were carried out with research respondents in order to understand individual experiences of micro-environments across the life course. Data show how moving house, changing living arrangements and housing type are guided by familial needs, personal expectations and financial resources, all these decisions being made alone, in partnership or with others. They illustrate architectural change alongside the ongoing development of domestic equipment and assistive technology over time within a significant space in the home. Housing histories vary, clearly, and while some people moved housing and location several times, others remained within one or two homes and locations. The reasons for staying put varied with time, life events and resources.

Teresa is a white British woman, who was living with her husband, Sidney, in an owner-occupied flat during the research. She was born in 1923 and was 87 years old when interviewed. She left school aged 16 and worked in various administrative posts, as well as undertaking army service from 1941 to 1946 during the Second World War. Living as a couple, Teresa and Sidney had an annual income through private and state pensions and had some financial resources. Teresa commented that her husband was 90 years old and had been diagnosed with Parkinson's disease in the previous year. She had had a heart attack 12 months prior to the interview, but did not count herself as having poor health – rather classifying it as good. Both Teresa and Sidney drove but only short distances, including to a supermarket for a 'big shop'.

Here, Teresa recalls aspects of the kitchen in the seven dwellings she had called home, starting with the first, a rented terraced house, where she lived from birth to about the age of 12:

'It was a Victorian house we lived in. The kitchen, I guess, really, in those days, was called a scullery rather than a kitchen. It had a back door but it had no heating system or very convenient cooking system; it had what was called a copper which the fire was lit under on washing days and bath nights [laughs]. And the water was heated in the sort of stone [...] which stood in the sort of alcove when the fire was lit. Otherwise water was boiled probably in the kettle on the fire. Quite a large sort of sink... [Q. Was it a butler sink?] Yes, I think is was white enamel but very thick and heavy and deep. You broke your back if you stood at it too long. It had stone [floor] ... a red ... not quarry tiles as they are now ... these were sort of quite big, which had to be scrubbed. Life wasn't easy in those days ... for women, I don't think.

There would probably have been a pantry ... where all the food stuff were kept ... I think there were sort of [a] marbly sort of slab that things were kept on and of course there was always a vent in the wall, so there was air.'

Teresa did not remember learning many kitchen skills, with the exception of ironing on the living room table. This was partly because her mother had mobility problems and so her father was the cook, and another member of the family, Dora, helped them in the kitchen and washing clothes with the 'jolly old dolly board'. She recalls that her father:

'lit the fire there and put the water into the sort of tub thing that was inside. It was what it was lined with … zinc or something like that would it have been? … Because there was no bathroom. We didn't have a bathroom, you know, the washing was done down there.'

In 1935, Teresa moved with her family to another part of town, to a newer terraced house that her father bought and where they lived until 1947. Here she recalls some changes in kitchen equipment. These were ongoing, and the larder or pantry still remained:

'it was quite luxurious compared with the house in […]. It was a more modern house. I mean it had a bathroom of course … and a kitchen, which, again, I think, if I remember rightly, was down a step. But I mean it didn't have a fridge and it didn't have a washing machine. It had the kitchen sink again and a gas cooker and cupboard space … I think it had what they called a kitchen cabinet in those days. It was sort of covered in the bottom and with shelves at the top. It had a larder. It had a larder, because we didn't have a fridge.'

Here she remembers 'I probably did do a bit of cooking and shopping and that sort of thing … but I mean six years of the time we were in that house [was the Second World War]', when Teresa did army service and they had 'a huge indoor shelter' and many visitors, especially family members in danger of being bombed. Teresa married Sidney after the war years and, having moved briefly with her mother and father on their retirement to a seaside resort, they bought a new bungalow in a village just outside a city in 1960. She says:

'It was only a two-bedroom house. But it had a nice little kitchen and it was a nice cooker. It didn't have a fridge or a washing machine when we first got married. But I worked for an electrical contractor and eventually, you know, we sort of … If things sort of went slightly out of date, we got them [laughs]. So we did have a fridge there and we did have a washing machine … it was a sort of kitchen-cum-dining room.'

The couple then adopted their son, and as Teresa's mother was now a widow, they wanted more space to accommodate everyone if necessary. 'So that was when we moved further down the lane to a three-bedroom house', in 1965. Sidney was working: 'he was extremely busy. So he wasn't at home. Six days a week he was working.'

This was very much a relationship where the husband was out of the home at work and the wife, even if working, managed the kitchen. The kitchens in these two properties were her responsibility and in the 1960s new ideas were formulated:

'well, yes. It was yours … It was much more modern, really … I think it's the same with young people these days. They think, oh, you know, they aren't having a hard time but it's their time and they're coping with it in the same way that we coped with what was our time … I think we sort of added to it as we wanted.'

The three-bedroomed house, where the couple lived for 12 years until 1978, was semi-detached, but the kitchen wasn't any larger: it just had a more interesting layout, with a hatch from kitchen to dining room. Here there was the full range of kitchen equipment: cooker, cupboards including a broom cupboard, fridge and a washing machine. However, Teresa preferred city life, and owing to their son's schooling, they returned to live in the centre of the city, in a bigger four-bedroomed semi-detached house, built in 1930. Yet she thought the kitchen 'was horrendous', and it was completely redone. Sidney was helped by his brother as well as outside help in this venture. The kitchen was changed twice, because of a mistake with a colour scheme that made it very dark and needing more light. Throughout this kitchen history, Teresa says she was never a great cook!

They had really liked this house but recognised a need to downsize:

'When [son] had gone, we were rattling round in a four-bedroom house, really. It was a bit ridiculous, I suppose. And the garden was getting a bit much, of course. [Q. Did the kitchen get problematic?] No, no, no really it was nothing really to do with the kitchen … We really needed to scale down.'

This led the couple to move one more time, in 2009, to a flat that was part of two blocks of 30 and 40 units built in 2005. While it was a mixed-age residence, there were a number of retired owners, and although it was a good location with a walkable shop, they felt the accommodation was not designed with older people in mind, and that their flat may possibly be too big for one person if left on their own. At this point Sidney joined Teresa in the interview:

'First sort of impressions of the kitchen were that it was neat, it was handy (T). It was, you know, it looked quite attractive (S) … I think when you first see something and when you live in it, it's quite different in a lot of ways. (T) … Because now, you know … I think … why do they always have cupboards so high that you need a stool to stand on to get to the shelves? (T) Which they tell you that you shouldn't do when you get older? (S) I have never had a kitchen before that didn't have a window … on the most brilliant sunny day, I have to have the light on (T) And that is something you don't think about … (S) Until you live in is. That's right (T). The last kitchen I had at […], I had everything white … Whereas I've got this dark … it's quite dark wood. The working top is dark. [Int. So nothing is reflecting the light or maximising the natural light in any way?] That's right (S).'

In the interview concerning their current kitchen, Teresa comments that she is 5 ft 2 in tall, and that while the bottom shelves are satisfactory, the higher shelves require her to stand on a stool. For lower cupboards she says:

'the cupboards down below, there's plenty of cupboard space but again, it's, you know … I can get down on my knees and I can't get up … [laughs] …. I did damage the cartilage in both my knees when I used to play hockey years and years ago … as long as I can bend, I'm okay…'

Teresa and Sidney also made a general point about recycling and the lack of options for getting rid of food waste for all 70 flats. They thought that this needed to be tackled, as it had to go into general waste.

In this narrative focusing on the kitchen, it is evident how personal changes across almost a century demonstrate how social characteristics – gender, family relations and family changes, location, housing type, employment and cultural difference – can all contribute to where and how a person lives (see Thompson et al, 2014). At the same time, architectural, engineering and technological change influence how the material environment changes, and the health and well-being of the individual influences how it is used. On the whole, the couple were pleased with their downsizing move, but raised a number of issues about living in a smaller apartment in a mid-rise block.

The following narratives were provided by participants in the Environment and Identity in Later Life study, who were interviewed in 2000/01 (Research summary 6.1).

In this second example, taken from Peace et al (2006, pp 139–42), the practicalities of home adaptation raised in Chapter 5 are explored alongside early experience of living alone. Bertie, a white British 84 year old, was interviewed at his owner-occupied semi-detached house in Bedford, where he had been resident for 50 years. He was a retired architect and recently widowed. His wife had experienced a series of strokes in the early 1990s, leading to poor mobility, other impairments and the need to bring her bed downstairs into the living room. Bertie shows what can be done by someone with particular professional skills who wishes to redesign their home. He

---

Research summary 6.1: Environment and identity in later life

This study was conducted in 1999–2003 by Peace, Holland, The Open University; Kellaher, CESSA, London Metropolitan University.

Aims: to understand the relationship between environment and identity in later life.

Location: the research was undertaken in three locations: in semi-rural, urban and metropolitan locations within middle England and London.

Methods: a detailed ethnography undertaken in two stages. First, a participative approach used nine focus groups with older people living in the three locations who discussed the meaning of environment in later life. Findings were used to develop the Facets of Life wheel (Peace et al, 2006, p 26) (see Chapter 9). Second, in-depth qualitative research took place with 54 older people, aged between 61 and 93, 63 per cent women, living in housing ranging from detached houses to a residential care home. The Facets of Life wheel was used by individual participants to direct conversations in in-depth interviews discussing how environment influenced self-identity. Further narratives from these participants are given in Peace et al (2006, pp 131–52) and Peace et al (2011).

Funded by: the Economic and Social Research Council, Growing Older Programme, 1999–2004.

---

was a self-funder for whom 'do-it-yourself' was the way forward, following an assessment from the local authority. He says:

'I had a letter which said that if by any chance we were lucky enough to get a grant I would be expected to pay between £6,000 and £7,000. Well I was horrified, so I called the whole thing to a halt and said "fair enough", so I went it alone and … I put a shower in myself, I had a lavatory basin put in, took a cupboard out and had the boiler put in the kitchen … but, she was interested in her clothes and so of course when she wanted to get dressed in the morning, what did I have to do? Go upstairs and I would bring the wrong one down and she said what she wanted and I wouldn't have a clue [laughs], so I trundled up and downstairs and the first thing we did was bring down the wardrobe and stuck it here behind me … She got all her clothes down here.

One of the things that I don't think is always appreciated is how important access and doors are. You came in this morning through the front wall where the first thing I did was widen it by three feet because if you've got the car in the drive you couldn't push a wheelchair right by it.

I got to the position in the end where the only way to get her out of here [front room] in a chair was to go out through here, through that porch where there was considerable congestion, down a ramp into the garden into a door at the back of the garage, back through the garage right around the front wall … It was a major issue…

So, I decided that we can't go on like this … we'd get jammed with the chair in that back door couldn't get her in or out and I thought I'd have to change the drive.

You can see yourself if you're with a person and perhaps that's where I had the advantage on the OT, I was with her all the while and so I could see whether a handle was needed and one of the vital ones is at the top of the stairs, you have a handle to grasp … [when getting on and off a stairlift].

Upstairs we've got a toilet and the very same situation arose, I put handles on both sides, but then you've got a 2 ft 6 in door swing in and you sterilise 2 ft 6 in of the floor space and so I put bi-fold doors up there and I did the same in the bathroom because there we wanted additional room. You see it wasn't only the patient, we wanted a carer alongside her and there wasn't room or if there was room the door swing was in the way, so I put bi-fold doors in there.

I would say that the authorities have been very helpful but I do believe that a lot of things … if you do have the inclination to be a do it yourself, you can do it yourself and I have done a lot. I shouldn't say it really but I have.'

This is an example of someone with a fervent understanding of the materiality and spatial dimensions of the built environment. Obviously without the voice of his partner we do not know how she found these changes, but Bertie did his best to make sure that their environment was enabling. In this situation, if we reconsider Lawton and Nahemow's (1973) environmental docility hypothesis, we can see how changes to environmental press increased the comfort zone for the carer(s) and hopefully the cared for, through Bertie's proactive actions (Lawton, 1983).

Bertie's comments begin to reveal his thoughts on staying put and moving following his wife's death. He is centred both in his locality and immediate environment, and recognised that some of his material changes would help himself. He says:

'I can get up whatever time I like. One of my worries is that if my curtains aren't drawn certain neighbours of mine are wondering what is happening [laughs] and they will come and diplomatically tap the front window or door. I am grateful for that ...

One thing people have said to me 'are you going to move?' and I won't move until we have got buses on the doorstep [...] really, the church is near, people you know are here, I have got a son ... not far away, they were here last night with two of his girls. I don't know some things in life you don't know until you face them do you?...

We go through life where we haven't got enough room, extensions here, there, and everywhere, and then you get to a point in life where you want to shrink everything really, although you can never have too much space. It is like a greenhouse, it is never big enough ... I don't go in the other two bedrooms much, but I use everything else.'

His comments about the pluses and minuses of place and space are sometimes heard when older people talk to researchers about possible choices over accommodation and support that may, or may not, be possible. There is a tension: future planning at a time of loss includes a recognition of personal mortality and the immediacy of certain needs that sees Bertie both want to remain engaged in his locality while at the same time managing space that is comforting even if somewhat unused. This is central to his comment that 'It is like a greenhouse, it is never big enough', drawing a parallel with the gardener who is always nurturing growth in situ. But, continuing, he talks about living alone and how this has made him inward looking:

'I will tell you one thing that is worrying, and I said it only recently, one of the things with living on your own, it can make you very selfish ... I am certain that is the case. I have seen it in other people, I suppose it is easy to do that than see it in yourself. But instead of having to think about the result of this or that, you only think about yourself.'

Bertie does not say that he is lonely or socially isolated, but at this point his reflection on withdrawing into himself may demonstrate both an important recognition of this possibility or an ongoing reflection about self at the end of a long life – or both (Victor et al, 2002).

This is a point that is picked up in the following narrative by Nancy (from Peace et al, 2006, pp 142–5). Born in Northampton, 77-year-old Nancy moved in the early 1950s to the smaller town of Burton Latimer with her husband. They lived in a three-bedroomed council house (social rented) that had been built after the Second World War. Towards the end of the 1980s, they moved to a purpose-built retirement bungalow also rented from the council. This had two bedrooms and central heating as well as doors wide enough to take a wheelchair. When interviewed, Nancy had been widowed for 12 years. She lived with a number of long-term limiting health conditions including osteoporosis, while recently a broken femur had added to mobility problems. She spoke about changes over time in Burton Latimer:

'People used to come to Burton to work, but now there's nothing, there's no shoe factories [there were four or five when she first came to live there]. You've still got the Weetabix factory [breakfast cereal] but there's not a lot of what used to be. Most people go out of town to work, there are little pockets of employment, little tiny factories that have grown up, but nothing to speak of. Of course, we've got no police station now, you never see a policeman the same as everybody else you know.'

Such changes in the infrastructure of a place are not unusual in 21st-century Britain, but can have an impact on the ambience; this may affect some people in terms of issues of safety and security much more than others, particularly as their health and well-being changes. Nancy and her husband had already decided to downsize by moving to a bungalow built for older people, and although she had not originally liked the approach – an aspect of liminal space too near the main road – she loved the interior, and being a gardener the back garden was appealing:

'When I first saw it behind the wall, I said "Oh if it's behind that wall I'm not going behind there, I'm not going to be shut behind there …" But when we walked in and saw how nice and light and that we saw this room looking onto the garden … I thought "oh yes that will do, we'll come here" and of course, we were only here just over a year when my husband died unfortunately so …'

Not only did Nancy lose the love and support of her husband, but her own health was also causing problems. Her comments here show that she tried to seek support to adapt her own housing without success:

'Well, I mean … At the moment I am all right as I am. I did think about moving because I wanted a walk-in shower, because I cannot get … I mean before my husband died I couldn't get in the bath … well, I could but you couldn't get out. But then when he died I thought I couldn't have a bath, so my son fixed a shower up over the bath. But now since I have done this [broken femur], and my back again, I can't get in to have a bath. And I have put in to the council to see whether I could have a walk-in shower, but oh no that was it, I am not disabled enough. They wouldn't even consider it … I don't know how you are supposed to be before you get one of them.'

Nancy had also looked at other more specialised housing options. When asked if she would move again, she talks through aspects of the environment that are important to her, and her overwhelming attachment to her dog and her home:

'No, not now. I … had a chance to have a flat in [sheltered housing scheme] … there's not a warden actually lives there but you've got the emergency bells you know if you wanted any help … I had the chance of one … my friend lives in one, and the one she's in is on the opposite side of the building and you look over the fields and it's lovely, you know it's really nice and bright and sunny. But this one I went to see … was on the other side of the building just looking at the walls of the other flats and it was dark and dreary and as soon as I walked in I thought oh no that's not for me. I'd have to let me daughter have the dog 'cos you know you're not allowed animals there … My home means everything, mine, I mean it's well it's not mine, it's the council bungalow but you know … I really am fond of my little bungalow and my dog … I love my big patio windows and I can see the weather and see my garden, and you know down there you have got smaller windows and I think I would get a bit claustrophobic … Although it's right in the middle of Burton, so I know this isn't far but it is far enough when you are in pain, you know. I don't know … I will weigh it up. I might consider it actually if I hadn't got the dog, but I don't think I want to part with her, bless her.

I love my garden it's just big enough for me, until I got osteoporosis and then I fractured my femur it was … I could do it myself … but I can't get down to do it now and me neighbour helps, he has to come and do it now, it's very kind of him, so that gets done. I … I've started putting things in pots and I can have a pot [around] myself …'

One senses that Nancy has been thinking of the future; her comments on staying or moving are heartfelt especially about her dog, yet without a choice of options through financial resources she weighs the advantages and disadvantages – the locational, social, psychological, personal – and decides it is not the time to move. She manages through the support of others – family and friends – and says this about her weekly routine:

'I can walk for about a quarter of an hour I should think and then I have to have a little sit but you know coming back is the worst up the hill … it's a bit of a drag especially if you've got shopping but I don't carry a lot of shopping because either me neighbour fetches things for me if I need anything heavy or me relatives take me shopping you know, so I manage.

So we have a local taxi down and he pick us up about an hour later. On Thursdays we go down … and pay our rent, pick our pension up, have a little waddle round Gateway … do a bit of shopping, and go and have a cup of coffee … and he comes and picks us up there and brings us home again [laughs]. Then we go to our clubs, on Monday it is the Monday Club, Fridays we've got Darby and Joan. One Monday a month in the evening we go to the British Legion, and we usually have taxis then, but he don't charge much.

I used to go every Tuesday morning to [church] … that is 9–10 am, it is a communion, but I am afraid I haven't been lately because of kneeling down and getting up [laughs] you know…

I do have a little lass on Fridays, she comes and hoovers all through for me, that's about the only thing really that I can't manage … I can't push the hoover and walk on a stick at the same time … and sort of climbing up to change a light bulb … I can't do that but eh either me neighbour or me son-in-law when he comes over does things for me. Oh I've got plenty of help. I've got some good friends and neighbours – not too bad …'

When considering UK policy development, Nancy's comments are particularly rich, ranging from accessibility to adaptability, housing options to friendship, social support and keeping her pet, safety to security, the importance of the natural environment to community involvement – all explored beside changes in her own health and well-being. At the point we left her, Nancy had decided to stay put, and had put moving 'out of her mind'. Her financial position does not give her a range of options, but her social capital enables her to continue her interdependent living while she is able to maintain a level of control and autonomy.

We turn now to a research participant who was coping with vision impairment alongside other health conditions. Raymond from Liverpool was a participant in the Needs and Aspirations of Vision Impaired Older People research from 2014 that is outlined in Research summary 4.3. He is a Biafran/Nigerian, who came to England in 1973 following a period of conflict. An educated man, he trained for the Church and also has qualifications in philosophy. He stayed first with a cousin in Manchester and then moved to Liverpool, where he lived in a number of places before finding his current house in 1992, which he owns with a mortgage. Raymond says the property has been remortgaged to release housing equity, indicating some financial difficulties. Officially aged 78 (though he says he may be 80 as he is unsure of his early history), he lives alone, even though a cousin and his wife live on the second floor. He has five children, four of whom (two girls, two boys) live in Liverpool and one (a boy) in Birmingham. His partner, 'the mother of the children', died in 2004. His own mother, aged 100, was still living with cousins in Nigeria.

Raymond describes his health as being 'quite good': 'I would say I am reasonably healthy. I don't put myself down and my quality of life is good.' Yet he has complex health conditions: having had high blood pressure since 2005 for which he takes medication, this was followed by a diagnosis of glaucoma in both eyes in 2007. Despite this being operated on, he is registered as having severe sight impairment. More recently, prostate 'trouble' led to catheterisation, followed by an operation in 2015. Nevertheless, Raymond manages most of his daily activities, which have been made easier since the removal of the catheter. He is usually able to move between floors, using an upstairs toilet, bathroom and shower. He has made some changes to the bathroom and certain windows, and a back kitchen has been extended.

His children help him to maintain his independence. Raymond says: 'Well my children visit me regularly, help me with shopping. I cook for myself but they help me with preparing the ingredients and purchasing them as well.'

His second daughter comes frequently to clean the kitchen and the house generally: 'She spent four days last week trying to organize me.' He would 'like to have someone to help me clean the house as the children are busy and are not local'. Yet there is usually someone who visits most days: 'My son comes here regularly almost every day, to take out the bin out and bring it in, and make sure that I'm sound anyway ... Either they phone me to ask me how I am and come here to assist.' The family has done this since 2007, for almost eight years at the time of the interview, and he has grandchildren who also come to visit. As he put it, his children have all studied and trained for different professions – electrical engineering, quantity surveying, social work – whereas he is someone with a relatively low annual income of around £14,000 (2015) whom they all support in different ways.

Raymond is a member of an African Caribbean group for people with vision impairment: one staff member acts as a go-between with other organisations, including the African Elders Association that meets in Toxteth Town Hall. The latter, a community organisation, has a lunch club and offers activities such as fitness exercises and speakers from visiting agencies. Raymond has been a long-term member of the Labour Party and the Brotherhood of the Cross and Star, which he no longer attends.

He says that he has never felt lonely and can use the telephone. He cannot use a computer because of his sight, but one of his sons helps with this. Through staff at the African Caribbean group, he has gained access to an occupational therapist, resulting in rails being put beside his stairs to prevent him from mis-stepping. When asked if there was anything else that he would like to change, Raymond says: 'Yeah, I think I would like to have a toilet on the ground floor.' He is also aware of various gadgets that are available through the Royal National Institute of the Blind shop, but has never visited the shop and only has a liquid level monitor for drinks and fluids. He thinks his home met most of his needs, and says:

'… the home is where, others say that a white man's home is his castle, where you relax. Yeah … where you feel comfortable. Myself I use artefacts★ that keep me happy. (Int. Have you ever thought of living somewhere else?) I haven't thought of moving although my children, some of them, are thinking that way. I think something like sheltered accommodation could be considered.'

[★The African artefacts were a shield and spears that were displayed in the main living room]

But they had never researched anything, and Raymond continues: 'Well, under normal circumstances I would like to stay here but things change. The house could be too big for me. I think that could be one of the considerations.' The garden is in a very bad state, even though his second son had 'had a go at it'. On reflection, Raymond says he gets by with the ongoing support of his children who live in the city. His comments are those of a man who draws strength from his culture, skills, beliefs, family and lifelong experience.

Finally, I turn to Helen, who was living in north London at the time of the Environment and Identity study. She spoke about neighbourhood change and how her relaxed sense of being in the community during the day and after dark was altered by the following incident (from Peace et al, 2006, pp 67–8):

'I suppose it was in April just before I was ill and I had to come home by bus … and [as] I walked up … I was very conscious of somebody following me. And I wouldn't look around, but I got quite het up within and I crossed over … and I felt the footsteps coming nearer and nearer. And I couldn't resist it, I turned around, I had to you know, and it was a young fellow. So I went on walking and suddenly he brushed past me, just touched my arm and said "you needn't be so scared, I am only going home" and it was a young man […] Whether he intended doing anything or not and decided not to … I don't know. But you see until then I never thought about it, but ever since then it has just left me with that uneasy feeling … and you see there wasn't a soul around … […] near to help me, if he decided to mug me. I had a handbag of course … […] but it was a very uneasy feeling. And it has left me, this is the trouble, it has left me … I suppose I was lucky and got away with it, but another time it could happen. So [today] I thought 'I must get those two letters in the post' and so I went in the car, which is ridiculous because it is only around the corner, and the walk would have done me good, but I thought 'no, I am not walking round there'. It is such a shame because we never used to feel like that, did we.'

This comment adds to our understanding of how the meaning of place can change. Safety and security are not issues specific to age, gender or mobility, but all contribute to vulnerability in such circumstances. Elsewhere, it has been discussed how traumatic life events within specific spaces can impact on the ways in which people avoid particular locations, and this can continue across the life course (Peace, 2009). In Helen's example, this experience also changed her behaviour.

Option recognition

Teresa, Sidney, Bertie, Nancy, Raymond and Helen, living in different types of general housing and community, indicate some variation in their need for more accessible environments given their health, mobility and emotional attachments. They talk about the importance of social relations within their immediate neighbourhood, their ability to maintain routines with different levels of support, the value of continuity within their lives, and their confidence in place. In the mid-2000s, Peace et al reanalysed data from the Environment and Identity study, developing the theoretical concept of option recognition to provide a framework for such experiences:

As people get older, the significance of place and the importance of situating the self appropriately have implications for self-esteem, health and wellbeing. The interaction between environmental context and personal identity is reflected in a wide range of social, psychological and physical issues. The social dimensions often centre on the micro- and macro*-environments of the community and entail personal, family and housing histories. Psychological factors may be seen in displays of attachment, loss and emotions concerning security and safety, which can impact on morale. The physical or material setting itself may continue to be supportive or become challenging. At the micro level of the individual's dwelling, this can lead to re-investment, adaptation or re-configuration. At the [...] level of the community, it may lead an individual to maintain, increase or reduce levels of engagement. The interface between these factors generates the complexity of person-environment interactions that may lead to the environmental tipping point that demands action and which we have called 'option recognition'. (Peace et al, 2011, pp 734–5).

  *In this quote, 'macro' is used as the wider community in which the dwelling is situated. In the definition outlined in this text it would be seen as a meso-level, whereas macro- is considered to be national to global – see Figure 0.1.

In this quote, the use of 'tipping point' should not be seen as comparable to the professional perception of crisis intervention, which usually leads to environmental change or hospitalisation instigated through cognitive and/ or physical co-morbidity, and may take decision-making away from the individual (see Chapter 8).

Figure 6.1 visualises balancing continuity and change, so some tipping points may be stabilised, thus bringing the social, physical/material and psychological dynamics of the person and environment back to a level of manageability for that particular individual or couple. This may involve changing the complete living environment – community, housing and personal support – or only certain parts of it; alternatively, such rebalancing may not be possible or desired.

Figure 6.1: Balancing issues of person–environment in general housing

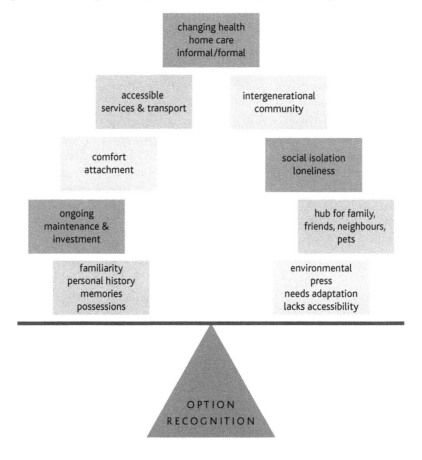

These vignettes introduce people for whom biopsychosocial factors all contribute to environmental tipping points that may lead to a change in dwelling over time. There are different levels of environmental normality in which people maintain their self-identity through routines enabling levels of autonomy and participation that are sometimes delegated to others.

What the future holds for these older people is unknown, yet all interactions were situated within a particular temporal and spatial context – such as Bertie's recognition of the value of his housing adaptations, his acceptance of neighbours who wonder whether he's all right, the importance of his social network that maintains him in place, and how being alone led him to being inward thinking; a position he saw as selfish. Some, such as Teresa and Sidney, are forward planners. Their housing history shows how specific life events impact on moving options, which are made easier through personal competence and financial assets. They take this experience of 'building up and scaling down' into advanced old age and are already thinking of further downsizing if either is left living alone, and are considering how age-proofing the environment is important.

A difference is seen between making decisions as a couple or alone, even if supported by family. Changing health and well-being, particularly for Nancy and Raymond, brings recognition of the possible need for alternative lifestyles. Yet their knowledge of other ways of living, and possibilities available thanks to social and financial resources, varies. Only Nancy has viewed a property where she has a friend, and here the limited choice available has led to a reassertion of home values and what she can and can't replace, especially her pet. Although her mobility affects her engagement with the wider community and immediate environment, she points out the benefits of current social networks. Weighing up advantages and disadvantages produce real tensions. Raymond brings a global understanding to the meaning of home and what he values. Culturally, he appreciates the support of local groups, and keeps contact with his mother and homeland, also demonstrated by his prized possessions. He talks about the support of his children and the possible potential of sheltered accommodation. Yet as a family they have not pursued this or sought advice. Lastly, Helen brings the issue of being settled to the fore. She has lived in her neighbourhood for a long time, during which she has witnessed change, but it was this event that was personally unsettling – and although the consequences are unknown, it can be seen as a potential tipping point.

Parallel thinking

These are views from those living in various parts of England that begin to unlock the complex issues experienced in later life. These challenges lead people to make ongoing compromises within their environment, re-establishing a best fit in housing, neighbourhood and community that links to Keating and Phillips's (2008) earlier critical human ecology. To broaden this view, we return to the meaning of home – but first turn to findings from ENABLE-AGE.

The ENABLE-AGE project

The ENABLE-AGE project was a major piece of international research (2002–04) that was funded by the EC. Five multidisciplinary teams studied the lives of very old people in three West European and two East European nations – Sweden, Germany, UK, Latvia and Hungary. The main objective was to research subjective and objective aspects of housing and their impact on health in very old age. Importantly, healthy ageing is not just related to biomedical aspects of ageing but also includes subjective experiences and meanings of autonomy, participation and well-being (Iwarsson et al, 2004, p 79, Sixsmith et al, 2014, p 2; Iwarsson et al, 2016).

This was a two-stage mixed methods study involving a survey with 1,918 older adults (national samples of n=376–450), providing a comprehensive assessment of the objective environment, followed by an in-depth study with a sub-sample of 190 people diverse in terms of age, gender, social class, dwelling type, accessibility issues, health status and ability to perform activities of daily living (117 women; 73 men) (Sixsmith et al, 2014; also Dahlin-Ivanoff et al, 2007; Fänge and Dahlin-Ivanoff, 2009). Given variation in life expectancy between nations, the definition of very old age varied, and participants ranged from 75 to 85 (Hungary, Latvia) and from 80 to 89 (Sweden, Germany, UK). All were single households in urban areas. The research used the Swedish research tool 'The Housing Enabler', and raised particular issues regarding cross-national research – as discussed in Chapter 9.

At a time when ageing in place has become an important policy initiative globally, the views of the very old living alone are especially valid. The researchers demonstrate how, despite variation in levels of personal engagement between those living in West and East European countries, three factors are particularly important:

- sociocultural care and service provision can facilitate interdependent living;
- as functional capacity may change, the physical environment can be adapted to be more enabling; and
- safety and familiarity within the wider community environment can make participation easier to maintain.
  (see Iwarsson et al, 2007; Wahl, et al, 2009; Sixsmith et al, 2014; Iwarsson et al, 2016)

Analysis of the qualitative data enabled understanding of healthy ageing within the context of home and everyday lives, questioning whether this environment plays an active part in maintaining or limiting quality of life (Sixsmith et al, 2014, p 1). People were engaged to different degrees in keeping active, involved and being seen as independent, sometimes through modifying behaviour to accomplish tasks. Gender differences existed: men were more concerned with physical exercise, decorating and gardening as ways of maintaining activity; while women saw a balanced diet as part of a healthy lifestyle alongside maintaining social and family relationships. Loneliness, feelings of depression and inactivity were commented on by some, while for others solitude was valued, and the home provided continuity through possessions that were familiar and enabled connectivity.

Additionally, an East–West comparison showed how financial limitations could prevent home maintenance, and how healthy ageing focused on getting by for those in East Europe. Nevertheless, home was seen as a place where people could maintain a sense of control and agency, and the researchers concluded that in all locations 'the home environment plays a significant role in developing and supporting personal strategies for healthy ageing' (Sixsmith et al, 2014, p 8). In contrast, Granbom et al (2014) question ways of understanding people's residential reasoning over staying put or considering changes in where they should or could live.

These are all issues that have been raised earlier, but discussion was extended across diverse developed countries, and thus inequalities were indicated. There is a continuing synergy between the theoretical perspectives outlined in Chapter 2, allowing us to draw parallels with work on place attachment and relocation that appears in earlier North American research from Rowles, Rubinstein and Chaudhury; their collaboration with Europeans Wahl and Oswald that considered belonging, agency and autonomy; and the particular work of Golant in the US that discussed residential normalcy, coping strategies and potential relocation (Golant, 2011, 2015, 2018b). The latter perspective links closely with the concept of options recognition.

Reflecting on home: the lens of general housing

At the beginning of Chapter 4, there was concern expressed about how home is perceived in terms of both place and accommodation as people grow older in different types of environment. Later, when looking at rural and urban environments, a wide-ranging meaning of place from urban deprivation to the aesthetics of nature to common concerns of connectivity was considered (Fig 4.6). Chapter 5 moved to mainstream housing where the majority of older people live in intergenerational communities. For many, their current dwelling is part of a complex housing history where people, place and housing all change, as seen with Teresa and Sidney; for others, their housing and neighbourhood may be part of a long residence as part of a family, couple or on their own, and where they may now wish to stay. Personal experience has shown the positive meaning of home through feelings of belonging, green space, history through possessions, interaction with pets, maintenance of social relations and ownership, not necessarily financial but in terms of well-being and ontological security. The stories outlined in this chapter, alongside findings from the ENABLE-AGE research, capture the ways in which living in ordinary housing as part of an intergenerational community can help people age well through maintaining the continuity of their everyday lives.

Figure 6.2 builds on Fig 4.3 by adding this lens to the meaning of home. We should remember the different ways of living that were outlined in Chapter 1, where changes to family structure were noted, along with the increasing number of older people, especially women, living alone and the balance between individualistic and family cultures. Figure 6.2 presents issues raised through research in age-integrated environments. As outlined,

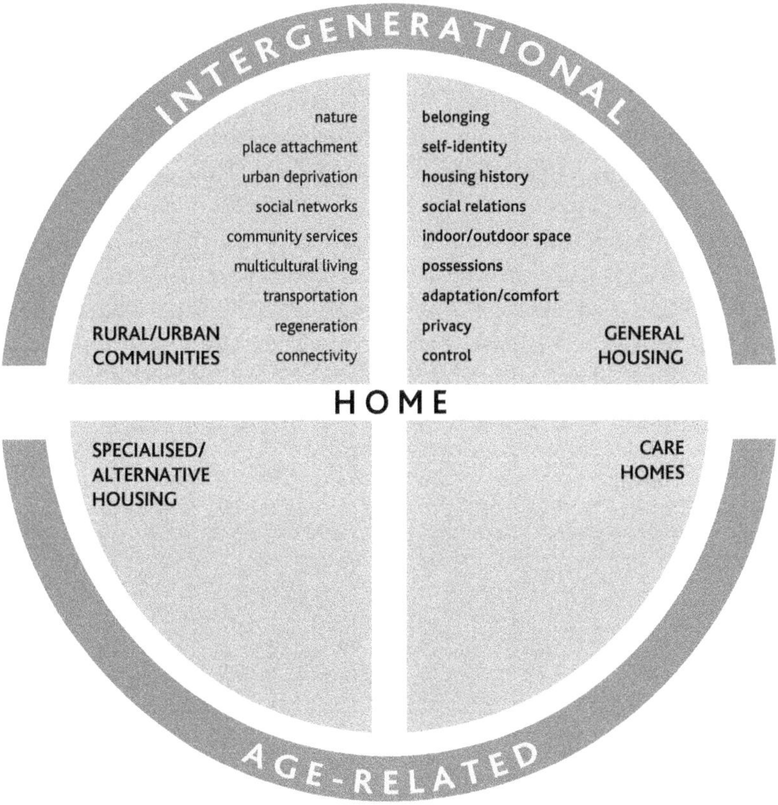

Figure 6.2: Reflecting on the meaning of home: the lens of general housing

they become more home-centred, which raises the earlier question from Chapter 4 about whether the meaning of home can embrace a sense of social inclusion or exclusion, or both; where people may feel part of a community but are not totally engaged with it. The issues raised have to sit alongside those tipping points highlighted in Figure 6.1. which indicate how continuity and change are also part of the meaning of home. For some, their environment – housing/neighbourhood – no longer meets their needs: retrofitting or adapting parts of their housing would be needed to maintain comfort; living alone may be isolating; services may be too distant. People may develop a greater acceptance of personal support through delegating autonomy to others, whether family members and home carers, and in some cases this may lead to a consideration of alternative housing that is age-related. It is a point at which those respondents who said they would stay put for as long as possible may consider the meaning of this phrase, and decide whether familiarity, attachment and social relations will enable them to see out their lives in the same place. These issues feature in the discussion of new housing that engages people in co-design and relate to perceptions of the ageing self (see Grenier, 2005; Hillcoat-Nallétamby and Ogg, 2014). The question now becomes whether the issues of meaning raised within mainstream housing and age-integrated communities are also seen in age-related environments.

Conclusions

For some older people, community living in housing they have lived in for some time may be maintained or change, either through an intentional move or resulting after a period of poor health and often a stay in hospital. Central to the discussion of option recognition is the potential contrast between personal and collective living. As life expectancy extends globally, alternative living environments beyond ordinary housing will continue to develop as part of the balance between health, housing and social care in later life. This is a transition period that researchers are already considering. In Chapters 7 and 8, we look at living in age-related environments, housing (with care) and care home, questioning the ongoing construction of the meaning of home.

7

Alternative environments: specialised housing (with care)

Introduction

Motivation, agency and choice are key when people make decisions about changing where they live. The concept of option recognition was introduced as a forerunner to this decision, for some being part of rightsizing their accommodation or changing their location, for others a consequence or concern for their health and well-being; the reasons are entangled. As already acknowledged, older people's housing is part of the public debate about intergenerational relations, the lack of family housing and financial transfers. Independent Age (2016) report that talking to the family about housing, care and end of life are some of the most difficult conversations older people may have that may encourage change. This chapter focuses on alternative environments of housing and care that for some are the outcome of that change.

While discussions may range from good ideas to recognising insufficient knowledge about alternatives, the ability or motivation to move may never be considered by those who decide to stay put. Living with others who are non-family members in a form of communal living is experienced by many across their lives, yet they may not make the comparison with arrangements in later life. Heywood et al, (2002, p 118) comment on collective living in student halls of residence, shared residences in early adulthood, assisted living in later life and (in advanced old age) the experience of residential care and nursing homes. Nevertheless, to date a relatively small percentage of people aged 65 and over in the UK make a change to age-related housing (with care). Chapters 7 and 8 offer parallel scenarios for those who live in environments where age and ageing form a commonality, and where key experiences are coping with transition and developing a new lifestyle. When people move, either as a couple or alone, to different forms of housing (with care), their motivation may be intentional, purposeful and planned, or may occur as a consequence of ageing within particular circumstances – financial, health related, familial – that influence the outcome. The term (with care) is put in parenthesis as the need varies with time and place.

This chapter gives a brief history of housing (with care), also known as specialised housing (Park and Porteus, 2018), seen as an alternative to the care home that is less institutionalised and focused on independent living (Heywood et al, 2002, pp 118–36). Evolving through the public and voluntary (not-for-profit) sector, sheltered housing and private sector retirement housing, a diversity of properties for rent and for sale are discussed. The advantages and disadvantages of living in these environments are indicated through findings from recent empirical research, and co-housing as an alternative way of living is also considered. To conclude, as seen in Chapters 4 and 6, we return to the meaning of home when viewed as living in age-related housing (with care).

Case study: living to the fourth age in retirement housing

To begin, we turn to the story of Jo, who made this move and lived in retirement housing for 20 years. This case is based on an interview taken from a study of people with high support needs, which is outlined in Research summary 7.1. This narrative shows how living in specialised housing is not just about the physical environment but affects social relationships, as well as feelings about safety, security, comfort, well-being and self-identity.

Jo, a 93-year-old widow living alone, took part in an interview for the A Better Life research in 2010 (then aged 85), and this was followed by a more recent interview with the author in 2018. On retirement, Jo (various part-time employment) and her husband Trevor (school teacher) moved from London to a bungalow in a small semi-rural town, and then as they got older moved to be nearer to their two daughters, who were both living in London. She lives in a ground-floor flat in retirement housing owned

---

Research summary 7.1: A Better Life: the needs and aspirations of people with high support needs

The Open University (2009–11)

Aims: to understand the meaning of 'high support needs' as defined by organisations, practitioners and professionals through the lives of primarily older people so defined. **Location:** Participants living across England.

Methods: This qualitative study involved in-depth interviews with 26 older people – aged 85 and over. The researchers used an adapted version of the Facets of Life Wheel, a tool developed in the Environment and Identity study (see Research summary 6.1). Further discussion of this instrument is given in Chapter 9 (See Katz et al, 2011, 2013).

Funded by: Joseph Rowntree Foundation, A Better Life programme, 2011.

---

and managed through a housing association (HA). At the first interview, she had moved into the flat 12 years earlier with her husband. They bought their one-bedroomed flat in 1998 through a shared leasehold arrangement, where they paid for 80 per cent of the property and the HA owned 20 per cent. This means that executors will sell the 80 per cent share. At this scheme there are six relatively modern blocks of eight flats plus others within an adapted older property, making 56 in total.

When they moved from ordinary housing, a manager and her partner lived on site, who got to know residents and routinely checked certain people with health needs. Jo comments on a sense of 'ongoing support for residents especially for the older members', which made her feel secure. Over time, she thinks that the scheme has become less supportive, and now there is a part-time peripatetic housing officer, who is primarily responsible for communal events and building maintenance. More managerial control has been taken by a central team based in a larger HA formed by the merger of two HAs in 2010. While there is a residents' association and all contribute through a service charge to the upkeep of the buildings, grounds and community lodge, where activities take place and visitors may stay, all care needs are organised individually, often with family support.

In terms of the immediate physical environment, Jo's flat has an L-shaped living and dining area with a galley kitchen leading from it. Early in their occupancy, the couple had had the windows along one wall in the sitting area extended, with French windows providing a door that leads to a small rockery where they planted flowers and shrubs and had a bird feeder. The one bedroom is on a short corridor to the front internal door and the combined bathroom and toilet. The traditional bath now has a seat attached that enables Jo to sit, swing around into the bath and be showered from overhead. A raised seat has been put on the toilet. While Trevor was alive, discussions took place with the local authority and a recommended occupational therapist regarding the removal of the bath and installation of a walk-in shower. At that time, the discovery of concrete floors and drainage issues proved a stalling point, which was not resolved before Trevor's death. The flat has an emergency alarm system with cords to pull in all areas, and Jo wears a telecare pendant around her neck.

During the earlier research, Jo was seen as someone with high support needs owing to health issues. Over the last 15 years, she has gradually developed age-related macular degeneration with some peripheral vision, and is registered as vision impaired. She also has osteoporosis, which impedes her mobility, pre-diabetes and marginally high blood pressure. She was, and still is, mobile and oriented within the flat, can wash her face and hands and go to the toilet without assistance, can answer the telephone, but will not go outside unaccompanied. This was the situation in 2012 when organising delivered shopping and maintaining some level of cooking was feasible, but home care support was already needed for Trevor and indirectly herself.

By 2018, Jo's personal circumstances had gradually changed, although having been widowed she decided to stay put in her familiar environment. At this time she could no longer: bathe herself, dress without some support, organise her medication, cook or make a hot drink for herself. All shopping was brought to the flat through a local shop delivery, her daughters and a frozen food delivery service. A cleaner came once a week, and a gardener and hairdresser at regular intervals, all self-funded. Following an assessment of her personal needs and finances, she was awarded an individual budget/ direct payment through local authority adult social care that paid for half of the home care service that visited three times a day. Her daily routine was managed through this paid assistance of home carers, working for local independent agencies. She comments that while at some times of the day the same carer attends, at other times it is always a different person, and this lack of continuity for someone with vision impairment required an advance schedule. The carers make very large print notes of people's names so Jo knows who will be next to arrive, and let themselves into her flat through the use of an external key safe.

In addition, the weekly visits of her two daughters deal with shopping, financial issues, medical appointments and all household issues. They have lasting power of attorney, and can make decisions on her behalf about her health and welfare, property and financial affairs (and liaise with the home carers). Interestingly, only one aspect of Jo's lifestyle seems to concern her neighbours: the car parking of carers and family members, which takes up limited allocated space at different times of the day, can lead to notes of complaint from other residents.

This is a combination of support within an environment that Jo values as her home and can navigate easily. When asked if she worried about moving around at night, she says, 'Oh no, I put lights on wherever I go, I'm fine', and in the more recent interview she adds: 'I am happier being here because I know my own things and where things are and I can walk to the toilet myself in my own time.' This comment personalises both time and space. To an extent, obviously, her routines are directed by the home carers' schedules. At lunchtime, Jo says she is busy preparing a tray for her carers. She is totally oriented in her flat, and when asked about her situation she says this:

'I can't live without the carers and my family. If I have the same person [home carer] then they know what to do though they have rules about using food beyond certain dates. [At lunch time before they come] ... I can prepare things [in the kitchen] and engage with who is coming and that is important. It occupies my mind. I know in advance what

I would like someone to cook [microwave]. I know what is there [in the freezer], chicken, salmon, broccoli to be defrosted. I get the same knives and forks out that I like. [Int. Do you feel in control?] Oh yes, I am quite in control of things, myself I cannot see the time but I get the time from my radio, and I have a talking clock by my bed.'

Jo says she never feels bored 'because of my radio, especially music and Classic FM' (a classical music station), and knowing the wider environment of the grounds from past memories and short walks to a nearby seat with her daughters. She says: 'I can look out at the beautiful surroundings and feel content and that's important to me.' A pertinent example of the value of autobiographical memory.

Her comments indicate the position of interdependence that some people live by, where they are able to feel they retain a sense of control over different aspects of their lives and value their privacy, even if other people would see this as a very limited existence. She protects her own routines, maintaining agency and delegating degrees of autonomy to others within her own housing (see Leece and Peace, 2010). Jo's situation at this time offers an example for which we do not know the outcome, whether she spends the rest of her life in this setting, or if a further health problem may cause her to move. A tension is portrayed between doing things as you like when you like within the limits of your ability and being alone for periods of time, which you may, or may not, sense as loneliness. The circumstances shown here provide an example of the types of experience discussed in other empirical research.

Housing, support and care

Table 7.1 lists various forms of age-related specialised housing in the UK alongside age-integrated services where older people may be dominant users, such as intermediate care. Expressions more common in other economically advanced nations are italicised. It does not relate to independent living settings for younger people with disabilities. There is no standardised terminology, and Howe et al (2013), reviewing literature from the US, UK, Canada, Australia and New Zealand, found nearly 100 terms with some commonality that use the umbrella term 'service integrated housing'. Their analysis identified similar issues within and between nations relating to policy, legislation, flexibility in housing and services through different regulatory frameworks, a need for clarity of information and a common research base underpinned by shared conceptual development (Howe et al, 2013). It is a scenario that was outlined in the HAPPI document in 2009 (Barac and Park, 2009, p 10) and remains complex (see Park and Porteus, 2018, p 13).

Table 7.1: Forms of housing (with care)

General housing + formal/informal support and care	intergenerational
Home-sharing + informal support	intergenerational
Lifetime homes (inclusive design)	intergenerational

S P E C I A L I S E D   H O U S I N G

Sheltered housing	age-related
Congregate housing	*age-related*
Very sheltered housing/extra care/enhanced care	age-related
Extra-care housing	age-related
Retirement housing + formal/informal support and care	age-related
Assisted living – with personal and healthcare	*age-related*
Retirement villages/*continuing care retirement communities*	*age-related*
Campus model housing	*age-related*

Co-housing	intergenerational or age-related
Small care homes (in general housing)	independent living or age-related

Care homes – residential	age-related
Care homes – nursing	age-related

Intermediate care	intergenerational
Respite care	Intergenerational
Hospice	intergenerational
Hospital geriatric wards	age-related
Hospital acute wards	intergenerational

The national voluntary organisation Age UK England offers this typology for the levels of support or care that may be provided in different types of housing:

- 'age-exclusive' housing, where residents have to be over a certain age to qualify, but little or no support is provided;
- 'housing-with-support', where residents receive support services such as an emergency alarm system, but staff do not provide care;

- 'housing-with-care', where staff provide care services such as help with washing, dressing, toileting and taking medication.

(Age UK, 2017, p 3)

The different forms of age-related accommodation (with care) could be described in terms of their proximity to general housing and community living as – integrated or remote – all are dependent on site, size, planning procedures and guidance. While an integrated site may be part of the vision for an intentional co-housing group, a larger site would be essential for the integration of extra-care housing (ECH) alongside care home facilities. This may impact on living in an age-related setting. Additionally, age-related housing may be qualified by the terms integrated care, flexi-care, close care, specialist or separate extra care. For example, specialist extra care may accommodate specific people such as those living with dementia, while separated extra care may mean a separate wing or unit for people living with learning difficulties or dementia, and close care may describe flats or bungalows linked to a care home (Riseborough et al, 2015; Wood and Vibert, 2017; Which, 2020). With this diversity in mind, we turn to historical policy development.

From almshouses to sheltered housing

While retirement communities for residents with a common bond, such as military personnel, can be traced back to Roman times, in the UK the combination of housing and care for older people appeared in the Middle Ages when the Christian Church drew on alms (money and services) to provide housing and support for the poor, old and distressed. Today, most almshouses have charitable status, being run by volunteer trustees, with some becoming HAs, and continuing to support those, particularly older, people who live in a defined area and are financially vulnerable (Pannell et al, 2020). The Almshouse Association currently represents more than 1,600 almshouses member charities providing homes for over 35,000 residents with similar schemes in the US, Belgium and Scandinavia (see Glossary).

The emergence of almshouses sits within four centuries of British legislation, with implications for housing people in need through the Poor Law, its amendments and associated legislation (1601, 1834, 1929, 1930), the workhouse system and indoor relief, discussed further in Chapter 8 (Peace et al, 1997; Peace, 2003). As Butler et al (1983) show (Research summary 7.2), the 1909 Royal Commission on the Poor Law acknowledged the need for special housing for 'the elderly' – the term then used in policy documents – in particular through 'cottage homes', often bungalow schemes provided by local authorities.

The combination of accommodation for the older poor and employment of workhouse staff led to the development of sheltered housing, a form of

---

Research summary 7.2: Sheltered housing in England and Wales

The University of Leeds (1977–81)

Aims: quality of life of local authority sheltered housing residents.

Methods: carried out in a representative sample of 12 local authority areas (7 non-metropolitan district councils, 3 metropolitan district councils, 2 London boroughs), where samples of local authority and HA schemes were drawn, and samples of tenants listed in 51 schemes. In the 'first tenant interview survey', summer 1978, 600 tenants discussed 'their history, experience, attitudes and their assessment of sheltered housing and other services'. A second in-depth interview survey of 200 tenants in 26 schemes in 4 of the original 12 study areas was carried out in 1980, developing themes from the first survey.

Funded by: Department of Health and Social Security (DHSS).

(See Butler et al, 1983; Butler, 1997)

---

rented social accommodation (Nocon and Pleace, 1999). This was, and remains, 'housing-with-support' in the Age UK typology. Butler et al (1983) report that at least two schemes were developed before the Second World War, and while the word 'sheltered' is now analogous with safeguarding, they trace the term to the 1944 Housing Manual (Ministry of Health, 1944) which referred to appropriate sheltered siting.

After the Second World War, the role of sheltered housing, the allocation of tenancies and questions of responsibility were all state supported, predominantly local and emerged slowly. Ideas concerning variation in housing and care needs were considered more than 60 years ago alongside care home developments. A design bulletin entitled 'Flatlets for Old People' said this:

> Most old people wish to remain independent for as long as possible, but for many the time comes when, although they are not so infirm as to be 'in need of care and attention', a fully self-contained bungalow or flatlet becomes too much of a burden. What is needed is accommodation mid-way between self-contained dwelling and hostels providing care. (Ministry of Housing and Local Government, 1958, p 3)

The point 'in need of care and attention' was made in the National Assistance Act 1948 regarding care home provision. Local government housing departments were encouraged to build low-rise blocks of bedsits or small one-bedroomed flats where a warden had accommodation on site linked to tenants by alarm systems and where there were communal sitting rooms. The development of local authority sheltered housing continued across the century, and some provision is still in use though adapted and refurbished.

The Housing Act 1961 subsidised HAs as not-for-profit organisations to develop such schemes. Data for units of sheltered housing indicate the gradual shift in development between 1950 and 1980 from local authorities to HAs, which provided 22 per cent (65,670 units) of housing in 1981; 500,000 units were reached by 1983 (Butler et al, 1983, pp 3, 54–63). This form of public housing for low-income older people was gradually influenced by provision from not-for-profit organisations and later the private sector. In addition, following Townsend's (1962) seminal critique of residential care homes, *The Last Refuge* (1962) (see Chapter 8), he voiced support for sheltered housing as a replacement to what was deemed institutional care, suggesting that 50 dwellings per 1,000 people over the age of 65 were needed to meet the demands of those with no family support, who lived alone or may live with a moderate or severe disability (Townsend, 1981; Butler et al, 1983, p 56).

In the 1960s and 1970s, particular policy documents drew attention to issues of design, care, funding and partnership working, from the Ministry of Housing and Local Government (MHLG, 1962, 1966) and jointly with the Ministry of Health (MHLG/MoH, 1961). The MHLG Circular 82/69

Figure 7.1: Almshouses

(1969) considered housing for older people that 'will enable them to maintain an independent way of life as long as possible', and offered minimum design specifications, including:

- outward-opening lavatory doors;
- window ledge heights;
- space standards;
- heating requirements;
- a lift to access dwellings more than one storey from the point of pedestrian or vehicular access;
- siting close to shops and transportation;
- the need for a common room in particular types of Category 2 scheme.

(MHLG, 1969)

Thirty units was the suggested optimum size, with HA schemes being seen as slightly smaller (17–30 units, 1965–77). The aim here was to resist age segregation (Butler et al, 1983, p 58). The circular established 'Category 1' schemes for the more 'active' older person, commonly self-managed bungalows with a small garden, and 'Category 2' sheltered housing schemes for the 'slightly less active' who were on their own and needed more labour-saving accommodation. Here a communal area, laundry and public telephones were seen as valued alongside the warden's accommodation and/ or office and a guest room. (MHLG, 1969). These terms are sometimes recalled, but should not be confused with categories of ECH.

During the 1970s, the number of sheltered housing residents began to rise. This provision was still primarily for older people with limited financial resources and social needs who may have been tenants of council (social) housing. The 1972 Housing Act brought both local authority and HA rents into a 'fair rent system', yet gradually, as HA provision developed, local authority provision began to suffer. The Housing Corporation, established in 1964, was allowed to lend to HAs encouraging their involvement; a pattern central government continued to support (Butler, 1997). In contrast, finance available for warden services was discontinued, hitting local authority development at a time when some were introducing 'extra-care sheltered' or 'very sheltered housing', both seen as requiring additional staffing. While sheltered housing was not seen as replacing the care home system, 'enhanced sheltered units' were for those tenants wishing to remain in sheltered housing yet needing more support as their health and well-being changed. Some local authorities talked of Category 2½ (Butler et al, 1983). While the National Federation of Housing Associations gave a cautious response to these ideas (in 1979), organisations such as the Abbeyfield Society developed a form of extra care. Such schemes involved: greater levels of staffing, communal services such as meals, a more accessible environment and arrangements for dealing with medication. It was becoming 'housing with care'.

Policy developments: community care and housing (with care)

As seen in Chapter 5, from 1979 onwards the Conservative era of New Right thinking was based on free market principles and service privatisation. The view that older people wished to stay put within general housing and avoid moving particularly to residential care became an entrenched position that was supported by the continuing development of domiciliary services provided and accessed through local authorities (Means and Smith, 1998a; Heywood et al, 2002). However, access to home care services was to change with the development of a community care policy – via the Griffiths Report, 1988, the subsequent White Paper (Department of Health, 1989) and legislation – the NHS and Community Care Act 1990 (Department of Health, 1990). The governance of adult social care through local authorities developed care management, where needs assessment and means testing direct service provision. Financial support through direct payments or an independent budget can be used to pay or contribute to home care where there are means below a financial limit, as seen in Jo's case study. In addition, there has been a growth in private sector home care agencies and an increase in those who self-fund these services (Heywood et al, 2002, pp 62–4; Henwood et al, 2018).

Research for the Department of the Environment throughout the 1990s commented on the development of very (or enhanced) sheltered housing; problems of 'hard to let' sheltered housing, where a dated environment could be sub-standard and inconveniently located; and practice-related issues surrounding remodelling provision (Tinker, 1989; McCafferty, 1994; Tinker et al, 1995; Tinker et al, 2008). Such evidence contributed to the discussion of alternative models of care for older people in a research volume accompanying the report of the Royal Commission on Long Term Care (Tinker et al, 1999). Since this time, a co-ordinated ageing policy that locates housing within the broader context of income, health/social care, transport and planning, all impacting social relationships, has continued to develop. The future funding of social care remains to be solved, and the crucial position of housing alongside health and social care while recognised in the Care Act 2014 needs further integration.

Housing (with care) in later life: into the 21st century

Retirement housing

Across the late 20th century and into the 21st, the provision of housing for older people has diversified. While settings commissioned through local authorities may be for rent, other facilities are owned outright or in part through leasehold schemes with shared tenure (more commonly through HAs), which may appeal to owner occupants downsizing from general housing as seen in the earlier case study (see Croucher et al, 2006, Which, 2020). Park and Porteus highlight a dramatic growth of retirement housing for sale between 1984 and 1990, with over 60 per cent of 28,000 housing units built since 1989 for sale. They describe ECH as being, from 1997 onwards, a "home for life" with on-site access to care and support' (Park and Porteus, 2018, p 12). Across the 21st century, the growth of retirement and ECH units has been slower and slightly more for rent than for sale. How facilities differ can also relate to whether the scheme is offering housing with support or housing with care. In Jo's situation, it was housing with support, as she had a telecare alarm service. Her home care through an external agency was organised by her family as if she was living in mainstream housing. She called it retirement housing rather than assisted living.

Retirement housing is used as a generic term here. Corporate developers such as McCarthy and Stone report the growth of this market, with evidence from polls of downsizers that people in the 55–64 age group may consider such a move, with releasing equity to pass on the their children and having less maintenance being factors (McCarthy and Stone, 2018). Churchill Retirement Living, in a recent study of the company provision, comments that a 'typical customer is a 79 year old widow moving after her husband has passed away; usually leaving an older, large house for a one or two bedroomed apartment' (Clark et al, 2017, p 4, Clark, 2018). The language for these types of facilities is confusing, as ECH is a form of retirement housing, yet the boundary between them relates to the funding, provision and management of care, and it depends on the scale of scheme whether there is a range of accommodation and care on one site that people may choose to move between.

HAPPI 1, 2, 3 – alternative living environments

Here we return to the Housing Our Ageing Population: Panel for Innovation (HAPPI) and three influential documents that have been published since 2009 (Barac and Park (HAPPI), 2009; Best and Porteus (HAPPI 2), 2012; Best and Porteus, 2017 (HAPPI 3)). The first HAPPI report was based on a study of 24 housing schemes in 6 European countries, including the UK, 'to ensure that new build specialised housing meets the needs of older people of the future'. The panel (see Glossary) determined ten design components, outlined in Chapter 5, that were concerned with developing sustainable energy efficient buildings, enabling flexible use of communal and private space, and embracing the natural environment. The second and third reports

Figure 7.2: Retirement housing

were concerned with the implementation of the recommendations. HAPPI 2 (2012) systematically called on key stakeholders to take up the challenge of developing quality housing for older people, while HAPPI 3 (2016) stressed concerns that to date there had only been modest specialised housing development, calling witnesses to present at an inquiry. Examining why people may not engage with retirement properties they considered: 'concerns about loss of autonomy and control; the costs of services and affordability of charges; the availability, quality and choice of care and support services, and the imposition of institutional and old fashioned management practices' (2012, p 9).

While many housing with care settings predate these initiatives and the guidance has greater influence on the design of new builds, good practice in management of living arrangements is central to the HAPPI reports and is considered in all sectors of provision.

Introducing ECH

Funding, information and guidance

Following the discussion document 'Lifetime Homes, Life Time Neighbourhoods', 2008 (see Chapters 4 and 5), a move was made under the Coalition government (2010–15) to fund ECH. In 2012, through a social care White Paper ('Caring for Our Future: Reforming Care and Support'), the government through the Department of Health (DoH) announced additional funding for new specialised affordable housing for older and disabled people; the £300 million Care and Support Specialised Housing Fund (CaSSH). The Housing LIN former overseer of the Department of Health's Extra Care Housing Fund currently reports on new arrangements for the CaSSH administered through the Homes and Communities Agency, Homes England and the Greater London Association. Most recent funding focuses on specialised housing for older people and people with dementia, learning disabilities, physical and sensory disabilities, and mental health problems, as well on the development of housing that meets the HAPPI design criteria and their definition of 'specialised housing models'; alongside under-represented co-operative housing or co-housing schemes.

The Housing LIN has developed particular expertise regarding ECH, including information and guidance on: investment issues, capital funding and operating costs or revenue funding for support and care; innovative design, lifestyle and resident evaluation; and more recently guidance on issues relating to the COVID-19 pandemic (see Housing LIN Extra Care Housing COVID Hub, 2020; Dutton, 2020; Nicholson et al, 2020)

Facilities

Riseborough et al (2015) define ECH as:

> housing with care primarily for older people where occupants have specific tenure rights to occupy self-contained dwellings and where they have agreements that cover the provision of care, support, domestic, social, community or other services. Unlike people living in residential care homes, extra care residents are not obliged as a rule to obtain their care services from a specific provider, though other services (such as some domestic services, costs of communal areas including a catering kitchen, and in some cases some meals) might be built into the charges residents pay. (2015, p 3)

It is a housing model that has had considerable government subsidy, and legally the housing is separate from the care. The tenure rights are what makes ECH different from the care home sector. The coming together of housing, care and support may postpone or remove living in residential care. However, in terms of planning, ECH can be classified as either C3 (Dwelling Houses) and/or C2 (Residential Institution), depending on issues relating to tenure, needs assessments and care provision, meals provision and communal facilities (Riseborough et al, 2015, p 13). The overlap between the sectors may be narrow in some senses, even if not perceived that way.

ECH or housing with care (also including enhanced/very sheltered housing) is diverse, being anything from a small block of apartments and/or bungalows (10–30 units) to a facility that is part of a retirement village or continuing care retirement community with 300–400 resident owners. However, while size and scale may vary, several features are common to most ECH schemes:

- Purpose-built, accessible building design that promotes independent living and supports people to age in place
- Fully self-contained properties where occupants have their own front doors, and tenancies or leases which give them security of tenure and the right to control who enters their homes
- Office for use by staff serving the scheme and sometimes the wider community
- Some communal spaces and facilities
- Access to care and support services 24 hours a day
- Community alarms and other assistive technologies
- Safety and security often built into the design with fob or person-controlled entry

(Riseborough et al, 2015, p 4)

In larger schemes, additional facilities – restaurant, gym facilities, meeting rooms, public areas – may be open to the public for a fee, and other individualised telecare devices may also be used, such as fall detectors.

Figure 7.3: Extra-care housing

The specialised housing stock

Statistics regarding retirement housing units (called homes by other authors) including ECH, vary owing to the database and methodology used (Knight Frank, 2018; Best and Martin (HAPPI 5), 2019). Wood (2013), in a report for the think tank Demos, commented that retirement housing (all categories) provided 2 per cent of the UK housing stock, 533,000 homes, with around 100,000 to buy. In more recent analysis, both Wood and Vibert (2017) and property consultant Knight Frank (2018) report expansion of provision to 720,000 homes, the latter commenting on survey research suggesting that 19 per cent of the population aged 50 and over see themselves living in retirement housing at some future point. Data from the Elderly Accommodation Counsel in 2018 suggesting 726,000 specialist homes for older people of all tenures in the UK is seen in the fifth HAPPI report (Best and Martin, 2019, p 13). They comment that, depending on the housing stock figures used, this would see between 6 and 9 per cent of older person households living in forms of specialised housing, higher than the earlier estimate of 5–6 per cent.

Commissioners, developers and providers see the future as maintaining current provision, developing new schemes, variation in tenure, variation in payment for care and ongoing training and development for care staff. Local authorities as commissioners outline housing for older people in their strategic housing needs assessments, and many have ECH in partnership with or alongside other providers, with the number of facilities varying according to location and availability of resources. A greater number of small developers and large-scale housebuilders are also moving into this area: the picture is fluid (Croucher et al, 2006, Local Government Association, 2017a; Park and Porteus, 2018).

Current problems faced on the supply side need to be viewed alongside demand from older people. While the availability of accommodation varies and may be targeted at those with the financial resource to make a choice, there is ECH for rent, and in the main those who relocate see this as a positive decision rather than as a result of a crisis. Riseborough et al (2015) comment on the SHOP@ tool (Strategic Housing for Older People Analysis Tool (SHOP) developed by the Department of Communities and Local Government (DCLG) and the Department of Health, and available through the Housing LIN (2008). They report that using data from the Elderly Accommodation Counsel (EAC), the demand for ECH in 2015 was 25:1,000 units for a population aged 75-plus, and 20:1,000 units of enhanced sheltered housing (Riseborough et al, 2015, p 11). The SHOP instrument can be used to assess need at unitary/county and local levels.

Such statistics continue to illustrate the selective nature of this type of living arrangement.

The proprietors (for profit and not for profit)

The EAC offers information concerning all forms of accommodation (with care) provided by a wide range of for profit/not-for-profit development companies/Has, some of whom are members of the following professional organisations:

Retirement Housing Group (RHG) – 16 members in November 2021. The RHG aims to influence policy development and includes members with expertise in planning, design and the law. For example, they would like to see Stamp Duty, a tax paid by those buying new properties, reduced for people aged 55 and over moving either to specialist retirement housing or a property smaller in room numbers than that currently occupied, encouraging downsizing. https://retirementhousinggroup.com.

Associated Retirement Community Operators (ARCO) (2020) – has 29 members in November 2021, including provisional or prospective developers. Members follow ARCO's Standards and Compliance self-regulatory framework and external assessments as part of their Consumer Code, developed in 2015. Members such as ExtraCare Charitable Trust and Anchor/Hanover have supported a range of academic research programmes discussed in due course. https://www.arcouk.org.

Building developments are funded both independently and through government grants for ECH.

Housing and care research

From the turn of the 21st century, substantial empirical research has begun to report the lived experience of British age-related housing (with care). Research summary 7.3 outlines ten studies in ECH and retirement villages, many using mixed methods – either cross-sectional at fixed points in time or with a limited longitudinal element. The value of and need for longitudinal research is recommended (see Evans, 2009a; Netten et al, 2011; Bernard et al, 2012; Kneale and Smith 2013; Holland et al, 2015; Cameron et al, 2019). While the aims of research vary, they form the basis for the following analysis, where attention is given to the impact of an alternative lifestyle on health maintenance, quality of life, social interaction and the physical environment, and where the present and future role of varied forms of retirement housing are discussed.

Research summary 7.3: Empirical research on ECH and retirement communities

1. Hartrigg Oaks
University of York (2000–02)

Aim: to gain views concerning living at the first continuing care retirement community in the UK.

Location: York

Scale: 152 bungalows built to LTN standards clustered around central complex with services, café, amenities and an attached 42-bed residential care home. Developed through the Joseph Rowntree Housing Trust.

Methods: mixed methods – two postal surveys with residents; face-to-face interviews and discussion groups with residents and staff, plus discussion groups with residents from nearby village of New Earswick (Croucher et al, 2006; Croucher and Bevan, 2010; Croucher and Beven, 2014).

Funded by: Joseph Rowntree Foundation.

2. Berryhills
Keele University (2000–03)

Aim: to examine the lives of those living in a purpose-built retirement village regarding health, identity and well-being (n=159) living in 148 rented flats and compare with older people living in a local public housing estate (n=98).

Location: Staffordshire.

Scale: the retirement community was a single purpose-built three-storey building retirement community housing in Stoke on Trent.

Methods: multi-method, participative action research including three waves of structured questionnaires, community conferences, diary-keeping (Biggs et al, 2000; Bernard et al, 2004; Bernard et al, 2007).

Funded by: NHS Executive (West Midlands).

3. Westbury Fields Retirement Village
University of the West of England (2004–06)

Aim: to explore the extent to which residents with diverse housing and care histories and different socio-economic backgrounds can integrate in one setting.

Scale: opened in 2003, 149 one-, two- and three-bedroomed apartments plus a communal area with a range of facilities, and a 60-bed care home with a specialist dementia unit.

Methods: in-depth interviews with 37 residents and 8 staff, a housing questionnaire to 34 additional residents and profile data on the living arrangements and health and social care needs of residents (Evans and Means, 2007; Evans, 2009a, 2009b).

Funded by: St Monica Trust, Bristol.

4. ECH
Personal Social Services Research Unit (PSSRU) (2008–11), University of Kent

Aim: to examine costs and outcomes in 19 ECH schemes funded through Department of Health ECH Fund.

Methods: information through interviews was collected at 6, 18 and 30 months. Comprehensive costs estimated for individuals based on capital costs, care and support costs and living expenses. Comparative work undertaken with data relating to care home residents (Darton et al, 2008; Darton and Callaghan, 2009; Baumker et al, 2011; Netten et al, 2011; Darton et al, 2012).

Funded by: Department of Health.

5. EVOLVE (Evaluation of Older People's Living Environment)
Universities of Sheffield, PSSRU Kent, Manchester (2010–13)

Aim: a study of the relationship between building design and residents' quality of life in ECH schemes linked to no. 4.

Location/Scale: stratified sample of 23 ECH schemes in England – small new build, remodelled, extra care villages identified through the EAC and ranging from 30 to 246 living units.

Methods: cross-sectional survey with 163 participants, plus use of the EVOLVE tool to evaluate quality of building design (Lewis, at al., 2010, Lewis and Torrington, 2012; Barnes et al, 2012; Orrell et al, 2013).

Funded by: Engineering and Physical Sciences Research Council, supported by DoH, Housing LIN and EAC.

6. LARC (Longitudinal Study of Ageing in a Retirement Community)
Keele University, (2006–10)

Location: Denham Garden Village (DGV), Buckinghamshire. Originally owned and managed from the late 1950s by the Licensed Victuallers National Homes, where terraces and bungalows alongside a nursing home were offered to those from the profession. From the 1980s, residents included those outside the industry, and in 2001, the site was taken over by Anchor for redevelopment.

Aim: exploring the development and implication of the new purpose-built retirement village.

Scale: at the time of research, DGV had 326 properties, both apartments and houses.

Methods: the mixed methods research involved biannual surveys of the resident population (longitudinal element) plus qualitative methods – ethnography, diary-keeping, individual/group interviews, annual community conferences, directed writing, photography and audio visual work (Bernard et al, 2012; Liddle et al, 2014).

Funded by: Anchor Housing.

7. ExtraCare Project
University of Aston (2012–15, extension to 2018)

Aim: to evaluate whether the ExtraCare approach gives positive outcomes for healthy ageing which result in measurable health and social care cost savings.

Scale: 14 locations (across housing units and villages) supported by ExtraCare Charitable Trust.

Methods: three-year longitudinal study. a cohort of volunteer new residents were assessed prior to moving in 14 locations, and then 6, 12, 18 months after entry using measures regarding cognitive functioning, mobility, psychological health outcomes (N= 162 at baseline). Comparison with community volunteer panel members living in Aston area of West Midlands (Holland et al, 2015, 2019; Shaw et al, 2016; West et al, 2017).

Funded by: Extra Care Charitable Trust.

8. ECHO – The Provision of Social Care in Extra Care Housing Universities of Bristol, Worcester, PSSRU, Kent. with Housing LIN (2015–17)

Aim: to examine how care is negotiated and delivered in ECH schemes.

Scale: four ECH schemes.

Methods: a qualitative longitudinal study involving 51 residents interviewed four times, interviews with the manager and five members of care staff at each scheme. Explored in depth how process and experience off care and implications for future developments in ECH (Smith et al, 2017; Cameron et al, 2020).

Funded by: National Institute for Health Research, School for Social Care Research.

9. **Adult Social Services Environments and Settings (ASSET)** (2012–2014) PSSRU
   University of Kent, University of Worcester, Housing LIN

Aim: to consider how adult social care services are commissioned and delivered in ECH and retirement villages.

Methods: a survey of 64 LA commissioners and 99 housing with care schemes plus in-depth case studies in 9 schemes based on interviews with 6 commissioners, 25 scheme staff, 144 residents. 138 residents completed the Adult Social Care Outcomes Tool (ASCOT) plus cost data from the 9 case studies (Evans et al, 2014a).

Funded by: National Institute for Health Research, School for Social Care Research.

10. **Extra Care Housing: Can it be a Home for Life?** (2011–15) International Longevity
    Centre UK: London

Aim: to consider the outcomes of living in ECH.

Scale: working with three providers of ECH in East and West Midlands, North-West England. Settings include villages and courtyard developments.

Methods: using longitudinal data records from 4,000 residents in ECH plus use of data from the British Household Panel Survey and the English Longitudinal Study of Ageing to compare outcomes with those in the community and in receipt of domiciliary care. Further study of data utilising records for one large not for profit ECH provider considering the potential of being 'home for life (N=1,188) (Kneale, 2011; Kneale and Smith, 2013).

Funded by: ILC-UK.

Source: Keyword search regarding forms of ECH through Google Scholar, Housing LIN and informal contacts

A new way of living

Moving into different forms of age-related housing is for many a new beginning, a location in which one can age actively in a purposively designed environment combining independent living in self-contained housing, often an apartment, with opportunities for communal services, activities and social events. The safety and security of a managed community and the potential for access to flexible levels of care in a purposively designed environment are seen by many as important reasons for moving (Croucher et al, 2003; Evans and Means, 2007; Kneale, 2011; Liddle et al, 2014, Holland et al, 2015). In these studies, there is variation in the size and type of environment, from a single block of one- or two-bedroomed apartments defined as ECH in a downtown location to a larger retirement village with a combination of ECH, bungalow/semi-detached housing and a nursing home. Apartment blocks may contain communal public spaces or there may be a separate hub for activities such as hairdressing, gym, café, restaurant or medical facilities; these may be open to people living outside the site, and levels of integration between residents and non-residents may be seen as important.

Interesting variations in tenure and financial arrangements are seen in three of the earliest studies. Croucher et al (2003) report on the way that residents' fees at Hartrigg Oaks are pooled to create a shared resource, which funds care and support for all according to an accepted philosophy. Berryhills, with predominantly working-class residents, provided rented accommodation where some needed financial support for both housing and/or personal care, and increasing rent was a noted concern for some (Bernard et al, 2007). A growing diversity of tenure was remarked on at Westbury Fields (Evans and Means, 2007), from renting to leasehold purchase, and this varied the range of residents' socio-economic status. The fact that many concerns levy service charges on residents is an area for future research into perceptions of value for money.

Who are the residents? Impact on aspects of health.?

While housing with care may be marketed at those aged over 55 or 60, in the main residents/tenants are aged in their mid- to late 70s and older, and they form the focus of research – with some studies making comparison to matched groups of older people living in the wider community (Bernard et al, 2004; Evans and Means, 2007; Kneale, 2011; Holland et al, 2015a). Findings from PSSRU research comparing ECH and care home participants in 2005 show entrants to ECH as healthier than those moving to care homes, with their move to a more social and supportive environment not being in response to a crisis (Baumker et al,

2011; Darton et al, 2012). ECH residents are predominantly white British, middle- or lower middle-class elders, predominantly women, with the ILC-UK large sample showing a majority living alone with three out of ten being couples (Kneale, 2011).

Research in ECH by Holland et al (2015) reports positive findings for those whose health was assessed prior to a move and then post-move, indicating improvement in cognitive function, well-being and a reduction in functional limitations. Through their longitudinal approach, Holland et al (2015, pp 22–5) report on the importance of maintaining wellbeing through connectivity with others in and beyond ExtraCare accommodation, yet also show the complexity of health maintenance where over time declining mobility impacts negatively on social engagement and self-reported health (Kay et al, 2015). An attitudinal perspective is voiced at retirement community Berryhills, where some who were relocating from a working-class community commented that environmental change was a privilege, with their health and well-being improving in comparison with the poorer health status and increased functional limitations of those in the community (Biggs et al, 2000; Bernard et al, 2004).

Housing with care as 'age-friendly' communities

The Keele University team researching DGV used the Age-Friendly Cities and Communities (AFCC) domains (see Table 4.2) to test the assumption that retirement communities are following, or could follow, the age-friendly model (Liddle et al, 2014). They considered whether the DGV had potential for being an age-friendly community, using this definition: 'an age-friendly community is engaged in a strategic and ongoing process to facilitate active ageing by optimising the community's physical and social environment and its supporting infrastructure' (2014, p 1622).

The researchers considered the AFCC domains in relation to some of the studies outlined earlier (see Liddle et al, 2014, pp 1610–11), while acknowledging important within-site issues, noting, for example, for DGV that 'social divisions are rooted in a complex mixture of class, tenure, age, health status and size of the village' (Liddle et al, 2014, p 120). Taking up the AFCC concept, other researchers have since developed a measurement tool for age-friendliness in settings (Garner and Holland, 2020). In this discussion, the AFCC domains are highlighted.

Alongside the outcomes for health maintenance, analysis relates to the social and physical environment. In the EVOLVE research, a majority of respondents report a good quality of life and high satisfaction with place, even though the physical environment is not rated as highly as social participation, relationships, maintaining independence and being active (Orrell et al, 2013). Joining a communal environment with opportunities to develop interests and meet others, and make friends if wished, is a common theme, and seen in the discussion of developing 'communities of interest' in DGV (Bernard et al, 2012). Yet some preferred activities may not be available, and for those with mobility issues accessibility can be problematic, especially on a large site (Barnes, et al, 2012; Liddle et al, 2014; Shaw et al, 2016), a feature considered in the design at Westbury Fields. Research has indicated that loneliness and social isolation may be more common than expected in retirement housing, and greater attention is needed to developing organised activities that can involve community organisations and volunteers (Evans, 2009b, Gray and Worlledge, 2018).

Even though outdoor spaces and buildings are viewed positively, further consideration regarding wheelchair access, visual impairment and signage to aid orientation particularly for people with dementia is indicated as desirable, especially on large sites. In the DGV research, the need for greater accessibility by residents whose health may gradually change over time is noted, which may contribute to internal discrimination between residents (Liddle et al, 2014, pp 1623–4). In contrast, as discussed earlier, ways of facilitating access to amenities and services for all through shared financial arrangements is an innovative approach adopted at Hartrigg Oaks. Such comparisons indicate the tensions that can exist between the individual and the collective, and ways of enabling communal ownership. These are issues picked up by the EVOLVE assessment tool. Access also relates to transportation. Where public transport or car access is unavailable, a minibus is often used to take residents regularly to a local shopping centre.

The balance between public and private living is a common research theme. Housing with your own front door, where individual or couple autonomy and independence is central, is greatly valued, alongside a gradation of privacy between public and private spaces (Orrell et al, 2013). All forms of age-related setting encourage levels of social activity. The larger retirement village can include a wider range of leisure facilities that are valued, alongside on-site community support and health services (Bernard et al, 2012; Liddle et al, 2014). Communication and information are central to many residents. On-site staff have a role that is 'seen and unseen' and dependent on recognising individual needs.

The AFCC domain of civic partnership and employment raises the relationship between overlapping communities – the age-related retirement village and the surrounding intergenerational location – where exchange and levels of integration are possible, but research shows that intensity and direction of flow may vary. Forms of housing with care can offer employment and facilities for the local population, while residents may become members of churches, parish councils and other wider community organisations. Liddle et al (2014) note in their research at DGV that the regular routines of retirement community residents – visits to the on-site

GP, use of the gym – could feel threatened by wider community access, leading to a tension between different community members. Evans et al (2017) comment on how the siting of older people's housing can provide a hub for greater community integration. Here, social and financial problems between proprietors, residents and the wider community link to issues of territoriality and ownership.

For those whose previous environment was challenging, such a move may result in new personal relationships where attitudes towards 'being a burden' on the family or anxiety about changes in health may be side-stepped for an increase in comfort, safety and security. To a degree, this option could become a cultural norm for certain people.

Alternative housing (with care): the issues

This brief evaluation raises a number of issues for housing (with care), including: ongoing role, recognising diversity, co-housing and future design.

Purpose – replacing the care home?

Health and social care needs are central concerns for many residents and the review of state -supported ECH (Darton et al, 2008), ASSET and ECHO studies (Evans et al, 2014a), raise questions over whether such schemes could replace the care home sector. The ASSET study considered the care profile of 138 residents across 9 ECH schemes (including a retirement village), and while residents in housing (with care) were less dependent than care home residents 'a minority of residents have similar levels of dependency' (Evans et al, 2014a, p 2). These residents reported having 'longstanding illness', and yet many did not receive planned care so were not seen as needing to live in a care home. Nevertheless, the research indicated that costs for both accommodation and care/support varied widely, reflecting the profile of resident need, the type of facility and the proportion needing higher levels of care. This led the researchers to consider that 'as a general rule smaller schemes might need to be more focused on a high care mix in order to justify the fixed costs of 24/7 care services, while larger schemes can more easily cater for a varied care mix with a high percentage of low/no care needs' (2014a, p 2). Such comments highlighted variation in settings, yet housing (with care) was not seen as replacing the care home.

The experience of older people living in these different environments is relatively recent, and although limited comparisons were made over time in the DGV and ExtraCare Charitable Trust studies, further longitudinal research is needed to enhance the picture developing here. The ILC-UK study working with the largest sample and comparative data reports that those living in ECH were less likely to move to the care home sector than those living in the community with home care, estimating about 10 per cent of the former and 19 per cent of the latter through a matched analysis of people aged 80 and over. Kneale comments: 'This highlights the efficacy of extra care in supporting people with a diverse range of support needs. Furthermore this can represent substantial savings in social care budgets' (Kneale, 2011, p 4).

At this point, it is worth noting that in ECH, accommodation and care may, or may not, be provided by the same proprietorial organisation even if care planning is undertaken by on-site staff. Also, the overall environment is not regulated in the same way as the care home sector (see Chapter 8) although the Care Quality Commission (CQC) does regulate the care provided and external home care agencies if used. Most supported living and ECH services that provide personal care will need to be registered with CQC to carry out the regulated activity of personal care. For this to apply, there must be separate legal agreements for the accommodation and the personal care.

Ongoing variation in health and well-being, accompanied by social change, will need different forms of support. As seen with Jo, the individual and in many cases the affected family may need to deal with financial, service and lifestyle issues. For people with forms of cognitive impairment, their situation may lead to moving to a care home or specialist dementia care unit, on or off site, or to staying put with on-site home care. In comparing lifestyles across ECH, community living and care homes, Phillips et al (2015, p 963) indicate that satisfaction is not dependent on setting, although their respondents living in ECH were more satisfied with financial matters and their access to personal services. The balance between accommodation and care may influence the overall milieu, and financial support for care provision and other facilities (through public or private resources) is crucially important.

Recognising diversity

Darton et al (2012) point to the lack of diversity among housing with care residents in terms of ethnicity, with little evidence regarding sexuality and culture. Research concerning the cultural diversity of residents is limited, and here attention is drawn to issues and experiences raised for Black, Asian, Minority Ethnic (BAME) groups, Jewish elders and LGBTQ elders.

Harjit, who lives in ECH and is a long-term migrant, was a participant in the Environment and Identity study outlined in Chapter 6 (Peace et al, 2006; Research summary 6.1). He came to the UK from India in the 1960s as a student, living first in Scotland and then London. Owing to life-long health issues leading to poor mobility, he came to live in local authority ECH. By moving into specialised housing, he no longer lived with his own community, although they were part of his social network. He says:

In many ways mentally and in my thinking processes I am more like British but culturally I am Indian, so I am in sort of limbo, in between, so I could say that I belong to both of them or none of them, completely. So it's just one of those states you've got to make the best of the situation and adapt yourself.

... to be truthful, many people like us here who after being here for such a long time, if you go to India we are out of place there because India has evolved and developed in a different direction and a different way to the way we have done here. In other words we have got British values, it is not only the language but other things as well about law, standards and other things. And we are out of place there. We don't belong there, you see. And that is why ... and sometimes at odd times we feel we don't belong here, so we are in limbo sort of thing, you get that feeling. But most of the time I feel this is my home ... we take part in politics, we back a football team, we do anything that any British citizen would do, which when you go to India we are foreigners. And it stands out a mile.

Recently, quite a few years now, there have been Indian channels in Britain, television channels and radios and I've got two Indian channels on my television which are directly from India so I get the news and entertainment and everything – what they get, I get and so it's not too bad – it's like being in India when you are watching that ... (Peace et al, 2006, p 147)

Harjit talks about the common experience of belonging in two places at one time – a place he calls 'limbo'. He is an educated Hindu businessman without immediate family, but with supportive friends in the community who do his shopping – while he reciprocates by offering help with financial services. He moves slowly, but uses a mobility vehicle and can reach his health service appointments. The ECH is newly built, having replaced very sheltered housing. While restaurant-style meals can be purchased, Harjit spoke of the lack of communal activities that he might have found sociable. His comments about television and Indian channels show the way in which virtual mobility has become common for those with resources. Harjit lives between cultures, and yet there is a sense of attachment in his words. In cases of both long-term and short-term migration within diverse localities, little is known about older people moving to housing (with care).

Historically, older BAME members living in specialised housing have been residents of rented sheltered or very sheltered housing schemes run by local authorities owing to their lower economic status (Jones, 2006). People from minority ethnic groups have higher levels of poor health and disability than their white British counterparts, and this is particularly the case for Asians – especially Bangladeshi and Pakistani elders aged 65 and over (de Noronha, 2019). Consequently, a concern for future accommodation and care outside the care home sector has seen organisations including Age Concern and Help the Aged (now Age UK), the Policy Research Institute on Ageing and Ethnicity, and the Race Equality Foundation support special housing reviews (Patel and Traynor, 2006; Jones 2006, 2008).

Jones (2008, p 42) found an absence of specialised housing, including ECH, and identified these issues when reviewing the literature:

- lack of awareness or understanding among BME elders of housing options
- lack of appropriate promotional material
- lack of understanding among service providers of specific religious and/or cultural needs
- lack of staff with appropriate language skills and/or cultural knowledge
- inconsistent allocation policies between service providers
- scheme location (for example the importance of being near community facilities such as shops selling appropriate foodstuffs and places of worship)
- inappropriate design of accommodation
- unevidenced assumptions made by service providers regarding what individual preferences will be
- the need to involve BME elders in the service development process.

Jones goes on to raise the need for anti-discriminatory practices and partnership working between providers and BAME communities (Jones, 2008, pp 42–3).

In 2010, a further call to commissioners and providers of ECH (Institute of Public Care, Oxford, 2010) highlighted good practice case studies from Jones and Bignall (2011) for the Race Equality Foundation. Nevertheless, almost ten years later, the cultural needs of older BAME groups with regard to choice over appropriate housing and care are still only being considered on a limited scale. Economic and social disadvantage continues, and Nigel de Noranha notes that 'the extent to which extra care housing and retirement housing can meet the needs of BME older people would also benefit from investigation of what works well' (2019, p 24).

Ideas of 'what works well' for BAME elders may gain from a comparison with the views of Jewish elders. The Jewish charities that are funding research have consulted their community regarding the concept of ECH because of concern over deterioration in general housing stock and the increasing costs of care (Research summary 7.4). Like all groups, their characteristics and history vary, and compared with the wider population these London-based Jewish community members were seen as older and relatively well educated. The majority of participants taking part in focus groups were aged between 50 and 70, and were from a variety of religious and cultural backgrounds.

Research summary 7.4: Is extra-care housing an attractive concept to older Jewish people living in Britain?

The Open University (2010)

Aims: to consult the community concerning the future development of ECH.

Methods: 16 recorded focus groups with 105 participants, in groups of 3–9 members followed by thematic analysis of transcriptions. Purposive and snowball sampling gained access to community members from a range of religious affiliations – traditional to orthodox as well as liberal and progressive.

Location: South-East England.

Funded by: four separate independent Jewish Charities providers of housing and care interested in the future development of ECH.

(Holland and Katz, 2010)

Following a short briefing concerning the diversity of housing with care and the characteristics of ECH, the researchers focused on a range of topics regarding future ways of living to stimulate discussion (Holland and Katz, 2010, p 62). Analysis showed that the knowledge of housing with care was diverse, and while some lived in sheltered housing, few were considering a move, delaying any form of planning for the future. A majority had family living relatively nearby, while some had relatives in other parts of the UK and across the world. The changing nature of families looking after their own was discussed, with participants feeling that housing and care services should take a more personal approach to cultural issues. Financial arrangements were key, with participants wanting to know how the care aspects of ECH would be affordable, recognising differences between settings. They also asked what a 'lifetime home' actually meant.

Members of the focus groups were particularly concerned over issues to do with locality, community and facilities, and could see that living in a town had advantages in relation to transport and access to shops within walking distance, healthcare and wider cultural amenities. They thought it was important 'that a Jewish facility was "seen to be Jewish" by the outside world, so kosher food should be provided' (Holland and Katz, 2010, p 67), yet they felt they could be a mixed community if other non-Jewish people would fit in with them. Some of the participants lived in the Jewish community in north and north-west London, and Holland and Katz report that 'most participants did not wish to move out of their current comfort zone, their own geographical neighbourhood, for a "Jewish extra care scheme" somewhere else – especially if that somewhere else was "miles out of town" ... all sixteen groups were keen to age close to an active Jewish community' (2010, p 66).

In discussing issues that could relate to members of different minority groups, the researchers raised the important relationship between global and local; having a sense of belonging; staying local but being able to reach out to their community of all ages; and living somewhere that was affordable. They wanted to maintain their self-identity as ageing Jewish people within a physical and social environment that enabled more (Holland and Katz, 2010). It seems that these elders had the confidence to use their difference to capture issues that many would agree to.

In turning to views from LGBT+ elders, these comments also have resonance with other minority groups. Research shows that many are either living alone, with their partner or with their partner living separately in ordinary housing. In general, they wished to stay put, valued privacy and wanted to maintain their independence by drawing upon their family of choice. Some have discussed discriminatory issues of ownership of space and place outside the urban environment, impacting on issues regarding the meaning of home (Willis et al, 2018). Discussion of specialised housing in later life is limited, even though it is raised in broader analyses of health, social care and housing needs (Addis et al, 2009; King and Stoneman, 2017; Kneale et al, 2019; Almack and King, 2019). Westwood (2017) suggests that these are heternormative settings where voices of lesbian, gay, and bisexual women are unheard. Two early American papers (Lucco, 1987; Johnson et al, 2005) identify discrimination with regard to sexual orientation within retirement communities, and comment on how LGBT+ members did not wish to come out within such settings and kept their sexuality to themselves. However, discussion with respondents highlight a desire for a gay or gay-friendly retirement community or continuing care for older homosexuals. There appears to be some support for specialist housing schemes, even though different attitudes may exist within or between groups, as research from the UK shows (Willis et al, 2016). King and Stoneman, reporting on the Secure, Accessible, Friendly and Equal (SAFE) Housing Study (2017) with LGBT+ participants, discuss issues of safety, comfort and trust in different housing situations. They utilise forms of social capital to consider bonding and bridging, concluding 'This means that policy makers and housing practitioners need to consider not only individual needs – important as these are – but how individuals are connected to others and, as importantly disconnected from others' (2017, p 98).

Given the diversity of the ageing population, discrimination through racism, homophobia, and antisemitism will contribute to fundamental attitudes that influence support for separate specialist facilities where particular groups maintain levels of control and autonomy. There is an ongoing need for awareness raising. The support of community providers is an asset when discussing specialist housing, and although not based on shared religion, ethnicity or sexuality, other schemes have the backing of a profession or trade that supports its members, such as those from the licensed victuallers trade who were the first residents at DGV before redevelopment (Bernard et al, 2012). Similarities exist across this discussion where common bonds can aid mutuality between people and where location, communities of association, cultural difference, and sensitive care practice are all important.

Co-housing

Consideration of the diversity of residents who may live in housing (with care) indicates the potential for intentionality in other housing alternatives. A number of people across the UK are already considering or experiencing other intentional ways of living; these include co-housing that is either intergenerational or to a limited development age-related. Researchers Fernández Arrigoitia and West see senior co-housing as:: 'intentional, collaborative and bottom-up co-housing and co-living, with informal forms of mutual aid at its core' (2021, p 1674). It is not independent living or an ECH community, and although limited in the UK at present it is more widespread in other European countries and in North America (Glass, 2012; Susinovic et al, 2019).

As a lifestyle, this type of environment is now being recognised by UK policy makers supporting alternative living arrangements in later life (DCLG, 2009; Chartered Institute of Housing and Housing LIN, 2014; Best and Porteus, 2016), acknowledging earlier developments in other Western developed countries, particularly Scandinavia, the Netherlands, France and in North America (see: Brenton, 2001, 2013, 2017; Durrett, 2009; Glass and Vander Plaats, 2013; Jarvis, 2015; Labit, 2015; Hammond, 2018). The UK CoHousing Network, established in 2007, had a membership of over 80 groups in 2015 with 19 built cohousing communities, and says this about co-housing – so-called intentional communities:

> Cohousing schemes are intentional communities run by their residents. Each household has a self-contained home as well as shared community space and facilities. Cohousing can be a great way to live balancing privacy and highly sociable neighbourhood life. Originating in Denmark in the 1960s the movement has grown across Scandinavia, Germany and the United States. Cohousing is attracting a lot of interest across the country and UK Cohousing Network is proud to be at the heart of this growing movement. (UK Co-housing Network, nd)

These groups are categorised as:

- *Established* – where residents are living in their cohousing community
- *Developing* – where the group is developing its cohousing project
- *Forming* – where the group is initially forming its membership
                                        (Cohousing Directory, see Glossary)

Many of the schemes are intergenerational, but those defined as 'senior' relate to potential residents who are aged 50 or 55 and over, and when writing in 2021 there were 30 groups/schemes across the UK: five are established, fourteen developing, seven were forming and four were yet to define themselves.

This first established senior group is the Older Women's Cohousing Community (OWCH) based at New Ground in High Barnet, north London (see Brenton, 2017). This scheme houses 26 women (including one couple) ranging in age from 52 to 89 and living predominantly in one-bedroomed apartments (there are a limited number that are two-bedroomed), with a shared communal hub plus a laundry, a guest suite, a shared garden with allotments and car share with a small parking space. There is an annual maintenance change that varies according to flat size.

OWCH began moving into the scheme in November 2016 after a development history of 18 years, which included regular meetings to discuss their value base and mission. They sought to:

- marry interdependence and communal living through self-management of the shared areas through working groups and a revolving management committee;
- offer friendship rather than responsibility for each other; and
- be inclusive in terms of mixed tenure: 17 owner-occupier leasehold apartments and 8 social rented apartments.

To get to this point, the development phase had involved everything from the practicalities of initiating new builds to finding a London site, to partnership working with an HA for initial site finance, to gaining planning permission, co-designing the environment with an architectural practice and negotiating with the local authority regarding opportunities for social renters – apartments that came to be owned and managed by the small HA Housing for Women. The various issues faced during this development phase indicate just how complex housing development can be when something non-familial and self-managed is attempted. There are no staff members on site, and once through the front door you have ownership of public space as well as private.

From the start, OWCH was fortunate in having the motivation of founder member and facilitator, Maria Brenton, who has a long history of

Figure 7.4: New Ground, cohousing

promoting and endorsing the value of this form of intentional living, more recently developing a guide to development (Brenton, 1999, 2001, 2013, 2017). Brenton highlights particular benefits for older people, especially the personal and social connectedness between members who may have felt isolated or lonely living on their own, as widowers, divorcees or singles. Ongoing activity and engagement with others can enhance well-being and provide a form of active ageing.

During the period of transition before and after moving into New Ground in 2016–18, Fernández Arrigoitia and West carried out mixed methods partnership research with a majority of the new residents, involving questionnaire surveys, diary records and in-depth interviews before and after the move, and focus group work in situ (Fernández Arrigoitia and West, 2020). Thematic analysis of qualitative data has enabled consideration of whether co-housing is a generalisable model 'beyond the dedicated, activist and privileged few' or 'a mode of later life living that rests on co-operation and mutuality' (2021, p 1690), and what it tells us about 'post-traditional ageing' through this group of older women.

First, it is worth noting how the OWCH women defined their community:

A form of group living set up and run by the people who live in it. Occupants subscribe to a set of defined values and aims; they enjoy their own accommodation, personal space and privacy, but in addition have common areas in which to meet and share joint activities. The aim is to promote neighbourliness, combat isolation and offer mutual support; residents will also be encouraged to become involved with the local community. The OWCH scheme is not in any way sheltered housing, nor a gated retirement community cut off from the outside world. (OWCH, 2018)

Interestingly, the in-depth interviews revealed involvement in forms of social activism by the longer standing OWCH members who are currently residents – housing activism, trade unions and the Campaign for Nuclear Disarmament. However, the questionnaires revealed the diversity of the 26 women in terms of age (16 now aged over 70); employment, with four working full or part time; varied partnership status, from divorced and separated to widowed, co-habiting or never married; socio-economic diversity in terms of income, with former professionals mixed with others distinctly less privileged; and health status that, while reported as 'good/ very good', could be unpacked to indicate daily problems and revealed some chronic health issues.

The research findings already shatter a few myths about the co-housing experience. For example, these are not all people with capital resources and experience of co-living, they are diverse and not all 'activists', and they are able to use their ability to connect with each other both formally (working groups and committee) and informally to examine and re-examine on an ongoing basis issues that will continue to change for the group over time. For example, on a practical level, while the aim and early reality was for all the women to share the cleaning of the public spaces, the challenge of this led the group to involve a property management company to handle this task. At some point, they will also face the experience of health problems for different members. Fernández Arrigoitia and West report that the women don't look after each other, but they are 'looking out for each other' (2021, p 1691), suggesting that this is 'a flexible spectrum of everyday informal care that constitutes their forms of mutual aid'. The authors ask, 'But will it hold this place in perpetuity?' (2021, p 1691) The OWCH women have all agreed to sign a power of attorney for health and financial issues, and this could be seen as one way of defining issues of responsibility should they be needed. The impact of co-housing in terms of the use of health and social services requires ongoing longitudinal research.

The researchers note how many members do not want to be a burden on their children and families because of their own caring experiences, yet there is evidence of family involvement through visiting – and they may find a new role. It is interesting that scheme members see their new environment as empowering for ageing individuals who draw on the strength of the group: they do not deny their ageing. Joanne says:

'What's happening here is we are thinking individually and taking some courage to actually accept that we're getting older [...], acknowledging that it is a process and we can become victims, or we can use our power, both within ourselves and [...] and the courage we get from each other is inspiring.' (Fernández Arrigoitia and West, p 1688)

Finally, it should be noted this is a women's environment, and Fernández Arrigoitia and West are beginning to question whether this makes a difference within senior co-housing, drawing on the feminist ethos of gender equality and ethics of care that underpins some European writing concerning co-housing, whether intergenerational or senior (for example, Sargisson, 2012; Vestbro, 2010). They recognise empowerment coming from 'everyday cooperation associated with women's way of working together' (Fernández Arrigoitia and West, 2021, p 1691). The research at New Ground considers the balance between individualism and interdependence, where interdependence relates to both the inside group as well as family and friends outside, which they see as 'double streams' whose association may, or may not, support them in the future. One might hope for a three-way partnership.

Cohousing is a way of living that offers a very different pathway to the forms of retirement housing discussed previously. While there may be some similarities in views, concerning living independently and not being dependent on family members, the word 'commitment' referring to managing, maintaining and defending co-living is not one that Jo or Nancy (Chapter 6) would recognise. It is still a minority venture within an infrastructure and culture dominated by the development of independent living and an acceptance of a range of age-related housing with or without on-site care facilities. Choice concerning alternative ways of living can be biased towards certain groups, with the intersectionality of socio-economic status, gender, race/ethnicity and sexuality being key indicators of inequality with regard to decisions over housing, health and social care. Even though the OWCH co-housing scheme has begun to enable a consideration of the role of gender in developing a less patriarchal way of living, older women and an increasing number of couples are the dominant resident group in diverse forms of housing with care.

Design and late life housing

This final section extends the discussion on building design from Chapter 5 to consider specialised housing (with care) within diverse integrated/segregated locations. The interface between physical and social environments forms part of a growing body of design-related work. In *Age-Friendly Housing*, Park and Porteus (2018) discuss ways of rethinking housing in later life building on the HAPPI project and the annual Housing Design Awards reported by Housing LIN (2021). They consider 15 case studies from the UK, Holland, Denmark and Finland that include cohousing, bungalows and later life apartments, forms of ECH, contemporary almshouses and combined independent living and residential care. Certain topics come to the fore. Co-design between architects and older potential residents is most common in relation to co-housing, and New Ground outlined earlier forms one of the case studies. The architects were Pollard Thomas Edwards, and through workshops with early OWCH members they sought to answer the following questions:

- How should this ideal community be laid out?
- What's the route to my flat and the view from it?
- Where are the shared spaces and what will they be used for?

A key feature emerging through the workshop process was that 'a common outlook over a shared garden' (Park and Porteus, 2018, p 127) might be central for as many apartments as possible (see Figure 7.4); also that there should be a single entrance that was near to the settings' communal hub. How the building would sit within the residential street was important, and whether the environment could be seen as many 'little houses' was discussed. This shows how the vision for New Ground also comes from the conceptual development of the building.

The second example here identifies complexity by examining the replacement of an existing 40-bed residential care home to create an ECH with 86 two-bedroomed apartments and 3 two-bedroomed bungalows plus on-site and outreach services for older people. This development was initiated through a borough council in St Helens, Merseyside, who gifted land to developers Helena Partnerships. Design discussion involved all parties, including the healthcare provider (MHA) and DK-Architects. Park and Porteus (2018, p 135) note that 'The layout has to work for three distinct users: the visitor must feel welcome, the self-reliant resident should not feel institutionalised, the more dependent should feel secure.' Park and Porteus's text is a valuable addition regarding the built environment, alongside design guidance for ECH produced by the DWELL research team (2016) featured in Chapter 5; architect Sam Clark's discussion of retirement living though the 'guide for planning and design professionals' (Clark et al, 2017, Clark, 2018), and the EVOLVE building design instrument (Lewis et al, 2010) included in Research summary 7.3.

The EVOLVE measurement tool enables researchers to consider in detail the relationship between the built environment and personal well-being. Developed in ECH, this includes a series of checklists to be used across varied housing types – general to special – through a comprehensive walk-through evaluation. It covers all spaces, both public and private areas, where the level of detail in living units captures features such as the minutiae of drawer handles in considering aspects of inclusive design. This assessment may last up to 36 hours for a retirement village (Lewis et al, 2010). Detailed development and testing indicates the value of the tool and highlights issues that could be improved; for example, designers becoming more attuned to sensory issues. Through a scoring system, the instrument can aid understanding of all areas enabling comment on universal needs such as 'dignity and privacy', where it might be seen that 'there is a WC which can be accessed without going through a bedroom', or 'accessibility', where 'there is space inside the hallway for a wheelchair turning circle more than 1500mm' (Lewis et al, 2010, p 40).

Reflecting on their research, Orrell et al (2013) make this important comment regarding environmental determinism and the domains of safety, accessibility and working care: 'where buildings perform highly on these domains, the resulting effect on residents is of a living environment that is over-institutionalised in appearance and not home-like' (p 60). As discussed in Chapter 5, the question then becomes whether more inclusive design tests our understanding of normalcy. Issues of scale, age segregation and community integration can affect where people wish to live in later life, and recognition of diversity between older people who are relatively independent and those who are more frail may impact on how the material environment reflects the ageing process. With regard to new build, the relationship between physical and social environments should be central to an informed planning process with community participation to develop a strong brief; sustainable housing development that facilitates privacy while enhancing interaction; the potential for revitalising existing buildings and community spaces; and a recognition that design can contribute to perception of home. There is an important relationship between academia and practice disciplines here, and dementia-friendly design, discussed in Chapter 5, is returned to in Chapter 8.

Reflecting on home: the lens of age-related housing (with care)

To conclude, we return to the ongoing consideration of the meaning of home, this time from the lens of age-related alternative housing (with care); the lifestyle options increasingly chosen by some older people and marketed as a 'home for life'.

In Figure 7.5, this sector is foregrounded, while enabling the reader to consider broader contextual issues both locational and in terms of themes raised in mainstream housing. In reviewing the literature on these alternative environments the question about how home is perceived in a new environment is not asked directly, yet views are seen indirectly through

Figure 7.5: Reflecting on the meaning of home: the lens of age-related housing (with care)

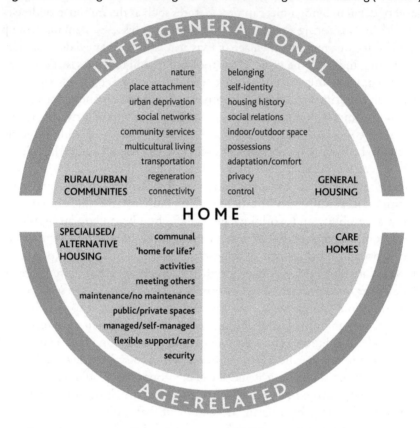

qualitative research and longitudinal perspectives (Biggs et al, 2000; Evans, 2009a, 2009b; Shaw et al, 2016; West et al, 2017; Johnson et al, 2020; Fernández Arrigoitia and West, 2021). Older residents react in different ways to initial transitions from a lifetime of age-integrated community living to a decision to move and an ongoing experience of an alternative form of age-related housing (with care). For some, the decision has been made because they feel their health needs will be better met by such a change. There may be a nervousness or a relief coupled with excitement about a new lifestyle. For some, engagement in on-site activities with the potential for making new acquaintances is part of the reason for moving, while others wish to maintain connections with family and friends in the wider community. They value independent living and having their own front door, as well as the ability to bring possessions with them to maintain continuity; yet they are thankful for less ongoing maintenance and desire greater security. How far this is an intentional form of housing will vary, and reflects different levels of interdependency.

Research shows that people come to settle and develop new routines over time. Some begin to recognise how physical and cognitive change in their health can lead to a different pace of life, with individual endeavours taking on greater meaning. They may become less engaged in organised activities and ontological security may be more greatly valued. West et al (2017), with regard to longitudinal analysis of ECH, discuss a period of liminality when people find themselves moving between the third and fourth ages of life, and it is here that the potential to conceal frailty as discussed in relation to general housing becomes more visible and a public concern. The ability of proprietors of specialised housing to maintain a diversity of residents with different levels of need will also impact on those who are ageing in place within communal settings. As seen with Jo, if someone has vision impairment, orientation within a known space in their own time can be important to maintaining a sense of home. Discussion by Johnson et al (2020) gives further consideration to how people maintain an agentic lifestyle in ECH as their abilities change. They recognise the need for a physical/material environment that is enabling alongside opportunities to make choices regarding levels of support that facilitate maintenance of control and agency. In this way, housing (with care) may embrace the meaning of home.

For those who have taken the decision to live in co-housing, they may face similar issues but in a totally different self-managed environment – where factors such as personal care or housing maintenance are discussed collectively. Here, decision-making is both individual and collective. The energy given to developing a co-housing environment may enable members to experience different levels of agency; this is ongoing and part of the emotional support from people in place that is seen as central to the meaning of their home. They value their age-related environment located in an intergenerational location, where they are recognised for being an individual in a wider community as well as a group member. This is also part of the meaning of home. The example discussed here was developed by older women, and the dominance of women in age-related housing has already been noted. The imbalance of gender and age is also seen in care home living, and this is returned to in the final discussion of home in Chapter 10.

Conclusions

While a majority of older people in the UK continue to live in mainstream community-based housing, certain policy initiatives have encouraged alternative living arrangements for people in later life, especially the generation of 'active agers'. At the same time, there have been calls for people to downsize general housing and, if owner occupiers, to use the capital resource in different ways, either as renters or new owners of smaller accommodation. During a period when younger people are finding it difficult to raise capital as first-time home buyers or, depending on their location, afford to be private renters or gain access to social housing, available housing transfers between generations are valuable and need ongoing discussion (Wood and Vibert, 2017).

Consequently, specialised housing (with care) and cohousing offer different ways of living for some older people. They are still a relatively small percentage of predominantly white British, middle- or lower middle-class renters and owner occupiers, who have decided to spend their later years living in a managed or self-managed community where social interaction may guard against social isolation and planned care may be available on site (Atkinson et al, 2014). Ongoing support and care in UK senior cohousing is yet to be studied. The development of retirement housing and ECH are forms of collective independent living (with potential for care services) that are seen as a positive new start. This can be an environment of ageing that encourages a sense of belonging within a new place through the maintenance of individual agency and the support of personal identity. But reflecting on the meaning of home across settings continues to raise complex issues of person–environment congruence that are individual, social, familial, economic, emotional and material – and greater understanding of the ageing process and how agency is maintained is needed. In contrast, the care home (residential and nursing) as a more institutionalised long-term care service provides a stereotype of reduced autonomy that many seek to avoid. Consequently, Chapter 8 turns to this setting to see whether or not it has been typecast within the environments of ageing.

Care home living: a form of long-term care

Introduction

Chapter 8 begins by returning to the case study of Jo. You may be wondering what happened next. Eventually, Jo became a little more vulnerable, developed a form of pneumonia and had to be admitted to an acute hospital for a week, followed by three weeks within a community rehabilitation hospital. Members of her family visited almost every day, and in rehab she regained her mobility through daily exercises with a physiotherapist. Eventually, through her insistence, she returned to her home in retirement housing; to the flat she knew well, and with 24-hour care, provided through a combination of daily home carers and her daughters who covered the nights, she lived out the last six weeks of her life before dying in her own home. Her daughters and formal carers felt this was the 'peaceful death' that in many ways she had been determined to achieve. She did not have to move to a care home.

The need for long-term care

Jo's experience can be seen as a period of long-term care (LTC). This phrase relates to forms of health and social care, formal and informal, for people in need of medical support and personal care such as washing, dressing, meals, assistance with toileting and medication, across a range of contexts. It is defined in this way by the National Institute of Aging in the USA:

> Long-term care is provided in different places by different caregivers, depending on a person's needs. Most long-term care is provided at home by unpaid family members and friends. It can also be given in a facility such as a nursing home or in the community, for example, in an adult day care center. (National Institute of Aging, 2017)

The future development of LTC is key to global health and ageing, and the World Health Organization (WHO, 2015a) also draws attention to the role of family caregivers alongside formal carers, predominantly women or spouses. They note how in low- and middle-income countries LTC services may be limited or non-existent, and while there are positive examples from high income countries, all need to rethink issues of quality of care. The aim is to provide older people in need with care that is not 'depersonalised, degrading or abusive in manner' [rather it should] 'facilitate older people's dignity, autonomy and personal wishes, while keeping them connected to their community and social networks' (WHO, 2015a, p 149).

There is a growing need for financial investment in this area, and governments need to adopt sustainable and equitable models. Examples from OECD countries (2011, 2015) indicate variation in gross domestic product funding, alongside adoption of insurance systems and tax revenues (WHO, 2015a, pp 144–6). The WHO suggests that national plans are needed that rethink the integrated service aims of LTC; the human rights of the older care dependent; the value of family carers who need respite options; and greater investment in low paid, under-skilled carers, for whom such work is often devalued by societal attitudes and needs recognition.

The diversity of LTC in the UK includes home care, housing with care (Chapters 5 and 7) and the care home. The nature of changing demography contributes to the need for different services, and the growth of longevity sees the population aged 85 and over projected to double between 2014 and 2041 (see Research summary 1.1). Changing care needs in advanced old age can be related to co-morbidity and the incidence of cognitive impairment, with the Social Care Institute for Excellence (SCIE) reporting that 39 per cent of people over 65 years with dementia live in care homes and that this forms an estimated 80 per cent of residents living with dementia or severe memory problems (SCIE, 2020).

'Care home' is the term used for both residential care homes and nursing homes in the UK. The term 'nursing home' is more commonly used in other countries, where they may form a separate service or are found alongside other forms of housing and care in continuing care communities, assisted living or retirement villages (Golant, 2015). To a degree this is seen in the UK, although forms of care home development vary and a brief history is given here. This service forms a context for views voiced particularly by Higgs and Gilleard (2015) as part of their 'social imaginary' for the fourth age (Chapter 1), where people may fear living a life of vulnerability coping with chronic ill health in LTC. Yet negativity regarding the care home sector is not all embracing, and Johnson et al (2010) identify evidence that as people get older their views may change. They comment:

> More recently, an ICM poll revealed that people between the ages of 35 and 64 were more afraid of the prospect of moving into a care home (72 per cent) than those aged 65 or more (56 per cent) (Carvel, 2007).

These findings suggest that older people develop a more nuanced view of ageing and residential options for later life. (p 214)

This chapter seeks to understand how this UK environment may have evolved over time. First, the coming together of residential care and nursing home care is considered; then details of current residents and staff and the physical environments in which people live and work. Finally, reflection is given to whether such settings can produce a life of quality that meets the WHO aims raised previously. Specific attention is given to living with dementia in LTC settings including housing with care, before final deliberation on the focus of current research concerning what is for many a place to live and die – and the impact of this on understanding the meaning of home.

The development of the care home

Historical context is important for a nation such as the UK where residential care and nursing home environments, though physically similar, emerged in different ways that came together in terms of policy and practice in the 1990s (see Figure 8.1). This is primarily a discussion based in England as developments

Figure 8.1: Parallel trends in the history of residential care and nursing homes

Residential care homes		Nursing homes
Victorian workhouses	working poor	Victorian workhouses
reform of the workhouse		
Public Assistance Institutions (PAIs)		
National Assistance Act 1948		
Voluntary sector institutions	Pre-Second World War	Private Convalescence Homes Nursing Homes Registration Act 1927
	Post-Second World War	
Public and voluntary sector Residential care homes	1960s	Private nursing homes
Independent residential care homes	1980s	Independent nursing homes
Regulation of care homes	1990s onwards	Regulation of care homes with nursing
Non-nursing care staff, medical care provided through general		State registered nurse alongside non-nursing care staff
Practitioners in community		First contact for nursing care

vary across the four UK nations (unless stated), and links to the development of housing and care are evident. Material is drawn from a range of research by the author and colleagues (Kellaher, 1986; Peace, 1986, 2003; Willcocks et al, 1987; Peace et al, 1997; Peace et al, 2006; Gopinath et al, 2018).

Workhouse beginnings versus private convalescence

In the UK, the development of social institutions such as care homes evolved over several centuries in a nation where demographic change, employment patterns, socio-economic status and emerging middle-class development all contributed (see Abel-Smith, 1964; Townsend, 1981; Means and Smith, 1983). The history of residential care homes can be traced back to the workhouse system – noted in Chapter 7. The New Poor Law of 1834 and subsequent amendments introduced a centralised system that encouraged the development of workhouses, institutions that each housed up to 100 people and were operated by Poor Law Unions that imposed strict discipline (Townsend, 1981) (see Poor Law in Glossary).

Under the Poor Law Amendment Act of 1851, Boards of Guardians, who oversaw the workhouses at parish level, were empowered to subscribe to voluntary hospitals to which they could send pauper patients. However, few did this and hospitals for the poor, later seen as public hospitals (Abel-Smith, 1964), came to cater initially for those with acute rather than chronic illness. Life expectancy at the turn of the 19th century was 47 for men and 50 for women, and in 1901 only 3.1 per cent of the total population was over the age of 65, with and 0.1 per cent 85 and over (Table 1.7 in Laing, 2018).

The debate over whether to pay or not to pay directly for healthcare has a long history in the UK, occasionally advanced by the need for hospital care for all owing to epidemics such as smallpox in the late 19th century, which led to a growth of convalescent homes and later nursing homes. The diverse quality of these homes came to be questioned, especially regarding the care of the chronically sick, and this led in the 1920s to the appointment of a Select Committee on Nursing Homes (Registration) (Abel-Smith, 1964, pp 338–42; Peace, 2003, p 17). This resulted in the Nursing Homes Registration Act 1927, which introduced a system of registration and inspection for these privately run nursing homes. In parallel, changes were being made to workhouses, with the Local Government Act 1929 abolishing the Poor Law Unions and transferring the administration of poor relief to local government. Legislation in 1930 abolished the workhouse, though many were renamed public assistance institutions (PAIs), which were controlled by local county councils. At the time of the Second World War, older people formed a majority of their residents owing to both poverty and poor health (Willcocks et al, 1987, pp 17–18), alongside war casualties who needed hospital provision and people who came to be housed in PAIs owing to homelessness caused by air raids, all leading to further overcrowding (Peace, 2003, p 17).

Post-war to present day

It was not until the post-war period that health, accommodation and care for older people became a policy issue. Voluntary organisations, such as the Nuffield Foundation in 1947, undertook a review of institutional solutions to the care needs of older people, and a case was made for developing small purpose-built hostels (Means and Smith, 1983) – small settings of 25–30 places run primarily by local authorities and the voluntary sector, and not large institutions. Consequently, 'Section 21 of the National Assistance Act 1948 placed a duty on local authorities to provide 'residential accommodation for persons who, by reason of age, infirmity or any other circumstances are in need of care and attention not otherwise available to them' (Part III Section 21(1) – see Department of Health and Welsh Office, 1990, pp 12–13). The framing of this Act resulted in a distinction between residential care homes and nursing homes that focused on 'board, lodging and personal care' in relation to residential homes, and meeting health-related needs in nursing homes. Nursing care relates to having a registered nursing staff member and financial support through the NHS. The annual report of the Ministry of Health (MoH) 1948–49 described the demise of the workhouse with these words: 'The old master and inmate relationship is being replaced by one nearly approaching that of hotel manager and his guests' (MoH, 1950: 311). This concept has been picked up in research addressing quality of life issues over time (Bland, 1999).

Nevertheless, the small home ideal did not emerge as a form of community-based LTC, and in the post-war years, many local authorities utilised converted buildings and upgraded workhouses or PAIs to develop residential homes for older people. While the National Assistance Act 1948 had not sought to exclude ambulant older people from publicly supported residential care homes, shifts in policy targeted those who were more frail. Guidance issued in the 1960s and 1970s drew distinctions between healthcare and social care, and residential care homes were seen primarily for those people failing to cope at home even with domiciliary care (now home care), yet not in need of 'continuous care by nursing staff' (Judge, 1986: 7). At this time, concern was not focused on care needs but rather on developing new homes for a large number of people, and the issue of costs led to economies of scale and a proposal for 60-bed homes (MoH, 1955; Peace, 2003). Although local authorities became the major providers of residential care homes until the late 1970s, a small but growing number of older people lived in nursing homes and residential homes run by owners/ proprietors in the private and voluntary sectors and registered with local authorities. In the post-war period, these were the smaller homes, commonly large domestic houses often with purpose-built extensions (see Glossary for small care homes) (Peace and Holland, 2001b).

During this period, concerns regarding quality of life within care homes were raised following ground-breaking research by sociologist Peter Townsend in *The Last Refuge* (1962), mentioned in Chapter 7. In 1960, Townsend surveyed all 146 local authorities in England and Wales to draw a stratified sample of 173 residential care homes for detailed ethnographic research. He did not include nursing homes. While homes ranged from large former PAIs in cities, with more than 1,000 residents, to small privately owned homes with six or fewer residents, Johnson et al (2010, p 5) report that at the time of his research three fifths of people living in care homes were accommodated in former PAIs. While those over pensionable age formed the vast majority (86 per cent) of residents, it was common for younger people who were seen as chronically ill or physically disabled to be included. Over 110,000 people were accommodated (Peace, 2003), and Townsend's observations reported institutional living at its most extreme – large overcrowded dormitories that were bleak and lifeless; little privacy or dignity; commonplace loneliness; and a collective form of organised living that could be harsh (see Thompson and Townsend, 2004).

The 1960s, 1970s and 1980s saw the growth of a 'literature of dysfunction' regarding the lives of older people, people with mental health issues and learning disabilities living in communal settings (see Barton, 1959; Robb, 1967; Meacher, 1972; Miller and Gwyne, 1972; Clough, 1981; Booth, 1985), leading to growing discussion of the protection of human rights and the need for person-centred care within institutional settings (see Jack, 1998).

Central to many arguments was Goffman's definition of 'institutional totality' following research in American mental health settings. This outlined:

- **Batch living** – the rigidity of routine where people were not treated as individuals, had little privacy and followed the rules of the institution.
- **Binary management** – the maintenance of social distance between staff and residents (then known as 'inmates'), with certain areas being out of bounds. Only staff members had keys and access to all rooms alongside their own living areas.
- **Inmate role** – the adoption of a depersonalised role by residents, who were reliant on the goodwill of staff if individual preferences were to be acknowledged. This behaviour could be maintained through a system of rewards or penalties, including medication.
- **Institutional perspective** – actively regulation of their own behaviour by residents, adopting the institutional perspective as a way of getting by and not getting into trouble.

(see Goffman, 1961, pp 17–22)

The legacy of this body of research certainly added to the critique whereby the care home became synonymous with institution, as seen in continuing policy discussion. In the late 2000s, Johnson et al (2010) replicated aspects of Townsend's study, aiming to rediscover his original sample of homes. The participatory methodology associated with this study is discussed in Chapter 9. Their findings, based on interviews with residents and staff in 20 care homes visited in 2005–06, more than 40 years after Townsend, report both continuity and change, and show the development of large non-profit trusts and private for-profit companies within the sector.

For more than 30 years, statistical sources for this sector have come to rely on analysis by Laing and Buisson (see Glossary), who have undertaken annual reviews of the care home market (see Laing, 2018, 2019). Table 8.1 outlines the period from 1970 to 2018, highlighting dramatic changes in social policy. Policy led by the Conservative government from 1979 to 1996,

Table 8.1: Care homes for older people, 1970–2018

Year	Residential places			Nursing places		NHS places		All
	LA	FP	NFP	FP	NFP	GLS	OMILS	Total
1970	114,534	23,559	37,308	19,261		52,000		
1975	135,186	25,646	38,145	22,771		49,000		
1980	141,719	37,177	39,634	25,523		46,100		
1983	143,826	54,374	42,146	27,515		46,900		
1985	144,458	84,791	41,960	36,054		46,300		
1987	142,772	113,916	39,261	50,000	7,212	43,000		
1990	123,600	148,800	36,700	108,600	9,300	46,000	26,800	499,800
1995	78,900	176,400	53,200	188,600	15,900	29,200	15,200	557,400
1998	67,700	187,800	50,700	198,100	16,200	18,700	10,400	549,600
2000	59,300	188,100	51,400	182,400	16,000	14,400	8,500	520,100
2005	42,600	180,800	49,800	157,400	12,600	12,100	5,600	460,900
2010	33,000	186,000	44,000	163,600	13,600	9,600	2,900	452,700
2015	22,800	197,200	43,700	180,800	15,200	8,000	1,900	469,600
2017	18,200	194,900	43,900	180,700	15,700	7,600	1,600	464,100
2018	17,100	198,600	44,400	177,400	16,700	7,400	1,600	464,800

Note: NHS care homes – there are no places recorded until 2017 when there were 1,500 places and 2018 when there were 1,615 places

LA – local authority, FP – private for profit, NFP – voluntary not for profit, GLS – geriatric long stay, OMILS – older mentally ill long stay

Source: Adapted from Table 1.3, Laing (2018), pp 30–1

(see Glossary and Laing and Buisson)

including the Thatcher years (1979–90), saw the commodification of the
care home industry, with the following trends:

- Public sector residential care homes run by local authorities are dominant
until the mid-1980s, then decline by 59 per cent between 1985 and 2000.
- Residential care homes dominate provision in 1990, with 309,100 places
alongside 117,900 nursing home places, with a particular rise in the
independent/private (for-profit) sector.
- Between 1983 and 1990, the for-profit sector increased from 23 per cent to
48 per cent of all residential places and 87 per cent of all nursing home places.
- Independent (not-for-profit) voluntary residential care homes show some
stability across this period, with a particular increase from 1990 to 1995.
- Since 2002 residential facilities defined as 'care homes' and nursing homes
became 'care homes with nursing'.
- In 2018, there were 260,100 residential places and 194,100 nursing places,
with an overall total of 454,200 care home places at that time.

These trends reflect specific policy decisions and drivers. The privatisation
of residential care homes began with changes to the 1980 Supplementary
Benefit (Requirements) Regulations, which allowed people to obtain financial
support for care home provision through board and lodgings payments (Challis
and Bartlett, 1988). This led many low-income older people who qualified
for income support to enter homes more easily in the private and voluntary
sectors using public funds channelled through the benefits system, without
a requirement that a local authority should assess their care needs.

Following 1990, there was a lower percentage growth overall in residential
care home places. The implementation of the NHS and Community Care
Act 1990 sought to reduce the 'perverse incentive' towards institutional
care by redirecting financial support for care homes through local authority
budgets, alongside the development of local care management practices to
assess individual needs and financial means-testing for home care and care
home placements. These arrangements developed during the period of
the Royal Commission on Long Term Care (Sutherland Report, 1999a,
1999b) considered in Chapter 7, which proposed funding LTC provision
through partnership between public funds and personal finance. In 2000,
the Labour government made nursing care free in care homes in England,
Wales and Northern Ireland, funded through NHS budgets, but social care
(personal care) was to remain means tested and chargeable (Wanless, 2006;
Jarrett, 2017). In contrast, free personal and nursing care in care homes was
adopted in Scotland in the Community Care and Health (Scotland) Act
2002 (Scottish Government, 2005).

Table 8.1 details the care home profile into the 21st century. In 1985,
the ratio of residential care home places to nursing home places stood at

7:1 moving to 3:1 in 1990, with figures for 2018 putting this ratio at 1.3:1. In 2018, the market value of the overall care home sector was reported as £16.9 billion (Laing, 2018, pp 30–1). The ongoing decline of NHS long-stay hospital places (geriatric, older mentally ill) is reflected in these changes, with the gradual increase in care home residents also linked to the growing number of older people living with forms of dementia (Alzheimer's Society, 2020). In 2000, the Department of Health (DoH) National Beds Inquiry reported that two thirds of NHS hospital beds were occupied by people aged 65 or over and that a proportion of older people occupying acute hospital beds could have been treated in alternative facilities. This led to the development of intermediate care and rehabilitation services, enabling a phased return for some from hospital to their own home or to a residential or nursing home for a short- or long-term stay that might offer respite care for informal carers (Laing, 2002; Peace, 2003). The value of intermediate care and rehabilitation was seen in Jo's case study.

Another issue seen in Table 8.1 is the ongoing growth of the for-profit independent sector. In early decades, a residential care home or nursing home in this sector might have been owned by a husband and wife team who were also managers. In 2005, the Office of Fair Trading expressed concern over the lack of information potential residents received over financial arrangements either through local authorities or directly from the homes. Greater transparency was needed concerning value for money and what fees covered; these issues were picked up by the Commission for Social Care Inspection (CSCI), the regulators at that time (CSCI, 2007). The Competition and Markets Authority (CMA) reported that in 2016 approximately 5,500 providers in the UK were operating 11,300 care homes for older people, and that around 80 per cent of providers were single home businesses supporting 29 per cent of care home beds (CMA, 2017, p 33). More recently, statistics show that by 2018 the for-profit sector owned and ran 83 per cent of care home beds in England, with 13 per cent not for profit and only 4 per cent run by local authorities (Laing, 2019).

The past 50 years have seen a complete reversal in care home ownership between state and independent sectors. Care home managers in the not-for-profit sector could be working for organisations such as Abbeyfield, Methodist Homes and Anchor Hanover, which also provide retirement housing, shared (sheltered) housing, housing with care and retirement villages (see Glossary). In the growing corporate for-profit sector, some providers have merged to form larger businesses, and material from Savills (2020) indicates that five care home operators, HC-One Ltd, Four Seasons (Health Care), Barchester Healthcare, BUPA Care Homes and Care UK, now provide 13 per cent of the market, or 62,000 care home beds.

Historic trends relating to the demand (occupied places) and supply (registered bed capacity including some NHS long stay) indicates that in March 2018 there was a capacity of approximately 465,000 places across all providers, with over 90 per cent occupancy rate primarily in independent sector care homes (Laing, 2018, p 48). Yet Laing, utilising inspection reports from the regulator – the Care Quality Commission (CQC) – also indicates that resident numbers may be 5 per cent lower than estimated (Laing, 2018, p 48), owing to regional variation in home closures and openings. During the summer of 2020, the impact of the COVID-19 pandemic, from January 2020 onwards, and the mortality of care home residents means that reduced occupancy rates are an ongoing concern (Institute for Government, 2020).

Social care within domestic and communal settings and further development of integrated care remains pressing. Following the Sutherland Reports (1999a, 1999b), reviews into the future of social care funding continue (Croucher and Rhodes, 2006 for the Joseph Rowntree Foundation; Wanless Report, 2006), with ongoing discussion regarding independent living, personalisation, the expense of residential care with the Green Paper 'Shaping the future of care together' (DH, 2009) identifying options regarding different insurance systems. This led to the Dilnot Commission Report, 'Fairer care funding' (2011), which developed a system based on social insurance and collective provision. The earlier discussion in Chapter 5 about owner-occupied housing as a welfare asset reappears here, yet the care home resident and/or their family do not become owners of their care home place; rather they pay a fee.

Paying for care

Since the Care Act 2014, local councils have been required to provide information and advice for all those seeking social care within their own home or a care home. For many older people, becoming a care home resident will result in a care needs assessment through their local adult social care service. A financial assessment will be carried out or can be requested, indicating the means-tested threshold for personal savings and assets – currently £23,250 in England – above which people will be required to pay their own fees, and the sliding scale of contributions based on an income to the lower limit of £14,250 (NHS, 2020; Beck, 2021). Table 8.2 outlines the three main types of residents in 2018, based on their care home funding alongside Laing's valuation of weekly costs for nursing and residential care homes, indicating the role of self-funders.

Although fees will have increased since this analysis, the trends remain. There is a financial differential between residents in any care home, and while some self-funders and their supporters may feel more in control of decision-making, they may also still lack information and support (Tanner et al, 2018; Baxter et al, 2020). Local authorities, whose funding from

Table 8.2: Resident type based on financial resources, UK, 2018

	All care home residents	Weekly fees all care homes	
		Nursing	Residential
'pure' state-funded	137,000 (35%)	£730	£555
'quasi' self-pay (pay top ups)	44,000 (11%)	£873	£622
'pure' self pay	176,000 (45%)	£1000	£750

Source: Laing (2018), p 34

central government has been reduced through austerity measures over the past decade, pay a lower rate for a care home place than do self-funders and those who top up state supported fees. The local authority only has access to certain care homes for those who are totally state supported. If an individual and their family wish for greater choice, they must have the financial resources to do so, with deferred payments being settled in some cases after a person's death. This form of means testing is constantly being questioned, and is central to the discussion of social care and LTC. Self-funders may be supporting the viability of care homes and the quality of provision that is achieved for all residents (Henwood et al, 2018). It is interesting to note here that self-funders are seldom seen as owners of personal space; all are seen as residents.

The UK still needs a workable solution for paying for social care. As of September 2021, the Conservative government announced a social care levy part of the Health and Social Care Bill 2021–22; a 1.25 per cent tax on earnings, similar to National Insurance Contributions (NICs), aiming to commence in April 2023 (Seely and Keep, 2021). Allied to this proposal, a raised means test threshold of £100,000 including housing assets will determine those paying for all their care home fees from October 2023, with individuals starting to contribute if assets are more than £20,000. The proposals also set a cap of £86,000 for lifetime contributions, based on local authority costs for care home places rather than those individuals choose. Care costs would be taken over by government at this point (Bottery, 2021). The debate concerning these proposals is ongoing (see Which, 2021).

Changing characteristics of residents and staff

Care home residents

In 1981, Peter Townsend wrote a leading article on the structured dependency of older people, in which he reflected on the social dependence of certain people living in residential care (not nursing homes). He made an interesting statement about familial and gendered care based on his earlier research (1962):

the chances of institutionalization for a bachelor or spinster of advanced age were higher than those for a widowed or divorced childless person, and the chances then decreased, step by step, for a married but childless person, then for someone with one son only, someone with one daughter only, someone with sons and daughters but living at a considerable distance from them or having little contact with them and finally, the chances were least for someone with sons and daughters and having daily contact with them. (1981, p 18)

Sixty years on, this recognisable trend may remain, but without detailed profiles for all residents in a care home sample over time we turn to comparative research regarding resident characteristics across settings. Studies undertaken by the Personal Social Services Research Unit, University of Kent (Research summary 7.3), considered findings from 2005 for samples of older people living as care home residents in 19 extra-care housing (ECH) schemes. (Darton et al, 2012) indicates the following trends:

- a distinct difference in mean age, with care homes residents predominantly in their 80s, with an average age of 85 rather than in the late 70s in ECH;
- a higher number of female residents in both sectors;
- residents in ECH include a range of single, married, divorced/separated and widowed; in care homes nearly three quarters are widowed and 17.2 per cent married;
- dominance of white British ethnicity in both settings, with only a very small percentage from non-white populations;
- 65 per cent of ECH residents formerly lived in private households, over a third of residents in other supported housing and care homes; 45 per cent of care home residents were admitted from hospital or intermediate care and 27 per cent from private households;
- high percentage in both settings previously lived alone; ECH residents were more likely to have lived as part of a couple than care home residents.

A similar pattern was found in Wales through a comparison of older people living in residential care homes, ECH and the community (Phillips et al, 2015). A majority of participants in all environments were female (73 per cent). Care home residents were slightly older than other participants, with a greater percentage single and divorced than the ECH sample, which was dominated by widowed participants. The highest percentage of those married were living in the community. It has also been noted that just over 8 per cent of ECH residents may move to more institutional settings including care homes (Kneale and Smith, 2013).

Direct comparison with the Townsend quote regarding marital status and assistance is not available, although evidence shows that families continue to support their older relatives even if they do not live together; and without their care, the future cost and nature of LTC would change dramatically (Carers UK, 2021). Moreover, using census data for England and Wales (ONS, 2013), Laing indicates that non-married people aged 85 and over are almost three times as likely to live in a communal establishment (mainly care homes) than married people of the same age. (Laing, 2018, p 31), reflecting informal care between couples and family members in the community. Gopinath et al (forthcoming) note that primarily owing to chronic health conditions and/or moderate/severe dementia, married residents living in care homes while their partner lives in the community are a growing but invisible group.

Age itself may partly be a driver for the care home sector, and Laing comments that 'Demand for care in residential settings escalates rapidly with age. Approximately 0.6% of the 65–74-year-old UK population live in a care home or long stay hospital setting (at March 2018). This rises to 14.7% of those 85 years and over' (Laing, 2018, p 31). Increased life expectancy cannot be the only reason for these changing living arrangements. Levels of chronicity and co-morbidity in health conditions are particularly important. The continuing incidence of cognitive impairment and dementia in later life underpins the ongoing demand for care home services, with the picture regarding dementia care being complex.

Laing (2018) reports that in the Laing and Buisson previous market reports for care homes, their consideration of 'population-based' demand assumed age specific rates as fundamental to the growth in this sector, whereas in the 2018 report they adopt a different methodology: 'This is based on the proposition that admission into a care home is a function of proximity to end of life, with a lag of about 2 years, rather than the number of older people in the population' (p 38). This decision was made following analysis of change in occupancy rates over the past 40 years where, by 2005, it was noted that demand for care home places was roughly in line with death-based projections rather than population projections of advanced age, which continues to outstrip the demand for care home places. Given the issues raised concerning mortality and living in a care home, the fact that Laing suggests 167,000 (42.3 per cent of all residents) are in receipt of provider-defined 'dementia care' (Laing, 2018, p 9) indicates levels of severity that sit alongside higher predictions. In 2008, Manthorpe estimated that 'over a third of people with dementia live in care homes and that two-thirds of care home residents have dementia' (2008, p 36) a similar estimate to the Alzheimer's Society's report of 70 per cent for residents with dementia and severe memory loss (2020) – no doubt indicating definitional differences. The diversity of care home residents by ethnicity or as LGBT+ members is not recorded.

Staffing in care homes

It has been estimated that care homes in the UK employ over 440,000 members of staff (Table 8.3) (Laing, 2018). The workforce for adult social care, including care homes, housing with care and home care staff and managers, is proving difficult to recruit and retain across England, as seen in the Adult Social Care and Workforce in England report (2018/19) (National Audit Office, 2018), which indicated an annual turnover of 27.8 per cent.

In the care home sector, all types of staff are essential and yet some, such as care assistants and domestic staff, are particularly low paid, which does not encourage recruitment – despite calls to meet the National Minimum Wage and National Living Wage during the past decade (Carr, 2014). Education and ongoing training for care staff is also an issue. Johnson et al (2010), in their comparative study of Townsend's work, offer their views on consistency and change in care home life over almost 50 years, saying this about staffing:

> We found that staff roles were more differentiated and that proprietors and managers were doing far less 'hands on" work and much more administration when compared with the past. This in part reflects the much closer regulation and inspection of care homes in 2005–6. Overall, staff […] were better trained, albeit still inadequately. While there is less reliance on casual and familial labour, staff remain poorly paid and often not protected by union membership. (2010, p 208)

Nevertheless, in terms of preventing care home closures, care home managers and qualified nurses (sometimes the same person) are key personnel (Table 8.3). The care home manager has a range of roles, with their skills being

Table 8.3: Estimated full-time equivalent (FTE) staff employed in care homes for older people and dementia (65+), UK, 2018

	FTE staff
Home managers (Including vacant posts)	11,000
Other supernumerary management, administration and reception staff	23,000
Qualified nurses	36,000
Carers	284,000
Domestic	63,000
Chefs/cooks	25,000

Note: excludes the small remaining in-house NHS provision of non-registered nurses in long-term and units for older people

Source: Table 1.16, Laing (2018), p 78.

essential to the quality profile of the care home and relied on by proprietors, indicated by their gradual increase in salary (Laing, 2018, p 92). Nursing homes need qualified nurses on the staff in order to maintain their registration, and there is a continuing shortage of qualified nurses in this sector (Meyer, 2015). Furthermore, in terms of all adult social care staff, while a majority of workers are British, Laing reports that in 2018 '7% (95,000) jobs had an EU nationality and 9% (125,000) a non-EU nationality' (2018, p 78). Change through Brexit, as the UK leaves the EU, may present a challenge to the continuing appointment of non-UK EU national staff. All these issues affect staffing for the care home sector, alongside other social care services, and in Chapter 10 consideration is given to the impact of the COVID-19 pandemic.

Design in communal settings

The built environment of current care homes in the UK has continued to change over time influenced by issues of size and scale, with premises varying from extended converted housing to new build with group-living units (see Willcocks et al, 1987, pp 80–1; Department of Health, 2003, p 20). Here consideration is given to specific design features – the single bedroom, the influence of the National Minimum Standards and design that can be therapeutic and dementia-friendly.

A room of your own

First, we return to 1980, when multidisciplinary social scientists Dianne Willcocks, Leonie Kellaher and the present author, founders of the Centre for Environmental & Social Studies in Ageing (CESSA), were commissioned by architects and policy officers from the Department of Health and Social Security (DHSS) to research the views of residents and staff in local authority care homes regarding their living and working environments (Research Summary 8.1), as they wished to rewrite the building regulations (notes) for care homes (MoH, 1962; DHSS, 1973, Peace, 1986). The 1960s had been a period of transition – a percentage of four-bed rooms was still noted in the 1962 Building Note, with units being used on occasion to accommodate 'residents who became mentally infirm, confused or restless' (p 3). In contrast, the 1973 revision of the Building Note (DHSS, 1973) built on 'one of three "collaboration in design" exercises during which teams from twelve local authority architect and social services departments worked with representatives of DHSS architects, Social Work Service officers and administrators on specific projects included in the local authority building programmes' (Peace, 1986, p 186). This revision advocated that care homes should be part of the wider community, and although supporting the idea of linking residential care homes with housing projects on larger estates, guarded against creating what were called 'elderly ghettos'. In terms of interior design, the domestic home was a model, and if new build care homes exceeded 40 places, self-contained units ('family groups' of eight individuals) were suggested, to encourage social interaction and cut down on distance between facilities, thereby aiding mobility (see Korte, 1966; Peace, 1986).

Between 1962 and 1973, the needs of residents and ideas for the multi-purpose use of residential care homes emerged. The 1973 revision:

> also took on board the growing complexities of residential living: the needs of different groups of long-stay residents; the move to a multi-purpose home with the introduction of day care, short stay and meals services; the importance of community integration, and the needs of residents for both greater privacy and more self-determination. (Peace, 1986, p 143)

Later in the 1970s, and the early 1980s, with the coming of the Thatcher government (DHSS, 1978; DHSS, 1981), contradictions in political philosophy that affected residential care homes linked to reduced capital investment for local authority provision and the growth of the independent sector. This period saw the White Paper 'Growing older' report the importance of design for care homes that 'contributes greatly to efficiency and to the quality of life of residents' (DHSS, 1981, p 46), announcing that 'consumer research had been commissioned by the DHSS to discover the attitudes of elderly residents to the homes in which they live'.

Research summary 8.1: The National Consumer Study of Local Authority Homes for Older People (NCS)

Centre for Environmental and Social Studies in Ageing, Polytechnic of North London, 1980–81

Aims: a study of the views of care home residents and staff on the environments in which they were living and working; to revise LA Building Note No. 2. 1973.

Location: throughout England

Methods: a mixed methods approach including (a) a stratified sample of 100 local authority old people's homes (the current dominant sector) where 23 homes incorporated some form of group-living design – a structured/semi-structured survey of 1,000 residents and 400 staff members (N=10+4) was undertaken in each home; (b) in-depth case studies in four homes in which two researchers (Kellaher and Peace) each spent a week, six months apart, living and researching the interior environment and the external interaction with the wider community.

Funded by: Department of Health and Social Security (DHSS)

See: the main findings are found in research reports Peace et al (1982), Willcocks et al (1982) and the book *Private Lives In Public Places: A Research Based Critique of Residential Life in Local Authority Old People's Homes* (Willcocks et al, 1987).

The word 'consumer' reflected a more individualised policy and the gradual marketisation of the care home sector. Research was directed by the DHSS with a large survey component and in–depth case studies. In essence, this became a discussion of person–environment (P–E) fit at the communal level, in which architectural design, in material form, was brought alongside everyday living and working experiences of residents and staff within public and private spaces. Institutional aspects of working practice were considered alongside the well-being of residents and the need for person-centred care (see Peace, 1986, p 145; Willcocks et al, 1987, pp 84–139), showing the way in which there was a need for a more 'balanced life' in terms of spatial allocation. In 1981, a total emphasis on sitting space and public shared rooms was found, with fewer than a third of private rooms being single bedrooms.

While acknowledging the point made by Townsend (1981) that at that time a number of people living in residential care could have been living in a form of sheltered housing, the 'normalisation' of the physical/material environment was advocated, responding to a call from 67 per cent of participants for people to have the personal space of a single room in what the researchers called the 'residential flatlet' (Willcocks et al, 1987, p 133; Figure 8.3) – a place for individual ownership, control and autonomy with organisational support. While the layout of single and double rooms had been discussed in the earlier building regulations, the interaction between the person and their care home environment had only been studied by a small number of architects and psychologists (Lipman, 1968; Harris et al, 1977; Lipman and Slater, 1977a, 1977b). In the preface for the book from this research, *Private Lives in Public Places* (Willcocks et al, 1987), M. Powell Lawton commented:

> They reject environmental determinism. They develop at length the idea that physical environment is only one component of a larger whole, one that is shaped by ideology as well as professional caregivers. Under some conditions, the way homes for the aged are designed may inhibit or facilitate certain behaviours. Their analysis of how thoughtful design can make more probable the resident's achievement of personal goals

Figure 8.2: The residential flatlet

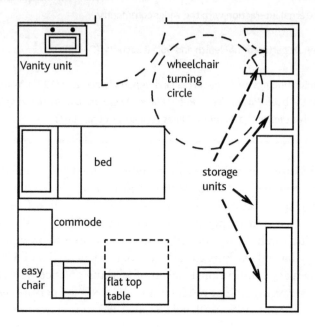

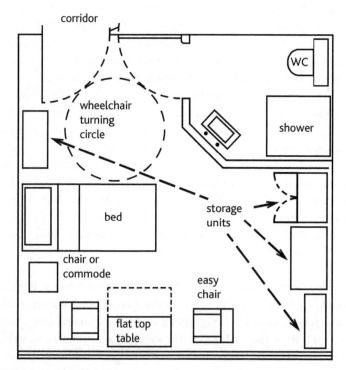

Source: Willcocks et al (1987), p 150

is thought-provoking and directly useful to the designer. (Willocks et al, 1987, p x)

The national consumer study sought to understand ways in which individual lives within communal settings could be enhanced through P–E interactions, both internal and external, that brought together physical, social and psychological experience. It was concluded that:

> broad shifts in care patterns are necessary: a transformation of spatial arrangements between public and private space; a positive reorientation of the relationship between the old age home and the wider community; and the introduction of practical support for a new philosophy in residential living, that is organizational change based on substantially revisited staff-training programmes. (Willcocks et al, 1987, pp 146–7)

For the CESSA team, this led to developing diverse training resources such as the board game 'Images of Residential Life', which enabled care staff to consider the viewpoint of residents and vice versa, and 'Inside Quality Assurance' – a quality assurance tool for care home insiders and outsiders to initiate their own assessment of resident views and the potential need for change. This was part of the Caring in Homes initiative following the Wagner review of residential care (Wagner, 1988; Youll and McCourt-Perring, 1993; Kellaher, 1998a).

Making change through National Minimum Standards

Twenty years after the National Consumer study began, The Care Standards Act 2000 set up the Commission for Social Care Inspection, establishing new National Minimum Standards (NMS) for all residential and nursing homes and domiciliary care alongside the regulation of care homes (Department of Health, 2003). In terms of design, a recommendation of at least 80 per cent single rooms was advised through Standards 23 and 24 even though spatial dimensions were slightly smaller than those suggested for the residential flatlet – 12 m² of usable floor space excluding en-suite facilities (see Appendix 1) (Department of Health, 2003). While there were delays in providing single rooms for the majority of residents, it is now common provision in all care homes. This was a period when spatial change enabled the potential for greater personalisation of private space alongside more person-centred care. Yet the material environment can only support cultural change. The small percentage of double rooms has given choice to people who wish to share, though the potential for use of two single rooms is also noted in Standard 23 (Appendix 1). In present times, potential choice does not reflect partnerships in later life (married and partnered), as noted earlier (Gopinath et al, 2018, forthcoming). The changing characteristics of residents are central to how ways of living develop and the physical environment should develop.

The characteristics of residents who took part in the National Consumer Study in 1980–81 reveal similarities and differences to those outlined by Darton et al (2012) 25 years later. They were slightly younger, with a mean average age of 80 rather than 85.2, and while similarly predominantly female, there were more male residents who had been childless and living alone prior to moving to a care home. The major difference lies in issues of changing health, co-morbidity and particularly mental infirmity, with residents less likely to have been admitted through a hospital discharge. In the earlier research, 14–34 per cent of respondents were classified as showing some signs of infirmity on five dimensions of mental status, utilising the Crichton Royal Behavioural Rating Scale (Willcocks et al, 1987, p 40), without comparable data we note a much higher percentage of current residents with dementia and severe memory loss.

Care home design

The early 1980s saw the demise of the architectural department within the DHSS, and the building guidance for care homes was not revised. Instead, CESSA was allowed to publicise a short report (Peace et al, 1982), but on reflection the interface between social scientists and architectural practice was limited. It was not until 1996 that Judith Torrington, a practising architect and academic (University of Sheffield), developed a design guide seen as a 'desk top reference book' (Torrington, 1996, p vii), which noted:

> There is anthropometric information, space by space check lists which include illustrated space standards and items of commonly used equipment. There is a section on interior design dealing with colour, lighting and acoustics. Services and systems are covered where they are specific to the building type. The design guide concludes with the design of external spaces. (p vii)

Particularly interesting was the way in which Torrington contextualised design through a suggested diversity of current residents in a 40 place care home, where she comments:

> If such a home did exist and was representative of the entire care home population the following statements could be made about the residents:

- 13 would have established dementia.

- 28 would show mild/severe dementia.
- 13 would have no living spouse or children.
- 3 would have no relatives at all.
- 16 would suffer urinary incontinence.
- 16 would be male.
- 24 would be female.
- 1–2 would be aged 65–74, of whom 1 would be male and 1 female.
- 9 would be aged 75–84, of whom 4 would be male and 5 female.
- 30 would be aged 85+, of whom 11 would be male and 19 female.
- Most would have limited mobility.

(Torrington, 1996, pp 1–2)

The design failures she noted were also identified in the National Consumer Study. Torrington says:

> The design defects listed here are common:
> - bathrooms unused because of poor access to bath and lack of lifting aids;
> - empty lounges too remote from the central areas for residents with limited mobility;
> - overcrowded dayrooms where the only possible furniture arrangement is a circle of chairs round the perimeter of the room;
> - residents eating off trays in lounges because dining rooms are too small or inaccessible;
> - toilets near the main dayrooms with inadequate screening;
> - insufficient space for staff to assist residents walking around the home, in bathrooms and toilets;
> - identical or similar bedroom corridors which are disorienting to the staff as well as to residents;
> - fire escape stairs used as storage areas (particularly for wheelchairs);
> - a group of exiled smokers (residents and staff) round the service entrance;
> - old people sitting in uncomfortable draughts at the front door in order to see something going on;
> - en-suite toilets which do not get used because they are too small.

(Torrington, 1996, p 2)

Dementia-friendly environments

Torrington based her understanding of P–E interaction for people with particular limitations on detailed observations regarding lighting, acoustics, how colour schemes aid orientation and ways to reinforce reality, recognising issues that are dementia friendly. She notes particular issues that are summarised here:

- 'Experts in the field advocate small homes for 30 or at the most 40 residents organized in family groups.'
- 'Groups may be segregated according the severity of their condition.'
- 'People with dementia behave in a way which involves risk to themselves and to others.'
- 'The attitude towards risk needs to be addressed at the outset; it has consequences for all aspects of the building design, from the choice of ironmongery to design of landscape and enclosure.'
- 'As the disease progresses memory failures become very marked.'
- 'Successful therapies for dementia sufferers can relate to reinforcement of the familiar.'
- 'Clarity of form and layout and good visibility are important. This is not particularly easy to achieve in a large residential building.'

(Torrington, 1996, pp 12–20)

In subsequent years, Torrington's guidance was extended through research with colleagues at Sheffield University concerning the relationship between building design (residential care homes, extra care housing, domestic housing) and quality of life (see Chapters 5 and 7). Design in Caring Environments research funded by the EPSRC EQUAL programme (Barnes, 2002, Barnes et al, 2012) saw the development of the Sheffield Care Environment Assessment Matrix, where 11 user-related domains measure the physical environment. Through research in 38 care homes it was possible to identify underused spaces, spatial confusion and barriers to activity. Significant positive associations were seen between aspects of the built environment, such as accessibility to the garden, resident choice, control and quality of life, while this was not the case in buildings seen as risk averse through a concentration on health and safety (Parker et al, 2004, p 957). Supporting good links with the community also enhanced well-being (Torrington, 2006) – a point made by Evans (2009a, 2009b) regarding ECH in Chapter 7. Judith Torrington was a member of the HAPPI panel for innovation contributing to the design issues for specialised housing outlined in Chapter 5, and as noted earlier, the HAPPI design principles have been extended with regard to housing for people with dementia (Twyford and Porteus, 2021).

Internationally, qualitative research regarding P–E interaction for people with cognitive impairment provides further evidence of positive outcomes for residents and staff living and working in specific environments. For example, researchers in Northern Ireland, Scotland and Canada have indicated the value of access to outdoor spaces and way-finding aids that enable a greater level of autonomy (Innes et al, 2011; Chaudhury and Cooke, 2014). Positive aspects of design are central to Davis et al's (2009) work, which considers everyday experiences for seven people with dementia living in different therapeutic environments, showing how they can be active participants rather than just recipients of care.

Alongside this work, multidisciplinary centres of excellence in dementia-friendly design and ways of living have developed. The early and ongoing work of the University of Stirling, based at the Iris Murdoch Dementia Services Development Centre, is recognised globally as a centre of research, offering a range of information, guidance, a library, hints for householders, consultancy advice for new design and retrofit. Their website has a virtual care home, which demonstrates features that will make a difference for people with dementia who may also have additional sensory, visual and mobility problems. The environment is seen as less stressful, and more secure, with potential for minimising falls and incontinence, enabling wayfinding through engaging signage (see Marshall, 2001; DSDC, 2011, 2021). Additional sources of information are also found via the King's Fund Centre, the Alzheimer's Society and the Housing LIN (see Glossary). While this research and guidance aims to influence new design for dementia-friendly buildings, similarities are seen in Maggie's centres and hospice environments where collaboration with expert users shows how architects take into account nature, privacy, spatial experience and homeliness (Worpole, 2010; Van der Linden et al, 2016; Park and Porteus, 2019). Maggie's centres do not replace conventional cancer treatment, but they are models of good practice that are creatively designed by key architects (Maggie's, n.d.).

Quality in care homes – the impact of regulation

While the value of being a therapeutic environment is clear, the need to protect the health and safety of frail adults is also recognised. This tension is central to care homes as regulated settings, with implications for quality of life and quality of care. A system of regulation, through registration and inspection, for group care services has emerged across the last century. As noted earlier, in England and Wales registration began in relation to private sector nursing homes, then voluntary providers, before moving to public provision (Department of Health and Welsh Office, 1990). Figure 8.3 outlines the development of care home regulation in England across almost a century of legislation, codes of practice and organisation, indicating the powers of central government, which devolved to local government and more recently to executive non-departmental public bodies. In 1975, the regulation of nursing homes and mental nursing homes merged, and gradually issues were defined such as the qualifications and residency of the 'person in charge' and the level and qualification of nursing staff (Health Service Act 1980). As Peace (2003) notes:

> All nursing homes had to be in the charge of either a registered medical practitioner, or qualified nurse ... where a nurse was in charge of the home, they had to be a registered nurse and health authorities were able to determine staffing levels given the number and types of patients within particular homes. (p 31)

The NHS and Community Care Act 1990 integrated residential care and nursing homes regulation. Until then, the registration and inspection of residential care was undertaken by local authority-based 'arm's length' registration and inspection teams. Kellaher et al (1988) carried out the only study of this system, funded by Joseph Rowntree Trust, and this resulted in the training module 'Making sense of inspection' (Department of Health and Welsh Office, 1990), in which the centrality of the service user was developed.

The central significance of quality of life and quality of care was developed through Codes of Practice (Figure 8.3b); first for residential care homes in 'Home life' (1984) sponsored by DHSS and then updated for all settings in 'A better home life' (1996), taking into account the work of the National Association of Health Authorities by the Centre for Policy on Ageing that hosted advisory groups chaired by Kina, Lady Avebury. The principles of good practice were underpinned by personal rights to:

- fulfilment;
- dignity;
- autonomy;
- individuality;
- esteem;
- quality of experience;
- understanding of emotional needs;
- risk and choice that would maintain quality of life.

The Care Standards Act 2000 replaced the Registered Homes Act 1984, removing responsibility for regulation from local authorities and setting up the National Care Standards Commission (NCSC) from 2002, leading to the Commission for Social Care Inspection (CSCI) – non-departmental public bodies (Figure 8.3c). The Codes of Practice were influential in the development of the National Minimum Standards for Care Homes for Older People (Department of Health, 2003), introduced by CSCI and already noted in relation to design issues.

There were 38 standards related to seven key topics that were seen as achievable outcomes that related to aspects of quality of life:

Figure 8.3: The regulation of care homes (residential and nursing): legislation, codes of practice, regulators

---

(a) Legislation

Residential care homes	Nursing homes
	Nursing Homes Registration Act 1927
National Assistance Act 1948	Public Health Act 1936
Mental Health Act 1959	Mental Health Act 1959 (beginning of regulation for mental nursing homes)
	Nursing Homes Act 1963
	Nursing Homes Act 1975
Residential Homes Act 1980	Health Services Act 1980
Health and Social Services and Social Security Adjudications Act 1983	Health and Social Services and Social Security Adjudications Act 1983
Registered Homes Act 1984	

NHS and Community Care 1990
Sections 42–45,46,47,48 relate to the LA's use of voluntary and private organizations to provide welfare services; protection for people already using these services as LA's develop and assess people for community care services. Also, initial development of inspection for community care services alongside the care home sector.

The Care Standards Act 2000

The Health And Social Care (Community Health and Standards) Act 2003

Health And Social Care Act 2008

Regulated Activities Regulations, 2014

The Care Act 2014

Note: Major legislation in bold alongside contributing legislation

(b) Codes of Practice

Residential care homes

Home Life: A Code of Practice for Residential Care. Report of a Working Party sponsored by the DHSS and convened by the Centre for Policy on Ageing under the Chairmanship of Kina, Lady Avebury. CPA 1984

Nursing homes

A Handbook on the Registration and Inspection of Nursing Homes (1990) – National Association of Health Authorities. London

Care homes (merged residential care and nursing homes)

A Better Home Life: A Code of Practice for Residential and Nursing Home Care. (1996) Centre for Policy on Ageing, London

Care Homes for Older People: National Minimum Standards. Care Home Regulations (Department of Health, 2003). First published in 2001. Third impression 2006

(c) Regulators

Local Authority based Registration and Inspection teams (from 1984 to 1999)

Social Services Inspectorate (SSI)

National Care Standards Commission (NCSC) (2002–2003)

Commission for Social Care Inspection (CSCI) created by the **Health and Social Care (Community Health and Standards) Act 2003**; launched in 2004 as a single inspectorate for social care in England. CSCI combined the work of:

Social Services Inspectorate (SSI)

SSI/Audit Commission Joint Review Team

The National Care Standards Commission (NCSC)

CSCI established a new system of **national minimum standards** for all residential and nursing homes, and domiciliary services alongside The Care Home Regulations, 2001 (Department of Health, 2003).

Care Quality Commission operating since April 2009 was set up as a single integrated regulator for England's health and adult social care services through the **Health and Social Care Act 2008** replacing the following three bodies:

Healthcare Commission

Commission for Social Care Inspection (CSCI)

Mental Health Act Commission

Source: Adapted and extended Module 3, p 19. DHSS (1990); Centre for Policy on Ageing (1996); Peace, 2003; Johnson, et al 2010; CQC, n.d.)

- choice of care home (1–6);
- health and personal care (7–11);
- daily life and social activities (12–15);
- complaints and protection (16–18);
- environment (19–26);
- staffing (27–30);
- management and administration (31–8).

CSCI argued that the standards were qualitative but measurable, and that all issues needed to be met in order for the registered setting to meet compliance. They emphasised the need to 'maintain and promote independence wherever possible, through rehabilitation and community support' (Department of Health, 2003, p x). Each standard was justified through a statement of good practice that was seen as the intended outcome.

In light of Laing's comment concerning morbidity and mortality regarding current care home residency, here we consider NMS 11 regarding death and dying, found in the section devoted to health and personal care (Department of Health, 2003, pp 6–12) (see Appendix 2). This had the following outcome: 'Service users are assured that at the time of their death, staff will treat them and their family with care, sensitivity and respect.' This standard was considered by Froggatt (2007) in research that involved the content analysis of 352 inspection reports undertaken by NCSC for 226 care homes in South Yorkshire, England in 2002–03. She analysed findings regarding Standard 11 in comparison with WHO (2002) principles of palliative care and other UK palliative care policy documents (National Council for Hospice and Specialist Palliative Care Services, 2002; National Institute for Clinical Excellence, 2004). While many of the areas regarding physical, social, psychological and spiritual needs were covered by all parties, WHO (2002) regards dying as a 'normal' process. Froggatt comments:

> There is also no mention in the Standards of the balance to be kept between life and death, as prescribed in the WHO principles, which state that death is to be 'neither hastened not postponed'. The time-frame for palliative care is much longer in the WHO principles, where its applicability at an earlier stage of illness is recognized, though Standard 11 recognizes the process of deterioration (11.9). (Froggatt, 2007, pp 237–9)

In developing an argument for greater acknowledgement of openness regarding death and dying, Froggatt (2007), recognising the structural, cultural and staffing environments of care homes, shows how 'the regulated death' positioned in inspection reports through consultation, where communication with a dying resident may be difficult, observation (which may not occur) and records, offers a particular perspective and a different view than the one given through palliative care in the wider research literature (see Komaromy et al, 2000; Katz, 2003; Mathie et al, 2012). She closes her early discussion by stating that 'all care in care-homes is end-of-life care' and, importantly, that 'the standards of care outlined ... are applicable regardless of whether an individual is known to be dying or not' (Froggatt, 2007, p 245), views developed in more recent European research (Froggatt et al, 2017).

The relationship between ageing, dying and environmental context is complex, and raises the issues of social imaginaries of place and ethics of care that are discussed in Chapter 1. There are parallels here with regulated hospice environments, giving supportive and pain free care to people in the last six months of their lives, focusing on comfort and quality of life, so every day can be fulfilled to personal capacity whether at home, as a day visitor, in respite or as an in-patient. Privacy and dignity are central to the philosophy of palliative and hospice care, and enabling spiritual expression is also recognised (Gerry, 2011). Additionally, the 30 Maggie's centres (including three in Hong Kong, Barcelona and Tokyo), offering free practical, emotional and social support for people with cancer and their family and friends, are noted as therapeutic environments, and are not regulated by the CQC.

During the period of Froggatt's initial research, the CSCI oversaw care home regulation. The Care Quality Commission (CQC) took over from CSCI in

2009, forming the current independent regulator of Health and Social Care in England that ensures the quality and safety of care in various settings including care homes, and the care given in people's own homes (CQC, n.d., 2016, 2021a). Through registration, they assess that proprietors are appropriately qualified, and have sufficient staff with the right skills, qualifications and experience. The size, layout and design of premises needs to be suitable, and policies, systems and procedures should be effective in terms of management and decision-making. For care homes, the number of inspections undertaken each year varies depending on ongoing ratings as outstanding, good, requires improvement, inadequate. For outstanding and good homes this may be every 30 months, while others may be inspected every 12 or 6 months.

In March 2021, the CQC website indicated that while topics found in the NMS are still addressed, they aim to maintain the following fundamental standards to which everyone has a right:

- Person-centred care
- Dignity and respect
- Consent
- Safety
- Safeguarding from abuse
- Food and drink
- Premises and equipment
- Complaints
- Good Governance
- Staffing
- Fit and Proper Staff
- Duty of Candour
- Display of Ratings

(CQC, 2021a)

The focus of inspection across all settings considers:

- Are they safe?
- Are they effective?
- Are they caring?
- Are they responsive to people's needs?
- Are they well-led?

Each of these areas lead to different lines of inquiry. For example, 'Are they effective?' considers how care, treatment and support achieves outcomes that maintain quality of life. The inspection process includes both comprehensive and focused inspections, collecting a range of data through discussion with service users, family and friends, staff, managers and other professionals, observations of everyday life and consideration of local information, written policy and records. For care homes, a single inspector and an 'expert by experience' (person who has either been or cared for a service user) visit the home unannounced. Service ratings are given for the five areas of questioning, and following feedback the care home develops an action plan addressing particular issues. These points are monitored through the more focused inspection, which can be unannounced. Inspection reports and ratings are available for the public to review through the CQC website (CQC, n.d.).

For other settings such as small care homes (up to four residents), supported living schemes and ECH, inspections are sometimes announced so that the relevant staff and people using the service are available. Hospice services will have both unannounced and announced visits, also dependent on staffing issues. In addition, the CQC produces a wide range of publications addressing issues such as inequalities in end-of-life care (CQC, 2016) and developing shared innovation in health and social care homes (CQC, n.d.). Owing to the COVID-19 pandemic, which has seen an increase in mortality among care home residents (Burton et al, 2020), CQC discontinued inspections in March 2020 and adopted a transitional regulatory approach). During the summer 2021, a consultation was taking place regarding future regulation procedures (CQC, 2021a, 2021b).

The regulation of communal living indicates the importance of recognising the care home as an environment where a range of people live, die, work and visit. Yet it is also a place where for the resident 'individual needs and preferences should not be overwhelmed by institutional or organisational forces' (Department of Health and Welsh Office, 1990, p 67). In the late 1990s, Peace and Holland (2001b) carried out a pilot study of small registered care homes with up to four residents within three English counties. Although this category was a minority of care homes, the authors demonstrated how they presented a hybrid between informality and formality, domestic and institutional. More recently, in an Australian discussion of the impact of living in a regulated care setting for people with dementia, Carr and Biggs (2020) develop a valuable continuum approach, showing how levels of regulatory intensity vary between standards surrounding medication to practices regarding food and daily routines, indicating that flexibility in care practice is possible within a regulatory framework that appears reductionist. The issue of regulation in specialised housing (with care) was introduced in Chapter 7, and the impact of living in regulated settings reappears at the end of this chapter following discussion of more recent care home research.

Care home research

Over time, international research concerning care home experience, policy and practice has been substantial. To consider the current research agenda, a literature review of refereed journal articles from 2010 onwards was undertaken by Gopinath (August 2019) and updated by Peace (October 2020), using the keywords 'care homes', 'residential', 'nursing', 'quality of life', 'residents', 'person-centred care', 'admission', 'family', 'environment' to search the Google Scholar database and the journal *Ageing & Society*. This located 163 refereed journal articles – international (66), UK (97) – and even though there were overlapping issues, the main topics identified through content analysis were:

- quality of life (32);
- transition to care home from community home or hospital (26);
- abuse in care homes (25);
- LTC policy (18);
- person/relationship-centred care (including medical/occupational therapy practice, and end-of-life care) (17);
- characteristics of care home residents (including health) (17);
- family and care homes (16);
- issues of design and outdoor environments (9);
- miscellaneous (research agenda, climate change, media and stereotyping) (3).

As of January 2021, further searches revealed more than 20 articles concerning COVID-19 and UK care homes that have contributed to discussion in Chapter 10 yet not included in this analysis. Findings from this limited review consider transitions to care home living taking into account social relationships and self-identity, care practice, quality of life and abuse/mistreatment. Certain publications have already been discussed in relation to LTC, design and outdoor environments, while papers concerning UK care home residents confirm characteristics already reported (see Johnson et al, 2010; Gordon et al, 2013; Cook et al, 2015; Zubair et al, 2017), with the exception of more recent discussion regarding older LGBT+ residents, the heterosexualised milieu of residential care homes and the impact of this on practice (Westwood, 2016; Willis et al, 2016; Simpson et al, 2018). Further papers contribute to reflections on the meaning of home.

More than two thirds of publications regarding *transitions* relate to discharge from hospital to care home. Here, policy development, practice issues and family involvement are commonly discussed. Various stakeholders are involved in discharge planning from hospital settings (Mitchell et al, 2010; Waring et al, 2014), as well as the assessment of needs for those moving from the community (Johnson and Bibbo, 2014). In the UK, changes to care home capacity, hospital 'bed-blocking' by those waiting to be discharged, and the impact on health economics and personal finance are discussed (Gaughhan et al, 2015). Authors report positive effect on personal well-being through involvement in decision-making and greater acceptance of care home living

(Brownie et al, 2014; Johnson and Bibbo, 2014), impacting on re-establishing self through the personalisation of space (van Hoof et al, 2016).

Where the person has dementia, decision-making and choice over transition can be limited (Emmett et al, 2014). Koppitz et al (2017) report that in many developed industrial countries, people aged 85 and over may find themselves 'relocated involuntarily', with 43 per cent in Switzerland admitted to nursing homes after hospital discharge, a figure stated as higher than in the US. In contrast, Ray et al (2015), through their own literature review, consider planned care transitions and seek to develop a guide for best practice.

The contribution of *social relationships* with spouse/partners, children and other members across rural and urban locations in this transition is seen across the international literature (Sussman and Dupuis, 2012; Ryan and Mckenna, 2013). Many older care home residents with dementia will have lived at home with their spouse/partner. In recent years, couples living apart but remaining together through visiting has become more common (Høgsnes et al, 2014; Gopinath et al, 2018). Biographical knowledge of the person with dementia and the value of maintaining relationships is discussed. At the same time, visitors will have ongoing views on the quality of care being received, which could be used as a monitoring role (Emmett et al, 2014).

For older residents, qualitative research indicates the impact of this transition on *self-identity* (Thein et al, 2011; Naess et al, 2016) through the loss of usual routines, treasured belongings and social networks, and the importance of care practice that recognises socio-cultural identity, especially when living with dementia. Lee et al (2013), through interviews with eight older adults (65–97) who had been living in a residential setting for three months to a year, revealed through narrative analysis feelings of uncertainty and confidence over maintaining levels of control and assertiveness. The authors comment on the need for staff to have greater understanding of residents' life histories to enable the maintenance of self-identity aspects through more person-centred care, nurtured by talking, listening and reminiscing. As Willemse et al (2014) indicate, this may relate to positive changes in staff job satisfaction in a smaller setting. This is also where family members could act as go-betweens, communicating with care staff about health, everyday routines, personal habits, likes and dislikes (see Bauer et al, 2014; Dorrell and Sundin, 2016). This is associated with the concept of connectedness proposed by Cooney et al (2014).

In contrast, Paddock et al (2019), through qualitative case studies across three care homes over 12 months, show how able residents react to their ongoing sense of ageing within an environment where independence and personal autonomy are restricted and collective routines deny the expression of their diverse personalities. The researchers discuss how residents without dementia may use social comparison to those with dementia as an adaptive strategy to reflect on self. This important finding relates to the concern seen in specialised housing (with care), where more vulnerable residents could be stigmatised by others. The proportions of people with different needs across settings may make forms of social comparison more or less likely. Finally, Hafford-Letchfield et al (2020) discuss the concept of 'giving up' with care staff, and how they respond to a person's withdrawal from everyday living, focusing on loss and willing death with the potential for depression or self-harm. They comment on using distraction and their knowledge of the person to recognise moods, carrying out functional care tasks rather than being able to offer end-of-life care and recognising their need for training and support.

Issues relating to the *quality of life* and the psychological well-being of residents dominate papers in this research review across a wide range of topics, including: mealtimes, food and nutrition, use of Information Technology, sexual intimacy and sexuality, healthcare and over-medication, spirituality, experience of leisure activities and end-of-life care, each with a concern as to how person-centred needs are identified and responded to (see Fernadez-Mayoralas et al, 2015; Smit et al, 2016). Discussion is also given to developing a household model of care encouraging domestic activities for people with dementia (Morgan-Brown et al, 2013) and how the WHO active ageing concept can be transferred to residential long term care (Van Malderen et al, 2013).

Discussion continues regarding *care practice* and the importance of relational work to recognise the need for cultural change, ongoing support and investment. Nolan and colleagues extend their debate regarding the Senses Framework by reflecting on compassionate *relationship-centred care* that embraces security, belonging, continuity, purpose, achievement and significance for older people, their families and care staff within LTC and acute hospital environments (Nolan and Allan, 2012; Dewar and Nolan, 2013; Brown Wilson et al, 2013). INTERACT, conducted by the My Home Life North East network in England (see Glossary), a care home practice development network, encourages meaningful relationships on a daily basis through social connections, interactions and communication (Cook and Clarke, 2010), to prevent social isolation within a communal setting through visual, hearing and cognitive impairments.

Finally, the *abuse or mistreatment* of older residents and staff – physical, medicinal, social, psychological, financial, and heightened where people with dementia are involved (see Bennett et al, 1997) – sadly continues as a strong research theme. Burns et al comment that 'institutional abuse is a global issue' (2013, p 514) and Stevens et al (2013) report how UK examination of the mistreatment of older people has been growing since the 1990s (also see Biggs, 1996; Biggs and Haapala, 2010), with specific scandals in LTC settings. Twenty-five publications were identified that offer theoretical, conceptual and empirical responses to why abuse takes place, identifying how residents can suffer 'recurring neglect, mistreatment and loss of dignity' (Burns et al, 2013, p 526). Four papers focus on resident-to-resident abuse, with Backhouse et al, 2018 discussing how care-home staff manage dementia-related behaviours such as aggression or agitation that put the individual, other residents and staff themselves at risk. Other authors offer perspectives from family and staff, and indicate changes to practice.

Two publications outlining theoretical perspectives analyse empirical material from national studies of abuse and neglect in institutional care in the UK. First, Burns et al (2013) adopt Grint's conceptualisation of 'wicked', 'tame' and 'crisis' problems (Grint, 2005) through comparative case studies across eight care homes involving mixed methodologies. One example shows how greater menu choice – seen as good practice – extended the time taken by care staff at mealtimes, leading to toileting issues after lunch, as outlined here:

'After lunch is a particular example of high demand. Everybody wants the toilet but there are only three staff and there are 20 residents, so somebody's got to wait. Somebody's got to be last. But everybody's like, "Oh, I need to go now" and that's a really stressful time.' (Ruby, care worker) (Burns et al, 2013, p 523)

Issues of staffing, environment (toilet on first floor, restaurant ground floor, one lift that will only accommodate one wheelchair user) and management concern for developing good quality care that will meet inspection standards are all discussed here. Their immediate solution may be seen as 'tame' in trying to reduce the immediate issue rather than confront the 'wicked' problem, where interconnecting factors create further stress in care processes.

The second perspective comes from Stevens et al (2013), who utilise positioning theory (Sabat, 2008) and interactionist approaches to consider mistreatment in LTC settings. Through examination of research involving people with dementia and care workers, they show how different forms of communication – language, eye contact, gestures, tones of voice – are used to develop meaning and storylines to understand everyday interactions when some people are seen as 'not worthy of interaction' and the organisational culture leads to negative positioning.

Such research indicates how the complexity of P–E interactions contributes to forms of practice within communal settings.

This brief snapshot of current literature focuses on empirical work within individual settings where quality of care and quality of life are central to understanding how levels of institutionalisation persist, encouraged through attitudes that deny how a lack of resources impacts on staffing, training and infrastructure, preventing true personalisation and relationship-centred ways of being for residents, their families and staff. This issue is central to the development of LTC for the oldest members of society, bringing the individual and the communal together in what is a true test of creating P–E relationships, where partnership working and end-of-life care are part of daily living.

Reflecting on home: the lens of the care home

Certain factors have emerged as common to the current care home environment: residents are predominantly people in their mid-80s or older; a high percentage are living with cognitive impairment and/or a chronic health condition and will experience end-of-life care. They are individuals no longer part of a domestic home. In recognising the concerns of authors such as Gilleard and Higgs (2010, 2013), for people in very old age living in settings perceived poorly by many, we should reconsider the perspective taken earlier on the meaning of home in a care home. The research review shows that many residents have moved to a care home from hospital, with others having relocated from community-based or specialised housing. They come to live in a communal setting that offers accommodation for around 20 to 80 people, or more, where their personal space is commonly a single room, either with or without en-suite facilities, and daily routines involve the use of a range of public spaces. While the number of male residents has increased over time, the environment is dominated by women, both as residents and staff. Design varies, with more or less accessibility to internal and external spaces – gardens and the wider community. Some people living with dementia may move to a separate special unit within a larger setting. As has been seen, these are also regulated settings – living and working environments – where the provision of care is central, and staff aim to address individual needs and aspirations within the collective nature of their routines. Family members and other friends are commonly welcome and play an important role in the continuity of social relationships. As discussed in Chapter 10, the recent experience of the COVID-19 pandemic has challenged these interactions.

With this scenario in mind, it would be surprising if residents did not, or had not, reconsidered their understanding of the meaning of home in this transition; yet it is an under-researched area. Oswald and Wahl (2005) have drawn attention to the physical, social, behavioural, cognitive and emotional features of home in later life that are central to this changing context, with Chaudhury and Oswald (2019) (as seen in Chapter 2) focusing on issues of agency, identity, belonging and autonomy in their recent discussion of P–E exchange. Rowles and Watkins (2003) comment that when some older people relocate they engage with a new place through the reinstatement of routines and habits that may need adjustment, while others note the importance of objects, furniture and other possessions in re-establishing self in personal space (Sherman and Dacher, 2005; van Hoof et al, 2016; Lovatt, 2018).

Here, five studies concerned with redefining home in nursing and care homes are drawn on to explore these themes. Johnson and Bibbo (2014) use an interpretive phenomenological approach to learn from eight older adults who recently moved into American nursing homes who are also interviewed two months later. Findings show that control over the decision to move was central to initial feelings of loss over previous home and possessions, their ability to maintain autonomy, how they reconstructed a sense of home and how they adjusted to different ways of living. The authors show how different people acknowledged their need for care with different levels of acceptance, with some seeing their care home as a place for end of life (2014, p 59). In adjusting to living in the nursing home, the authors comment on the dichotomy between safety and what they call 'restricted living', where the control by staff may prove limiting.

Over time, respondents have adapted to this new environment in different ways. Some still find it difficult to eat or sleep, while others are adjusting to a lifestyle where they recognise more clearly that the importance of 'being cared for' and 'interpersonal interactions' sit alongside 'safety' and 'restricted living'. The authors state: 'home was no longer expressed as a desired ideal to return to … but as a place where individual autonomy could be expressed' (2014, p 61). While some will never see the nursing home as 'home', others who feel they have made the right choice report satisfaction. This research confirms the work of Hammer (1999), in which place, possessions, safety and autonomy are key issues in the redefinition of home. While people have come to accept the nursing home as their accommodation, some would like more private space. The duality of safety and autonomy also remains important, yet the 'rules and processes' of the nursing home do not facilitate autonomy seen as central to personal adjustment (2014, p 62). On reflection, the researchers call for further longitudinal research and more explicit questioning on the meaning of home.

This research has similarities to that of Cooney (2011) in Ireland, which aims to understand older people's perceptions of 'finding a home' in LTC settings through qualitative research in seven diverse health and care environments. Here a larger (N=61) purposive sample of able residents is interviewed over time, and through thematic analysis four areas emerge as central: continuity, preserving personal identity, belonging, and being active and working. There are slightly different perceptions among what appear to be more active participants, which may also indicate cultural difference. Issues of continuity in terms of routines and habits alongside the importance of preserving identity are similar, while belonging relates to group experience of comradeship and activities to levels of participation. The researcher usefully discusses how mediating factors such as life experiences and contextual factors such as the physical or social environment can facilitate or constrain resident adjustment. There is a certain mutuality linked to ways of defining quality of life in care settings (see Kellaher, 2000; Cooney et al, 2014).

Later, in a British study, Kenkmann et al (2017) build on *Private Lives in Public Places* (Willcocks et al, 1987) through five in-depth case studies of care homes. They consider how residents and staff experience the duality of the care home as living and working environments. Here, we focus on their analysis regarding the discourse of home. There is no common view as to how care homes equate with the 'domestic home'. They report: 'residents were more likely to refer to their rooms as "home", but not to the home as a whole' (p 13), even though there is attachment to the place where 'a sense of community existed' (p 13). In the main, community refers to both external group identity through personal relationships, friendships, particular staff and joint activities. Where a care home has spare capacity in terms of internal communal areas, residents report a degree of ownership of both public and private spaces, giving greater choice over interaction with others from both inside and outside the home, making the boundary more fluid. In contrast, staff do not consider the residents' discourse on home; for them it is a place of work. 'A good home' is compared with other care homes, and related to effective teamwork and a friendly atmosphere' (p 14). For some staff, the meaning of a homely place means more person-centred care, where residents have more choice over issues such as 'time to get up' or 'have breakfast'.

Finally, Wada et al (2020) in Western Canada discuss the perception of home by residents, family members and care staff before and after a move is made from two older and more institutional LTC settings to one new and more home-like 260-bed facility divided into 13 units of 20 resident rooms. This involves an ambitious qualitative methodology, with 210 interviews carried out over a two-year timeline before and after relocation. The findings show how differences in the physical environment can underpin issues regarding privacy, personalisation, autonomy, choice and flexibility, as well as degrees of connectedness and togetherness. Moving to a physical environment with more spacious communal areas and larger bedrooms with en-suite bathrooms, absent from previous settings, offers greater opportunity for personalisation and privacy. Some residents say it feels more like a 'hotel' than a home. Staff can see advantages of the move from the residents' perspective, and they are changing work practices to offer greater flexibility over some daily living routines such as time of 'getting up' and 'meal availability'.

The new physical environment facilitates greater social engagement with family and friends, although this relocation prevents continuity with former familiar staff and residents. The move also sees less interaction between

Figure 8.4: Reflecting on the meaning of home: the lens of the care home

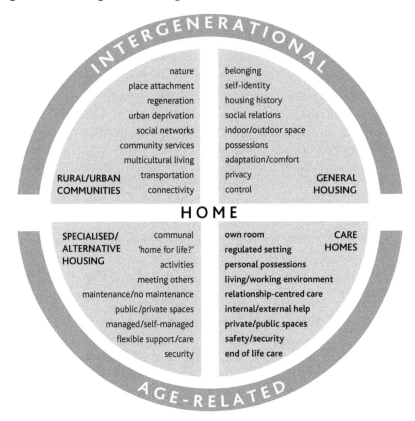

residents and staff, and limited activities are provided in the new setting. This is partly because of a shortage of staff, who are more commonly committed to certain professional care tasks, and the authors conclude that 'combining the requirements of both care and home in a single physical space creates tension and requires unique negotiations between residents and staff' (2020, p 1287). They suggest that in future innovative technology may facilitate changes in lifestyle.

Alongside these useful findings, thoughts on how a care home resident considers the meaning of home return us to the Environment and Identity study (Peace et al, 2006), in which, through environmental biographies, participants are always 'pacing the self' in terms of where they want to live:

> They may think about their futures but defer action. While they are not waiting for a crisis to occur and make that decision for them, they also realize that relocation to 'special' housing will make them 'special' and in the main this is not what they want. However the rhetoric of 'being a burden' to family members often hangs over people and for some

it may also foreshadow end-of-life care. Throughout this discussion we are aware of tensions between issues of security, companionship, autonomy, frailty, dependence, independence. Sometimes personal identity may be affected by stereotypes attached to places such as care homes. (2006, p 157)

For these reasons a combination of self-identity, acknowledged life history, embodied vulnerability, continuing relationships with valued others, levels of personal agency and individual philosophy all contribute to how 'home' can be redefined within a care home.

The acceptance of delegated autonomy for certain activities of daily living enables different forms of attachment between people and place, influenced by factors displayed in the final part of Figure 8.4 that relate to physical, social and psychological aspects of environment where the individual recognises self in place which may, or may not, be internalised as home. We return to the meaning of home across time and environments in Chapter 10.

Conclusions

This chapter has addressed the complexity of care home living in the UK from historical development to the current characteristics of this environment for residents and staff. A regulated setting, this is both a living and working environment that can lead to restrictions in everyday life, both personal and communal, where P–E interaction is pivotal. In looking at the current research literature, it is apparent that concerns about developing a life of quality while avoiding issues that may lead to abusive practice are ongoing. This is an environment of ageing that cares for many people living with dementia and/or other health conditions until the end of their lives, and recognising this experience as part of a personal biography within a broader relational history is fundamental. While research has been central to this analysis, in Chapter 9 methodological developments in environmental gerontology come to the fore, aiming to show the value of participatory and interdisciplinary working in this field.

Appendix 1

DoH (2003)

Environment

Individual accommodation: space requirements

OUTCOME
Service users' own rooms suit their needs

STANDARD 23

23.1 The home provides accommodation for each service user which meets minimum space as follows:

23.2 In all new build, extensions and first time registrations, all places are provided in single rooms with a minimum of 12 sq metres usable floor-space (excluding en-suite facilities).

23.3 Pre-existing care homes, with rooms which provided at least 10 sq metres of useable space for each service user as at 16 August 2002, continue to provide that amount of space in those rooms. Pre-existing care homes with rooms which did not provide that amount of space as at that date, provide at least the same useable floor space in those rooms as they provided as at 31 March 2002.

23.4 Single rooms accommodating wheelchair users have at least 12 sq metres usable floor space (excluding en-suite facilities).

23.5 Room dimensions and layout options ensure that there is room on either side of the bed, to enable access for carers and any equipment needed.

23.6 Where rooms are shared, they are occupied by no more than two service users who have made a positive choice to share with each other.

23.7 When a shared place becomes vacant, the remaining service user has the opportunity to choose not to share, by moving into a different room if necessary.

23.8 Rooms which are currently shared have at least 16 sq metres of usable floor space (excluding en-suite facilities).

23.9 In new build, extensions and all first time registrations, service users wishing to share accommodation are offered two single rooms for use, for example, as bedroom and sitting room.

23.10 Pre-existing care homes, which provided at least 80 per cent of places in single rooms as at 16 August 2002 continue to do so. Where they did not provide that percentage of places in single rooms as at that date, they provide at least the same percentage of places in single rooms as they provided as at 31 March 2002.

Environment

Individual accommodation: furniture and fittings

OUTCOME
Service users live in safe, comfortable bedrooms with their own possessions around them.

STANDARD 24
24.1 The home provides private accommodation for each service user which is furnished and equipped to assure comfort and privacy, and meets the assessed needs of the service user.
24.2 In the absence of service users' own provision, furnishings for individual rooms are provided to the minimum as follows:

- a clean comfortable bed, minimum 900mm wide, at a suitable, safe height for the
- service user, and bedlinen;
- curtains or blinds;
- mirror;
- overhead and bedside lighting;
- comfortable seating for two people;
- drawers and enclosed space for hanging clothes;
- at least 2 accessible double electric sockets;
- a table to sit at and a bed-side table;
- wash–hand basin (unless en-suite wc and whb provided).

24.3 Adjustable beds are provided for service users receiving nursing care.
24.4 The service user's room is carpeted or equivalent.
24.5 Doors to service users' private accommodation are fitted with locks suited to service users' capabilities and accessible to staff in emergencies.
24.6 Service users are provided with keys unless their risk assessment suggests otherwise.
24.7 Each service user has lockable storage space for medication, money and valuables and is provided with the key which he or she can retain (unless the reason for not doing so is explained in the care plan).
24.8 Screening is provided in double rooms to ensure privacy for personal care.
(Department of Health, 2003, pp 24–5)

Appendix 2

DoH (2003)
Death and Dying

Standard 11

OUTCOME
Service users are assured that at the time of their death, staff will treat them and their family with care, sensitivity and respect.

STANDARD 11

11.1 Care and comfort are given to service users who are dying, their death is handled with dignity and propriety, and their spiritual needs, rites and functions observed.

11.2 Care staff make every effort to ensure that the service user receives appropriate attention and pain relief.

11.3 The service user's wishes concerning terminal care and arrangements after death are discussed and carried out.

11.4 The service user's family and friends are involved (if that is what the service user wants) in planning for and dealing with increasing infirmity, terminal illness and death.

11.5 The privacy and dignity of the service user who is dying are maintained at all times.

11.6 Service users are able to spend their final days in their own rooms, surrounded by their personal belongings, unless there are strong medical reasons to prevent this.

11.7 The registered person ensures that staff and service users who wish to offer comfort to a service user who is dying are enabled and supported to do so.

11.8 Palliative care, practical assistance and advice, and bereavement counselling are provided by trained professionals /specialist agencies if the service user wishes.

11.9 The changing needs of service users with deteriorating conditions or dementia – for personal support or technical aids – are reviewed and met swiftly to ensure the individual retains maximum control.

11.10 Relatives and friends of a service user who is dying are able to stay with him/her, unless the service user makes it clear that he or she does not want them to, for as long as they wish.

11.11 The body of a service user who has died is handled with dignity, and time is allowed for family and friends to pay their respects.

11.12 Policies and procedures for handling dying and death are in place and observed by staff.

(Department of Health, 2003, pp 11–12)

9

Methodological development

Introduction

This chapter returns to considering the ways in which environmental gerontologists address key issues. Although the earlier discussion of theoretical development in Chapter 2 did not detail a methodological approach, we are drawn here to the qualitative work of Gubrium, Rowles, Rubinstein and de Mederios, for example, who have developed ethnographic methods and phenomenological approaches that help us to understand the minute detail of everyday living in later life. Like other gerontologists in this field such as Oswald, Wahl, Chaudhury, Golant, Bernard and Burholt, the current author has experience of mixed methods research, in which in-depth perspectives can be viewed within a bigger picture. This may include innovative measurement and the triangulation of data in analysis (see Kellaher et al, 1990; Mertens and Hess-Biber, 2012).

In addition, the approach to research here has been influenced by the author's colleagues at The Open University (OU) who have expertise in biographical studies, oral history and autobiographical writing (Johnson, 1978; Atkinson and Williams, 1990; Bornat, 1994, 2001; Holland, 2001; Bytheway, 2009, 2011). While these methods emerged through social history and sociology (Chamberlayne et al, 2000; Thompson, 2000), they underpinned the need for in-depth knowledge of personal narrative, leading in 1995 to the launch of the Centre for Ageing and Biographical Studies at the OU's then School of Health and Social Welfare. Through bringing these traditions together, this author has continued her interest in how environmental experience, both individual and group, can be understood through environmental biography and participatory research that is grounded in place. Consequently, the interaction between people and their environment requires continued consideration of context, three areas are studied: participatory methods involving older people within the research process; the effects on research practice of interdisciplinary and interprofessional study; and issues of measurement, through subjective, objective, conceptual and applied research, with potential for further translation. Figures are drawn from research fieldwork.

Participatory research: involving older people

In Chapter 2, the discussion of photo-walks, a joint approach between the older person and the researcher that facilitated non-representational theory (Barron, 2019) reminded this author of an earlier experience. During graduate studies in the mid-1970s, cognitive mapping of place was developed with older people in Swansea (Peace, 1977), influenced by Lynch (1960), Regnier (1974) and others. The map was the instrument on which people were asked to draw their activity and neighbourhood space, which spurred discussion about history, boundaries and attachment to place – even if it also pointed to how well, or not so well, people read maps. It enabled the collation of views to represent community definition and usage in different locations, as seen in Fig 9.1. Were these participatory methods or just innovative forms of methodology that brought the views of respondents closer to the research aims and objectives?

More recently, interdisciplinary researchers such as Kaspar et al (2015) have adopted more technological methods to understand how the mood of people with or without cognitive impairment varies in relation to day-to-day out-of-home mobility. Here, a multi-method approach involves older people wearing GPS tracking systems and reporting their views through directed daily diary records. While research has indicated that a positive mood is associated with activity and social engagement in later life, when these datasets were combined they found people with Alzheimer's Disease

Figure 9.1: Neighbourhood consensus, Oystermouth, Swansea

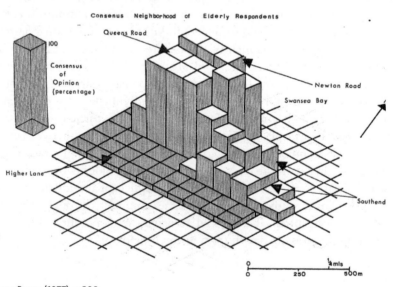

Source: Peace (1977), p 398

or mild cognitive impairment had lower levels of mood than cognitively healthy older people. Nevertheless, compared with the total aggregated data, people with Alzheimer's showed positive links between mood and out-of-home behaviour that was either particular to their own condition or in relation to specific occasions such as walking on a weekday, indicating the importance of individual experience of cognitive status.

An interest in methodological innovation drew this author's attention to participatory research. This epistemological approach is concerned with ways of knowing from a particular perspective. It can also be known as participatory action research (PAR) and covers a range of approaches at either end of the participative and action continuum. From the geographical perspective, Kindon et al (2010) define PAR simply as 'researchers and participants working together to examine a problematic situation or action to change it for the better' (p 1). They also comment on the variation between what some see as participative research and others as action research. Ideas surrounding this type of approach within social research challenge traditional scientific methods and open up wider recognition of knowledge production through post-positivist approaches, which originated particularly in development studies and feminist research, where the experience of social inequality and marginalisation was voiced (see Hall, 1981, 2005; Stanley and Wise, 1983; Roberts, 1990; Greenwood, 2004; Ray, 2007).

It can be argued that given the inequalities experienced by many older people and the ways in which ageism can be faced by a majority, it is not surprising that academic researchers have been attracted to the participatory approach, thereby involving older people in the research process (Osborn and Willcocks, 1990; Peace, 2002b; Bytheway et al, 2007). Kindon et al's action-based definition may be an aim, yet participative methods can also unpack conceptual thinking, with implications for measurement, rather than finding ways to solve problems. In both cases, the academic researcher may maintain control and manage the process: where older people initiate the research topic and draw on academics' expertise, knowledge transmission and partnership working are based on greater equality. Clark et al (2012), whose work features later, have considered the impact of participatory approaches on research outcomes, particularly on the efforts to produce knowledge.

In social gerontology, researchers have been encouraged by funding bodies to consider participative research. During the 1980s and 1990s, UK policy in health and social care saw a call to acknowledge the older consumer (Barnes and Walker, 1996; Audit Commission, 2004), which in practice supported recognition of the person-centred approach to disability and aged care (see Peace, 1999, 2002b; Carter and Beresford, 2000). These trends developed through different ideologies, which foregrounded the older and the disabled person for very different reasons, and the expression 'user involvement' became a common phrase (Hickey and Mohan, 2004; Ray, 2007). For those

Table 9.1: Characteristics of emancipatory, empowering and action research approaches

Empowering research	Emancipatory research: disability movement	Action research
Personal development/ control of 'knowers'	Control rests with 'knowers'	Problem-focused
Equal balance of power	Surrender of objectivity	Context-specific
Develops partnership	Linked to political action	Involves change intervention
Supported within wider system	Brings about change	Aims at improvement / involvement
Maintains ownership of responsibilities	Research skills utilised	Cyclic process – research, action, evaluation
Supported by adequate resources	Interlink personal/political individual/collective	Participation through research
Collective as well as individual process	Recent recognition of methodological plurality	Future-oriented

Note: Peace, 2002b, p 232.

Source: These characteristics were brought together from readings within the fields of disability, social care, ageing and health.

in disability studies, the growth of participative research has continued to be seen as empowering (Oliver, 1990; Beresford, 2005, 2021), and Table 9.1 indicates the characteristics of different research approaches that underpin the over-arching heading 'participatory'. Here, the shift in the balance of power between researcher and researched is central, and in 2002 'common characteristics around participation, empowerment, shared expertise, the link between the personal and the political, and the importance of outcome in terms of implementation and change' were recognised (Peace, 2002b, pp 231–3).

Over the past 30 years, different types of participatory research have developed, involving older people not just as service users but as citizens or knowers who wish to contribute to knowledge as experienced experts or co-researchers, learning research skills, becoming fieldworkers, analysts and disseminators. Changing roles can lead academic researchers to work in different ways as facilitators, trainers, mentors and supporters, with the level of partnership often guided by the support of research funders (see Peace, 2002b, p 229).

From the late 1990s, there was a more formalised arrangement of consultation with older people offered by UK research funding bodies – for example, the Joseph Rowntree Foundation's Older People's Programme Steering Group; the Older People's Advisory Committee for the Economic and Social Research Council's Growing Older Programme (1999–2004); and the Older People's Reference Group for the New Dynamics of Ageing

Programme (2009–15). It is fair to say that proposal development often considers the value of participatory methods in answering a research question, recognising the advantages and disadvantages.

Here, arranged chronologically, consideration is given to four projects that were introduced earlier and involved older people as co-researchers, before looking at the generic benefits and challenges of participatory approaches. The issue of co-design is also a form of participative method commonly led by architectural scholars, as seen in the DWELL project and the Older Women's Cohousing Community scheme.

Social interaction in urban public places (2004–06)

A study of the English town of Aylesbury, introduced in Chapter 4, showed how everyday interactions in public spaces highlight different intergenerational behaviour patterns that are temporal, diurnal and seasonal (Holland et al, 2007). While this research included interviews with local stakeholders and street surveys, the main database was a unique piece of participatory observation that was undertaken by members of the community (Research summary 4.2). As Clark et al (2009) show, the researchers chose this method in order to fully understand, through the observations of local people, the context in which daily activities took place, bringing something different to the semi structured interview data.

To undertake this form of research, the academic team developed 'a non-participative, semi-structured observation method […] devised for recording basic data about the characteristics, location and activities of groups and individuals within selected observation sites' (Clark et al, 2009 p 348). Members of the public, aged 16 and over, were invited to take part in the research, being recruited via contact with local voluntary groups, which was followed by snowballing through initially recruited volunteers, later called co-researchers. At an initial training day, 60 people came to the OU to learn about the aims of the study, and they were invited to earn a small fee for carrying out observations. This proved to be a key motivator important, as some people would not have been able to take part without the payment. This unusual situation relied on a funding body, which agreed to provide this support, and a host university that was willing to organise a standard consultancy rate for the final 46 intergenerational co-researchers (aged 16–73).

The co-researchers worked in pairs for safety reasons, and carried out observations at one or more of the nine chosen micro-sites; these included a shopping mall, a central park, town squares, a canal pathway and two residential area. One person used an observation sheet with an outline diagram of the site and a matrix for recording demographic characteristics of people using the site (gender, visible ethnicity and approximate age) and any social interactions, while the other completed an 'ethnographic diary' extract to capture activity more broadly; co-researchers could do either task (see Figure 9.2). Most sites were observed for an hour at a time between 8 am and 9 pm, with observations split into 10- or 15-minute slots (see Clark et al, 2009 for further details). While some co-researchers originally came to the training with a friend, over time people became used to being paired with other co-researchers, and this was not problematic.

The aim of the research was for observations to be made daily across a 12-month period (October to October 2004/05), with weekend observations undertaken by the academic team. The co-researchers included people who stayed with the project for many months as well as those who could only commit a short period of time. Seven training events were held across the year, the earlier sessions being focused on observational research with practice in the classroom and the town. Discussions ranged across a wide range of issues: 'participants [...] were introduced to the rationale of the project, the observation method and research ethics and safety procedures.

Figure 9.2: The tools of observation

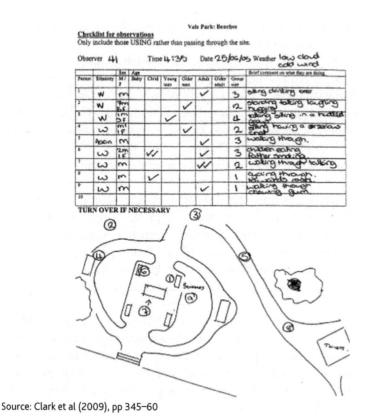

Source: Clark et al (2009), pp 345–60

Confidentiality was taken very seriously and co-researchers received instruction on the importance of not identifying known individuals in their data' (Clark et al, 2009, p 350).

The co-researchers were given a project handbook, and once the observation period began, members of the academic team were always on call either by phone or in person. Ongoing training sessions focused on reflections of experience, discussion of key issues or training for new members. Final debriefing sessions were also held. While the analysis was carried out by the academics, a small number of co-researchers were keen to learn how analysis was undertaken, and spent time looking at trends within and between sites, temporal issues and intergenerational patterns. The research team considered the non-participatory observational research successful, and felt it combined well with other methods.

The participatory nature of the research approach was not without criticism (Cooke and Kothari, 2001), and this included public scrutiny to judge whether the research and its purpose were robust. On reflection, the balance of power between the research team and the co-researchers had a direct influence on the rigorous nature of the approach and the variable quality of the data. The principal researcher developed important management skills that were conveyed to the rest of the academic team; these concerned being available to the co-researchers, guiding and directing them, yet enabling a flexibility so that they could develop their strengths in observing and recording within an ethical framework.

The co-researchers were both 'insiders' and 'outsiders', and on occasion they wanted to report the extraordinary rather than the mundane. Ongoing reflection and discussion was important, and here similarities may be seen with the Manchester study outlined later, with important issues of power balance. For the Age-Friendly Cities and Communities (AFCC) research, the potential for action was at its heart. In the Aylesbury study, an understanding of interaction in public places was central to the funding body's programme of work, and a research advisory group including local government officials was regularly informed of the research and its methods. Locally, one of the town squares was going through a period of regeneration, which was completed during the study, and so the findings would prove valuable even if not directed towards a particular call for action.

The co-construction of knowledge proved pivotal to the outcome of the Aylesbury study, even though this was not a true participatory research process in which lay members commission, design, conduct, analyse and present research; rather, each side brought different skills to the table, as summed up by this participant:

'I think my views are that there [is] so much behind the scenes that they need people like you to do the analysing. You people would have an overview. Lay people have a particular interest – they will be interested in a particular activity. Some people wouldn't like children running around. I have grandchildren and may think a different way. Some people will not be keen on teenagers. I think academics need to be more objective than lay people who may have a particular point of view' (PF). (Clark et al, 2009, p 356)

For the academics, lay knowledge was essential to the analysis, and the participants' comments showed that they had learnt new skills and now had a better understand of their town.

Revisiting The Last Refuge – the tracing study (2005–07)

Research by Johnson et al (2010) that revisited data from *The Last Refuge* (Townsend, 1962) was discussed in Chapter 8. They aimed to 'develop a longitudinal study' that focused 'on a single cohort of homes' from the original sample to 'explore the historical processes of continuity and change' (Johnson et al, 2010, p 12). The study built on past data and method rather than replicating the study, and drew on a new random sample of care homes. The researchers were able to examine material from the study of 1958/59, which is archived in the Peter Townsend Collection at the National Social Policy and Social Change Archive. Townsend drew a stratified sample of 180 residential care homes (RCHs), with 173 forming the final sample from all local authorities in England and Wales (Table 9.2).

Material from Townsend's study was organised carefully; it included a list of all 173 homes with names and broad location but no exact addresses. The first two categories in Table 9.2 were merged and labelled 'local authority'. Reports written by Townsend and colleagues on each home were archived alphabetically in 11 files by place and/or name. The research team began by successfully compiling levels of data for the 173 RCHs, checking and rechecking the original list, reports and locational definitions – in the process

Table 9.2: Sample of care homes and PAIs, Townsend, 1958–9

Former Public Assistance Institutions (PAIs)	39
Other local authority homes	53
Voluntary homes	39
Private homes	42
Total	173

Source: Adapted from Johnson et al (2010), Table 3.1, p 41 and Townsend (1962), Table 1, p 10

finding that 40 reports were missing, mainly for public assistance institutions and local authority homes (see Johnson et al, 2010, pp 40–1).

The research could now progress to what the researcher team called the 'tracing study' where the aim was to 'find out what happened to the 173 homes visited in 1958–59' (p 41). They began by using the regulatory systems in England and Wales (National Care Standards Commission and Commission for Social Inspection), discovering that, while some homes still existed in the same place, changes in ownership, location and residents will likely have occurred, even if the final care home had the same name. They needed to trace surviving and non-surviving homes to find out why some had closed, what had happened to the residents, whether there had been a change in ownership and if the building had been demolished or there had been a change in usage. The team decided that this tracing study would be helped greatly by people with local knowledge, who could visit the site, talk to local people and consult local records. Before and after they gained funding for the research, they began to explore whether older people would be interested in volunteering to help with the research – gaining a good response from the University of the Third Age in England and Wales, and from a member of a local history association who carried out a pilot tracing study of two homes. His work was used as a model in the information pack for volunteers. Following funding, the team contacted other organisations, and this led to 100 volunteers, 79 of whom carried out tracing studies (Johnson et al, 2010, pp 44–9).

The volunteers completed a personal profile form, which showed that they: 'were on the whole highly educated and skilled and committed in some way to lifelong learning' (Johnson et al, 2010, p 47). Over three quarters were aged between 60 and 79, with a further 10 per cent aged 80 and over; just under three quarters were women. Education and employment histories led the researchers to describe almost all of the volunteers as middle class, with 44 per cent having worked in health, social work or social care, and 60 per cent having a first degree and/or higher degree. When asked why they had volunteered, their comments show 'skills, knowledge and experience' from their previous employment in the field, their knowledge of Townsend's work, their skills in historical research, knowledge of the local area, a growing awareness of ageing experience and having the time to learn new skills.

As the volunteers were recruited over time and across England and Wales, the research team did not set up a training programme; rather, they briefed and supported each volunteer – members of the team individually acting as contacts. A briefing pack was developed, including guidance on how to gain information, letters of introduction and a standard form for completing their report alongside examples from pilot work. While the research team had gained ethical approval for the research and had Criminal Record Bureau checks (now Disclosure and Barring Service), the volunteers were not to engage with the care homes. The volunteers were only investigating one or a few homes, and the researchers received very full reports (see Johnson et al, 2010, Appendix 2 for examples). At the end of this participatory research, 39 homes were agreed to be 'survivors' of the Townsend study, based on location, continuous population of residents (through deaths and admissions), building (modified and extended), name, tenure and provider. All issues relating to changes in policy through greater privatisation and corporatisation were noted. The research team considered that the tracing study gave the volunteers the 'opportunity to engage in the kind of detective work that characterizes research at its most exciting' (2010, p 49). It enabled them to draw random stratified samples of non-surviving and surviving homes matched for size and tenure, and these formed the basis of the more focused follow-up study.

Researching age-friendly communities (2013–15)

Population ageing and urban living come together at the local level, and the expertise of Buffel and colleagues in researching AFCC demonstrates the involvement of older people through participatory research in both Manchester and Belgium (Buffel et al, 2012), learning community development skills from the national Belgian Ageing Study (De Donder et al, 2013).

In Manchester, the study can definitely be called PAR (Buffel et al, 2015, 2018); the research aimed to examine 'how older residents, especially those in disadvantaged positions, perceive their neighbourhood (both the physical-spatial and social characteristics of their area) and how the neighbourhood influences (promotes or obstructs) active ageing' (Buffel, 2015, p 29). This was a qualitative ethnographic study based in three contrasting neighbourhoods, with a central research team of three who involved local older people through becoming part of the community and gaining people's trust.

The project methodology developed into a hands on guide, which was described in the following terms: 'a collaborative process of research, training and action towards social transformation, i.e. to improve the area's age-friendliness. A key feature ... is the active involvement of older people as co-investigators in all stages ... including the planning, design, execution and implementation phases of the research' (Buffel, 2015, p 31).

As the research unfolded, it showed the process of action and reflection, and being locality based within a major city it gained from enlisting the networks of its research advisory board (academics, community stakeholders, policy makers) and an age-friendly steering group (older people and local community stakeholders). City-wide stakeholders were interviewed and 123 older residents were recruited from the three areas, as well as local community stakeholders who took part in 14 focus groups. The focus groups considered how people perceived age friendliness for their neighbourhoods, and discussed resources and barriers, seeking to raise awareness (Buffel et al, 2015, p 35)

Reflection on this process showed that the focus groups were over-represented by older people who were socially active, and that they needed to include a wider range of people. Through the steering group and local advertising, 18 older people from a range of ethnic groups volunteered to become co-researchers, thereby helping to extend the project. Buffel notes:

> We used a volunteer profile for their recruitment: it was stipulated that co-researchers should have good communication skills; show a commitment for the full duration of the project; were capable of listening attentively; take responsibility; and have links with more vulnerable groups of older people in the neighbourhoods selected in the research. (2015, p 36)

The co-researchers took part in two certificated community-based training sessions organised through the University of Manchester Institute for Collaborative Research on Ageing, covering the participatory research process, research purpose, designing interview questions, interview practice, ethical issues (information giving, informed consent); data analysis, sharing with others, translating into practice and consideration of impact. While the training was structured around these issues, it also provided opportunities to practise interviewing skills.

Through their own networking and snowball methods, the co-researchers located and interviewed 68 'hard to reach' older people, including those who were isolated, living in social housing, people from different ethnic groups and those experiencing health conditions, mobility issues and poverty. This partnership approach involved the university insuring the co-researchers during the project, and the research team thanked them for their work by giving each co-researcher a gift voucher.

During this interviewing period, the project held two meetings, first for reflection on progress – agreeing some changes to questions and issues to follow-up – and second when key findings were discussed. A third session focused on participatory data analysis and how to develop a 'joint framework for the interpretation of qualitative data' (Buffel, 2015, p 40), explaining issues of data immersion, developing and using coding, and how prior agreed codes differed from the codes emerging from the data. The co-researchers and the research team worked together and then in pairs to assign codes to their transcribed interview data.

To complete the process, researchers and co-researchers came together to discuss dissemination, which led some to develop findings leaflets and events for diverse audiences in each of the localities. Findings were numerous, including – the importance of strong neighbourhood attachments, reliable and frequent local transport, the value of local meeting spaces, fear of crime that might limit engagement, and public toilets – which will continue to lead to ongoing work in Manchester – while the research guide highlighted both advantages and challenges in involving older residents in being co-researchers (Buffel, 2015, pp 75–119). The advantages of this PAR were numerous, focusing on issues such as developing confidence building skills, and how ageism may be counteracted through showing participants' years of experience and local knowledge. There were also inevitably challenges: co-researchers having difficulties with the technology of recording interviews, a blurring of the boundaries between researcher, researched, academic and activist, issues of privacy and confidentiality when interviewing known people and a raising of expectations about future change in times of austerity. These are all useful points concerning the development of participatory research with older people.

Dementia-friendly environments (2016–19)

The final example is the research Neighbourhoods: Our People, Our Places, collaborative cross-cultural research by Ward et al (2018) that concerned the lived neighbourhood of people with dementia, asking how neighbourhoods can support people with dementia and their carers to remain socially and physically active. While the potential of dementia-friendly environments to facilitate activity through more inclusive design both indoors outdoors was raised in Chapter 4 and discussed further in Chapter 8, this research has sought to move beyond issues of accessibility to capture more complex environmental issues through forms of participatory qualitative research. The study was based in three localities in Scotland, England and Sweden, involving up to 15 co-habiting dyads from each locality (not necessarily couples), where one person has a diagnosis of dementia, five people with dementia are living alone and five are carers whose partner or relative has moved into a care home.

The research team asked respondents to take part in three forms of interview that were seen as co-participatory. They were described as:

1. A walking interview, where we ask participants to take us on a walk to or through a place of their choice.
2. A social network mapping interview, where we ask participants to 'map' the people in their lives who are important and to describe the nature of each relationship.
3. And finally, we're asking people to take us on a tour of their home, which we are either filming or audio-recording. (Ward et al, 2018, p 7)

To develop a longitudinal aspect to the research, interviews 1 and 2 were repeated after 6–12 months. The interviews and other documents, including film footage, form part of a case study dossier for each respondent with open coded analysis. In addition, at each field site a group of eight to ten practitioners and small groups of people with dementia and their carers come together as an 'action learning set' to consider findings and co-design an intervention (see Campbell et al, 2020).

In terms of participatory research, these respondents agreed to allow the researcher into their lives to walk and talk about places they wished to be in. This enabled them to talk about the past and present, about things they valued and how their experience of dementia could cause problems of disorientation – but also how place-making could provide a strength that was reinforced through routines and associations of people and place. The research has shown how people with mild to moderate dementia can be embedded within what the researchers call a 'lived place', connecting their meaning of home with both housing and neighbourhood that is seen as relational (Clark et al, 2020). For some, it gave them the confidence needed to inform those they did not know about their condition and how they could help to make a place more friendly for them. The researchers acknowledged that only by being in situ, and hearing people talk of place, can they understand how this practice is important for all.

The second participatory method involved social network mapping as a way of enabling respondents to focus on either the social network that supported them as a person with dementia or as a social carer. The mapping was part of the interview process, and people were asked to construct a social map. This started with the people they knew, how they knew them and where they lived. Interestingly, the word mapping once again caused some people to wonder how to start, but unlike with the use of actual maps mentioned earlier, various forms of networks emerged as written lists, family tree formats, categorised lists and temporal lists directed by daily or weekly routines.

Depending on whether you were a person with dementia or a carer, the network could include people whose role was social in the sense of being a friend rather than someone who offered some kind of social support for a person in need of care. People therefore had different roles and relationships. While most lists were made during the interview process and could become tools for discussion, one person made a list in advance of the interview, and this proved useful for creating a second map or layer that looked in more detail at emotional support (see Campbell et al, 2019).

The researchers say this about the method:

> We argue that such forces are at play in the production and reappraisal
> of the maps and can be understood in the context of the emotional

reflexivity required to produce the maps, such that the maps themselves take on particular resonance as 'affective artifacts' through the emotionally charged, performative work of the method. (Campbell et al, 2019, p 8)

For people with dementia, creating a social network map could also be life enhancing. Rather than being disengaged, they are seen as people who remain agentic through routine, social networks, neighbourliness and continued practice of engagement. In talking about one respondent, it is noted that 'she recognized that her world had not shrunk as she had initially thought but had in fact grown because of living with dementia' (Campbell et al, 2019, p 8).

These are interdependent lives, and the research team engaged with other professionals, practitioners and community members to visualise how place can support the lifestyle and well-being for people with dementia, and also how ongoing community development can help to maintain a dementia-friendly community. While the World Health Organization AFCC domain of outdoor space and buildings may have led to a focus on the built environment, we see here a broader understanding of the term 'age-friendly' and the need to integrate the social with the physical environment, thereby contributing to psychological well-being.

Issues from participatory action research

These examples of different forms of PAR provide a base for considering epistemological issues that highlight advantages and disadvantages when developing parallel forms of knowledge. In two of these studies, lay members became co-researchers, and took part in group training sessions concerning the research process and specific research methods (interviewing skills, non-participant observational skills), which were then put into practice. These studies used taught and experiential sessions. In the Manchester study, this took place locally, while the Aylesbury study invited participants to the OU in Milton Keynes, just over 20 miles away, while practice sessions were held both at the university and on the streets of Aylesbury. In contrast, the social network mapping exercise for people with dementia and the tracing study both involved individual communication and support. This was a different type of skills development – the one perhaps more formal than the other yet also a social process, one that is common and develops a form of partnership working.

In projects involving lay members as co-researchers, there were two fundamental concerns that were of importance to the rigorous nature of the research process and to the developing knowledge base. First, people needed to understand the ethical issues that surrounded the research, and especially the need for information giving, informed consent from participants, confidentiality, anonymity and data protection. These issues were all discussed in training sessions and one-to-one discussions, and needed to be robust procedures that protected the rights of research respondents who were being questioned or observed, as well as co-researchers themselves. The academic researchers sought ethical approval through university and other research ethics committees, and for co-researchers this was another area of skills development that allowed them to discern the boundaries between their involvement and the work undertaken by the academic research teams.

The tension that may exist between maintaining confidentiality and anonymity in parallel with personal experience, familiarity and knowledge is often one of the more difficult things for the lay co-researcher to work through, raising important issues of reliability and validity in terms of data collection. It is easier for the professional researchers to be distanced, both because they may not be a part of the locality or community and/or because they are able to sustain greater impartiality. In the Aylesbury study, Clark et al (2009) recognise the objective and subjective dimensions of the study and issues of positionality. They seek to challenge research practices within the social sciences and, as noted here, feel their research benefits from including this approach within a mixed methodology:

> We learned to look at research and our own attitudes to knowledge in different ways, gaining clearer insight into the tacit knowledge that lay participants can bring to research and how that can and cannot be used. The co-researchers in various ways shared this experience of discovery and many of them felt that they had become equipped with new skills, learned to look at the world around them with more attention, and to see their town in a new light. (Clark et al, 2009, p 357)

The final topic raised relates to the action within PAR, which was particularly relevant to the AFCC research and the work concerning neighbourhood within the lives of people with dementia. Both projects aimed to make a difference. In Manchester, this was certainly a motivating factor for the co-researchers, who sought to involve hard to reach older people and broaden the knowledge base, seeing themselves as part of an ongoing process engaging with diverse local and city-wide stakeholders with the potential to bring about change. Gaining research skills can empower lay researchers who may wish to carry on further researching (Leamy and Clough, 2006). In contrast, in the Neighbourhoods: Our People, Our Places research it was the nature of method itself that brought about change, by enabling the person with mild/ moderate dementia to lead the researcher through walking interviews and/

or using social network mapping to facilitate conversation about the social within the physical, thus potentially developing a useful tool for practice. This is also empowering.

Environmental gerontology: a field of interdisciplinary research

When considering the ways forward for environmental gerontology, Scheidt and Schwarz (2013, p 326) draw on a wide range of authors, with Pastalan (2013) commenting on the need for an awareness of paradigm shifts within sciences – examples being physics, medicine and communication technology that need assessment in relation to the ecology of ageing – thereby highlighting the importance of interdisciplinarity. In this text, we have not directly engaged with the sciences, yet when addressing environments of ageing it is important to always be conscious of how the diversity of issues provides the rationale for undertaking interdisciplinary research, including across the social sciences (Peace, 2018). It is not surprising that social gerontology is based either in multidisciplinary centres or where greater focus is placed on health and well-being in practice-based faculties and schools. However, as Hennessy and Walker outlined in 2011, there were, and perhaps still are, barriers to interdisciplinary collaboration in research: 'ideological differences in approaches to knowledge, the lack of training and dedicated funding for interdisciplinary research, academic and other disincentives, and inadequate peer review' (p 53).

Nevertheless, during the 21st century, there has been growing recognition of research questions that need to be addressed through interdisciplinarity, leading to discussion of the value of this development. In Ellie Bothwell's report on the growth of interdisciplinarity through interviewing senior academics, she highlights how researchers need to go outside their comfort zone of associated disciplines; that it is the research question that drives the combination of approaches, recognising that interdisciplinarity is possible even if challenging (Bothwell, 2019). She indicates that the development of interdisciplinarity has been initiated by political drivers seeking answers to big questions, with calls from research funders leading to multidisciplinary research, centres of excellence and inter-faculty research initiatives, alongside comment decrying solutions-focused research and attacks on the levels of academic rigour within individual disciplines.

Finally, with regard to interdisciplinarity within UK research in general, Bothwell (2019) notes that the assessment of university research – the Research Excellence Framework (REF) that occurs every four or five years – saw difficulties in positioning interdisciplinary research in the 2014 exercise, and that the Stern Review (post-2014, DBEIS, 2016) has called for greater inclusion of this type of research in submissions to the 2021 assessment.

Following the 2014 REF, evaluation of newly submitted impact case studies by social gerontologists indicated the importance of interdisciplinary work (Bangor et al, 2015) and in the current 2021 REF assessment, past president of the British Society of Gerontology Professor Judith Phillips, from Stirling University, is a member of the new Interdisciplinary Research Advisory Panel.

New dynamics of ageing programme

Since the turn of the millennium, one of the big research questions in the UK has focused on the quality of life in an ageing society. It is within this context that Walker (2014) reported on what he called 'the new science of ageing' emerging as a result of demographic change through patterns of mortality and morbidity in the developed world, which has recognised the importance of extending quality of life throughout a healthier later life. He notes that continuity and changes in health and well-being across the life course have advanced a different way of thinking:

> The new science of ageing seeks to question [...] the inevitability of decline: while ageing, old age and senescence are inevitable, at least for the foreseeable future, as far as the bulk of the lifelong ageing process is concerned, loss of function and capability is not. If this idea can be more widely accepted, it effects would be transformational. (Walker, 2014, pp 9–10)

Walker was involved in the National Collaboration on Ageing Research (2001–04), which brought both together researchers and funding bodies to consider interdisciplinary research on ageing and encourage UK research councils to develop joint sponsorship. He later became the director of the New Dynamics of Ageing (NDA) programme (2005–13), jointly funded by five research councils and aimed at promoting multidisciplinary research, involving the collaboration of people from different disciplines. The NDA programme had two major research themes:

- ageing well across the life course
- ageing and its environments

with particular sub-themes: locality, place and participation, the built and technological environment and the global dynamics of ageing, reflecting environmental issues that could be addressed through certain aspects of ageing – active, independent, extreme age, life course perspective.

Funding supported 11 large collaborative research projects (CRPs) and 24 smaller scale programme projects. Two of the large CRPs related to environments of ageing were SomnIA, concerning the optimisation of sleep quality mentioned at the end of Chapter 1 (Venn and Arber, 2011), and Grey and Pleasant Land, which concerned the connectivity of older people in rural civic society (Hennessy et al 2014a), as discussed in Chapter 4. To aid communication between researchers from very different backgrounds, the NDA funded 11 preparatory networks that enabled scoping reviews, networking, making contact with research end users and planning proposals that fed into the CRPs.

It was through this work alongside other funding developments that Walker saw the beginning of a paradigm shift in ageing research:

> the new science of ageing consists of an increase in the prevalence of multi-disciplinary research [...] a greater than previous emphasis on life course influences; the common use of the person-environment perspective which places the older or ageing person in a social, economic and physical context; a closer engagement with research end users, including older people; and an increased emphasis on knowledge exchange. (2014, p 11)

These are all issues that relate to the development of critical and cultural approaches within environmental gerontology. Here, a difference is suggested between multidisciplinary working, where different disciplines take into account separate aspects of research, and interdisciplinary working, where the research team work to the same methodology and learn new skills (Walker, 2018).

Transitions in Kitchen Living study

One of the small-scale NDA projects was the Transitions in Kitchen Living study raised earlier (Maguire et al, 2014; Peace et al, 2018). This research shows some of the benefits and challenges of interdisciplinary research, as the project was carried out by social gerontologists from the OU (Peace, Percival) and ergonomists/designers from the Design School at Loughborough University (Maguire, Marshall, Nicol, Sims, Lawton). Details are given in Research summary 9.1. The researchers carried out a comprehensive mixed methods approach that combined the skills of social scientists working in gerontology who had experience of undertaking in-depth biographical interviews with older people, and ergonomists and designers who were skilled in carrying out post-occupancy evaluation of human interactions within buildings, in particular for people with disabilities. This was an ideal combination to study the micro-environment of the kitchen (and places for eating) for a diverse sample of women and men living as couples or on their own, within a range of housing types and in two locations. However, to work seamlessly, all researchers developed new methodological skills: undertaking housing histories, in–depth and semi-structured interviewing, ergonomic assessment, environmental mapping, lighting readings and the use of photography.

Research summary 9.1: Transitions in Kitchen Living

The Open University and Loughborough University

Aim and Objectives: the study aimed to investigate historically and contemporarily the experience of the kitchen for people in their 60s, 70s, 80s and 90s living in a variety of general and specialised housing in England. The focus was material, social and psychological, and the main objectives were to:

• provide a historical understanding of the kitchen experience, guided by life events;
• provide contemporary understanding of the current kitchen, examining role, function and design, utilising mixed methods to understand activities;
• consider person–environment (P–E) fit through the juxtaposition of individual health and well-being, kitchen living and the potential for improving the kitchen to meet needs;
• extend theoretical development in environmental gerontology through focused multidisciplinary research and triangulation of data that are historical and contemporary, individual and contextual, qualitative and quantitative.

Methods: a comprehensive mixed methods approach involving meetings with 48 participants on two or three occasions during 2009–10 in Bristol and Loughborough. All in-depth interviews were recorded and transcribed. Material concerning past history of the kitchen involved an in-depth oral history interview prompted by a self-completion housing history record. A topic event guide focused attention on points of the life course, including first remembered home and setting up first home as an independent person. Following this interview, participants undertook a self-completion record of routine kitchen activities and provided basic demographic data. They were offered a digital camera to take pictures of the good and bad aspects of their kitchen. However, most preferred the researcher to do this, directed by them.

The second visit involved a semi-structured interview with multiple choice and open-ended questions regarding the current kitchen. It focused on how the kitchen met the person's abilities, needs and coping strategies; consideration was given to the person's health and well-being, discussing physical abilities (mobility, dexterity, vision, hearing). These interviews also focused on activities of daily living from washing to recycling to feeding pets, whether the person liked to cook and what they liked to eat. The conversation was comprehensive.

Finally, sketches were made of the kitchen layout; photographs were taken; measurements were made of the ergonomic 'kitchen triangle' (between the cooker, the fridge and the sink); the kitchen area was calculated, together with the height of the lowest cupboard shelf. Light recordings were made at different locations: the kitchen sink, where food was prepared, and where it was eaten with the lights on and off.

For further information see Sims et al (2012), Maguire et al (2014) and Peace et al (2018).

The mixed method approach led to different forms of analysis and triangulation of methods. The use of an inductive grounded theory approach to analyse the in-depth housing history interviews was undertaken by bringing the whole team together, with every member reading and analysing a number of interviews individually in advance to discuss and agree themes for further content analysis. This was a useful team-building process that proved essential to the project.

On reflection, it is clear there was some variation in research quality: some oral history interviews lacked the depth that can be given by more detailed prompting, while some drawings of the contemporary kitchen were not of expert quality. Nevertheless, the research flourished, and communication across the whole team led to material that continues to be used in discussion as inclusive design across the life course has become more topical. The team explored historical and contemporary difference in kitchen design and equipment, showing how people come to use this micro-environment across the life course – as seen in extracts from the kitchen/life history interview undertaken with Teresa and Sidney and quoted in Chapter 6.

With regard to the contemporary kitchen, the impact of design and individual competence gave a clear example of the environmental docility hypothesis – with windows that could not be opened, shelves that were too high to reach without a step-ladder, ongoing support needed for recycling waste and insufficient lighting. The triangulation of datasets enabled a greater understanding of how data confers or highlights difference. For people who wished to cook, sitting at a table was a luxury not seen in galley kitchens common to some specialised housing (with care). In terms of kitchen equipment, the microwave was the most common piece of 'new' machinery owned by all participants aged from 61 to 91; this was used primarily for reheating and not for direct cooking (Peace et al, 2018).

The research provides guidance, not only for older people, but also for designers and retailers for making the kitchen an easier place to manage and contribute to ageing in place and sustainable living. The study has been replicated in Mauritius with the methodology adapted for older people who are Creole, Hindu, Chinese and Muslim (Maguire et al, 2012; Peace et al, 2018; Ramsey-Iranah et al, 2020). While Scicluna, a post-graduate student in the original team, considered the kitchen as a place for older lesbian women (Scicluna, 2013). In addition, being a part of the NDA programme enabled researchers from across 35 projects to come together in sub-groups and discuss common themes that are seen as part of the new science of ageing. The Transitions in Kitchen Living team contributed to discussion of art and design centring on areas of designer competency, user interaction, improving image, communication between specialties (Timmins et al, 2014) and nutrition and food environments, where food, nutrition and environment were key to health and well-being and foregrounded multicultural issues and accessible, usable spaces (Thompson et al, 2014).

In recent years, UK Research and Innovation (UKRI) has launched an Industrial Strategy Challenge Fund to engage knowledge transfer between research and business partners. This initiative includes a healthy ageing challenge that involves a social, behavioural and design research programme, which will develop new research initiatives regarding environments of ageing from spring 2021 (UKRI, 2021).

Different forms of measurement

The last section of this chapter considers ways in which measurement develops with conceptual and applied focus. Over the years many research instruments used to assess generic measures of quality of life, morale, life satisfaction and loneliness (Lawton, 1975b; Victor et al, 2005; Bowling and Stenner, 2011) have been used in gerontology within different contexts alongside assessments of personal health, both physical and cognitive, and measures of (instrumental) activities of daily living to consider personal behaviour (see Hartigan, 2007 regarding the work of Sidney Katz and the Barthel Index, named after Dorothea Barthel). There has been a long history of assessment of different aspects of setting – community, neighbourhood, dwelling – through objective quantitative measurement and subjective qualitative ethnographic approaches. Golant's (1984, pp 61–98) early account of measurement in relation to the experiential environment of individual behaviour outlined the eclectic mix to which researchers could turn at that time. In the UK, the London-based Centre for Ageing Better has developed an online measurement bank, which although not solely relating to environment provides a useful resource (Centre for Ageing Better, accessed 2021, see Glossary).

Here, we focus on two initiatives where researchers address different forms of measurement regarding environment and ageing. First, there is a subjective approach, showing the way in which older people contribute to a research instrument that gives them greater control over the definitions of environment and personal identity; and second, there is an objective research measure developed through occupational therapy that advances assessment of P–E interaction of value to practice and research at the levels of individual and group.

The facets of life wheel

The Environment and Identity in Later Life study was introduced earlier, with details outlined in Research summary 6.1 (Peace et al, 2006, 2011). The aim of the study was to focus on the meaning of environment in terms of self-identity through detailed ethnographic methods. From the outset, the researchers decided that the study had to be situated in three ways:

- locations to include a diversity of community types from urban to rural including multicultural populations – three locations were identified;
- locations to include a range of housing types and tenures;
- a purposive sample of participants living in general housing, specialised housing and accommodation with care.

Recognising the development of participative methods outlined earlier, the researchers, having reviewed commonly used measures of quality of life in relation to environment, decided that the complexity of P–E interaction was best explored through an experiential approach. This involved listening to people speak about what mattered to them in the everyday, defining environment in whatever way they wished. To do this, the team worked with nine focus groups within the three locations:

> a decision was taken to begin this research with group discussions to identify themes and categories that older people themselves thought were significant about the places where they lived, both home and community. Two groups were assembled specifically for our discussions and the other seven consisted of 'naturally occurring' groups including: two social/luncheon clubs; a mother's union (Christian) group; a sewing circle; a black oral history group; a men's billiards group; and a (Sikh) cultural community group (for which a translator was used). Of the nine groups, four were all-white British and Irish; three were mixed race; one was all black-Caribbean and one was all Indian. Two of the groups were all male; four were all female; and three were mixed gender. The sessions were led by one or more of the researchers, depending on the size of the group, and they were audiotaped for later content analysis. (Peace et al, 2006, p 25)

Through detailed content analysis of the transcribed conversations, the researchers developed a research tool called the facets of life wheel (Figure 9.3),

Figure 9.3: Facets of Life Wheel

Name

Address

Date of Birth

Ehnic Group

Health/disability

Type of housing

Tenure

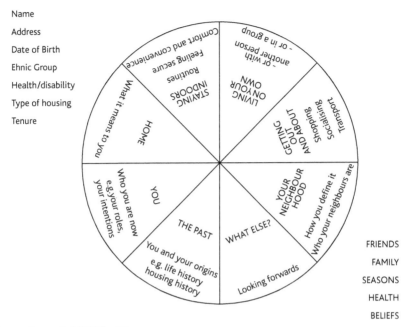

FRIENDS

FAMILY

SEASONS

HEALTH

BELIEFS

Source: Peace et al (2006), p 26

which was based on eight topics with prompts suggested by the groupwork. The tool became a moveable wheel mounted on a board that interview participants could place next to themselves or hold on their lap.

The eight areas under consideration were:

- the past (origins; life story; housing history);
- self (who you are now; roles);
- home (where is it? what it means to you?);
- staying indoors (routines, comforts, convenience, security);
- living arrangements (alone; with another person; in a group);
- getting out and about (shopping? socializing? transportation?);
- neighbourhood (how do you define it? who are your neighbours?);
- what else? (including future plans and projects).

Research participants could see the topics for discussion and choose where to start the conversation, elaborating as they wished, prioritising the topics that interested them and extending the discussion (Figure 9.4).

While the researchers realised they could be criticised for the lack of consistency in the areas covered by each in-depth interview, they wished

Figure 9.4: Using the Facets of Life Wheel

to let people speak for themselves prompted by the views of other older people. The researchers say this about the use of the wheel:

> The **facets of life wheel** seemed to enhance people's confidence in collaborating on these themes as they could anticipate the wider context and the ways their particular account might fit. We have already noted how previous approaches to measuring quality of life have tended to use sharply compartmentalized categories that do not allow the best representation of the mutability and continuity of life experience. While based on what can be described as domains of life and living, the **facets of life wheel** seemed, in piloting and in subsequent data collection and analysis, to permit expression of the interpenetration of social and material aspects of environmental life as might impact on identity. Moreover, it brings into focus the different and variable intensities that informants can attach to the meanings they ascribe to each of the topics. (Peace et al, 2006, p 27)

The researchers recognised that following an interview that was guided by the participant meant they would need to collect certain basic and supportive data through more structured questions, but these were displayed alongside the wheel so the interviewee knew they would follow. Through this process, a dossier was compiled for each of the 54 respondents who took part in the initial study, having been chosen purposively to cover the range of housing types across the locations. Through analysis of detailed datasets, the research outlined layers of environmental living, including location, neighbourhood and community, natural world, defining my/our place and belonging, meaning of home, security, routines, comfort, housing, garden, getting about, comfort and convenience, social engagement, self-agency and how environmental context was part of their self-identity.

One of the benefits of including this methodology in a discussion that has drawn attention to participative research lies in showing how older people can contribute to forms of measurement. Through ongoing analysis of data obtained in this way, the researchers could see how the breadth of narrative builds until reaching a point of exhaustion, which allowed them to discuss the issues of option recognition that are mentioned in Chapter 6. Since developing this tool, the researchers have developed the concept in research with older people who have high support needs and older people with visual impairment, where the topics were communicated orally (Research summaries 4.3 and 7.1) (Katz et al, 2013; Peace et al, 2016). Where possible, allowing research participants to use the figure to direct conversations has been empowering, and they see their comments as representing themselves. It is a truly subjective measure supported by more objective assessment of personal characteristics.

The Housing Enabler

In Chapter 5, attention is drawn to the current housing stock in the UK and how poor housing standards may affect the lives of older people whose personal health and well-being may benefit from greater housing adaptation (Nicol et al, 2016). These changing circumstances relate directly to the work of Iwarsson and colleagues in developing the Housing Enabler that was used in the Enable-Age study discussed in Chapter 6. This instrument was developed at the Centre for Ageing and Supportive Environments at Lund University, Sweden (Iwarsson and Isacsson, 1996; Iwarsson, 1999; Iwarsson and Slaug, 2010). The researchers come from professional/academic traditions in occupational therapy and gerontology, so accessibility is central, being defined as 'the relationship between the person's functional capacity and the demands of the physical environment', with the Housing Enabler developed to 'support practitioners in producing reliable and valid analyses as a basis for targeting housing accessibility problems' (Iwarsson et al, 2012, p S17).

The measure involves three phases of assessment and analysis (Figure 9.5). First, a functional profile is developed by interviewing and observing the older person, outlining particular difficulties – including use of mobility aids. Then an assessment is made through observation of their living

Figure 9.5: Example of the assessment and scoring principles of the complete Housing Enabler instrument

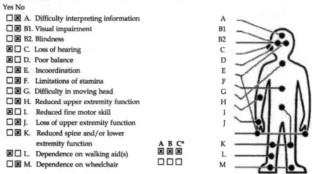

First mark the functional limitations and dependence on mobility devices that you have observed. Then transfer the crosses to all the rating forms concerning environmental barriers.

Yes No

☐ ☒ A. Difficulty interpreting information
☐ ☒ B1. Visual impairment
☐ ☒ B2. Blindness
☒ ☐ C. Loss of hearing
☒ ☐ D. Poor balance
☐ ☒ E. Incoordination
☐ ☒ F. Limitations of stamina
☐ ☒ G. Difficulty in moving head
☐ ☒ H. Reduced upper extremity function
☒ ☐ I. Reduced fine motor skill
☐ ☒ J. Loss of upper extremity function
☐ ☒ K. Reduced spine and/or lower extremity function
☒ ☐ L. Dependence on walking aid(s)
☐ ☒ M. Dependence on wheelchair

A B C*
☒ ☒ ☒
☐ ☐ ☐

A
B1
B2
C
D
E
F
G
H
I
J
K
L
M

*Section in the environmental component: A. Exterior surroundings. B. Entrance. C. Indoor environment

Mark the observed environmental barriers with a cross. Then circle the scoring points (1–4) found at the intersections between functional limitations etc. and environmental barriers. The total of these scores is a quantification of the magnitude of accessibility problems.

Personal component / functional profile	Yes				✘ ✘					✘		✘			
	No	✘	✘	✘		✘	✘	✘	✘		✘	✘		✘	
A. Exterior surroundings	Bygg ikapp	A	B1	B2	C	D	E	F	G	H	I	J	K	L	M	RATING
General A1. Paths narrower than 1.5 m. A width of 1.0 m is acceptable provided there are 1.5 m turning zones at least every 10 m.	p. 304					3	3							3	3	☐ Yes ☒ No ☐ Not rated
A2. Irregular/uneven surface. (irregular surfacing, joins, slop ng sections cracks, holes; 5 mm or more).	p. 305	2	3		①	1		3				1	③	3		☒ Yes ☐ No ☐ Not rated
A3. Unstable surface (oose greve, sand, clay, etc). Mark if it causes difficulties e.g. when using a wheelchair or rollator.		2	3			3	3	2				1	3	4		☐ Yes ☒ No ☐ Not rated

Source: Iwarsson and Slaug (2010). Reprinted with permission from Veten and Skapen HB and Slaug Enabling Development

environment, outlining any particular environmental barriers. Use is made of building standards or guidance if applicable to the settings. Finally, a score is calculated to quantify 'the magnitude of accessibility problems', and the levels of environmental barriers can be ranked to aid decision-making regarding potential for adaptation (Slaug et al, 2020, p 161). It was first developed in Swedish, an English version was produced in 2001, and Danish and Finnish translations followed. Where it is used in projects such as the ENABLE-AGE study, country-specific versions are developed.

The Housing Enabler has been developed over 25 years of research, and continues to be tested and retested for reliability, validity and alternative function (see Glossary). The ideas underpinning the instrument can be used in different ways. Work with individuals uses the complete instrument, while a screening tool is available to consider accessibility problems at a group level, building on datasets for groups that can involve people of all ages and functional capacity (Iwarsson and Slaug, 2010). The tool is based on a list of 'the 60 environmental barriers causing the most accessibility problems' in particular settings (Iwarsson et al, 2012, p S18).

Ongoing development of the screening tool has taken advantage of data from the ENABLE-AGE survey, using material from people aged between 75 and 89 living in Germany, Hungary, Latvia and Sweden. Here, Slaug et al (2011) were able to consider functional limitations and use of mobility devices for a combined group (N=1,542), indicating 14 items that were categorised into six broader themes:

- difficulty in interpreting information;
- severe loss of sight/blindness;
- severe loss of hearing;
- limitations in movement;
- limitations in upper extremity;
- use of mobility devices. (Table 2, Slaug et al, 2011, p 585)

Different group profiles were associated with particular environmental barriers, and when tested in simulated accessibility analyses raised potential for prioritising particular public health strategies. For example, 'limitations in movement' associated with barriers outdoors and at entrances, 'limitations in upper extremity' with indoor items such as 'wall-mounted cupboard/shelves placed extremely high' and 'no grab bars at shower/bath' (Slaug et al, 2011, p 591). These findings relate to those from the Transitions in Kitchen Living study although using very different research methodologies, and raise issues relating to home adaptation and inclusive design.

The Housing Enabler tool highlights possibilities for architects and planners in using simulation models to consider different solutions to housing accessibility problems, which are of value to those involved in real estate developments (Slaug et al, 2020). In addition, variations of this model have been pursued to develop forms of accessible transportation that could lead to further neighbourhood age friendliness (Iwarsson et al, 2000).

Conclusions

The aim of this chapter is to show how researchers whose work forms a part of environmental gerontology are thinking innovatively. They are developing a wide range of methods for understanding the physical, social and psychological environments contextualised economically and politically in which people live, both across the life course and more specifically as they grow older. The individual environmental biography is grounded in time and space, and we need new ways of capturing this dynamic. Multidisciplinary research aimed at social impact is foregrounded here, and it indicates a strong element of creativity in how this field embraces ways of working that are complex yet original, rigorous and ethically sound.

Ideas developed in one culture are replicated in others, and feedback between researchers is inspiring. The production and analysis of mixed approaches demands a wide-ranging skill base, and where methods are participatory then new forms of team-working are important. There is also a strong sense that researchers wish to make a contribution through their work to societal change and intergenerational connection, and that focusing on subject/object relations through robust quantitative and qualitative research methods aids this ambition. What are seen here as important methodological approaches come at a time of the COVID-19 pandemic, however, and future research (particularly participative) may need to draw on different ways of involving older people through greater use of technology and other innovative thinking to maintain communication. Contextual understanding is fundamental when researching environments of ageing, and in Chapter 10 we return to that wider picture.

10

Rethinking the spatiality of ageing

Introduction

When considering the journey made across different environments of ageing, and the wealth of literature covered, there are many paths and views that could have been taken. The aim of this chapter is to foreground contextual issues central to environmental gerontology. The spatiality of ageing started with a global perspective even if knowledge of person–environment (P–E) interaction is commonly local and national. Here a relational approach is taken to these spatial levels, looking at flows captured at different times through people and place. It returns to global concerns to reassess local and national impact that affects social exclusion and inclusion in later life, a part of the iterative theme of environmental living and the concept of home. In seeking a circularity of ideas with global to local, local to global influence relationality is used as a way to understand environments of ageing.

In Chapter 3, a discussion of global concerns focused on the big issues that are part of this challenging time. Thinking relating to global health focuses not only on definitions of active ageing and the ability of individuals to take personal responsibility for diet, exercise, activity and participation, but also the parallel incidence of long-term chronic ill health and end of life. Such experience varies within and between developed and developing countries where inequalities of personal and social health are related. When writing in October 2021, health for all ages is a chief concern as the COVID-19 pandemic has taken hold globally. By the summer of 2021, the third English national lockdown was coming to an end, with more than two-thirds of the adult population having had two COVID-19 vaccinations and later leading to booster vaccinations. What does this mean for the ways in which we will live in the future? Now, with several vaccines being rolled out at different speeds across the world, will things go back to how they were or will they change for ever – and could they change for the better?

This collective global experience has certainly moved centre stage, while other issues have moved to the wings. However, we are still living in an increasingly unequal world, where climate change continues unabated; there is growing intolerance of refugees and migrants; in the UK, EU withdrawal challenges identities as citizens of supranational collaborations; and technological change continues with benefits for some more than others. This concluding chapter reintroduces population ageing into this global turmoil, and reconsiders how the everyday lives of older people are impacted. As the global pandemic affects all other issues raised here, we begin with this moving picture.

Global health, global ageing – living during a global pandemic

On 11 March 2020, World health Organization (WHO) Director-General Tedros Adhanom Ghebreyesus declared that the outbreak of COVID-19, the disease caused by a zoonotic (animal to human) virus, known as SARS-CoV2, was now a global pandemic (WHO, 2020c). The outbreak, which was first reported from Wuhan, China, had by 23 March 2020, the date of the first lockdown in England, seen the number of COVID-19 cases surpass 300,000 globally (WHO, 2020d). At present, statistical data is changing daily, and the picture presented here provides only a snapshot to demonstrate trends.

As of 30 June 2021, WHO statistics on the Coronavirus Disease (COVID-19) Dashboard showed that globally by this date 'there have been 181,521,067 confirmed cases of COVID-19, including 3,937,437 deaths' and 'a total of 2,915,585,482 vaccine doses have been administered' (WHO, 2021a). The situation by WHO regions on 30 June 2021 is illustrated in Table 10.1. The US, India, Brazil, France, Russian Federation were the top five highest ranking nations in terms of confirmed cases of COVID-19 for 13 April 2021, with the UK being sixth (WHO, 2021a).

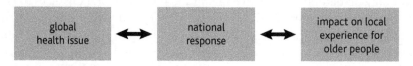

Globally, this pandemic is affecting people of increasing age more severely than younger people, and in the UK it is seen to have greater impact on those disadvantaged through ethnicity, disability and socio-economic status combined with age, gender and location. Data from the Office for National

Table 10.1: Data for confirmed cases of COVID-19, 30 June 2021 by WHO regions

Americas	72,186,963
Europe	55,906,897
South East Asia	34,851,968
East Mediterranean	10,985,785
Africa	4,035,208
Western Pacific	3,553,482

Source: WHO Coronavirus Disease (COVID-19) Dashboard, WHO (2021a).

Figure 10.1: Deaths registered weekly in England and Wales by age group, provisional, week ending 22 January 2021

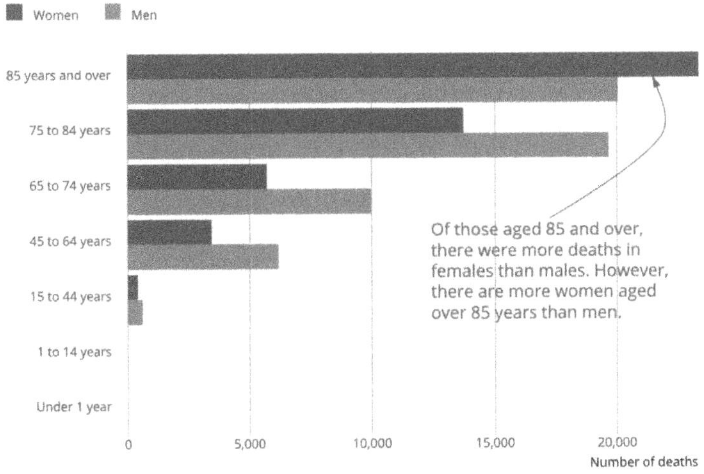

Source: ONS (2021), Open Government licence v.3.3.

Statistics (ONS, 2021) show that of the deaths registered by 22 January 2021, 103,394 mentioned COVID-19 on the death certificate. This was 15.5 per cent of all deaths in England and Wales. Nearly 73.0 per cent of deaths involving COVID-19 were for people aged 75 and over.

There have been more deaths in females aged 85 and over than males, reflecting population demography in the UK. However, as seen here, deaths by age and gender have been variable. Death by place of occurrence indicates that beyond hospitals, care homes form the second highest place of death, with a number of hospital deaths being among people whose place of residence is a care home (Burton et al, 2020; ONS, 2020g; ONS, 2021), a situation beginning to see detailed research (see Richardson et al, 2020). Finally, there is evidence that in the wider community the impact of the virus is locational, being dominant in urban areas, and that people from Black ethnic backgrounds in England and Wales are at greater risk of death involving COVID-19 than other groups (ONS, 2020h).

Across the world, national health systems are developing particular responses to the pandemic. The UK government introduced a series of staged strategies, with an initial lockdown from 29 March 2020 during which some 2 million people aged 70 and over across the UK who were seen as very high risk were asked to self-isolate for three months with assistance from family, friends and public support. There have been concerns that people living alone may be more isolated, and news reports for all ages continue to discuss the impact of lockdown on personal well-being (Steinman et al, 2020). This first experience was followed by periods of relaxation and then further restrictions involving both all and parts of the population. Scientific analysis of the impact of varied strains of the virus has been constant, with policy aimed at protection of the NHS to preserve capacity.

The initial approach, which targeted the older population through chronological age, was not common to all countries where populations have been targeted equally, and was seen by some in the UK as including people who are healthy and able to provide care and support for others. In March 2020, the British Society of Gerontology issued a statement objecting 'to any policy which differentiates the population by application of an arbitrary chronological age in restricting people's rights and freedoms', outlining the multiple roles that many older adults have in paid and unpaid work, with civic and voluntary groups and as carers for family members older and younger (BSG, 2020).

In confronting national needs in England, it appeared that greater knowledge was needed concerning the roles and requirements of older people living in different settings and their families. Visiting care homes initially proved difficult for many relatives and friends, and remains problematic for some – with social distancing during early months of the pandemic leading to social isolation and affective misunderstandings, especially for people living with dementia. Governments are being forced to find solutions to degrees of separation for people during a public health crisis, and requests have been made in the UK for family members to be recognised as equivalent to staff members, with regular testing and allocation of personal protective equipment for regular visits. During August 2021, revised guidance for visiting care homes indicated that every care home resident could have 'named visitors' for regular visits as well as a fully-vaccinated essential caregiver who may attend the home to undertake essential care needs (DHSC, 2021). Protocols also include maintaining physical distance, hand holding and hand washing and advise meeting in outdoor places. Guidance has also been given for supported living where residents have more independent living (DHSC/UK Health Security Agency, 2021). The position of visitor/resident relationships is still ongoing in 2021, raising complex human rights issues; this is a global issue (Zhou et al, 2020).

In a time of population ageing, how mortality and morbidity rates may change in the short or long term in response to the pandemic is unknown. Whether this will impact in different ways within developed nations with mature ageing populations than in developing nations that are ageing most rapidly will need ongoing monitoring.

In October 2021, the world was nowhere near an 'exit strategy'. Nations were working to prevent the spread of a virus for which a number of vaccines were being tested, approved and utilised. Global debate over the political, economic and humane distribution of vaccine is ongoing, and for a period of years this may affect the global development of population ageing, which may impact on aspects of social exclusion.

For this text, the current global pandemic takes the discussion of environment to a different level – where P–E congruence is not just a local experience but has to be reasoned globally. The WHO, when discussing Ageing and Health (2015, pp 27–30, 34–6), makes the case for a public health approach to health systems that recognises inequalities in varied environmental contexts. The lack of preventative health services in later life is commented on, as is how enabling and supportive environments are key. In developing nations and low-income regions, a structural resource base of water, energy, sanitation, housing development and healthcare systems continues to evolve alongside targeted international health intervention, especially regarding maternal and child health, malnutrition and infectious diseases (Lloyd-Sherlock, 2010). A decline in premature mortality means that death is now more synonymous with later life. Consequently, the context and environment of living with lifelong health conditions and end of life and palliative care is a growing contemporary issue. Adding to this pattern a virus that makes older people and those with particular health conditions more vulnerable to mortality reinforces the value of every human life.

This data highlights ongoing inequalities, and those reflecting on research developments regarding the impact of COVID-19 and later life recognise the need for further research and changes in methodology across ongoing epidemiology in the community and care homes in particular, hospital treatment, the management of COVID-19 and its complications, the impact of lockdown measures and issues relating to mental health, social isolation; public health interventions, vaccine delivery and the use of technology as a form of communication (Krendl and Perry, 2021).

Addressing climate change

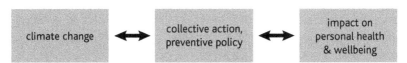

Prior to concerns about the COVID-19 pandemic, the main global challenge was the impact of climate change, and it will become so again in the future. It is the critical issue as already discussed that is affecting environments of ageing. Further reflection builds on The Lancet Countdown Report for 2019 concerning health and climate change (Watts et al, 2019), which as well as focusing on the future for younger generations draws attention to life course issues. The report indicates that environmental change will continue to encourage food poverty through declining crop yields caused through droughts and floods; there will be a continuing impact between increasing temperature and urbanisation; heatwaves and frequent fires will continue; older people with co-morbidities such as cardiovascular diseases, diabetes and chronic respiratory diseases will continue to be vulnerable to heat-related stress and premature mortality; and floods may cause immediate physical injuries, the loss of homes, infrastructure and livelihoods, impacting on well-being and leading to mental health problems (Watts et al, 2019). These are concerns at the extremes of environmental press.

Chapter 3 considered vulnerability with increasing age to heat mortality, especially among those living in cities (Hajat et al, 2007). More recently, extreme events in more rural locations have been witnessed. At the start of the 2019–20 Australian bushfire season, extensive fires across 18 hectares in Victoria and New South Wales led to the destruction of thousands of buildings and homes, and the deaths of humans and millions of animals (Handmer et al, 2019). In January 2020, the UN Environment Programme (UNEP) considered the implications: ongoing ecological and biodiversity impact; climate feedback loops; costs, economic, agricultural, well-being; and changing public attitudes. Climate feedback loops relate to the way in which global warming increases the likelihood of more severe bushfires, which then release greater amounts of CO_2 that feed back into greater global warming – while decomposing ash contains nutrients that can form algae and impact on marine life (UNEP, 2020).

Changing public attitudes is central to how climate change is recognised in national policy and local experience, and a united voice from all countries is required. The Paris Agreement on Climate Change set participating nations a target of 'holding the increase in the global average temperature to well below 2°C above pre-industrial levels and pursuing efforts to limit the temperature increase to 1.5°C' (adopted 2015; enforced 2016) (United Nations, 2016) (see Glossary). To carry this forwards requires phasing out fossil fuels and the use of other energy sources, turning to transportation powered by electricity, and behavioural change that brings down carbon emissions to meet these goals.

At present, nations are confronting this challenge in different ways, and there is a real need for shared global agreement. China, the US, India and the Russian Federation produce the highest levels of CO_2 emissions (Union of Concerned Scientists, 2020), with coal fired power stations still prominent. Their active involvement is essential (see Harris, 2011). While in 2018 the Intergovernmental Panel on Climate Change reported that the impacts of global warming of 1.5 °C above pre-industrial levels (IPCC, 2018) was possible with deep emissions reductions, the most recent Conference of the Parties (COP25) meeting in Madrid in 2019 did not result in ambitious forward planning.

COP26, Glasgow November 2021, was hosted by the UK with Italy and attended by members of nearly 200 countries and states. They agreed that current cuts in emissions were not enough to limit temperature rise to 1.5 °C by the end of this decade. The Glasgow Climate Pact made the following decisions:

- agreement to stronger national action plans with annual reviews;
- agreement to move away from fossil fuel and to phase down (not 'phase out') use of coal;
- agreement by developed countries to double financial support to developing countries for adapting to impact of climate change and protecting lives;
- voluntary agreements on reforestation; creating sustainable transport; controlling methane emissions. (UN Climate Change Conference UK, 2021)

Despite intense negotiations, the outcome appears disappointing, full of compromise even though acknowledgement of need for urgent response and of growing public acceptance of need for change is seen.

Prior to COP26, the UK Conservative government's response to the non-departmental public body, the Climate Change Committee (CCC), included: support for energy saving home improvements; active travel through maintaining cycling and walking (seen to have increased during the COVID pandemic); continued development of ultra-low emission vehicles; increased direct air capture using offshore wind capacity to develop electric power for home consumption; further research to cut emissions in heavy industry; investment in flood defences; and tree planting and restoration of peatland through a Nature for Climate Fund (HM Government, 2020).

These potentially positive moves aim to support a net-zero UK by 2050 through strategies noted in the Transport Decarbonising Plan of July 2021, the Net Zero Review report (HM Treasury, 2021) and government Net Zero Strategy (HM Government, 2021) of October 2021 that seek 'improved resource efficiency for businesses, lower household costs, and wider health co-benefits' (HM Treasury, 2021, p 2) across a transition period of 30 years through strategies relating to issues such as home insulation, installing low carbon heat sources, replacing polluting vehicles, cleaner air and changing industrial processes leading to new employment routes. These changes are across a longer time frame than the urgency of change by 2030 as requested at COP26.

As noted, a link is made between behavioural change as a consequence of the COVID-19 pandemic and climate change. In many developed countries, people have been asked to work from home during this period, and the virtual world has replaced the office for many; changes in movement and transportation have seen an initial reduction in flying and use of the car, with a reported 17 per cent reduction in CO^2 emissions in April 2020 compared with 2019 and greater time spent walking or biking (Le Quere et al, 2020). However, as developed nations returned to work in the summer of 2020 in the northern hemisphere, emissions rose and the United in Science report showed that 'COVID-19 has barely made a dent in the causes of climate change', with 2016–20 'set to be the warmest 5 year period on record'

(World Meteorological Organization, 2020). Internationally, there appears to be limited progress alongside reports of further higher temperature rises above 32°C, particularly affecting outdoor workers, older people and all those living with chronic health conditions, especially in European cities (Harper, 2019).

We cannot expect imposed behavioural change protective of health across all ages to automatically lead to ownership of environmentally friendly principles. Yet, as stated earlier, this need for P–E congruence is global. Recognition of its importance may not affect environments of ageing for current generations, but activism can bring to the fore how climate change makes lives more precarious.

These are reasons why those calling for attitudinal change maintain their commitment through activism, as Greta Thunberg stated to the European Parliament in Strasbourg in April 2019:

> Our house is falling apart. The future as well as what we have achieved in the past is literally in your hands now. But it is still not too late to act. It will take a far-reaching vision. It will take courage. It will take fierce determination to act now, to lay the foundations when we may not know all the details about how to shape the ceiling. (Thunberg, 2019)

The UK-based global environmental movement Extinction Rebellion, which developed in 2018, aims to use non-violent civil disobedience to induce government action. It was founded by people in their 40s and 50s with support from those of all ages, from 18 to 80 (Booth, 2019; Gunningham, 2019), and action staged in London in August 2020 forced governmental response. In an opinion piece for *The Guardian*, Anne Karpf made a call for solidarity:

> If climate activism is to stand any chance of succeeding, it needs to be intergenerational and multigenerational, based on the idea of stewardship of the commons – those resources shared by us all that we need to safeguard for future generations. That way we can be sure future generations will actually exist. (Karpf, 2020)

Intergenerational solidarity can enhance action for developing sustainability, persuading politicians to act – and many older people are committed to this engagement (Willis, 2020).

Transient populations

While the movement of migrant populations through conflict, disaster and ongoing displacement is very much a contemporary issue, the position of older migrants is far from visible and needs to be a recognised policy issue within ageing societies. For older people, different scenarios exist: being an active migrant, resettling and ageing in place, and remaining in your own home when other family members migrate (see Chapter 3). The Migration Data Portal special report entitled 'Older persons and migration' states: 'Older persons in migration contexts are at risk of being overlooked, which might perpetuate vulnerabilities and inequalities. In addition there is a lack of data on older persons left behind and their needs' (Migration Data Portal, 2021, p 1).

Both inter- and intranational comparison are needed between older migrants and non-migrants, as well as a greater understanding of similarities and differences within and between migrant groups across the life course. Such research is fundamental to appreciating how and why people live as they do, and recognising structural and biographical constructs in relation to age, ethnicity and cultural difference (Lievesley, 2010; Lloyd-Sherlock, 2010). Torres (2012, p 39), in discussing the variability of older migrants in relation to issues of social exclusion through the marginalisation of social resources and socio-cultural power, highlights how these issues can be pivotal in determining post-migration adaptation. The European Network Against Racism and the AGE Platform Europe in 2012 called on EU nations to recognise the needs of many older migrants and older ethnic and religious minorities in facing barriers to employment, healthcare needs, lack of access to adequate income, poor housing and a lack of knowledge concerning the society in which they live – where their specific needs may be neglected (Dwyer and Papadimitriou, 2006; UNECE, 2015).

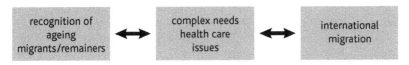

In 2015, research supported by HelpAge International interviewed 300 women and men aged 60 and over in cities, towns and camps in Lebanon, South Sudan and Ukraine whom they felt were 'living through some of the most acute global crises in the world today' (Gillam, 2016, p 1). For some, a short-term migration might turn into a long-term relocation, and as this report shows, older people were seldom asked about themselves or their needs, with many voicing a sense of helplessness and distress. Many older migrants are invisible not just to national policy makers in the countries where they might settle but also and more immediately to humanitarian aid organisations, who may overlook mobility issues and other age-related healthcare needs.

The report ends by calling on 'humanitarian responders' to hear the voices of older women and men in such circumstances, understand the diversity of such groups, recognising the isolation of many, and address the health service needs of those with chronic healthcare conditions and psychological distress. Such reports, as noted in Chapter 3, do not add to our understanding of belonging and homeland; rather, they address the immediacy of recognising the existence of older migrants in times of conflict. In addition, the consequences of continuing migration for older people left behind in multigenerational households needs recognition, and again HelpAge International is the source for empirical research evidence about their situation (HelpAge International/UNICEF, 2010; Cunningham and Dobbing, 2011). The various scenarios of moving and staying in later life are particularly relevant to older women who are caring for and supporting grandchildren and other family members.

In light of the COVID-19 pandemic, John Percival, reflecting on earlier work (2013b, 2020), has reconsidered the position of those wishing to be return migrants and go back to their homeland or place where family members are living in later life. He discusses the challenges to those for whom such travel is currently out of the question and those who face both a desire to return and the recognition of leaving an advanced healthcare system at such a time. In future, transnational migrants who see themselves as global citizens may not be exceptional, ageing in place beyond their homeland without family support or informal care.

Technological solutions

Chapters 3 and 5 highlight the importance of technology in environments of ageing, primarily being needs based. Globally, although the trajectory is uneven, communication through cell phone/internet systems is seen as ever more widespread across all age groups and of particular value during times of health crisis. Gerotechnology is a growing field, and Schillmeier and Domenech comment that 'If human beings lack the ability to perform in a socially "normal" way, technology helps to fill the gap of normality' (2010, p 1). This acceptance of the environmental docility hypothesis sees technology as assisting individual proactivity, a view recognising the complex interplay between personal, material, social and emotional environments. In terms of staying put in ordinary or specialised housing, Milligan et al (2010, p 21) discuss the value of assistive technology, both telecare and telemedicine. As noted earlier, such systems are common in specialised housing alongside the wider acceptance by all ages of a growing range of innovations, from robotic domestic equipment to health-related wearable tools that can monitor conditions such as temperature, blood pressure and blood glucose (Holland, 2012).

Research concerning ageing and technology is becoming more multifaceted, unpacking everyday experience and not solely concerned with health and safety. For example, longitudinal research undertaken in the Netherlands with city dwellers aged 70 and over living independently considers the purpose and results of acquiring all forms of technology. The researchers carried out an inventory of all electronic devices that may be added to over time (Peek et al, 2017). Across three interview periods, participants talk about their lives and social networks, indicating why they use all forms of technology (from chair lift to e-bike), whether they were purchased or given, and the advantages and disadvantages of different items. They consider the skills they needed to develop, being motivated, why they choose some things and not others, issues of reliability, the value of personal relations instead of technological solutions and perceptions of self when managing technology. The detail in this research allows for greater understanding of how older people come to include technology in their lives. Returning to Lawton and Nahemow's Press-Competence model, some items increase comfort or aid performance, while others may highlight changing levels of health-related competence with age.

Access to and use of technology and internet connection are not as common among the oldest old, although it appears that a 'needs must' approach has developed in the UK during the COVID-19 pandemic owing to restricted personal contact. Equipment has sometimes been given by others, and younger family members have provided support – enabling older people to learn new skills, particularly relating to smart phones or tablets (LoBuono et al, 2019; Freeman et al, 2020). However, this raises the value of personal communication (Gomez, 2015). Alongside family contact, technology has also replaced some face-to-face medical contact with GPs, medical consultants and hospital nurses, who offer telephone or online appointments. Once again, this may have been precipitated by the pandemic, but it is becoming more familiar and may, or may not, prove confidence building. Steinman et al (2020) make the point that 'hearing loss, cognitive impairment and unfamiliarity with new technology may compromise … ability to effectively use these modalities' (p S19). They feel that telemedicine can only go so far, and call on professionals to consider creative solutions, which may include socially distanced house calls. Nevertheless, the use of virtual reality has become diverse for all, from online shopping to exercise that promotes health and wellness, and to video games for entertainment (Marston et al, 2016). The question now is how far these different ways of living will become part of everyday life, and the implications for 'old age exclusion', voiced by Walsh et al (2017) in Chapter 3, recognising societal divisions.

Throughout this book, the definition of technology has been broad, with application at all environmental levels. This has led researchers Marston and van Hoof (2019) to ask why the WHO Age-Friendly City and Community (AFCC) initiative does not include technology as one of its key domains. The WHO (2018) have reported that technical assistance and support can aid AFCC development, yet given the participative development of this initiative since 2005, they uphold their model – which remains part of a new urban agenda adopted at the Habitat III Cities Conference (UN, 2017).

Nevertheless, for some, technology can be age friendly. Marston and van Hoof (2019) create a framework that offers technological solutions for the AFCC domains (Fig 4.2), and test ideas with people in the town of Milton Keynes, building on an infrastructure that has over 200 miles of shared-use paths, known as Redways, for cyclists and pedestrians, suggesting the use of outdoor spaces to consider delivery robots for shopping or accessible information for transportation. A similar recognition of technological potential also underpins the work of Reuter et al (2020), who examine the value of digitalisation through participatory action research methodology for the domains of communication and information, and civic participation. Working with an AFCC stakeholder group of older people in an age-friendly city in northern England, they tested digital methods for communicating and collecting news, feedback and concerns, to see whether citizenship can be developed through digital and non-digital methods. These innovative ideas need cross-national comparison to consider cultural and economic difference, and, as Waights et al (2019) discuss, the co-production of age-friendly standards around ICT.

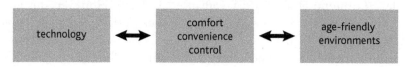

Connectivity: a meaning for age-friendly places

Concern over AFCC and technology has led to further reflection on the value of connectivity discussed in Chapter 4 in relation to rural ageing as the real key to age-friendly places, where community development builds on an infrastructure that enables participation. The diversity of the urban/ rural older population presents new challenges for spatial infrastructure such as transportation and walkability, service location, affordable housing options and diverse consumer and leisure services. Here we return briefly to local potential for social engagement, participation and housing sustainability before considering a more radical critique of what it means to be age friendly. These are local to global scenarios. In different ways, these examples have witnessed changes owing to the impact of COVID-19. However, we consider the positives before reflecting on the implications.

Accessible transport

Local transport and walkable neighbourhoods support personal well-being. Research in London provides evidence of the value of public transport in enabling social inclusion for all ages, while reducing car use and consequently having a positive effect on CO_2 emissions and air pollution.

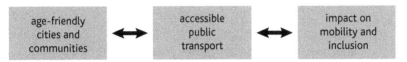

In 2014, Green et al (2014) reminded us that not only is free bus travel outside peak times (9 am or 9.30 am) available for older citizens throughout the UK but also that in London through the Freedom Pass 'older citizens resident in London boroughs are entitled to use all bus, tram and underground train services within the Greater London area with no time restrictions, and rail services at off-peak times' (p 474). The Freedom Pass is available to people whose principal residence is in London and meet the age requirement of being in receipt of their state pension or over 60 years of age (see London Councils, n.d.).

Through qualitative research focusing on bus travel across greater London, Green et al (2014) show how central the bus is to all older London citizens. They use the bus for everyday activities – shopping and healthcare visits – and are able to attend early appointments and engage with others. If car users, they speak of problems with parking, aggressive drivers and too much traffic. The bus is part of the relational space, which enables people to feel a part of the public and not isolated or lonely.

Not every experience is positive, of course, and some talk about not always feeling comfortable when seeking a seat or their encounters with younger people, who can sometimes be noisy and rude, but this does not put people off from using the bus. Even though buses are avoided by some and seen as having a class-based stigma (Clayton et al, 2017), this is definitely not the case in this research, which shows how strongly respondents feel the Freedom Pass supports their lifestyle. Green et al (2014) conclude by saying that for older people 'a public transport service used by a large cross-section of many of London's populations – provided a tangible and daily reminder of their position in society, rather than at its margins'(p 491). It is part of the age-friendly environment, enabling people to age in place.

This example is used to consider the future of transportation, and the impact of the COVID-19 pandemic. During the first period of lockdown in the UK, from March 2020, a majority of people except keyworkers were not using public transport, and as of 15 June 2020, older Londoners were no longer allowed to use their Freedom Pass or other transport access cards during the morning peak times (4.30–9.00 am Monday to Friday) to conserve space and aid social distancing for key workers. Passes were valid at all other times, and anytime at weekends and bank holidays. Those who qualify for a Disabled Freedom Pass continued to have access. The people who have fared worst from this ruling, which is ongoing in October 2021, are those aged over 60 who as key workers in health and other essential services have had to pay for their travel early in the morning.

The future of the transportation system across the UK is unclear yet central to the government's transport decarbonising plan and net zero review. During the pandemic, Transport for London have received central government financial support – currently extended to December 2021 – to maintain the system (Waitzman, 2021). Travel is one important part of association and well-being, and the importance for social inclusion through public transportation cannot be underplayed.

Community centres

In early pilot work for the AFCC initiative, older Londoners noted community centres as being important, particularly for people living alone (Biggs and Tinker, 2007). Since that time, austerity measures and local government cuts have seen changes to many schemes, and in 2014, a reduced number of 59,000 older people were said to attend those run by local authorities and other commissioned community services (NHS, 2014). This is an under-researched area in the UK that is considered by Orellana et al (2020a) through a rigorous systematic review and an empirical study. The review shows that the main users are 'women who lived alone or were widowed, divorced or single and older, without further education, with low income, comorbidities and who took multiple medications' (p 85), characteristics reflected in their study of four centres in south-east England (Orellana et al, 2020b). Although small in scale, this detailed research with a sample of 23 attendees shows how people who are able to maintain their lives in their own home with limited support find the day centre adds value to their lives.

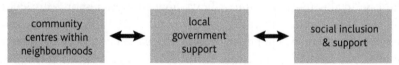

The researchers reported that people gained a sense of purpose, felt more in control and generally 'felt better' for attending day centres even if there were problems with delayed transportation or feelings of unease towards members with aggressive behaviour. In the discussion, the authors comment on the value of the congregate nature of centres which those attending valued, stating: 'It appears to counteract, to a degree the drawbacks of ageing in place in isolation, with its risks of loneliness, and is, therefore a strength' (Orelanna et al, 2020b, p 17).

In confirmation of these detailed findings, a larger research group undertook a UK-wide online and telephone survey of social support including day centres during the first period of COVID-19 lockdown between April and May 2020. This involved a convenience sample of 596 participants gained through diverse networks, including older adults (n= 223), people living with dementia (PLWD) (n=61) and carers plus past carers of PLWD (n=285) (Giebel et al, 2020). The focus was extensive, collecting demographic and locational data as well as social support service usage before and after the COVID-19 lockdown and measures relating to quality of life, anxiety and depression. Through quantitative analysis, the study found significant reduction in social support usage by all parties across this period, increased levels of anxiety among PLWD and older adults, and lower levels of mental well-being among carers and older adults. A more detailed study was undertaken with 50 carers and a small number of PLWD (Giebel et al, 2020). The number having no access to social support services stood at 212 pre-lockdown, rising to 352 after lockdown. These figures indicate the overall decline in participation and the researchers state: 'Social support services form a crucial part of post-diagnostic dementia care and meeting the needs of older adults, many of whom experience high levels of loneliness' (Giebel et al, 2020, p 7). These were facilities that also benefited present and past unpaid carers, for whom they are a place for maintaining relationships and networking.

These two examples highlight aspects of current normality used to show the value of access to public transport and meeting places that need to be taken into account in future when encouraging age-friendly environments. They are both part of connectivity within place. A further concern linking local to global environments is the future of ordinary housing.

Sustainable housing

In 2008, David Harvey said: 'the freedom to make and remake our cities and ourselves is […] one of the most precious yet most neglected of our human rights' (Harvey, 2008, p 1). This view resonates as the need for and future development of sustainable, age-friendly, although not necessarily age-related housing, is reconsidered. In 2013, the Royal Institute of British Architects (RIBA) published 'Silver linings: the active third age and the city', leading to the Design for an Ageing Population initiative (see RIBA, 2014), which brought together the public, architects, gerontologists, planners and other stakeholders to discuss and debate the age-friendly city (Handler, 2014). By asking for examples of innovative design, they questioned why evidence submitted focused more on residential projects such as specialised housing than on outdoor spaces and sustainable places that are car-free, bio-diverse and age integrated (see Chatterton, 2019).

Creating a built environment that enables people to age well while living within more sustainable housing has to be the way forward. One of a number of new developments that could provide models for general housing is the Future Homes Alliance project in Newcastle upon Tyne, which gained planning permission in 2020. It will use a co-design approach to develop intergenerational housing for 65 homes in three six- to eight-storey apartment buildings on a 24-acre site in the Newcastle Helix, a landmark city centre quarter. In this scheme, five 'demonstrator' homes will be used to test innovative ideas evaluated by researchers from Newcastle University. To benefit from solar energy, all homes will feature floor to ceiling south-facing windows; there will be moveable walls to enable change in interior space, and a range of communal facilities including gardens, mini-allotments and secure cycling storage will be provided. The aim is sustainability (Future Homes Alliance et al, 2020), formed through creative thinking and the lifetime commitment of the project's founding members, both public and professional (see Gilroy, 2021).

We should take into account an ecological approach, with issues of climate change leading to new build housing that can cope with radical changes in energy sources, insulation, flood proofing and air conditioning, all challenges that relate to global problems. Alongside these developments the Ministry of Housing, Community and Local Government (see Glossary for recent changes), through recent consultation regarding changes to building regulations, also aims to introduce a Future Homes Standard by 2025 for new builds to be future-proofed with low carbon heating and levels of energy efficiency: new and existing homes are said to account for 20 per cent of all CO_2 emissions. There will be further regulations for existing domestic and non-domestic buildings.

While these are new and exciting ideas, most older people continue to live in existing housing stock that, as seen earlier, may be able to be modified or adapted to meet particular health needs. This needs ongoing financial support, and although it could be argued that adapted housing becomes sustainable for the individual rather than being part of the new sustainable housing stock, such adaptation should result in an environment that is attractive to all. Poor housing design can produce heath inequalities (Marmot et al, 2010; Garrett et al, 2016), and housing adaptation is a public health issue – especially for those who wish to stay put in their own homes for as long as possible, and for younger generations who may also view these houses as home. The balance between the maintenance of older housing and the design of new builds that are inclusive is also a global challenge.

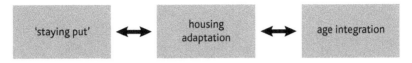

Each of these examples contributes to the understanding of being age-friendly, with connectivity and the link between people and place being demonstrated in different ways. Citizen engagement is made possible through the availability and affordability of services, overcoming aspects of old age exclusion, being part of future developments and enabling choice and control over levels of participation. There is a sense of popular acquiescence about the local being a place with opportunities for participation central to relational space and to intergenerational integration. Yet does such integration occur? As the HAPPI 4 report on rural housing reminds us, in England it is estimated that nearly half of rural households will be aged 65 and over by 2039, and a higher proportion of this population is aged over 75 years than in urban areas (Porteus, 2018 p 14). In the 21st century, the emergence of the WHO's AFCC and more recent age-friendly environments (WHO 2007, 2015a) lead us to believe that the position of older people still needs campaigning for.

In a recent discussion of how issues regarding age-friendly cities and communities can be more fully aligned, Buffel et al (2018) set out what they call 'a manifesto for change'. It incorporates the following areas:

- acknowledging urban complexity;
- prioritising home and neighbourhood;
- challenging social inequality and exclusion;
- increasing diversity;
- facilitating community empowerment;
- co-producing age-friendly communities;
- developing creative and participatory age-friendly design;
- encouraging multi-sectorial and multidisciplinary collaboration;
- integrating research with policy;
- strengthening international networking.

(Source: Buffel et al, 2018, pp 274–88)

These are issues raised across this text and they challenge the AFCC initiative locally to take into account the diversity of older people through forms of participation that enable them to be involved in how their community develops. This ownership is seen as empowering. It is easier to facilitate if a wide range of stakeholders are willing to come together, thereby leading to elements of coproduction and codesign for the environment. This requires everyone to recognise that inclusion is a good thing, and crosses the urban/rural landscape where international communication and co-operation are key.

A relational theory for environments of ageing

When writing a book that has the subtitle *Space, Place and Materiality*, it is difficult not to reflect on one's own spatial awareness. Two issues come to mind. First, when this author began research in this field almost 50 years ago, it was noticeable that the diversity of people of all ages brought variation to how place is created and understood. As a young white woman, it was necessary to consider interpretations of the narratives of others who were older, White British and male dominated. Now, it can be recognised that being an older woman affects perception and definition of space and place differently; this can be current, historic or imaginary, and can hold varying levels of emotional attachment. There is an interrelatedness here that can lead to an acceptance of difference and intergenerational synthesis, a form of personal relationality. In Chapter 2, theoretical positions of relationality and non-representational theory were introduced as being useful to environmental gerontologists. Individual agency can be affected by changes to control across time. In this section, relationality is used to examine two of the structural devices discussed in this text: first, the breadth of environments of ageing, primarily British, used to examine the meaning of home (Figure 10.2); and second, the association of population ageing with other global challenges that can be related to national and local experience (Figure 10.3). The use of a relational perspective here is limited to ongoing comparison, yet the aim is to bring wider spatial contextualisation to individual dialogue.

Environmental living and the meaning of home

Across the life course, the concept of home is a repository of self-identity, levels of association with certain people, things, possessions, built form and given voice through memory. As an older person, views on home contribute to the wider sense of place in which you live – a process with temporal elements that are positive, negative, variable or balanced. From Chapter 4 onwards, different aspects of environmental living and ageing were discussed to allow reflection on the meaning of home, with key constructs identified through cross-sectional research that would value from longitudinal study. No doubt there are issues raised here that will resonate globally, with important local nuances that are cultural and relating to specific intergenerational and age-related environments. Figure 10.2 brings together these findings, and research narratives from points of the life course have been used to explore issues of continuity and change. Drawing on the wealth of conceptual development in Chapter 2, the theoretical work of Wahl et al (2012) and Chaudhury and Oswald (2019) outlined in Figure 2.2 regarding PE exchange are particularly helpful in the interpretation of meaning of home through issues of agency and belonging, identity and autonomy explored over time.

When unpacking Figure 2.2, urban/rural communities are valued in different ways, yet connectivity of person in place is essential to place attachment and is seen to be missing for some older people, especially those in urban locations, who experienced ongoing disadvantage and social exclusion. The aesthetics of the green environment, whether through natural landscape, garden or balcony in contrast to urban change, has been noted. Issues displayed in this section of Figure 10.2 apply not only to those living in general housing,

Figure 10.2: Changing perceptions of meaning of home in later life: a cross-sectional view

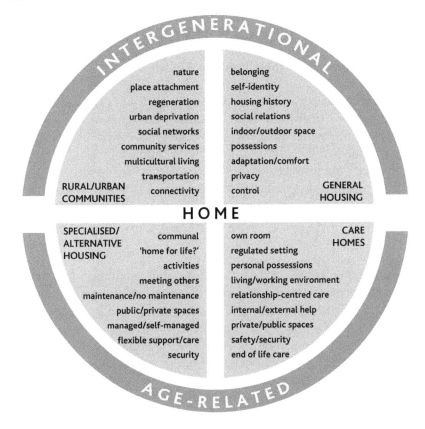

but also to age-related settings where location can be important to well-being and affects how people are seen as more or less part of the wider community. Age integration and segregation vary through location, access to transport, levels of association with community, personal health and well-being. In most cases, family and friends become the go-between across place.

The relational comparison is then with the living environment of general housing – home to a majority. In these settings, ageing in place and staying put were valued, with individual preference for continuity in lives that are emotionally and socially age integrated, even if the physical/material environment of a person's housing and private/semi-private outdoor space may vary in terms of personal congruence and requires adaptation. The empirical research in Chapter 6 gives voice to how people feel about their homes, indicating independence, personalisation of space, displays of comfort, ownership beyond tenure and relations within and beyond housing to neighbourhood and homeland. What is not seen here is an example of intergenerational living, which may add to these themes.

The concept of option recognition has been introduced, as well as the tipping points that can challenge continuity and lead to change. Negative issues or push factors related to health, particularly mobility, environmental barriers within the home, and living alone with or without local family support can all affect how people's lives develop. Abuse within the home has not been identified, yet hearing the views of Helen shows dissonance between home and neighbourhood as a place of safety that may seem hostile and home as housing where someone wishes to stay put. Others, such as Bertie, Nancy and Raymond, remain settled in their communities, yet Nancy in particular begins to comment on aspects of environmental press. These voices indicate how the meaning of home is gender specific and embedded in life histories, personal experiences and networks that centre belonging in forms of social construction (see Peace, 2015). It is worth noting here that while domestic housing as a place of women's work has been critiqued by feminist writers over time (Oakley, 1985; Bowlby et al, 1997), an emancipation of the concept of home has also been seen by feminist theorists (Young, 2005, p 142) as a context of self.

Consideration turns now to age-related settings and making a move. Relocation requires information, communication, motivation, financial and social capital to enable choice over decision-making. Looking across Figure 10.2, there is the first sense of individual (or coupled) daily life becoming communal, and not necessarily familial. A planned decision to move to an age-related housing environment is seen as more likely to maintain levels of autonomy and well-being for some and to enable the re-establishment of a sense of home; 'sense of' as references are still made to former home as home. Nevertheless, this is a more inclusively designed environment, where having your own front door and private space is part of a new lifestyle that can afford activity and potential companionship. When people move to housing (with care), the need for further support is accepted or denied until needed. However, there is recognition that a 'home for life' may not be possible owing to increasing levels of frailty for some residents/tenants, particularly through cognitive impairment, which leads to evidence of some stigmatisation between people.

Bringing these issues together shows how maintaining a sense of self involves an ongoing reconstruction of the meaning of home and recognition over how the culture of homeland can be maintained. This is certainly true of Hajit, who sums up his sense of living in limbo from a position of greater comfort in extra care housing and the maintenance of associations with others aided by access to transportation locally and culturally at a distance through technology. Over the passage of time, different values may have more or less meaning, and within age-related settings comparison between selves influences the ownership of personal ageing.

Chapter 8 turns to care homes, where maintaining self-identity in very old age is perhaps crucial to the ways in which residents experience a more restricted or managed lifestyle; a regulated setting where levels of personal autonomy for certain activities may be enabled or discouraged through the nature of the physical and social environment and are delegated to staff, partners, family members and other professionals. The recognition of delegation is central here, even if unspoken, and relates to issues of personal control which ultimately links to knowledge of end-of-life support and care. As with all environments of ageing, care homes are relational spaces where relationship-centred care can aid P–E interaction and communication. To different degrees, the balance between individual and communal living is a factor in all age-related settings.

The fact that these age-related environments are the residence of more older women living alone leads to reflection on gender difference and communal engagement, which requires further research. Companionship and activities within a secure environment may be welcomed by all, yet there will be different levels of friendship between men and women. Additionally, although couples may live together in housing (with care), in care homes it is seldom the case, and a spouse may become a visiting partner (Gopinath et al, forthcoming).

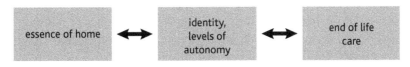

Focusing on this final scenario of long-term care recognises that globally this is an issue facing the political economy of all countries at different stages of development where family care is not able or willing to provide end-of-life care. An affordable solution is needed for people in extreme old age who can no longer maintain independent living through informal or formal home care and seek quality long term care embracing end of life. The WHO makes the case for smaller scale residential settings, particularly for people with dementia, which, although offering formal care, are able to draw upon family, friends and volunteers (WHO, 2015a, pp 127–36). If these settings were central to community living, then the experience of end of life could be supported more widely across generations. Additionally, small-scale and community integrated age-related housing (with levels of care) could affect how people perceive staying put in general housing, as moving within place may enable a sense of remaining in intergenerational communities.

This discussion is drawn primarily from British research concerning later life, and elsewhere with regard to the concept of home this author has stated: 'Perhaps it is somewhere that, when you lose the essence of it, you give up on life as you have lived it, whatever your situation' (Peace, 2015, p 452). This is based on the complexity of meanings, and how degrees of control, risk-taking and safety within place, alongside delegated support, enable an acceptable level of continuity. Here, being older associates home with well-being, which is linked to those issues of agency, comfort, belonging, identity and autonomy – constructs with degrees of value across these environments of ageing.

The spatiality of ageing

Finally, we turn to the boundaries between global to local, local to global interaction. As this writing advanced, there was concern that having concentrated on local experience of varied places and settings for older people primarily in the UK, the text would fail to return to the global challenges and initiatives raised earlier. However, the way in which these topics cross the levels of spatial scale (Figure 0.1) are relational and interchange with each other (Figure 10.3). As noted through the work of Massey in Chapter 1, they are 'part of ubiquitous social relations that give place multiple identities'. And, as the sociologist Beck comments, with regard to globalisation, 'Issues of global concern are becoming part of the everyday local experiences and the "moral life-worlds" of the people' (2002, p 17).

Figure 10.3 aims to indicate fluidity and how challenges to the spatiality of ageing relate, impact and influence across levels. There are both circular and direct actions. For example, at present, global directives on health issues from the WHO are developed through national (meso-) strategic initiatives which may connect the global (macro-) to the local (micro-). Various examples of interrelationships are discussed in this chapter, and the flow schemas indicate action within and between levels. They may seem local, but encompass different forms of relational space that may only be known through the detailed environmental biography of the individual. For

Figure 10.3: The spatiality of ageing: global to local, local to global

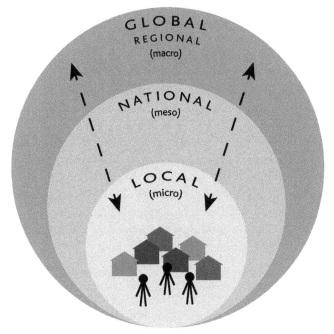

example, available and accessible public transport (local) will influence the development of the age-friendly community (local/national), which is part of a global network (global).

Other issues go directly from global to local or local to global, bringing together personal values and life histories with global issues that impact lives. Time is central to the way in which these relationships are ever changing, running alongside accessibility and availability. For example, the personal decision for a person with Type 1 diabetes to have a sensor in their arm in order to give constant glucose monitoring through a cell phone relates directly to the individual, their (local/national) health system, (global) technology and resources. Or the decision to become a climate change activist can be immediate, whether or not it can be directly put into practice. It is about ideology and commitment that at different levels can be recognised by national, local and individual governance. The comments from Greta Thunberg and Anne Karpf are witness to this.

These examples show an individual who is able to make choices – to consider holding and voicing a particular view or to have access to services, education, equipment and support. Here, cultural values, national infrastructure and personal agency are dependent on the drivers of change in place, the levels of development, where the power lies, the financial resources, educational opportunities, all of which will affect the social inclusion and exclusion of individuals directed by intersectional factors, including age. In a time of global capitalism, the global market is currently experiencing variation in growth. Owing to the global pandemic, internal businesses in many countries, including sectors such as hospitality, retail, and leisure, have suffered from degrees of lockdown, while other nations continue to manage to export goods. Nations are having to borrow money to support populations, and the future of this scenario is unknown debt. With regard to different employment scenarios, the impact in many areas is uncertain.

The future beyond the pandemic seems full of pluses and minuses, and solutions have to be social as well as political. This is a point when a health tragedy could influence more humane levels of governance – global to local, local to global – with a recognition of the value of democracy that involves the diversity of people of all ages. Utilising relationality across environments offers innovative ways of looking at the impact of the spatiality of ageing, not only in later life but also across the life course.

Conclusions

The complexity of the ageing self can be deconstructed in many ways, and the present author has focused on P–E interaction within locations and settings offering different contextual perspectives. This is a multidisciplinary field in which research can have practical applications. The concepts, frameworks and theoretical perspectives outlined earlier have been drawn upon, bringing together environmental and geographical gerontology, and leading to the adoption of the relational approach.

Reflecting on this detailed narrative, contribution is made to issues raised earlier by Scheidt and Schwarz (2013) in Chapter 2 and 9 that require further explanation or development in environmental gerontology. Central to discussions has been the concept of home and ageing 'in the right place' across different types of place, accommodation and care, to show how setting and location can contribute to the maintenance of autonomy through combined social, material and emotional environments that offer different levels of personal agency, comfort and belonging. By focusing on the built environment, attention is drawn both to the need for increased housing adaptation and the development of more sustainable housing, recognising the value of inclusive design for all ages and abilities, including those with dementia or other long-term conditions that impact on mobility and engagement. For movers to age-related housing (with care), how people acknowledge their ageing selves through comparison with others is also noted, and the harm caused by competence-related stigma in group living and group association is recognised; an issue that contributes to the discussion of the social imaginary of setting.

The introduction of global challenges highlights the interface between different environments of ageing. While the global COVID-19 pandemic foregrounds the relationship between global health and ageing, it cannot overwhelm other life-threatening concerns, as seen in relation to climate change and health as well as climate change and action. The relationship between levels of spatiality of ageing are noted – with connections from global to local, local to global. Attention is drawn to the age-friendly cities and communities initiative, and the value of community service provision regarding transportation and meeting places disrupted during the pandemic. The impact of technological development is underlined, with availability and affordability being central. Consideration is also drawn to transnational lives and the needs of older migrants and remainers, recognising the importance of understanding diversity within initiatives that aim to be age-friendly.

In terms of methodological development, there has been a focus on participatory research involving older people in determining research questions, being involved in data collection and in creating research tools grounded in reality. In learning new skills, co-researchers increase their social capital, enabling the research process and hopefully experiencing enjoyable levels of engagement. This development is also true for academic researchers involved in multi/inter-disciplinary/professional study, where the value of exchange needs to be greater than the sum of its parts.

To conclude, ongoing concern regarding environment and ageing and the synergy of issues at different levels of spatiality raises questions for future research content and method. While research in the local near environment is understandable, focus lies with both indoor and outdoor spaces. This association requires further research to examine the association or dissonance that may exist between these spaces in terms of belonging and agency, particularly for people living with dementia, and more broadly for understanding the meaning of home. New housing development has been noted, including co-design, and issues of sustainability through innovation are important. Initiatives should be monitored, post-occupancy evaluation carried out and understanding gained of both continued ageing in place and housing transitions between generations.

Technological development will transform aspects of daily living, and research must consider the impact on housing adaptation and whether staying put continues to be the preferred option in later life. Also of importance is the period of decision-making regarding relocation to different forms of housing – intergenerational and age-related housing (with care) across types of tenure. Little is known about these periods of transition or how these changes in housing types influence age segregation and integration between generations. The need for longitudinal research in new environments has been noted with a continued examination of the interface between housing, health and social care. These are issues with national implications where global comparison would bring greater explanation and where access to technology across populations will assist communication.

With regard to method, we must find innovative ways of exploring longitudinal perspectives where continuity and change over time can be captured. Could environmental biographies through oral history methods add detail to more factual records of housing history and housing design? Could mixed methods approaches extend to consider the triangulation of findings from 'big data' with those that capture the qualitative experience discussed and researched by non-representational theorists, in order to offer a different approach to how we understand affect, ageing and environment?

All these areas have potential for focusing on the diversity of the older population and examining the inequalities, gendered and culturally diverse, that are faced by those who are asset poor and face disadvantage. Environmental gerontology has an enormous capacity to continue to strengthen our knowledge of how people are living lives of social inclusion and exclusion. Finally, those working in this field should engage with a broader understanding of the spatiality of ageing, embedding older age within the wide demography that situates everyday lives not only in local and national contexts that are social, physical, economic and cultural, but also in relation to global challenges shared by all. These are all a part of the environments of ageing; it is an ongoing concern.

Glossary of terms

Abbeyfield
This was registered as a charity in 1956 and has operated supported (sheltered) housing since the mid-1950s, beginning with the work of Richard Carr-Gomm. https://www.abbeyfield.com

Age UK
On 1 April 2009, Age Concern England and Help the Aged merged to become Age UK. The leading charity for older people offering information and advice. https://www.ageuk.org.uk/

All Party Parliamentary Group (APPG) on Housing and Care for Older People is an officially registered APPG established in 2009 currently supported by Housing 21. It aims to highlight the importance of the role of housing alongside social care and health. Chaired by Lord Richard Best it has been responsible for developing the Housing our Ageing Population: Panel for Innovation (HAPPI) programme of work (see below).

The Almshouse Association
The Almshouse Association is a supported charity representing some 1600 independent almshouse charities across the UK. Some 36,000 people live independent lives in almshouses, low cost housing held in trust for local people in housing need. https://www.almshouses.org/

Alzheimer's Society
The Alzheimer's Society is the UK's leading dementia charity. They campaign for change and fund research. https://www.alzheimers.org.uk/

Anchor Hanover
Annchor Hanover Group is the largest provider of specialised housing and care for older people in England. It was formed in November 2018 when Anchor Trust and Hanover Housing Association merged. The group has housing for rent, sale, housing with care, retirement villages and more than100 care homes. https://www.anchor.org.uk/

Bedroom standard
This term is used by the government as an indicator of occupation density. A standard number of bedrooms can be calculated for each household in accordance with its age/sex/marital status composition and the relationship of the members to one another.

The Allocations Code of Guidance recommends that the following bedroom standard is adopted as a minimum measure of overcrowding: one bedroom for each adult couple, any other adult aged 21 or over, two adolescents of the same sex aged 10 to 20, two children regardless of sex under the age of 10. https://www.england.shelterd.org.uk

Households are said to be overcrowded if they have fewer bedrooms available than the notional number needed. Households are said to be under-occupying if they have two or more bedrooms more than the notional needed (MHCLG, 2020a, p 35).

Brexit

The term used for the withdrawal of the UK from the EU on 31 December 2020 after a referendum in June 2016. The UK joined the European Communities that later became the EU in 1973.

Centre for Ageing Better

The Centre for Ageing Better, a charitable foundation since 2016, is funded by the National Lottery Community Fund with a ten-year endowment. The centre's primary aim is to support a good quality of life in older age and promote the benefits of an ageing society by bridging the gap between research, evidence and practice. It forms part of the What Works Centres network in England.

The Ageing Better Measures Framework provides an accessible bank of tools to help individuals and organisations working on ageing studies. At present, there are '63 measures, survey scales and their associated data sources looking at outcome at the individual level related to ageing and later life' (CfAB, 2021). https://www.ageing-better.org.uk/publications/ageing-better-measures-framework

Economic and Social Research Council (ESRC) Growing Older Programme

The ESRC followed the EQUAL programme by running a social science-led Growing Older programme from 1998 to 2003.

Elderly Accommodation Counsel

A national charity that was set up in 1985 to help older people make informed choices about meeting their housing, support and care needs. In 2008, it launched FirstStop, an independent telephone service giving comprehensive information and advice covering care, housing and financial matters. http://www.eac.org.uk/

English Housing Survey (EHS)

The EHS is a national survey of people's housing circumstances and the condition and energy efficiency of housing in England. It was first run in

2008–09. Prior to this point, two surveys were undertaken: the English House Condition Survey and the Survey of English Housing. The EHS consists of two main elements: an interview survey with an annual sample of approximately 13,300 households and a follow up physical inspection of dwellings (see MHCLG, 2020h).

In 2016, a special report entitled 'Housing for older people' analysed EHS data 2014–15 (DCLG, 2016). Here, older households were defined as those where the oldest person was aged 55 or over. The younger households were those where the oldest person was under 55. Data was were also analysed by age group: 55–64, 65–74, 75–84, 85 years and over. Questions were answered by the **Household Reference Person**.

The 2018–19 EHS presented a life course analysis that was undertaken using the age group: 16–34, 35–64, 65 years and over.

EPSRC EQUAL

The Engineering and Physical Sciences Research Council (EPSRC) Extending quality of life of older and disabled people (EQUAL) research programme ran from 1997 to 2003/4.

EU–28

Data are given for 28 EU countries including the UK. As of 1 January 2021, the UK was no longer an EU nation and as of October 2021 there are 27 EU countries.

The Freedom Pass

The Freedom Pass is a concessionary travel scheme, which began in 1973, to provide free travel to residents in Greater London, who are aged 66 and over (the age of eligibility increased progressively from 60 in 2010 to 66 in 2020) or who have a disability. It is valid on London Underground and Overground and London Buses, and managed by the London Councils.

Housing Our Ageing Population: Panel for Innovation (HAPPI)

The HAPPI initiative is directed through the All-Party Parliamentary Group (APPG) for housing and care for older people chaired by Lord Richard Best·

The **HAPPI panel**, also chaired by Lord Best, included:
- members with direct architectural experience;
- senior executives concerned with urban regeneration, enabling environments and providing housing with care;
- older people – a Housing Association resident; a senior health activist; a social scientist; a journalist/TV presenter; a ministry representative.

In 2008, the panel viewed 24 housing schemes in 6 European countries, including the UK. Jeremy Porteus, Director of the **Housing LIN**, has acted as secretary to this group, and with others, including Richard Best, has authored reports. To date there have been five **HAPPI** reports, with a recent inquiry by the APPG into housing for people with dementia (Twyford and Porteus, 2021).

Homeshare UK

Homeshare enables two unrelated people to share a home for mutaual benefit. An older householder with a spare room will be carefully matched with a younger person who will provide an agreed amount of support for affordable accommodation.

There is a Homeshare UK Network of practitioners delivering Homeshare services around the UK and Ireland. https://homeshareuk.org/about-homeshare/about-us/

Households by area type in the English Housing Survey, 2014–15

All households are classified according to the ONS 2011 urban–rural classification system:

Urban: includes a built-up area with a population of more than 10,000 people.

Rural: includes town and fringe, village, hamlets and isolated dwellings.

Household Reference Person (HRP)

The person in whose name the dwelling is owned or rented or who is otherwise responsible for the accommodation. In the case of joint owners and tenants, the person with the highest income is taken as the HRP.

Housing 21

A leading not-for-profit provider of retirement housing and extra care for older people of modest means. https://www.housing21.org.uk

Housing Adaptation/Modification

In the UK, changing aspects of housing to meet the needs of people with an impairment or disability is called adaptation. The term home modification is used in the US, Australia and Sweden, while home adaptation is used in the UK and Spain; Sweden uses both terms.

Housing Corporation

This was established by the Housing Act 1964. It was a non-departmental public body that funded new affordable housing and regulated housing associations in England. Abolished in 2008, its responsibilities were split between the Homes and Communities Agency and the Tenants Services Authority. http://www.gov.uk/government/organisation/housing-corporation

Housing Enabler

Susanne Iwarsson and Bjorn Slaug, based at the University of Lund, Sweden, are the copyright holders for the Housing Enabler. The instrument is a commercial product sold by Veten and Skapen HB och Slaug Enabling Development.

Housing LIN

The Housing LIN knowledge and information exchange was originally supported by the Care and Support Specialised Housing Fund (2015–18). Currently, independent of the Department of Health, Housing LIN is now sponsored and supported by organisations such as the Nationwide Building Society. https://www.housinglin.org.uk/_assets/Resources/Housing/Support_materials

Index of Local Deprivation

The national assessment of indicators of multiple deprivation considers seven domains (income, employment, health, education, crime, access to services, living environments. (MHCLG, 2019a)

International Longevity Centre UK (ILC-UK)

ILC-UK is a specialist think tank on the impact of longevity. The centre established in 1997 is part of an international network on longevity. A small team headed by Chief Executive Baroness Sally Greengross organise events and have published over 250 reports. www.https.ilcuk.org.uk

King's Fund Centre – design care homes

In 2003, the Department of Health commissioned the King's Fund to develop specific programmes to enhance the environment of care as part of the department's work to improve patient experience. The most recent of these was a programme to improve the care environment for people with dementia in hospital, to support the implementation of the national dementia strategy and the prime minister's 'Challenge on Dementia'. https://www.kingsfund.org.uk/projects/enhancing-healing-environments

Laing and Buisson

Laing and Buisson is a leading business intelligence provider that has worked for over 30 years developing insights, analysis and data on market structures, policy and strategy across healthcare, social care and education. They have presented market reports across this time.

Tables in Chapter 8 from Laing and Buisson's reports 2018, 2019 are now presented for older people 65 and over. Earlier data analysis reported figures for elderly, chronically ill and physically disabled people, which resulted in a slight difference in figures but not in overall trends. https://www.laingbuisson.com/about-laingbuisson/

Methodist Homes (MHA)

Methodist Homes (MHA) was established in 1943 by a group of Methodists who wanted to improve the quality of life of older people. Their first residential care home was opened in 1945, and first specialist nursing care home built in 1989. They operate care homes offering nursing, dementia care and residential care, retirement housing, housing with care and retirement villages. https://www.mha.org.uk/

Ministry of Housing, Communities and Local Government (MHCLG) named in January 2018 (previously the Department of Communities and Local Government (DCLG)).

Its job is to create great places to live and work, and give more power to local people to shape what happens in their area. It is also successor to the Office of the Deputy Prime Minister, established in 2001.

In September 2021, the MHCLG was rebranded by government to become the Department of Levelling Up, Housing and Communities (DLUHC) dropping 'local government' from its title. The consequences of this change are yet to be seen. https://www.lgcplus.com/politics/mhclg-to-be-renamed-department-for-levelling-up-housing-and-communities-20-09-2021/

My Home Life

My Home Life was originally founded in 2006 by the National Care Forum in partnership with Help the Aged (now **Age UK**) and City, University of London with the goal of promoting care homes as important places to live, work and visit. There are regional network members. www.myhomelife.org.uk

Poor Law

The Poor Law system of relief for the poor was created in England and Wales in 1601, initially with responsibility in church parishes and later, in 1834, through unions of grouped parishes managed by Boards of Guardians. Workhouses provided dwellings for those without jobs or homes. Similar systems emerged in Scotland and Northern Ireland. The Local Government Act 1929 abolished the Poor Law Unions and transferred the administration of poor relief to local government. This saw the demise of the Poor Law system and legislation in 1930 abolished the workhouse even though many were renamed as Public Assistance Institutions, controlled by local county councils.

Power of Attorney

A power of attorney is a legal document that allows someone to make decisions for you, or act on your behalf, if you are no longer able to or if you no longer want to make your own decisions.
www.gov.uk/power-of-attorney

RNIB (Royal National Institute for the Blind)

A UK charity offering information, support and advice to almost two million people in the UK with sight loss.
http://www.rnib.org.uk/aboutus/research/statistics/Pages/statistics.aspx

Small care homes

Registered small residential homes have less than 4 residential places. Until the Registered Homes (Amendment) Act, 1991, small residential homes were not required to register with local authorities. When the Act came into force in 1993, many former adult family placements along with other establishments were reclassified as small homes and may accommodate a small number of older, or younger people with disabilities in forms of independent living. Provision for older people has been aggregated with other residential provision since the late 1990s. They are regulated through the Care Quality Commission.

Social Housing

In the UK, social housing is provided by the local authority for all ages. It used to be called council housing. Specialised social housing may be sheltered housing for older people, first provided by local authorities.

UK Cohousing and the Cohousing Directory

The UK Cohousing Network is discussed in Chapter 7. It can be found online at https://cohousing.org.uk and the Cohousing Directory is also part of the same site: https://cohousing.org.uk/members-directory/.

United Kingdom, Britain, British Isles – the United Kingdom is used in relation to England, Wales, Scotland and Northern Ireland. Britain, Great Britain and the British Isles are used in relation to England, Wales and Scotland. In this text some statistical data and legislation relates to England and Wales.

The current form of devolution in the UK goes back to the late 1990s. In 1997, voters chose to create a Scottish Parliament and a National Assembly for Wales. In Northern Ireland, devolution was a key element of the Belfast (Good Friday) Agreement and was supported in a referendum in 1998.

United Nations Framework Convention on Climate Change (UNFCCC)

A treaty was agreed in 1994 to stabilise greenhouse emissions and protect the earth from the threat of climate change. The **Intergovernmental Panel on Climate Change (IPCC)** is the UN body for assessing the science related to climate change. The **Conference of Parties (COP)** is the decision-making body of the **UNFCCC** and attends an annual conference. COP-26 was led by the UK in partnership with Italy in November 2021 in Glasgow.

United Nations Regions – The 5 UN regions are Africa, Americas, Asia and the Pacific, Europe and Central Asia, and Middle East.
https://www.un.org/en/sections/where-we-work/#:~:text=The%20UN's%20work%20is%20divided,Asia%2C%20and%20the%20Middle%20East.

United Nations (UN) Sustainable Development Goals

There are 17 sustainable development goals, which were set by the UN General Assembly in 2015 intending to be achieved by 2030. They cover the following areas: 1. No poverty. 2. Zero hunger. 3. Good health and well-being. 4. Quality education. 5. Gender inequality. 6. Clean water and sanitation. 7. Affordable and clean energy. 8. Decent work and economic growth. 9. Industry, innovation and infrastructure. 10. Reduced inequalities. 11. Sustainable cities and communities. 12. Responsible consumption and production. 13. Climate action. 14. Life below water. 15. Life on land. 16. Peace, Justice and strong institutions. 17. Partnership for the goals. They are subject to on-going consideration.

Warm Front

Relates to provision of heating services introduced in Wales and Northern Ireland.

White Paper/Green Paper

A government White Paper presents policy preferences before introducing legislation. It tests public opinion. Green Papers are more open-ended and may be issued more frequently.

World Health Organization (WHO) Regions

WHO member states are grouped into six regions: Africa, Americas, South-East Asia, Eastern Mediterranean, Europe, Western Pacific.
https://www.who.int/about/who-we-are/regional-offices

References

Abel-Smith, B. (1964) *The Hospitals 1800–1984*, London: Heinemann.

Aboderin, I. (2004) 'Modernisation and ageing theory revisited: current explanations of recent developing world and historical western shifts in material family support for older people', *Ageing and Society*, 24: 29–50.

Aboderin, I. (2005) 'Changing family relationships in developing nations', in M.L. Johnson, V.L. Bengtson, P. Coleman and T. Kirkwood (eds) *The Cambridge Handbook of Age and Ageing*, Cambridge: Cambridge University Press, pp 469–75.

Aboderin, I. (2016) 'Coming into its own? Developments and challenges for research an aging in Africa', *Journals of Gerontology: Social Science,* 72 (4): 643–5.

Aboderin, I. and Hoffman, J. (2012) 'Care for older adults in sub-Saharan Africa: Discourses and realities of family solidarity', invited Presidential Symposium, Taking care? Global discourses on intergenerational relationships and family support, 65th Annual Scientific Meeting, Gerontological Society of America (GSA), 14–18 November, San Diego, US.

Aboderin, I. and Beard, J.R. (2014) 'Older people's health in sub-Saharan Africa', *The Lancet*, 385: e9–e11.

Adams, S. (2016) *Off the Radar: Housing Disrepair & Health Impact in Later Life*, Nottingham: Care & Repair.

Adams, S. and Hodges, M. (2018) *Adapting for Ageing: Good Practice and Innovation in Home Adaptations*, London: Centre for Ageing Better.

Addis, S., Davies, M., Greene, G., Macbride-Stewart, S. and Shepherd, M. (2009) 'The health, social care and housing needs of lesbian, gay, bisexual and transgender older people: a review of the literature', *Health and Social Care in the Community*, 17 (6): 647–58.

Age Concern and Help the Aged (2009) *One Voice: Shaping our Ageing Society,* London: Age Concern/Help the Aged.

Age UK (2017) 'Factsheet 64: specialist housing for older people', London: Age UK. Available at: https://www.ageuk.org.uk/globalassets/age-ni/documents/factsheets/fs64_specialist_housing_for_older_people_fcs.pdf

Age UK (2019) *Later Life in the United Kingdom*, London: AgeUK.

Ahlin, T. (2017) 'Only near is dear? Doing elderly care with everyday ICTs in Indian transnational families', *Medical Anthropology Quarterly: International Journal of the Analysis of Health*, 32 (1): 85–102.

Alder, D. (2017) *Home Truths: A Progressive Vision of Housing Policy in the 21st Century*, London: Tony Blair Institute for Global Change.

Alexander Shaw, K. (2018) 'Baby boomers versus millennials & rhetorical conflicts and interest-construction in the new politics of intergenerational fairness', Sheffield Political Economy Research Institute, University of Sheffield, 18 January. Available at: http://speri.dept.shef.ac.uk/2018/01/18/baby-boomers-versus-millennials-new-paper-on-the-politics-of-intergenerational-fairness/

Almack, K. and King, A. (2019) 'Lesbian, gay, bisexual and trans aging in a UK context: critical observations of recent research literature', *International Journal of Aging and Human Development*, 89 (1): 93–107.

Alonso-Lopez, F. (2020) 'Filling the gaps of housing adaptation in Spain: is private expenditure an alternative to public support?', *Journal of Aging and Environments*, 34 (2): 141–55.

Altman, I. and Low, S.M. (1992) *Place Attachment*, New York: Springer.

Altus, D.E. and Mathews, R.M. (2000) 'Examining satisfaction of older home owners with intergenerational homesharing', *Journal of Clinical Geropsychology*, 6: 139–47.

Alzheimer Research UK/Dementia Statistics Hub (2021) 'Dementia statistics'. Available at: https://www.alzheimersresearchuk.org/dementia-information/dementia-statistics-hub/

Alzheimer's Society (2018) Caring for carers: Carers quality of life, *Care & Cure Magazine*, Autumn. Available at: https://www.alzheimers.org.uk/Care-and-cure-magazine/Autumn-18/caring-carers-carer-quality-life

Alzheimer's Society (2020) 'Growing number older people with dementia living in care homes'. Available at: https://www.alzheimers.org.uk/

American Institute of Architects (2014) *Design for aging review. AIA Design for Aging Knowledge Community*. Victoria, Australia: The Images Publishing Group.

Andrews, G.J. and Phillips, D.R. (eds) (2005) *Ageing and Place: Perspectives, Policy and Practice*, Abingdon: Routledge.

Andrews, G.J. and Grenier, A. (2015) 'Ageing movement as space-time: introducing non-representational theory to the geography of ageing', *Progress in Geography*, 34 (12): 1512–34. http://dx.doi.org/10.18306/dlkxjz.2015.12.003

Andrews, G.J., Evans, J. and Wiles, J. (2013). 'Re-spacing and re-placing gerontology: relationality and affect', *Ageing & Society*, 33 (8): 1339–73. http://dx.doi.org10.1017/S0144686X12000621

Andrews, G.J., Cutchin, M.P. and Skinner, M.W. (2018) 'Space and place in geographical gerontology: theoretical traditions, formations of hope', In M. Skinner., G.J. Andrews, and M.P. Cutchin (eds) (2018) *Geographical Gerontology: Perspectives, Concepts, Approaches*, Abingdon: Routledge, pp 11–28.

Andrews, G.J., Milligan, C., Phillips, D.R. and Skinner, M.W. (2009) 'Geographical gerontology: mapping a disciplinary intersection', *Geography Compass*, 3 (5): 1641–59. http://dx.doi.org/10.1111/j.1749-8198.2009.00270.x

Andrews, G.J., Cutchin, M., McCracken, K., Phillips, D.R. and Wiles, J. (2007) 'Geographical gerontology: the constitution of a discipline', *Social Science and Medicine*, 65 (1): 151–68. http://dx.doi.org/10.1016/j.socscimed.2007.02.047

Angus, J., Kontos, P.C., Dyck, I., McKeever, P. and Poland, B. (2005) 'The personal significance of home: habitus and the experience of receiving long term home care', *Sociology of Health and Illness*, 27: 161–87.

Aplin, T., Hayle, M., Fiechtner, E., Bailey, A. and Ainsworth, E. (2020) 'Home modification and service delivery in Australia', *Journal of Aging and Environment*, 34 (2): 190–209.

Apt, N.A. (2011) 'Aging in Africa: Past past experiences and strategic directions', *Ageing International*, 37 (1): 93–103.

Arber, S., Davidson, K. and Ginn, J. (eds) (2003) *Gender and Ageing: Changing Roles and Relationships*, Maidenhead: Open University Press.

Arendt, H. (1998) [1958] *The Human Condition* (2nd edn), Chicago: University of Chicago Press.

Atkinson, D. and Williams, F. (1990) *Know Me As I Am: An Anthology of Prose, Poetry and Art by People with Learning Difficulties*, Cambridge: Hodder Education.

Atkinson, T.J., Evans, S., Darton, R., Cameron, A., Porteus, J. and Smith, R. (2014) 'Creating the asset base – a review of literature and policy on housing with care', *Housing, Care and Support*, 17 (1): 16–25.

Atkinson, R.W., Anallitis, A., Samoli, E., Fuller, G.W., Green, D.C., Mudway, I.S., Anderson, H.R. and Kelley, F.J. (2016) 'Short-term exposure to traffic-related air pollution and daily mortality in London', UK *Journal of Exposure Science & Environmental Epidemiology*, 26: 125–32.

Atsushi, Seike (2005) 'Japan's baby boomers and the year 2007 problem', *Japan Spotlight*, Nov/Dec: 6–9.

Audit Commission (2004) *Older People: Implementing Telecare*, London: Audit Commission.

Bachelard, G. (1958) *The Poetics of Space: The Classic Look at How we Experience Intimate Places*, Boston, MA: Beacon Press Books.

Backhouse, T., Penhale, B., Gray, R. and Killett, A. (2018) 'Questionable practices despite good intentions: coping with risk and impact from dementia-related behaviours in care homes', *Ageing & Society*, 38 (9): 1933–58.

Bagnall, A-M. (2020) 'Final report: Leeds Homeshare local evaluation', project report, Leeds Beckett University. Available at: http://eprints.leedsbeckett.ac.uk/id/eprint/7231/1/FinalReportLeedsHomeshareLocalEvaluationPV-BAGNALL.pdf

Baily, J., Biggs, I. and Buzzo, D. (2014) 'Deep mapping and rural connectivities', in C.H. Hennessy., R. Means and V. Burholt. (eds) *Countryside Connections: Older People, Community and Place in Rural Britain*, Bristol: Policy Press, pp 159–92.

Baltes, P.B. and Baltes, M.M. (eds) (1990) *Successful Aging. Perspectives from the Behavioural Sciences*, Cambridge: Cambridge University Press.

Baltes, P.B. and Meyer, K.U. (eds) (1999) *The Berlin Aging Study*, Cambridge: Cambridge University Press.

Baltes, M.M., Maas, L., Wilms, H-U. and Borchelt, M. (1999) 'Everyday competence in old and very old age: theoretical considerations and empirical findings', in P.B. Baltes and K.U. Meyer (eds) *The Berlin Aging Study*, Cambridge: Cambridge University Press, pp 384–402.

Bangor, S. Hargreaves, S. and Mountain, G. (2015) *The Impact of Ageing Research within the Research Excellence Framework 2014: An Evaluation*, British Society of Gerontology.

Barac, M. and Park, J. (2009) 'Housing our ageing population: panel for innovation (HAPPI)', London: Homes and Communities Agency. Available at: http://www.housinglin.org.uk/Topics/browse/Design-building/HAPPI/

Barlow, J., Singh, D., Bayer, S. and Curry, R. (2007) 'A systematic review of the benefits of home telecare for frail elderly people and those with long term conditions', *Journal of Telemedicine and Telecare*, 13 (4): 172–9.

Barnes, M. and Walker, A. (1996) 'Consumerism versus empowerment: a principled approach to the involvement of older service users', *Policy and Politics*, 24 (4): 375–93.

Barnes, S. (2002) 'The design of caring environments and the quality of life of older people', *Ageing & Society*, 22: 75–89.

Barnes, S., Torrington, J., Darton, R., Holder, J., Lewis, A., McKee, K., Netten, A. and Orrell, A. (2012) 'Does the design of extra-care housing meet the needs of the residents? A focus group study', *Ageing & Society*, 32 (7): 1193–214.

Barnes, S., Park, A. and Wigglesworth, S. (2015) 'Designing for wellbeing in environments for later life', Available at: https://www.housinglin.org.uk/_assets/Resources/Housing/Blogs/HLIN_DWELL_blog.pdf

Barreto, M., Victor, C., Hammond, C., Eccles, A., Richins, M.T. and Qualter, P. (2021) 'Loneliness around the world: age, gender, and cultural differences in loneliness', *Personality and Individual Differences*, 169: 110066.

Barron, A. (2019) 'More-than-representational approaches to the life course', *Social and Cultural Geography*, 14 (5): 1–24.

Barton, C., Garton, G. and Grunwood, G. (2019) 'What next for planning in England?', research briefing, National Planning Policy Framework, House of Commons Library, London. Available at: https://commonslibrary.parliament.uk/research-briefings/cbp-8260/

Barton, R. (1959) *Institutional Neurosis*, 2nd edn, Bristol: John Wright and Son.

Bates, T. (2016) 'Why technology is not always the answer to your problem', Online Learning and Distance Education Resources. Available at: https://www.tonybates.ca/2016/01/30/why-digital-technology-is-not-necessarily-the-answer-to-your-problem/

Bauer, M., Fetherstonhaugh, D., Tarzia, L. and Chenco, C. (2014) 'Staff-family relationships in residential aged care facilities: the views of residents' family members and care staff', *Journal of Applied Gerontology*, 33 (5): 564–85.

Bäumker, T., Callaghan, L., Darton, R., Holder, J., Netten, A. and Tower, A. (2011) 'Deciding to move into extra care: resident's views', *Ageing & Society*, 32 (7):1215–45.

Baxter, K., Heavey, E. and Birks, Y. (2020) 'Choice and control in social care: experiences of older self-funders in England', *Social Policy & Administration*, 54 (3): 460–74.

Baylis, J. and Sly, F. (2010) 'Ageing across the UK', *Regional Trends*, 42: 2–28.

Beard, J. and Petitot, C. (2011) 'Aging and urbanization: can cities be designed to foster active aging?', *Public Health Review*, 32 (2): 427–50.

Beck, U. (2002) "The cosmopolitan society and its enemies', *Theory, Culture & Society*, 19 (1–2): 17–44.

Bengtson, V.L. (2016) 'How theories of aging became social: emergence of the sociology of aging', in V.L. Bengtson and R.A. Settersten Jr (eds) (2016) *Handbook of Theories of Aging* (3rd edn), New York: Springer, pp 67–86.

Bengtson, V.L. and Settersten, Jr, R.A. (2016) 'Theories of aging: developments within and across', in V.L. Bengtson. and R.A. Settersten Jr. (eds) (2016) *Handbook of Theories of Aging* (3rd edn), New York: Springer, pp 1–8.

Bengtson, V.L., Putney, N.M. and Johnson, M.J. (2005) 'The problem of theory in gerontology today', in M.L. Johnson. *The Cambridge Handbook of Age and Ageing*, Cambridge: Cambridge University Press, pp 3–21.

Bennett, G.J. and Ibrahim, S. (1992) *The Essentials of Health Care of the Elderly*, London: Edward Arnold.

Bennett, G., Kingston, P. and Penhale, B. (1997) *The Dimensions of Elder Abuse: Perspective for Practitioners*, New York: Springer.

Beresford, P. (2005) 'Service user': regressive or liberatory terminology?', *Disability & Society*, 20 (4): 469–77.

Beresford, P. (2021) *Participatory Ideology: From Exclusion to Involvement*, Bristol: Policy Press.

Berg, V. (2021) 'Care home fees and costs: how much do you pay?', Available at: https://www.carehome.co.uk/advice/care-home-fees-and-costs-how-much-do-you-pay

Bernard, M., Bartlam, B., Biggs, S. and Sim, J. (2004) *New Lifestyles in Old Age: Health, Identity and Well-Being in Berryhill Retirement Village*, Bristol: Policy Press.

Bernard, M., Bartlam, B., Sim, J. and Biggs, S. (2007) 'Housing and care for older people: life in an English purpose-built retirement village', *Ageing & Society* 27 (4): 555–78.

Bernard, M., Liddle, J., Bartlam, B., Scharf, T. and Sim, J. (2012) 'Then and now: evolving community in the context of a retirement village', *Ageing & Society*, 32 (1): 103–29.

Bernard, M. and Rowles, G.D. (2013) 'Past, present and future in designing private and public environments for creating and sustaining place', in G.D. Rowles and M. Bernard (eds) *Environmental Gerontology: Making Meaningful Places in Old Age*, New York: Springer Publishing, pp 283–304.

Best, R. and Martin, A. (2019) 'Housing our ageing population: rental housing for an ageing population (HAPPI 5)', All Party Parliamentary Group on Housing and Care for Older People, Housing LIN, London. Available at: https://www.london.gov.uk/what-we-do/planning/london-plan/current-london-plan/london-plan-chapter-seven-londons-living-space-7

Best, R. and Porteus, J. (2012) 'Housing our ageing population: plan for implementation (HAPPI 2)', All Party Parliamentary Group on Housing and Care for Older People inquiry report, Housing Lin, London. Available at: https://www.housinglin.org.uk/_assets/Resources/Housing/Support_materials/Other_reports_and_guidance/Housing_our_Ageing_Population_Plan_for_Implementation.pdf

Best, R. and Porteus, J. (2016) 'Housing our ageing population: positive ideas (HAPPI 3)', All Party Parliamentary Group on Housing and Care for Older People inquiry report, Housing LIN, London. Available at: https://www.housinglin.org.uk/_assets/Resources/Housing/Support_materials/Other_reports_and_guidance/HAPPI3_Report_2016.pdf (accessed February 2021)

Bevan, C. and Laurie, E. (2017) 'The Housing and Planning Act 2016: rewarding the aspiration of homeownership?', *Modern Law Review*, 80 (4): 661–84.

Bevan, M. and Croucher, K. (2011) 'Lifetime neighbourhoods', Department of Communities and Local Government, London. Available at: https://www.york.ac.uk/media/chp/documents/2011/lifetimeneighbourhoods.pdf

Bhatti, M. (2006) '"When I'm in the garden I can create my own paradise": homes and gardens in later life', *The Sociological Review*, 54 (2): 318–41.

Bichard, Jo-Anne., van den Heuvel, E., Jowitt, F., Gilhooly, M., Parker, S.G., Long, A., Ratcliffe, N.M., McKee, K. and Gaydecki, P. (2012),'Tackling ageing continence through theory, tools & technology', *Ageing & Society*, 1 (2): 83–96.

Bieber, M. (2003) 'The struggle for independence', in J. Clarkson, R. Coleman, S. Keates. and C. Lebbon (eds) *Inclusive Design: Design for the Whole Population*, London: Springer-Verlag, pp 50–7.

Biggs, S. (1996) 'A family concern: elder abuse in British social policy', *Critical Social Policy*, 16 (7): 63–88.

Biggs, S. and Tinker, A. (2007) 'What makes a city age friendly?', London: Help the Aged, King's College London, pp 171–84.

Biggs, S., Bernard, M., Kingston, P. and Nettleton, H. (2000) 'Lifestyles of belief: narrative and culture in a retirement community', *Ageing & Society*, 20 (6): 649–72.

Biggs, S., Phillipson, C., Leech, R. and Money, A. (2007) 'Baby boomers and adult ageing: issues for social and public policy', *Quality in Ageing and Older Adults*, 8 (3): 32–40.

Bildgardt, T. and Oberg, P. (2019) *Intimacy and Ageing: New Relationships in Later Life*, Bristol: Policy Press.

Blaikie, A. (2005) 'Imagined landscapes of age and identity', in G.J. Andrews. and D.R. Phillips. (eds) *Ageing and Place: Perspectives, Policy, Practice*, London: Routledge, pp 164–76.

Blakemore, K. (1999) 'International migration in later life: social care and policy implications. *Ageing & Society*, 19 (6): 761–74.

Bland, R. (1999) 'Independence, privacy and risk: two contrasting approaches to residential care for older people', *Ageing & Society*, 19 (5): 539–60.

Blozman, C. (2013) 'Ageing immigrants and the question of return: new answers to an old dilemma?', in J. Percival (ed) *Return Migration in Later Life: International Perspectives*, Bristol: Policy Press, pp 67–87.

Blozman, C., Poncioni-Derigo. R., Vial, M. and Fibbi, R. (2004) 'Older labour migrants' wellbeing in Europe: the case of Switzerland', *Ageing & Society*, 24 (3): 411–29.

Blunt, A. and Varley, A. (2004) 'Geographies of home', *Cultural Geographies*, 11: 3–6.

Boccagni, P. (2017) 'Addressing transnational needs through migration? An inquiry into the needs and consequences of migrants' social protection across borders', *Global Social Policy*, 17 (2): 168–87.

Bondi, L. (1998) 'Gender, class, and urban space: public and private space in contemporary urban landscapes', *Urban Geography*, 19 (2): 160–85.

Booth, E. (2019) Extinction Rebellion: social work, climate change and solidarity', *Critical and Radical Social Work*, 7 (2): 257–61.

Booth, T. (1985) *Home Truths: Old People's Homes and the Outcome of Care*, Aldershot: Gower.

Bornat, J. (ed) (1994) *Reminiscence Reviewed: Perspectives, Evaluations, Achievements*, Buckingham: Open University Press.

Bornat, J. (2001) 'Reminiscence and oral history: parallel universes or shared endeavour?', *Ageing & Society*, 21 (2): 219–41.

Bothwell, E. (2019) 'Is interdisciplinary research really the best way to tackle global challenges?', *Times Higher Educational Supplement*, December. Available at: https://www.timeshighereducation.com/features/interdisciplinary-research-really-best-way-tackle-global-challenges

Bottery, S. (2021) 'What will the government's proposals mean for the social care system?', London: The King's Fund. Available at: https://www.kingsfund.org.uk/publications/government-proposals-social-care-system

Bourdieu, P. (1977) *Outline of a Theory of Practice*, Cambridge: Cambridge University Press.

Bourdieu, P. (1998) *Practical Reason*, Stanford, CA: Stanford University Press.

Bourdieu, P. and Wacquant, L. (1992) *An Invitation to Reflexive Sociology*, Cambridge: Polity Press.

Bowes, A. and McColgan, G. (2013) 'Telecare for older people: promoting independence, participation and identity', *Research on Aging*, 35 (1): 32–49.

Bowlby, S., Gregory, S. and McKie, L. (1997) '"Doing home": patriarchy, caring and space', *Women's Studies International Forum*, 20 (3): 343–50.

Bowling, A. and Stenner, P. (2011) 'Which measure of quality of life performs best in older age? A comparison of the OPQOL, CASP-19 and WHOQOL-OLD. Research report', *Journal of Epidemiology & Community Health*, 65 (3): 273–80. Available at: https://jech.bmj.com/content/65/3/273.short

Boys, J. (2014) *Doing Disability Differently: An Alternative Handbook of Architecture, Disability and Designing for Everyday Life*, London: Routledge.

Boys, J., Bradshaw, F., Darke, J., Foo, B., Francis, S., McFarlane, B., Roberts, M. and Wilkes, S. (1984) 'House design and women's roles', in Matrix (1984) *Women and the Man Made Environment*, London: Pluto Press, pp 55–120.

Brenton, M. (1999) *Choice, Autonomy and Mutual Support: Older Women's Collaborative Living Arrangements*, York: Joseph Rowntree Foundation.

Brenton, M. (2001) 'Older people's co-housing communities', in S. Peace and C. Holland (eds) *Inclusive Housing in an Ageing Society: Innovative Approaches*, Bristol: Policy Press, pp 169–88.

Brenton, M. (2013) *Senior Cohousing Communities – An Alternative Approach for the UK?* (JRF Programme Paper: A Better Life), London: Joseph Rowntree Foundation.

Brenton, M. (2017) *Community Building for Old Age: Breaking New Ground. The UK's First Senior Co-Housing Community, High Barnet* (Housing LIN Case Study no. 139), London: Housing LIN.

Brezzi, M., Dijkstra, L. and Ruiz, V. (2011) 'OECD extended regional typology', OECD/EU. Available at: https://www.oecd-ilibrary.org/content/paper/5kg6z83tw7f4-en?crawler=true

Brooker, D. (2005) 'Dementia care mapping: a review of the research literature', *The Gerontologist*, 45 (1): 11–18. https://doi.org/10.1093/geront./45.Suppl_1.11

Bronfenbrenner, U. (1979). *The Ecology of Human Development: Experiments by Nature and Design*, Cambridge, MA: Harvard University Press.

Bronfenbrenner, U. (1999) 'Environments in developmental perspective: theoretical and operational models', in S.L. Friedman and T.D. Wachs (eds) *Measuring Environment across the Life Span*, Washington DC: American Psychological Association, pp 3–28.

Brown Wilson, C., Swarbrick, C., Pilling, M. and Keady, J. (2013) 'The senses in practice: enhancing the quality of care for residents with dementia in care homes', *Journal of Advanced Nursing*, 69 (1): 77–90.

Brownie, S., Horstmanshof, L. and Garbutt, R. (2014) 'Factors that impact residents' transition and psychological adjustment to long-term aged care: a systematic literature review', *International Journal of Nursing Studies*, 51 (12): 1654–66.

BSG (British Society of Gerontology) (2020) 'Statement from the President and Members of the National Executive Committee of the British Society of Gerontology on COVID-19'. Available at: https://www.britishgerontology.org/publications/bsg-statements-on-covid-19/statement-one. Accessed 27 Nov 2020

Buffel, T. (ed) (2015) *Researching Age-Friendly Communities: Stories from Older People as Co-Investigators*, Manchester: The University of Manchester Library.

Buffel, T. and Phillipson, C. (2011) 'Experiences of place among older migrants living in inner city neighbourhoods in Belgium and England', *Diversité Urbaine*, 11: 13–37.

Buffel, T. and Phillipson, C. (2016) 'Can global cities be "age-friendly cities"? Urban development and ageing populations', *Cities*, 55: 94–100. http://dx.doi.org/10.1016/j.cities.2016.03.016

Buffel, T. and Phillipson, C. (2019) 'Ageing in a gentrifying neighbourhood: experiences of community change in later life', *Sociology*, 53 (6): 987–1004.

Buffel, T., Phillipson, C. and Scharf, T. (2012) 'Ageing in urban environments. Developing age-friendly cities', *Critical Social Policy*, 32 (4): 597–617.

Buffel, T., Handler, S. and Phillipson, C. (2018) 'Age-friendly cities and communities: a manifesto for change', in T. Buffel, S. Handler and C. Phillipson (eds) *Age-Friendly Communities: A Global Perspective*, Bristol: Policy Press, pp 273–88.

Burholt, V. (2004) 'The settlement patterns and residential histories of older Gujaratis, Punjabis and Sylhetis in Birmingham, England', *Ageing & Society*, 24 (3): 383–409.

Burholt, V. (2012) 'The dimensionality of "place attachment" for older people in rural areas of South West England and Wales', *Environment and Planning A*, 44: 2910–21.

Burholt, V., Curry, N., Keating, N. and Eales, J. (2014) 'Connecting with community: the nature of belonging among rural elders', in C.H. Hennessy, R. Means. and V. Burholt. (eds) (2014) *Countryside Connections: Older People, Community and Place in Rural Britain*, Bristol: Policy Press, pp 95–124.

Burkitt, I. (2016) 'Relational agency: relational sociology, agency and interaction', *European Journal of Social Theory*, 19 (3): 322–39.

Burns, D., Hyde, P. and Killet, A. (2013) 'Wicked problems or wicked people? Reconceptualising institutional abuse', *Sociology of Health and Illness*, 35 (4): 514–28.

Burton, J.K., Bayne, G., Evans, C., Garbe, F., Gorman, D., Hanhold, N., McCarmick, D., Othiena, R., Stevenson, J.E., Swietlik, S., Templeton, K.E., Tranter, M., Willcocks, L. and Gutherie, B. (2020) 'Evolution and effects of COVID-19 outbreaks in care homes: a population analysis of 189 care homes in one geographical region of the UK', *Lancet Healthy Longevity*, 1: e21–31.

Butler, A. (1997) 'Sheltered housing: a case for joint planning', *Modern Geriatrics*, 9 (1): 60–3.

Butler, A., Oldman, C. and Greve, J. (1983) *Sheltered Housing for the Elderly: Policy, Practice and the Consumer*, National Institute Social Services Library no. 44, London: George Allen & Unwin.

Buttimer, A. (1980). 'Home, reach, and a sense of place', in A. Buttimer. and D. Seamon (eds) *The Human Experience of Space and Place*, London: Croom Helm, pp 166–87.

Bytheway, B. (2009) 'Writing about age: birthdays and the passage of time', *Ageing & Society*, 29 (6): 883–901.

Bytheway, B., Ward, R., Holland, C. and Peace, S. (2007) *Too Old: Older People's Accounts of Discrimination, Exclusion and Rejection*, London: Help the Aged.

Cadman, L. (2009) 'Nonrepresentational theory/nonrepresentational geographies', in R. Kitchen. and N. Thrift. (eds) *International Encyclopaedia of Human Geography*, London: Elsevier, pp 456–63.

Calasanti, T. (2004) 'Feminist gerontology and old men', *The Journal of Gerontology, Series B*, 59 (6): S305–S314.

Calasanti, T. (2020) 'On the intersections of age, gender and sexualities in research on ageing', in A. King, K. Almack and R.L. Jones (eds) *Intersections of Ageing, Gender and Sexualities: Multidisciplinary International Perspectives*, Bristol: Policy Press, pp 13–30.

Cameron, A., Johnson, E.K., Lloyd, L., Evans, S., Porteus, J., Darton, R. and Atkinson, T. (2019) 'Using longitudinal qualitative research to explore extra care housing', *International Journal of Qualitative Studies on Health and Well-being*, 14 (1):1–11. https://doi.org/10.1080/17482631.2019.1593038

Cameron, A., Johnson, E.K. and Evans, S. (2020) 'Older people's perspective on living in integrated housing and care settings: the case of extra care housing', *Journal of Integrated Care*, 28 (3): 281–90.

Campbell, S., Clark, A., Keady, J., Kullberg, A., Manji, K., Rummery, K. and Ward, R. (2019) Participatory social network map making with family carers of people living with dementia, *Methodological Innovation*, 12 (1): 1–12.

Canter, D. (1977) *The Psychology of Place*, London: Architectural Press.

Canter, D. (1991) 'Understanding, assessing, and acting in places: is an integrative framework possible?', in T. Gosling and G. Evans (eds) *Environment, Cognition and Action*, New York: Oxford University Press, pp 191–209.

Canter, D. (2012) 'The psychology of place revisited'. Available at: https://www.davidcanter.com/wp-content/uploads/2012/04/The-Psychology-of-Place.pdf

Competition and Markets Authority (2017) 'Care homes market study: final report', Available at: https://assets.publishing.service.gov.uk/media/5a1fdf30e5274a750b82533a/care-homes-market-study-final-report.pdf

Carers UK (2019) 'Facts and Figures'. Available at: https://www.carersuk.org/news-and-campaigns/press-releases/facts-and-figures

Caro, E.G. and Fitzgerald, K.G. (eds) (2016) *International Perspectives on Age-Friendly Cities*, New York: Routledge.

Carp, F.M. and Carp, A. (1984) 'A complimentary/congruence model of well-being or mental health for the community elderly', in I. Altman, M.P. Lawton, and J.F. Wohwill (eds), *Human Behavior and Environment: Elderly People and the Environment* (Vol. 7), New York: Plenum Press, pp 279–304.

Carr, S. (2014) 'Pay, conditions and care quality in residential, nursing and domiciliary services', Joseph Rowntree Foundation, York. Available at: https://myhomelife.org.uk/wp-content/uploads/2015/02/JRF-report-on-care-pay-conditions-summary.pdf

Carr, A. and Biggs, S. (2020) 'The distribution of regulation in aged and dementia care: a continuum approach', *Journal of Aging & Social Policy*, 32 (3): 220–41.

Cartensen , L.L. (1992) 'Social and emotional patterns in adulthood: support for socioemotional selectivity theory', *Psychology and Aging*, 7 (3): 331–8.

Cartensen, L.L. (2006) 'The influence of a sense of time on human development', *Science*, 312 (5782): pp 1913–15.

Carter, T, and Beresford, P. (2000) *Age and Change: Models of Involvement for Older People*, York: Joseph Rowntree Foundation.

Carvel, J (2007) 'Prospect of Moving into a Care Home Frightens Two Thirds of Britons', *Society Guardian*, 3 December, 2007.

Casado-Diaz, M.A., Kaiser, C. and Warnes, A.M. (2004) 'Northern European retired residents in nine southern European areas: characteristics, motivations and adjustment', *Ageing & Society*, 24 (3): 335–82.

Castells, M. (1996) *The Information Age: Economy, Society and Culture, Vol. 1: The Rise of Network Society*, Oxford: Blackwell.

Castells, M. (2009) *Communication Power*, Oxford: Oxford University Press.

Castle, N.G. (2001) 'Relocation of the elderly', *Medical Care Research and Review*, 58 (3): 291–333.

Castree, N. (2007) 'David Harvey: Marxism, capitalism and the geographical imagination', *New Political Economy*, 12 (1): 97–115.

Castree, N. (2011) 'David Harvey', in P. Hubbard and E. Kitchen (eds) *Key Thinkers on Space and Place*, London: SAGE Publications Ltd, pp 234–41.

Centre for Ageing Better (2017) *Room to Improve: The Role of Home Adaptations in Improving Later Life*, London: Centre for Aging Better.

Centre for Ageing Better (2019) 'Non-decent homes and later life in England: headline statistics'. Available at: https://www.ageing-better.org.uk/news/non-decent-homes-and-later-life-england-headline-statistics

Centre for Ageing Better (2020) 'UK network of age-friendly cities'. Available at: https://www.ageing-better.org.uk/uk-network-age-friendly-communities#:~:text=The%20UK%20Network%20of%20Age,enjoying%20a%20good%20later%20life

Centre for Policy on Ageing (1984) *Home Life. A Cope of Practice for Residential Care*, London: Centre for Policy on Ageing

Centre for Policy on Ageing (1996) *A Better Home Life. A Code of Practice for Residential and Nursing Home Care*, London: Centre for Policy on Ageing.

Challis, D. and Bartlett, H. (1988) 'Old and ill: private nursing homes for elderly people', Age Concern Institute of Gerontology, Research Paper 1. Age Concern England, Mitcham.

Chamberlayne, P., Bornat, J. and Wengraf, T. (2000) *The Turn to Biographical Methods in Social Science: Comparative Issues and Examples*, London: Routledge.

Champion, A. (2008) 'The changing nature of urban and rural areas in the United Kingdom and other European countries', United Nations Expert Group Meeting on Population Distribution, Urbanization, Internal Migration and Development, New York, 21–3 January 2008, United Nations DESA, New York.

Champion, A. (2012) 'Europe's rural demography', in L.J. Kulcsar and K.J. Curtis (eds) *International Handbook of Rural Demography*, Dordrecht: Springer, pp 81–94.

Champion, A.G. (2011) 'The changing nature of urban and rural areas in the UK and other European countries', in H. Zlotnik (ed) *Population Distribution, Internal Migration and Development: An International Perspective*, New York: United Nations, pp 144–60.

Chapman, S.A. and Peace, S. (2008) 'Rurality and ageing well: "a long time here"', in N. Keating (ed) *Rural Ageing: A Good Place to Grow Old?*, Bristol: Policy Press, pp 21–31.

Chartered Institute of Housing and Housing LIN (2014) *New Approaches to Delivering Better Housing to Older People*, London: Housing LIN.

Chatterton, P. (2019) *Unlocking Sustainable Cities: A Manifesto for Real Change*, London: Pluto Press.

Chaudhury, H. (2008) *Remembering Home: Rediscovering the Self in Dementia*, London: Blackwells.

Chaudhury, H. and Rowles, G.D. (2005) 'Between the shores of recollection and imagination: self, aging, and home', in G.D. Rowles and H. Chaudhury (eds) (2005) *Home and Identity in Late Life: International Perspectives*, New York: Springer, pp 3–20.

Chaudhury, H. and Cooke, H. (2014) 'Design matters in dementia care: the role of the physical environment in dementia care settings', in M. Downs and B. Bowers (eds) *Excellence in Dementia Care* (2nd edn), Maidenhead: Open University Press, pp 144–58.

Chaudhury, H. and Oswald, F. (eds) (2018). 'Environments in an aging society: autobiographical perspectives in environmental gerontology', *Annual Review of Gerontology and Geriatrics*, 38: 311.

Chaudhury, H. and Oswald, F. (2019) 'Advancing understanding of person-environment interaction in later life: one step further', *Journal of Aging Studies*, 51: 1–9.

China Power Project (2020) 'Does China have aging problem?', China Power Project, Center for Strategic and International Studies, Washington DC. Available at: https://chinapower.csis.org/aging-problem/#0c116559-4df5-cl

Christou, A. (2013) 'Ageing in the ancestral homeland: ethno-biographical reflections on return migration in later life', in J. Percival (ed) *Return Migration in Later Life: International Perspectives*, Bristol: Policy Press, pp 179–217.

Clark, A., Holland, C. and Ward, R. (2012) 'Authenticity and validity in community research: looking at age discrimination and urban social interactions in the UK', in Lisa Goodson and Jenny Phillimore (eds) *Community Research for Participation: From Theory to Method*, Bristol: Policy Press, pp 37–54.

Clark, A., Holland, C., Katz, J. and Peace, S. (2009) 'Learning to see: lessons from a participatory observation research project in public space', *International Journal of Social Research Methodology*, 12 (4): 345–60.

Clark, S. (in association with Churchill Retirement Living, Planning Issues Ltd and Housing LIN) (2017) *Retirement Living Explained: A Guide for Planning & Design Professionals*, London: Housing LIN.

Clark, S. (2018) 'Architectural Reflections on Housing Older People: Nine Stories of Retirement Living', PhD Thesis. School of Architecture, Planning & Landscape, Newcastle University.

Clark, A., Campbell, S., Keady, J., Kullberg, A., Manji, K., Rummery, K. and Ward R. (2020) 'Neighbourhoods as relational places for people living with dementia', *Social Science and Medicine*, First View: https://doi.org/10.1016/j.socscimed.2020.112927

Clarkson, J., Coleman, R., Keates, S. and Lebbon, C. (2003) *Inclusive Design: Design for the Whole Population*, London: Springer-Verlag.

Clayton, W., Jain, J. and Parkhurst, G. (2017) 'An ideal journey: making bus travel desirable', *Mobilities, Curated Issue: Transport Mobilities*. 12 (5): 706–25.

Click Energy (2020) Available at: https://www.clickenergy.com.au/news-blog/12-countries-leading-the-way-in-renewable-energy/

Clough, R. (1981) *Old Age Homes*, London: George Allen and Unwin.

Coffman, T.L. (1983) 'Toward an understanding of geriatric relocation', *The Gerontologist*, 23 (5): 453–6.

Coleman, R., Lebbon, C. and Myerson, J. (2003) 'Design and empathy', in J. Clarkson, R. Coleman, S. Keates and C. Lebbon (eds) *Inclusive Design: Design for the Whole Population*, London: Springer-Verlag, pp 478–99.

Collopy, J. (1988) 'Autonomy in long term care: some crucial distinctions', *The Gerontologist*, 28, Issue Supplement: 10–17.

Colquhoun, I. (1999) *RIBA Book of 20th Century British Housing*, Oxford: Architectural Press, Butterworth-Heinemann.

Conradson, D. (2005) 'Landscape, care and the relational self: therapeutic encounters in rural England'. *Health and Place* 11: 337–48.

Construction Industry Council (2017) *Creating an Accessible and Inclusive Environment. Essential Principles for Built Environment Professionals*, Manchester: Manchester Disabled People's Access Group/Manchester Women's Design Group.

Cook, G. and Clarke, C. (2010) 'A framework to support social interaction in care homes', *Nursing Older People*, 22 (3): 16–21.

Cook, G., Thompson, J. and Reed, J. (2015) 'Re-conceptualising the status of residents in a care home: older people wanting to "live with care"', *Ageing & Society*, 35 (8): 1587–613.

Cooke, B. and Kothari, U. (2001) *Participation: The New Tyranny?*, London: ZED Books.

Cooney, A. (2011) ' "Finding home": a grounded theory on how older people "find home" in long term care settings', *International Journal of Older People Nursing*, 7 (3): 188–99.

Cooney, A., Dowling, M., Gannon, M.E., Dempsey, L. and Murphy, K. (2014) 'Exploration of the meaning of connectedness for older people in long-term care in the context of their quality of life: a review and commentary', *International Journal of Older People Nursing*, 9 (3): 92–199.

Cooper, Marcus C. (1992) 'Environmental memories', in I. Altman and S.M. Low (eds), *Place Attachment, Human Behavior and Environment: Advances in Theory and Research* (Vol. 12), pp 87–111.

CQC (Care Quality Commission) (n.d.) https://www.qcs.co.uk/care-home-policies-and-procedures/

CQC (Care Quality Commission) (2016) 'A different ending: addressing inequalities in end of life care', Good Practice Case Studies. Available at: https://www.cqc.org.uk/sites/default/files/20160505%20CQC_EOLC_GoodPractice_FINAL_2.pdf

CQC (2021a) 'Fundamental standards'. Available at: https://www.cqc.org.uk/what-we-do/how-we-do-our-job/fundamental-standards

CQC (2021b) 'Enabling innovation and adoption in health and social care: developing a shared view'. Available at: https://www.cqc.org.uk?sites?default/files/20210208_InnovationPrinciples_report.pdf

Crane, M. and Joly, L. (2014) 'Older homeless people: increasing numbers and changing needs', *Reviews in Clinical Gerontology*, 24 (4): 255–68.

Crane, M., Byrne, K., Fu, R., Lipman, B., Mirabelli, F., Rota-Bartelink, A., Ryan, M., Shea. R., Watt, H. and Warnes, A.M. (2005) 'The causes of homelessness in later life: findings from a 3-nation study', *The Journal of Gerontology Series B*, 60 (3): S152–S159.

Cresswell, T. (2004) *Place: A Short Introduction*. Oxford: Blackwell Publishing.

Crimmins, E.M. and Zhang, Y.S. (2019) 'Aging populations, mortality, and life expectancy', *Annual Review of Sociology*, 45: 69–89.

Croucher, K. and Rhodes, P. (2006) *Testing Consumer Views on Paying for Long-Term Care*, York: Joseph Rowntree Foundation.

Croucher, K. and Bevan, B. (2010) *Telling the Story of Hartfields: A New Retirement Village for the 21st Century*, York: Joseph Rowntree Foundation.

Croucher, K. and Bevan, M. (2014) *Promoting Supportive Relationships in Housing with Care*, York: Joseph Rowntree Foundation.

Croucher, K., Pleace, N. and Bevan, M. (2003) *Living at Hartrigg Oaks: Residents' Views of the UK's First Continuing Care Retirement Community*, York: Joseph Rowntree Foundation.

Croucher, K., Hicks, L. and Jackson, K. (2006) *Housing with Care for Later Life: A Literature Review*, York: Joseph Rowntree Foundation.

CSCI (Commission for Social Care Inspection) (2007) *A Fair Contract with Older People? A Special Study of People's Experiences when Finding a Care Home*, London: CSCI.

Csikszentmihalyi, M. and Rochberg-Halton, E. (1981) *The Meaning of Things: Domestic Symbols and the Self*, Cambridge: Cambridge University Press.

Cummings, E. and Henry, W. (1963) *Growing Old: The Process of Disengagement*, New York: Basic Books.

Cummins, S., Curtis, S., Diez-Roux, A.V. and Macintyre, S. (2007) 'Understanding and representing "place" in health research: a relational approach', *Social Science and Medicine*, 65 (9): 1825–38.

Cunningham, R. and Dobbing, C. (2011) 'HelpAge project reduces negative impact of migration in Jamaica', HelpAge International. Available at: https://www.helpage.org/newsroom/latest-news/helpage-project-reduces-negative-impact-of-migration-in-jamaica/

Curl, A., Ward Thompson, C. and Aspinall, P. (2015) 'The effectiveness of 'shared space' residential street interventions on self-reported activity levels and quality of life for older people', *Landscape and Urban Planning* 139: 117–25.

Curry, N., Burholt, V. and Hennessy, C.H. (2014) 'Conceptualising rural connectivities in later life', in C.H. Hennessy, R. Means and V. Burholt (eds) *Countryside Connections: Older People, Community and Place in Rural Britain*, Bristol: Policy Press. pp 31–62.

Cutchin, M.P. (2013) 'The complex process of becoming at-home in assisted living', in G.D. Rowles and M, Bernard (eds) *Environmental Gerontology: Making Meaningful Places in Old Age*, New York: Springer, pp 105–23.

Cutchin, M.P. (2018) 'Active relationships of ageing people and places', in M.W. Skinner., G.J. Andrews and M.P. Cutchin (eds) (2018) *Geographical Gerontology: Perspectives, Concepts, Approaches*, London and New York: Routledge, pp 216–28.

Cvitkovich, Y. and Wister, A.V. (2001) 'Comparison of four person-environment fit models applied to older adults', *Journal of Housing for the Elderly*, 14 (1/2): 1–25.

Cvitkovich, Y. and Wister, A.V. (2002) 'Bringing in the life course: a modification to Lawton's ecological model of aging', *Hallyman International Journal of Aging*, 4 (1): 15–29.

Dahlberg, L. and McKee, K.J. (2014) 'Correlates of social and emotional loneliness in older people: evidence from an English community study', *Aging & Mental Health*, 18 (4): 504–14.

Dahlin-Ivanoff, S., Haak, M., Fänge, A. and Iwarsson, S. (2007) 'The multiple meaning of home as experienced by very old Swedish people', *Scandinavian Journal of Occupational Therapy*, 14(10): 25–33.

Dannefer, D. (2003a) 'Cumulative advantage and the life course, cross-fertilizing age and social science knowledge', *Journal of Gerontology*, 58b: S327–37.

Dannefer, D. (2003b) 'Toward a global geography of the life course: challenges of late modernity to the life course perspective', in J.T. Mortimer and M. Shanahan (eds) *Handbook of the Life Course*, New York: Kluwer, pp 647–59.

Dannefer, D. and Uhlenberg, P. (1999). 'Paths of the life course: A typology', in V. Bengston and W. Schaie (eds.). *Handbook of Theories of Aging*, New York: Springer, pp 306–26.

Dannefer, D. and Settersten Jr, R.A. (2010) 'The study of the life course: implications for social gerontology', in D. Dannefer and C. Phillipson, (eds) (2010) *The SAGE Handbook of Social Gerontology*, London: SAGE Publications Ltd, pp 3–19.

Darton, R. and Callaghan, L. (2009) 'The role of extra care housing in supporting people with dementia: early findings from the PSSRU evaluation of extra care housing', *Journal of Care Services Management* 3 (3): 284–94.

Darton, R., Bäumker, T., Callaghan, L., Holder, J., Netten, A. and Towers, A. (2008) 'Evaluation of the extra care housing funding initiative: initial report', PSSRU Discussion Paper No. 2506/2. Personal Social Services Research Unit, University of Kent, Canterbury.

Darton, R., Bäumker, T., Callaghan, L., Holder, J., Netten, A. and Towers, A-M. (2012) 'The characteristics of residents in extra care housing and care homes in England', *Health and Social Care in the Community* 20 (1): 87–96.

Davies, N. (1999) *The Isles*, London: Papermac.

Davis, S., Byers, S., Nay, R. and Koch, S. (2009) 'Guiding design of dementia friendly environments in residential care settings: considering the living experiences', *Dementia*, 8 (2): 185–203.

DBEIS (Department for Business, Energy and Industrial Strategy) (2016) *Building on Success and Learning from Experience: An Independent Review of the Research Excellence Framework*, London: DBEIS.

DCLG (Department for Communities and Local Government) (2006) *A Decent Home: Definition and Guidance for Implementation*, Wetherby: DCLG Publications.

DCLG (Department for Communities and Local Government) (2009) *The Future Home Improvement Agency; Handyperson Services Report*, Foundations: The National Body for Home Improvement Agencies, London: DCLG.

DCLG (Department for Communities and Local Government) (2015) *Technical Housing Standards – Nationally Described Space Standard*, London: DCLG.

DCLG (Department of Communities and Local Government) (2016) 'English housing survey: housing for older people report, 2014–15', Office for National Statistics, London. Available at: https://www.gov.uk/government/statistics/english-housing-survey-2014-to-2015-housing-for-older-people-report

DCLG/DH/DWP (Department for Communities and Local Government/ Department of Health/Department of Work and Pensions) (2008) 'Lifetime homes, lifetime neighbourhood: a national strategy for housing an ageing society', Office of National Statistics, London. Available at: http://www. cpa.org.uk/cpa/lifetimehomes.pdf

DEFRA (Department for Environment, Food and Rural Affairs) (2016) 'Rural urban classification, Government UK, July'. Available at: https:// www.gov.uk/government/collections/rural-urban-classification

Department of Health (1989) *Caring for People: Community Care in the Next Decade and Beyond*, Cm 849, London: HMSO.

Department of Health (1990) *Caring for People: Community Care in the Next Decade and Beyond Policy Guidance*, London: HMSO

Department of Health (2003) *Care Homes for Older People. National Minimum Standards and The Care Home Regulations 2001*, London: The Stationery Office.

Department of Health (2009) *Shaping the Future of Care Together: Care, Support, Independence.* Cm 7673. London: HM Government.

Department of Health & Social Care (2021) 'Guidance on care home visiting', Available at: https://www.gov.uk/government/publications/ visiting-care-homes-during-coronavirus/update-on-policies-for-visiting-arrangements-in-care-homes

Department of Health & Social Care/UK Health Security Agency (2021) 'COVID-19 Guidance for supported living', Available at: https://www.gov.uk/government/publications/supported-living-services-during-coronavirus-covid-19/covid-19-guidance-for-supported-living

Department of Health & Social Security (1973) *Annual Report 1972.* Cmnd 5352. London: HMSO.

Department of Health & Social Security (1981) *Growing Older.* Cmnd 8173. London: HMSO.

Department of Health & Social Security and Welsh Office (1978) *A Happier Old Age: A Discussion Document on Elderly People in Our Society*, London: HMSO.

Department of Health and Welsh Office (1990) *Making Sense of Inspection: A Training Course for Registration and Inspection Staff. The Registered Homes Act, 1984.* (written by L. Kellaher and S. Peace, CESSA, London Metropolitan University/Open University), London: HMSO.

Dementia Services Development Centre (2011) 'Life is not a game of skittles: some thoughts on meaningful activities', *Dementia Now ejournal*, Winter. Available at: https://dementia.stir.ac.uk/system/files/filedepot/ 58/dementianow-winter2011_activitiesarticle.pdf

Dementia Services Development Centre, University of Stirling, Dementia Design (2021) Available at: https://dementia.stir.ac.uk/about-dsdc

Department of Transport (2021) *Decarbonising Transport: A Better, Greener Britain*, London: Department of Transport. Available at: https://assets. publishing.service.gov.uk/government/uploads/system/uploads/ attachment_data/file/1009448/decarbonising-transport-a-better-greener-britain.pdf

Department of Transport/Rt. Hon. Grant Shapps MP (2021) *Local Transport Update: Tfl Funding Extended*, London: Department on Transport. Available at: https://www.gov.uk/government/speeches/ local-transport-update-tfl-funding-extended

de Donder, L., de Witte, N., Verte, D., Dury, S., Buffel, T., Smetcorn, A.-S., Brosens, D and Verte, E. (2013) 'Developing evidenced-based age-friendly policies: a participatory research project', in *SAGE Research Methods Cases*, London: Sage Publications.

de Noronha, N. (2017) 'The right to adequate housing: reflections on an avoidable tragedy', *Discovering Society*, 46. Available at: https://discoversociety.org/2017/07/05/the-right-to-adequate-housing-reflections-on-an-avoidable-tragedy/

de Noronha, N. (2019) 'Housing the older ethnic minority population in England', Race Equality Foundation and Housing LIN, Briefing BME Housing, Housing LIN, London. Available at: https://www.houisnglin. org.uk/_assets/Resources/Housing/Support_materials/Briefings/HLIN_ briefing_BME_housing.pdf

Devine-Wright, P. (2014) 'Dynamics of place attachment in a climate changed world', in L.C. Manzo and P. Devine-Wright (eds) *Place Attachment: Advances in Theory, Methods and Applications*, Abingdon and New York: Routledge, Taylor & Francis, pp 165–77.

Dewar, B. and Nolan, M. (2013) 'Caring about caring: developing a model to implement compassionate relationship centred care in an older people care setting', *International Journal of Nursing Studies*, 50 (9): 1247–58.

Dewsbury, J.D. (2000) 'Performativity and the event: enacting a philosophy of difference', *Environment and Planning D: Society and Space* 18: 473–96.

Dhital, A., Pey, T. and Stanford, M.R. (2010) 'Visual loss and falls: a review', *Eye,* 24 (9): 1437–46.

DHSC/UK Health Security Agency (2021) 'COVID-19 guidance for supported living', Available at: https://www.gov.uk/government/ publications/supported-living-services-during-coronavirus-covid-19/ covid-19-guidance-for-supported-living

Diaz Moore, K. (1999) 'Dissonance in the dining room: a study of social interaction in a special care unit'. *Qualitative Health Research*, 9 (1): 133–55.

Diaz Moore, K. (2005) 'Using place rules and affect to understand environmental fit: a theoretical exploration', *Environment and Behaviour*, 37 (3): 330–63.

Diaz Moore, K. (2014) 'An ecological framework of place: situating environmental gerontology within a life course perspective', *International Journal of Aging and Human Development*. 79 (3): 183–209.

Diaz Moore, K., Geboy, L. and Wiseman, G.D. (2006) *Designing a Better Day: Guideline for Adult and Dementia Day Service Centers*. Baltimore, MD: Johns Hopkins University Press.

Dilnot Commission Report (2011) 'Fairer care funding, July 2011. The report of the Commission on Funding of Care and Support'. Crown Copyright. Available at: https://webarchive.nationalarchives.go.uk/20130221121529/https://www.wp.dh

Dittmor, M. (2012) 'Nuclear energy: status and future limitations', *Energy*, 37 (1): 35–40.

Dobie, I. (2019) 'The Essex lorry deaths are not just 'tragic'. they're political', *The Guardian*, 8 November. Available at: https://www.theguardian.com/commentisfree/2019/nov/08/essex-lorry-deaths-tragic-political

Dorrell, A. and Sundrin, K. (2016) 'Becoming visible: experiences from families participating in family health conversations at residential homes for older people', *Geriatric Nursing*, 37 (4): 260–5.

Druta, O. and Ronald, R. (2016) 'Young adults' pathways into homeownership and the negotiation of intra-family support: a home, the ideal gift', *Sociology*, 51 (4): 783–99.

Dugarova, E. and Gülasan, N. (2017) *Global Trends: Challenges and Opportunities in the Implementation of the Sustainable Development Goals*. Joint report by the United Nations Development Programme and the United Nations Research Institute for Social Development, New York: UNDP and Geneva: UNRISD.

Duggan, S., Blackman, T., Martyr, A. and Schaik, P.V. (2008) 'The impact of early dementia on outdoor life: a 'shrinking world'?, *Dementia*, 7 (2): 191–204.

Durrett, C. (2009) *The Senior Cohousing Handbook: A Community Approach to Independent Living*. Gabriola Island, Canada: New Society.

Dutton, R. (2020) *Retirement Village and Extra Care Housing in England: Operators' Experience during the COVID-19 Pandemic*, St Monica Trust, London: Bristol/Housing LIN.

DWP (Department of Work and Pensions) (2015) *Households below Average Incomes (HBAI): An Analysis of the Income Distribution 1994/95–2013/14*, London: DWP.

DWP (2018) 'Pensioners' incomes series: financial year 2016/17'. Available at: https://www.gov.uk/government/statistics/pensioners-incomes-series-financial-year-2016/17

Dwyer, P. and Papadimitriou, D. (2006) 'The social security rights of older international migrants in the European Union', *Journal of Ethnic and Migration Studies*, 32 (8) Special Issue: Older Migrants in Europe: Experiences. exclusion and constructive accommodation: 1301–19.

Eales, J., Keefe, J. and Keating, N. (2008) 'Age-friendly rural communities', in N. Keating (ed) *Rural Ageing: A Good Place to Grow Old?*, Bristol: The Policy Press, pp 109–120

Earth Institute (2007) 'New research analyses countries at greatest risk from climate change impacts: study looks at vulnerability of populations in low elevation coastal zone', 29 March. Columbia University. Available at: https://www.earth.columbia.edu/articles/view/958

Ebeling, M., Rau, R. and Baudisch, A. (2018). 'Rectangularization of the survival curve reconsidered: the maximum inner rectangle approach', *Population Studies*, 72 (3), 369–79. https://doi.org/10.1080/00324728.2017.1414299

Edmonson, R. and Scharf, T. (2015) 'Rural and urban ageing', In J. Twigg and W. Martin (eds) *Routledge Handbook of Cultural Gerontology*, Abingdon: Routledge, pp 412–19.

Ekerdt, D.J. (2019) 'Things and possessions', in S. Katz (ed) (2019) *Ageing in Everyday Life: Materialities and Embodiments*, Ageing in a Global Context series, Bristol: Policy Press, pp 29–44.

Emmett, C., Poole, M., Bond, J. and Highes, J.C. (2014) 'A relative safeguard? The informal roles that families and carers play when patients with dementia are discharged from hospital into care in England and Wales',, *International Journal of Law, Policy and the Family*, 28 (3): 302–20.

Erikson, E.H. (1982) *The Life Cycle Completed: A Review*, New York: Norton.

Erikson, E.H., Erikson, J.M. and Kivnick, H.Q. (1986) *Vital Involvement in Old Age: The Experience of Old Age in our Time*, New York: Norton.

Estes, C. (1979) *The Aging Enterprise*, San Francisco, CA: Jossey-Bass Professional Learning.

Estes, C. (1993) 'The aging enterprise revisited', *The Gerontologist*, 33 (3): 292–8.

European Parliament (2020) 'Transformation of health and care in the digital single market'. Available at: https://ec.europa.eu/digital-single-market/en/european-ehealth-policy

Eurostat (1999) *Regional Population Ageing of the EU at Different Speeds up to 2025*. Statistics in Focus 4/1999, Brussels: Eurostat.

Eurostat (n.d.) 'Statistics explained. Urban Europe – statistics on cities, towns and suburbs – foreign born persons living in cities'. Available at: https://ec.europa.eu/eurostat/statistics-explained/index.php/Urban_Europe_—_statistics_on_cities,_towns_and_suburbs_—_foreign-born_persons_living_in_cities#Migration_in_metropolitan_regions

Eurostat (2016) *Quality of Life in European Cities 2015*, Flash Barometer 419. Luxembourg: Publications Office of the European Union. Available at: http://ec.europa.eu/eurostat/web/cities/publications

Eurostat (2019) *Ageing Europe: Looking at the Lives of Older People in the EU.* 2019 Edition. Luxembourg: Publications Office of the European Union. Available at: http://ec.europa.eu/eurostat/web/cities/publications

Evandrou, M. and Falkingham, J. (2006) 'Will the baby-boomers be better off than their parents in retirement?', in J.A. Vincent, C. Phillipson and M, Downs (eds) *The Futures of Old Age*, London: Sage Publications Ltd, pp 85–97.

Evans, S. (2009a) *Community and Ageing: Maintaining Quality of Life in Housing with Care Settings*, Bristol: Policy Press.

Evans, S. (2009b) 'That lot up there and us down here': social interaction and a sense of community in a mixed tenure UK retirement village', *Ageing & Society*, 29 (2): 199–216.

Evans, S. and Means, R. (2007) *Balanced Retirement Communities? A Case Study of Westbury Fields*, Bristol: St Monica Trust.

Evans, S. and Vallelly, S. (2007) *Social Well-Being in Extra Care Housing*, York: Joseph Rowntree Foundation.

Evans, S., Darton, R. with Porteus, J. (2014a) *What is the Housing with Care 'Offer' and Who Is it For?* London: Housing LIN.

Evans, S., Jones, R. and Smithson, J. (2014b) 'Connecting with older people as project stakeholders: lessons for public participation and engagement in rural research', in C.H. Hennessy, R. Means and V. Burholt (eds) *Countryside Connections: Older People, Community And Place In Rural Britain*, Bristol: Policy Press, pp 221–43.

Evan, S., Atkinson, T., Darton, R., Cameron, A., Netten, A., Smith, R. and Porteus, J. (2017) 'A community hub approach to older people's housing', *Quality in Ageing and Older Adults*, 18 (1): 20–32.

Fänge, A. and Dahlin-Ivanoff, S. (2009) 'The home is the hub of health very old age: findings from the ENABLE-AGE project', *Archives of Gerontology and Geriatrics*, 48 (3):340–5.

Fänge, A. and Iwarsson, S. (2005) 'Changes in accessibility and usability in housing: An exploration of the housing adaptation process', *Occupational Therapy International*, 12: 44–59.

Feng, W., Gu, B. and Cai, Y. (2016) 'The end of China's one-child-policy', *Studies in Family Planning*, 47 (1): 83–6.

Fernández-Arrigoitia, M. and West, K. (2021) 'Interdependence, commitment, learning and love. The case of the UK's first older women's co-housing community', *Ageing & Society*, 41 (7): 1673–1696.

Fernandez-Mayorala, G., Rojo-Perez, F., Martinez-Martin, P., Prieto, M.E., Roriquez,-Blazquez, C. and Martin-Garcia, S. (2015) 'Active ageing and quality of life: factors associated with participation in leisure activities among institutionalized older adults, with and without dementia', *Aging & Mental Health*, 19 (1): 1031–41.

Finney, N. and Harries, B. (2013) 'How has the rise in private renting disproportionately affected some ethnic groups: ethnic differences in housing tenure 1991–2001–2011'. Available at: http://hummedia.man chester.ac.uk/institutes/code/briefingsupdated/how-has-the-rise-in-priv ate-renting-disproportionately-affected-some-ethnic-groups.pdf.

Fisk, M. (2015) 'Surveillance technologies in care homes: seven principles for their use', *Working with Older People'*, 19 (2): 51–9.

Foo, B. (1984) 'House and home', in Matrix (ed) *Women and the Man Made Environment*, London: Pluto Press, pp 89–105.

Ford, R.G. and Smith, G.C. (2008) 'Geographical and structural change in nursing care provision for older people in England 1993–2001', *Geoforum*, 39 (1): 489–98.

Forster, D. (2021) 'Reform of Adult Social Care Funding: developments since July 2019 (England)', Briefing Paper, No.8001, London: House of Commons Library.

Forster, D., Sandford, M. and Harker, R. (2020) 'Adult Social Care Funding (England)', Briefing Paper, No.CBP07903, London: House of Commons Library.

Foster, L. and Walker, A. (2015) 'Active and successful aging: A a European policy perspective', *The Gerontologist,* 55 (1): 83–90.

Fox O'Mahony, L. and Overton, L. (2015) 'Asset-based welfare, equity release and the meaning of the owned home', *Housing Studies*, 30 (3): 392–412.

Francis-Devine, B. (2021) 'Poverty in the UK: statistics, briefing paper', No 7096, 31 March. Available at: https://researchbriefings.files.parliament.uk/documents/SN07096/SN07096.pdf

Freeman, S., Marston, H., Olynick, J., Musselwhite, C., Kulczycki, C., Genoe, R. and Xiong, B. (2020) 'Intergenerational effects on the impacts of technology use in later life: insights from an intergenerational, multi-site study', *International Journal of Environmental Research and Public Health*, 17 (16): 5711.

Friedrich, K. and Warnes, A.M. (2000) 'Understanding contrasting national patterns of late life migration: Germany, Great Britain and the United States', *Erdkundle*, 54: 108–20.

Froggatt, K. (2007) 'The "regulated death": a documentary analysis of the regulation and inspection of dying and death in English care homes for older people', *Ageing & Society*, 27 (2): 233–48.

Froggatt, K., Payne, S., Morbey, H., Edwards, M., Finne-Soveri, H., Gambassi, G., Roeline Pasman, H., Szczerbinska, B. and Van den Block, L. (2017) 'Palliative care development in European care homes and nursing homes: application of typology of implementation', *Journal of the American Medical Directors Association*, 18 (6): 550.e7–55.e14.

Future Homes Alliance (2020) 'Looking to the horizon with Future Homes', Available at: https://www.futurehomesalliance.com/2020/02/04/looking-to-the-horizon-with-future-homes

Gangopadhyay, A. (2017) 'Aging across worlds: examining intergenerational relationships among older adults in two cities in transition', *Ageing International*, 42 (4): 504–21.

Gann, D., Barlow, J. and Venables, T. (1999) *Digital Futures: Making Homes Smarter*, York: The Joseph Rowntree Foundation and Coventry: The Chartered Institute of Housing.

Garner, I.W. and Holland, CA. (2020) 'Age-friendliness of living environments from the older person's viewpoint: development of the Age-Friendly Environment Assessment Tool', *Age and Ageing*, 49 (2): 193–8.

Garrett, H., Roys, M., Burriss, S. and Nicol, S. (2016) *The Cost-Benefit to the NHS Arising from Preventative Housing Interventions*, Watford: IHS BRE Press.

Gaughan, J., Gravelle, H. and Siciliani, L. (2015) 'Testing the bed-blocking hypothesis: does nursing and care home supply reduce delayed hospital discharges?', *Health Economics, Supplement: Economics of Long-term Care*. 24 (S1): 32–44.

Geertz, C. (1993) 'Thick description: toward an interpretive theory of culture', in C. Geertz. *The Interpretation of Cultures*, London: Fontana Press, pp 3–30.

Geertz, C. (2000) *The Interpretation of Cultures* (reprint, revised), London: Fontana Press.

Gerry, E.M. (2011) 'Privacy and dignity in a hospice environment – the development of a clinical audit', *International Journal of Palliative Nursing*, 17 (2): 92–8.

Giarchi, G.G. (2006) 'Older people "on the edge" in the countryside of Europe', *Social Policy & Administration*, 40 (6): 705–21.

Giebel, C., Cannon, J., Hanna, J., Butchard, H., Eley, R., Gaughan, A., Komuravelli, A., Shenton, J., Callaghan, S., Tetlow, H., Limbert, S., Whittington, C.R., Rajagopal, M., Ward, K., Shaw, L., Corcoran, R., Bennett, K. and Gabbay, M. (2020) 'Impact of COVID-19 related social support service closures on people with dementia and unpaid carers: a qualitative study', *Aging & Mental Health*, 25 (7): 1281–8, DOI: 10.1080/13607863.2020.1822292

Gillam, S. (2016) 'Who will listen to the older voices in humanitarian crises?', *HelpAge International*, 5 May. Available at: https://.helpage.org/newsroom/latest-news/who-will-listen-to-the-older-voices-in-humanitarian-crisis

Gilleard, C. and Higgs, P. (2002) 'Concept forum – the third age: class, cohort & generation?', *Ageing & Society*, 22 (3): 545–57.

Gilleard, C. and Higgs, P. (2010) 'Aging without agency: theorizing the fourth age', *Aging & Mental Health*, 1 (2): 121–8.

Gilleard, C. and Higgs, P. (2011) 'Ageing abjection and embodiment in the fourth age', *Journal of Aging Studies*, 25 (1): 135–42.

Gilleard, C. and Higgs, P. (2013) 'The fourth age and the concept of a "social imaginary": a theoretical excursus', *Journal of Aging Studies*, 27 (4): 368–76.

Gilroy, R. (2021) *Planning for an Ageing Society*, London: Lund Humphries

Glaser, K. and Tomassini, C. (2000) 'Proximity of older women to their children: a comparison of Britain and Italy', *The Gerontologist*, 40 (6): 729–37.

Glaser, K., Price, D., Di, H., Gessa, G., Ribe, E., Stuchbury, R. and Tinker, A. (2013) 'Grandparenting in Europe: family policy and grandparents' role in providing childcare', Grandparents Plus, Calouste Gulbenkian Foundation, Kings College London.

Glass, A.P. (2012) 'Elder co-housing in the United States: three case studies, *Built Environment*, 38 (3): 345–63.

Glass, A.P. (2013) 'Lessons learned from a new elder cohousing community', *Journal of Housing for the Elderly*, 27: 348–68.

Glass, A.P. and Vander Plaats, R. (2013) 'A conceptual model for aging better together intentionally', *Journal of Aging Studies* 27: 428–42.

Glover, B.M. (2012) 'Accommodating older and disabled prisoners in England and Wales', in J. Katz, S. Peace and S. Spurr (eds) *Adult Lives: A Life Course Perspective*, Bristol: Policy Press, pp 161–72.

Goffman, E. (1959) *The Presentation of Self in Everyday Life*, London: Penguin Books.

Goffman, E. (1961) *Asylums: Essays on the Situation of Mental Patients and Other Inmates*, London: Penguin Books.

Golant, S.M. (1972) *The Residential Location and Spatial Behavior of the Elderly*, Chicago: University of Chicago Press.

Golant, S.M. (1984) *A Place to Grow Old: The Meaning of Environments in Old Age*, New York: Columbia University Press.

Golant, S.M. (2011) 'The quest for residential normalcy for older adults: relocation but one pathway', *Journal of Aging Studies*, 25 (3):193–205.

Golant, S.M. (2012) 'Out of their residential comfort and mastery zones: toward a more relevant environmental gerontology', *Journal of Housing for the Elderly*, 26 (1–3): 26–43,

Golant, S.M. (2015) 'Residential normalcy and the aging in place behaviors of older Americans', *Progress in Geography*, 34 (12): 1535–57.

Golant, S.M. (2018a) 'Explaining the ageing in place realities of older adults', in M.W. Skinner, G.J. Andrews. and M.P. Cutchin (eds) *Geographical Gerontology: Perspectives, Concepts and Approaches,* London and New York: Routledge, pp 189–202.

Golant, S.M. (2018b) *Aging in the Right Place*, Baltimore, MD: Health Professions Press, Inc.

Goldsmith, S. (1963) *Designing for the Disabled*, London: Royal Institute of British Architects.

Goldsmith, S. (2001) 'The bottom-up methodology of universal design', in F.E. Preiser and E. Ostroff (eds) *Universal Design Handbook.* New York: McGraw-Hill, pp 25.1–25.16.

Gomez, D.L. (2015) 'Little arrangements that matter. Rethinking autonomy-enabling innovations for later life', *Technological Forecasting Social Change*, 93: 91–101.

Goodwin, N. (2010) 'The state of Telehealth and Telecare in the UK: prospects for integrated care', *Journal of Integrated* Care, 18 (6): 3–10.

Gopinath, M., Peace, S. and Holland, C. (2018) Conserving habitus: home, couplehood and dementia, *Home Cultures*, 15 (3): 223–63.

Gopinath, M., Holland, C. and Peace, S. (forthcoming) 'Enduring commitment: older couples living apart', *Families, Relationships and Society*.

Gordon, A.L., Franklin, M., Bradshaw, L., Logan, P., Elliott, R. and Gladman, J.R.F. (2013) 'Health status of UK care home residents: a cohort study', *Age and Ageing*, 43 (1): 97–103.

Gov.UK Blog (2015) 'Public health matters. Bringing together housing and public health'. Available at: https://publichealthmatters.blog.gov.uk/2015/10/21/bringing-together-housing-and-public-health/

Gov.UK (2020) 'A green future?'. Available at: https://assets.publishing. service.gov.uk/government/uploads/system/uploads/attachment_data/file/693158/25-year-environment-plan.pdf

Gov.UK (2019) 'At a glance: summary of targets in our 25 year environment plan. Updated 16 May 2019'. Available at: https://www. gov.uk/government/publications/25-year-environment-plan/25-year-environment-plan-our-targets-at-a-glance

Granbom, M., Himmelsbach, I., Hack, M., Löfqvist., C., Oswald, F. and Iwarsson, S. (2014) 'Residential normalcy and environmental experiences of very old people: changes in residential reasoning over time', *Journal of Aging Studies*, 29, 9–19.

Gray, A. and Worlledge, G. (2018) 'Addressing loneliness and isolation in retirement housing', *Ageing & Society*, 38 (1): 615–44.

Greater London Authority (2018) 'The London health inequalities strategy', September, City Hall, London. Available at: https://www.london.gov.uk/sites/default/files/health_strategy_2018_low_res_fa1.pdf

Greater London Authority (2020) 'All London Green Grid'. Available at: https://www.london.gov.uk/what-we-do/environment/parks-green-spaces-and-biodiversity/all-london-green-grid

Green, J., Jones, A. and Roberts, H. (2014) 'More than A to B: the role of free bus travel for the mobility and wellbeing of older citizens in London', *Ageing & Society*, 34 (3): 472–94.

Greenwood, D. (2004) 'Feminism and action research: is resistance possible? And, if so, why is it necessary?, in M. Brydon-Miller, P. Maguire and A. McIntyre (eds) *Travelling Companions: Feminism, Teaching and Action Research*, Westport, CT: Praeger, pp 157–68.

Grenier, A. (2005) 'The contextual and social locations of older women's experience of disability and decline', *Journal of Aging Studies*, 19 (2): 131–46.

Grenier, A. (2012) *Transitions and the Lifecourse: Challenging the Constructions of 'Growing Old'*, Bristol: Policy Press.

Grenier, A. and Phillipson, C. (2013) 'Re-thinking agency in later life', in J. Baars, J. Dhomen, A. Grenier and C. Phillipson (eds) *Age, Meaning and Social Structure*. Bristol: Policy Press, pp 55–68.

Grenier, A., Barken, R. and McGrath, C. (2016) 'Homelessness and aging: the contradictory ordering of "house" and "home"', *Journal of Aging Studies*, 39: 73–80.

Grenier, A., Lloyd, L. and Phillipson, C. (2017) 'Precarity in later life: re-thinking dementia as "frailed" old age'. *Sociology of Health and Illness*, 39 (2): 318–30.

Grenier, A., Phillipson, C. and Settersten Jr, R.A. (eds) (2020) *Precarity and Ageing: Understanding Insecurity and Risk in Later Life*, Bristol: Policy Press.

Griffiths Report (1988) *Community Care: An Agenda for Action*, London: HMSO.

Grindle, B., Bang Nes, R., MacDonald, I.F. and Sloan Wilson, D. (2018) 'Quality of life in intentional communities', *Social Indicators Research*, 137: 625–40.

Grint, K. (2005) 'Problems, problems, problems: the social construction of 'leadership'', *Human Relations*, 58 (11): 1467–94.

Grundy, E. (1997) 'Demography and gerontology: mortality trends among the oldest old', *Ageing & Society*, 17 (6): 713–25. http://dx.doi.org/10.1017/s0144686X97006715

Gubrium, J.F. (1975) *Living and Dying in Murray Manor*, Charlottesville, VA, and London: University of Virginia Press.

Gubrium, J.F. (1986) *Oldtimers and Alzheimers: The Descriptive Organisation of Senility*, Greenwich, CT: JAI Press.

Gubrium, J.F. (2005) 'The social worlds of old age', in M.L. Johnson in association with V.L. Bengston., P.G. Coleman. and T.B. Kirkwood. (eds) *The Cambridge Handbook of Age and Ageing*, Cambridge: Cambridge University Press, pp 310–15.

Gubrium, J.F. and Holstein, J.A. (1997) *The New Language of Qualitative Method*, Oxford: Oxford University Press.

Gunningham, N. (2019) 'Averting climate catastrophe: environmental activism, extinction rebellion and collations of influence', *King's Law Journal, Special Issue: Environmental Justice,* 30 (2): 194–202.

Habinteg (2015) 'Briefing: 7 points about the new Housing Standards 2015', London: Habinteg, Available at: https://www.housinglin.org.uk/_assets/Resources/Housing/OtherOrganisation/7_points_housing_standards.pdf

Hafford-Letchfield, T., Gleeson, H., Ryan, P., Billings, B., Teacher, R., Quaife, M., Flynn, A., Zanone, P.S. and Vincentini, S. (2020) ' "He just gave up": an exploratory study into the perspectives of paid carers on supporting older people living in care homes with depression, self-harm, and suicide ideation and behaviours', *Ageing & Society,* 40 (5): 984–1003.

Hajat, S., Kovats, R.S. and Lachowycz, K. (2007) 'Heat-related and cold-related deaths in England and Wales: who is at risk?', *Occupational and Environmental Medicine, BMJ,* 64 (2): 93–100.

Halfacree, K. (1993) 'Locality and social representation: space, discourse and alternative definitions of the rural', *Journal of Rural Studies,* 9: 1–15.

Halfacree, K. (2006) 'Rural space: constructing a three situations fold architecture', in P. Cloke, T. Marsden and P. Mooney (eds) *The Handbook of Rural Studies*, London: Sage, pp 44–62.

Hall, B. (1981) 'Participatory research, popular knowledge, and power: a personal reflection', *Convergence,* 14 (3): 6–17.

Hall, S. (2017) 'Older people in situations of migration in Africa: the untold story', HelpAge International, policy highlight, February. Available at: https://samuelhall.org/publications/helpage-international-older-people-in-situations-of-migration-in-africa-the-untold-story

Hamilton, I.G., Philip, J., Steadman, H.B., Summerfield, A.J. and Lowe, R. (2013) 'Energy efficiency in the British housing stock: energy demand and the homes energy efficiency database', *Energy Policy,* 60: 462–80.

Hammer, R.M. (1999) 'The lived experience of being at home. a phenomenological investigation', *Journal of Gerontological Nursing,* 25: 10–18.

Hammond, M. (2018) 'Urban Ageing, Spatial Agency: Generating Creative Agency through the Medium of Cohousing'. PhD Thesis. Architectural Design, Manchester Metropolitan University.

Hammond, M., Walsh, R. and White, S. (2018) 'RIGHTSIZING: reframing the housing offer for older people', project report. Greater Manchester Combined Authority (GMCA) PHASE@ Manchester School of Architecture. Available at: http://e-space.mmu.ac.uk/621554/

Handler, S. (2014) *An Alternative Age-Friendly Handbook*, Manchester: The University of Manchester Library.

Handmer, J., Vande Merwe, M. and O'Neil, S. (2019) 'The risk of dying in bushfires: a comparative analysis of fatalities and survivors', *Progress in Disaster Science*, 1: 1–9. Available at: https://www.sciencedirect.com/science/article/pii/S2590061719300158

Hanson, J., Kellaher, L. and Rowlings, M. (2001) 'Profiling the housing stock for older people: the transition from domesticity to caring', Final Report of EPSRC EQUAL Research, University College London.

Harper, S. (2019) 'The convergence of population ageing with climate change', *Journal of Population Ageing*, 12: 401–3.

Harper, S. and Laws, G. (1995). 'Rethinking the geography of ageing',. *Progress in Human Geography*, 19 (2): 191–221. http://dx.doi.org/10.1177/030913259501900203

Harris, H., Lipman, A. and Slater, R. (1977) Architectural design: the spatial location and interactions of old people', *Journal of Gerontology*, 23: 390–400.

Harris, P.G. (ed) (2011) *China's Responsibility for Climate Change: Ethics, Fairness and Environmental Policy*, Bristol: Policy Press.

Hart, G.L., Larson, E.H., and Lishner, D.M. (2005) 'Rural definitions for health policy and research', *American Journal of Public Health,* 95 (7): 1149–55.

Hartigan, I. (2007) 'A comparative review of the Katz ADL and the Barthel Index in assessing the activities of daily living of older people', *International Journal of Older People Nursing* 2 (3): 204–12.

Harvey, D. (1973) *Social Justice and the City*, London: Arnold.

Harvey, D. (1996) *Justice, Nature and the Geography of Difference*, Oxford: Blackwell.

Harvey, D. (2000) *Spaces of Hope*, Edinburgh: Edinburgh University Press.

Harvey, D. (2008) 'The right to the city', *New Left Review*, 53. Available at: https://newleftreview.org/issues/ii53/articles/david-harvey-the-right-to-the-city

Hauderowicz, D. and Ly Serena, K. (eds) *Age-Inclusive Public Space*, Berlin: Hatje Cantz Verlag Gmbh.

Havighurst, R.J. (1961) 'Successful Aging aging', *The Gerontologist*, 1: 4–7.

Head, J., Garwood, S. and Laight, I. (2016) 'Funding extra care housing: technical brief', London: Housing LIN.

HelpAge/UNICEF (2010) 'Grandparents and grandchildren: impact of migration in Moldova', HAI/UNICEF project: findings and recommendations. Available at: https://www.helpage.org/silo/files/grandparents_and-grandchildren-impact-of-migration-in-moldova-helpage-project.pdf

Hennessy, C.H. and Walker, A. (2011) 'Promoting multi-disciplinary and inter-disciplinary ageing research in the United Kingdom', *Ageing & Society* 31 (1): 52–69.

Hennessy, C.H., Means, R. and Burholt, V. (eds) (2014a) *Countryside Connections: Older People, Community and Place in Rural Britain,* Bristol: Policy Press.

Hennessy, C. H, Means, R. and Burholt, V. (2014b) 'Countryside connections in later life: setting the scene', in C. Hagen Hennessy, R. Means and V. Burholt, *Countryside Connections: Older People, Community and Place in Rural Britain,* Bristol: Policy Press, pp 1–30.

Hennessy, C.H. and Means, R. (2018) 'Connectivity of older people in rural areas', in A. Walker (ed) *The New Dynamics of Ageing. Volume 1,* Bristol: Policy Press, pp 147–66.

Henwood, M., McKay, S., Needham, C. and Glasby, J. (2018) *From Bystanders to Core Participants? A Literature and Data Review of Self-Funders in Social Care Markets,* University of Birmingham: Health Services Management Centre.

Hetherington, K. (2003) 'Spatial textures: place, touch and praesentia', *Environment and Planning A: Economy and Space,* 35 (1): 1933–44.

Heywood, F. (2005) 'Adaptation: altering the house to restore the home.' *Housing Studies,* 20 (4): 531–47.

Heywood, F., Oldman, C. and Means, R. (2002) *Housing and Home in Later Life,* Buckingham: Open University Press.

Hickey, S. and Mohan, G. (2004) *Participation: From Tyranny to Transformation? Exploring New Approaches to Participation in Development,* New York: Zed.

Higgs, P. and Gilleard, C. (2015) *Rethinking Old Age: Theorising the Fourth Age,* London: Palgrave.

Hillcoat-Nallétamby, S. and Ogg, J. (2014) 'Moving beyond "ageing in place": older people's dislikes about their home and neighbourhood environments as a motive for wishing to move', *Ageing & Society,* 34 (10): 1771–96.

Hillcoat-Nallétamby, S. and Sardani, A.V. (2019) 'Decisions About the "If," "When," and "How" of Moving Home: Can a Relocation Service Help? A Welsh Case Study', *Journal of Housing For the Elderly,* 33 (3): 275–97.

Hillier, B. and Hanson, J. (1984) *The Social Logic of Space,* Cambridge: Cambridge University Press.

Hillier, J. and Rooksby, E. (2002) *Habitus: A Sense of Place,* Farnham: Ashgate Publishing.

Hitlin, S. and Elder, G. (2007) 'Time, self and the curiously abstract concept of agency', *Sociological Theory,* 25 (2):170–91.

HM Government (2020) The Government Response to the Committee on Climate Change's 2020 Progress Report to Parliament: Reducing UK emissions. London: Open Government License. https://assets.publishing. service.gov.uk/government/uploads/system/uploads/attachment_data/ file/928005/government-response-to-ccc-progress-report-2020.pdf

HM Government (2021) 'Net Zero Strategy: Build Back Greener', October, presented to Parliament pursuant to Section 14 of the Climate Change Act 2008. London: HMSO.

HM Treasury (2021) *Net Zero Review Final Report: Analysis exploring the key issues*, London: HM Treasury, Available at: https://www.gov.uk/government/publications/net-zero-review-final-report

Hoffman, J. and Pype, K. (eds) (2018) 'Introduction: spaces and practices of care for older people in sub-Saharan Africa', in J. Hoffman and K, Pype (eds) *Ageing in Sub-Saharan Africa: Spaces and Practices of Care*, Bristol, Policy Press, 1–20.

Høgsnes, L., Melin-Johansson, C., Gustaf Norbergh, K. and Danielson, E. (2014) 'The existential life situations of spouses of persons with dementia before and after relocating to a nursing home', *Aging & Mental Health*, 18 (2): 152–60.

Holland, C. (2001) 'Housing Histories: Older Women's Experiences of Home Across the Life Course'. PhD Thesis. Faculty of Health & Social Care, The Open University.

Holland, C. (2012) 'The role of technologies in the everyday lives of older people', in J. Katz, S. Peace and S. Spurr (eds) *Adult Lives: A Life Course Perspective*, Bristol: Policy Press, pp 151–60.

Holland, C. (2014) 'ICT and twenty-first century ageing', conference proceedings: *Meaning and Culture(s): Exploring the Life Course: 8th International Symposium on Cultural Gerontology, 2nd Conference of the European Network in Aging Studies (ENAS)*, 10–12 April, Galway: Ireland.

Holland, C. (2015) 'Public places and age', in J. Twigg and W. Martin (eds) *Routledge Handbook of Cultural Gerontology*. Abingdon: Routledge, pp 455–62.

Holland, C., Clark, A., Katz, J. and Peace, S. (2007) *Social Interaction in Urban Public Places*, Bristol: Policy Press/Joseph Rowntree Foundation. Available at: https://www.jrf.org.uk/sites/default/files/jrf/migrated/files/2017-interactions-public-places.pdf

Holland, C. and Katz, J. (2010) 'Cultural identity and belonging in later life: is extra care housing an attractive concept to older Jewish people living in Britain?', *Journal of Cross-Cultural Gerontology*, 25: 59–69.

Holland, CA, Carter, M., Cooke, R., Leask, G., Powell, R., Shaw, R and West, K. (2015) 'Collaborative research between Aston Research Centre for Health Ageing (ARCHA) and the ExtraCare Charitable Trust. The final report', Aston University. Available at: www.aston.ac.uk/archa

Holland, C.A., Garner, I., O'Donnell, J. and Gwyther, H. (2019) 'Integrated homes, care and support: measurable outcomes for healthy ageing', the ExtraCare Charitable Trust research report, ExtraCare Charitable Trust, Coventry.

Homeshare UK (n.d.) Available at: https://homeshareuk.org/

Homeshare International (n.d.) Available at: https://homeshare.org/

Hopkins, P. and Pain, R. (2007) 'Geographies of age: thinking relationally', *Area*, 39 (3): 287–94.

House of Commons (2018) 'CLG Committee housing for older people', second report of sessions 2017–2019. 5 February, HC 370.

Housing LIN (n.d.) 'Extra care housing', Housing LIN, London. Available at: https://www.housinglin.org.uk/Topics/browse/HousingExtraCare/

Housing LIN (2008) 'Strategic Housing for Older People analysis tool (SHOP)'. Available at: www.housinglin.org.uk/SHOPAT)

Howard, E. (1902) *Garden Cities of Tomorrow*, Cheltenham: Attic Books (reprint, 1977).

Howe, A.L., Jones, A.E., and Tilse, C. (2013) 'What's in a name? Similarities and differences in international terms and meaning for older peoples' housing with services', *Ageing & Society*, 33 (4): 547–78.

Huber, A. and O'Reilly, K. (2004) 'The construction of *Heimat* under conditions of individualised modernity: Swiss and British elderly migrants in Spain', *Ageing & Society*, 24 (3): 327–51.

Huppert, F. (2003) 'Designing for older users', in J. Clarkson, R. Coleman, S. Keates and C. Lebbon (eds) *Inclusive Design: Design for the Whole Population*, London: Springer-Verlag, pp 30–49.

Hyde, M. and Higgs, P. (2016) *Ageing and Globalisation*, Ageing in a Global Context series, Bristol: Policy Press.

IDEAL (n.d.) *Improving the Experience of Dementia and Enhancing Active Life*, University of Exeter/ERSC.NIHR/Alzheimer's Society. Available at: https://www.idealproject.org.uk

I'DGO Inclusive Design for Getting Outdoors (n.d.) Available at: https://www.idgo.ac.uk/

IMF (International Monetary Fund) (2020a) 'World economic outlook report; a long and difficult ascent', October. Available at: https://www.imf.org/en/publications/weo

IMF (2020b) 'IMF research perspectives'. Available at: https://www.imf.org/external/pubs/ft/irb/archive.htm

Imrie, R. (1996) *Disability and the City: International Perspectives*, London: Sage Publications Ltd.

Imrie, R. and Hall, P. (2001) *Inclusive Design: Designing and Developing Accessible Environments*, SPON Press, London, New York.

Independent Age (2016) *The Overlooked Over 75s: Poverty among the 'Silent Generation' who Lived through the Second World War*, London: Independent Age.

INED (Institute National D'Etudes Demographiques) (ined) (2019) 'World population prospects, 2019'. Available at: https://www.ined.fr/en/everything_about_population/demographic-facts-sheets/focus-on/world-population-prospects-2019/#:~:text=By%202050%2C%20one%20in%20four,to%20426%20million%20in%202050

Innes, A., Kelly, F. and Dincarsian, O. (2011) 'Care home design for people with dementia: what do people with dementia and their carers value?', *Ageing & Mental Health*, 15 (5): 548–56.

Institute for Government (2020) 'Adult social care. Performance tracker 2020'. Available at: https://www.instituteforgovernment.org.uk/publication/performance-trscker-soso/adult-social-care

Institute of Public Care (2010) *Meeting on the Supported Housing Needs of BME Communities*, Oxford and London: Race Equality Foundation.

IPCC (Intergovernmental Panel on Climate Change) (2018) 'Global warming of 1.5°C' [ed V. Masson-Delmotte, P. Zhai, H.O. Pörtner, D. Roberts, J. Skea, P.R. Shukla, A. Pirani, W. Moufouma-Okia, C. Péan, R. Pidcock, S. Connors, J.B.R. Matthews, Y. Chen, X. Zhou, M.I. Gomis, E. Lonnoy, T. Maycock, M. Tignor and T. Waterfield]. Available at: www.ipcc.ch/sr15/

IPCC (2019a) 'Global warming of 1.5 C'. Available at: https://www.ipcc.ch/sr15/

IPCC (2019b) 'Climate change and land'. Available at: https://www.ipcc.ch/srccl/

IPCC (2019c)'The ocean and cryosphere in a changing climate'. Available at: https://www.ipcc.ch/srocc/

Iwarsson, S. (1999) 'The Housing Enabler: an objective tool for assessing accessibility', *British Journal of Occupational Therapy*, 62 (11): 491–97.

Iwarsson, S. and Isacsson, A. (1996) 'Development of a novel Instrument for occupational therapy for assessment of the physical environment in the home – a methodologic study on "The Enabler"', *The Occupational Therapy Journal of Research*, 16 (4): 227–44.

Iwarsson, S. and Slaug, B. (2010). *Housing Enabler – A Method for Rating/Screening and Analysing Accessibility Problems in Housing. Manual for the Complete Instrument and Screening Tool* (2nd revised edn), Sweden: Lund & Staffanstorp; Veten & Skapen HB och Slaug Enabling Development.

Iwarsson, S., Jensen, G. and Ståhl, A. (2000). 'Travel chain enabler: development of a pilot instrument for assessment of urban public bus transport accessibility', *Technology and Disability*, 12 (1): 3–12.

Iwarsson, S., Wahl, H-W. and Nygrem, C. (2004) 'Challenges of cross-national housing research with older persons: lessons from the ENABLE-AGE project', *European Journal of Ageing*, 1: 79–88.

Iwarsson, S., Haak, M. and Slaug, B. (2012) 'Current developments of the Housing Enabler methodology', *British Journal of Occupational Therapy*, 75 (11): 517–21.

Iwarsson, S., Sixsmith, J., Oswald, F., Wahl, H-W., Sixsmith, A., Szeman, Z. and Tomsone, S. (2007), 'Importance of the home environment for healthy aging: conceptual and methodological background of the European ENABLE-AGE Project', *The Gerontologist*, 47 (1): 78–84.

Iwarsson, S., Löfqvist, C., Oswald, F., Slaug, B., Schmidt, S., Wahl, H-W., Tomsone, S., Himmelsbach, I. and Hask, M. (2016) 'Synthesizing ENABLE-AGE findings to suggest evidence-based home and health interventions', *Journal of Housing for the Elderly*, 30 (3): 330–43.

Jabereen, Y. (2005) 'Culture and housing preferences in a developing city', *Environment & Behaviour*, 37 (1): 134–46.

Jack, R. (1998) *Residential versus Community Care: The Role of Institutions in Welfare Provision*, Basingstoke: Macmillan.

Jarrett, T (2017) 'Social care: government reviews and policy proposals for paying for care since 1997 (England)', Briefing Paper, No. 8000, 23 October, House of Commons Library, London.

Jarvis, H. (2015) 'Toward a deeper understanding of the social architecture of cohousing evidence from the UK, USA and Australia', *Urban Research and Practice*, 8: 93–105.

Johnson, B. (2021) 'Response to Prime Minister's questions in Hansard Columns 154/155', Health and Social Care Volume 700, 7 September. London: House of Commons Library.

Johnson, E.K., Cameron, A., Lloyd, L., Evans, S., Darton, R., Smith, R., Atkinson, T.A. and Porteus, J. (2020) 'Ageing in extra-care housing: preparation, persistence and self-management at the boundary between the third and fourth age', *Ageing & Society*, 40 (12): 2711–31.

Johnson, J. (2020) 'Internet usage in the United Kingdom, by age group', Statista. Available at: https://www.statista.com/statistics/707890/internet-usage-in-the-united-kingdom-by-age-group/

Johnson, J., Rolph, S and Smith, R. (2010) *Residential Care Transformed: Revisiting 'The Last Refuge'*, Basingstoke: Palgrave Macmillan.

Johnson, M. (1978) 'That was your life: a biographical approach to later life', in V. Carver and P. Liddiard (eds) *An Ageing Population*, Sevenoaks: Hodder & Stoughton Ltd in association with The Open University, pp 99–113.

Johnson, M.J., Jackson, N.C., Kenneth Arnette, K. and Koffman, Steven D. (2005) 'Gay and lesbian perceptions of discrimination in retirement care facilities', *Journal of Homosexuality*, 49 (2): 83–102.

Johnson, R.A., and Bibbo, J. (2014) 'Relocation decisions and constructing the meaning of homes: a phenomenological study of the transition into a nursing homes', *Journal of Aging Studies*, 30: 56–63.

Jones, A. (2006) 'Beyond sheltered accommodation: a review of extra care housing and care home provision for BME elders', December, Age Concern/Chinese Housing Consultative Group, Housing Lin, London.

Jones, A. (2008) 'Meeting the sheltered and extra care housing needs of Black and Minority Ethnic older people: a Race Equality Foundation briefing paper', *Housing Care and Support,* 11 (2): 41–8.

Jones, A. (2020) 'Equity release: what are the options for older people?', *The Guardian*, 7 February. Available at: https://www.theguardian.com/money/2020/feb/07/equity-release-what-are-the-options-for-older-people

Jones, A. and Bignall, T. (2011) 'Meeting the supported housing needs of black and minority ethnic communities', Race Equality Foundation Briefing Papers, December. London: Race Equality Foundation Available at: https://raceequalityfoundation.org.uk/wp-content/uploads/2018/02/housing-brief19.pdf

Jones, A., Geilenkeuser, T., Helbrecht, I. and Quilgars, D. (2012) 'Demographic change and retirement planning: comparing households' views in the role of housing equity in Germany and the UK', *International Journal of Housing Policy*, 12 (1): 27–45.

Jones, I.R. (2015) 'Connectivity, digital technologies and later life', in J. Twigg and W, Martin (eds) *Routledge Handbook of Cultural Gerontology*, London: Routledge, Taylor & Francis Group, pp 438–46.

Jones, I.R., Hyde, M., Victor, C.R., Wiggins, R.D., Gilleard, C. and Higgs, P. (2008) *Ageing in a Consumer Society: From Passive to Active Consumption in Britain*, Bristol: Policy Press

Jones, M. (2009) 'Phase space: geography, relational thinking and beyond', *Progress in Human Geography*, 33 (4): 487–506.

Jones, T., Chatterjee, K., Spencer, B. and Jones, H. (2017) 'Cycling beyond your sixties: the role of cycling in later life and how it can be supported and promoted', in C. Musselwhite, (ed.) *Transport, Travel and Later Life (Transport and Sustainability, Vol. 10)*, Bingley: Emerald Publishing Limited, pp 139–68.

Joseph Rowntree Foundation (1997) *Foundations: Building Lifetime Homes*, York: Joseph Rowntree Foundation.

Joseph Rowntree Foundation (2021) *UK Poverty 2020/2021*, York: Joseph Rowntree Foundation.

Judge, K. (1986) 'Residential care for the elderly: purposes and resources', in K. Judge and I. Sinclair (eds) *Residential Care for Elderly People Research Contributions to the Development of Policy and Practice*, London: HMSO, pp 5–20.

Kahana, E. (1982) 'A congruence model of person-environment interaction', in M.P. Lawton, P.G. Windley and T.O. Byerts (eds) *Aging and the Environment: Theoretical Approaches*, New York: Springer, pp 97–121.

Kahana, E., Lovegreen, L., Kahana, B. and Kahana, M. (2003) 'Person, environment, and person-environment fit as influences on residential satisfaction of elders', *Environment and Behaviour*, 35 (3): 434–53.

Kalache, A., Barreto, S.M. and Keller, I. (2005) 'Global ageing: the demographic revolution in all cultures and societies', in M.L. Johnson, V.L. Bengtson, P. Coleman and T. Kirkwood (eds) *The Cambridge Handbook of Age and Ageing*, Cambridge: Cambridge University Press, pp 30–46.

Karpf, A. (2020) 'Don't let prejudice against older people contaminate the climate movement', *The Guardian*, 18 January. Available at: https://www.theguardian.com/commentisfree/2020/jan/18/ageism-climate-movement-generation-stereotypes

Kaspar, R., Oswald, F., Wahl, H-W., Voss, E. and Wettstein, M. (2015) 'Daily mood and out-of-home mobility in older adults: does cognitive impairment matter', *Journal of Applied Gerontology*, 34 (1): 26–47.

Katz, J. (2003) 'Practical applications of the principles and practices of palliative care to the residential sector', in J. Katz and S. Peace (eds) (2003) *End of Life in Care Homes: A Palliative Approach*, Oxford: Oxford University Press, pp 131–56.

Katz, S. (2005) *Cultures of Aging: Life Course, Lifestyle and Senior Worlds*, Ontario: Broadview Press.

Katz, S. (ed) (2019) *Ageing in Everyday Life: Materialities and Embodiments*, Bristol: Policy Press.

Katz, J., Holland, C. and Peace, S. (2013) 'Hearing the voices of people with high support needs', *Journal of Aging Studies*, 27 (1): 52–60.

Katz, J., Holland, C., Peace, S. and Roberts, E. (2011) *A Better Life: Needs and Aspirations of People with High Support Needs*, York: Joseph Rowntree Foundation.

Katz, S. and Calasanti, T. (2015) Critical perspectives on successful aging: does it "appeal more than it illuminates"?', *The Gerontologist*, 55 (1): 26–33. doi:10.1093/geront/gnu027

Kay, A., Lambie, J. and Holland, C.A. (2015) ' "Getting out and about"; can ExtraCare reduce the negative impact of low mobility?', Factsheet 2, collaborative research between Aston Research Centre for Health Ageing (ARCHA) and the ExtraCare Charitable Trust. Available at: www.://www.aston.ac.uk/lhs/research/centres-facilities/archa/extracare-project/

Kearns, R.A. and Andrews, G.J. (2005) 'Placing ageing: positionings in the study of older people', in G.J. Andrews and D.R. Phillips (eds) *Ageing and Place: Perspectives, Policy and Practice*, London: Routledge, pp 13–23.

Keates, S. and Clarkson, J. (2003a) 'Design exclusion', in J. Clarkson., R, Coleman., S, Keates and C, Lebbon, *Inclusive Design: Design for the Whole Population*, London: Springer-Verlag, pp 89–102.

Keates, S. and Clarkson, J. (2003b) 'Countering design exclusion', in J. Clarkson, R. Coleman., S. Keates and C. Lebbon, *Inclusive Design: Design for the Whole Population*, London: Springer-Verlag, pp 438–57.

Keating, N. (2008) 'Revisiting rural ageing', in N. Keating (ed) *Rural Ageing: A Good Place to Grow Old?*, Bristol: Policy Press, pp 121–30.

Keating, N. and Phillips, J. (2008) 'A critical human ecology perspective on rural ageing', in N, Keating (ed) *Rural Ageing: A Good Place to Grow Old?*, Bristol: Policy Press, pp 1–10.

Keating, N., Eales, J. and Phillips, J.E. (2013) 'Age-friendly rural communities: conceptualizing "best fit"'. *Canadian Journal of Aging*, 32 (4): 319–32.

Keglovits, M. and Stark, S. (2020) 'Home modifications to improve function and safety in the United States', *Journal of Aging and Environment*, 34 (2): 110–25.

Kellaher, L. (1986) 'Determinants of quality of life in residential settings for old people', in K. Judge and I. Sinclair (eds) *Residential Care for Elderly People. Research Contributions to the Development of Policy and Practice*, London: HMSO, pp 127–38.

Kellaher, L. (1998) 'When and how institutions do work – Caring in Homes initiative', in R. Jack (ed) *Residential versus Community Care: The Role of Institutions in Welfare Provision*, London: Macmillan, pp 185–201.

Kellaher, L. (1998b) *Quality Matters*, St Albans: The Abbeyfield Society.

Kellaher, L. (2000) 'A choice well made: 'mutuality' as a governing principle in residential care', Centre for Policy on Ageing/Methodist Homes for the Aged. London: Blackwells.

Kellaher, L. (2002) 'Is genuine choice a reality?', in K. Sumner (ed) *Our Homes, Our Lives: Choice in Later Life Living Arrangements*, London: Housing Corporation/Centre for Policy on Ag and 8.eing, pp 36–59.

Kellaher, L., Peace, S. and Willcocks, D. (1990) 'Triangulating data', in S. Peace (ed) *Researching Social Gerontology: Concepts, Methods and Issues*, London: Sage Publications, pp 115–28.

Kellaher, L., Peace, S. and Holland, C. (2004) 'Environment, identity and old age: quality of life or a life of quality', in A. Walker and C. Hagan Hennessy (eds) *Growing Older: Quality of Life in Old Age*, Maidenhead: Open University Press, pp 60–80.

Kellaher, L., Peace, S., Weaver, T. and Willcocks, D. (1988) 'Coming to terms with the private sector: regulatory practice for residential care homes and elderly people', Report 1, PNL Press, London.

Kelly, M. (2001) 'Lifetime homes', in S. Peace and C. Holland (eds) *Inclusive Housing in An Ageing Society*, Bristol: Policy Press, pp 55–76.

Kelley, J.A., Dannefer, D. and Issa Al Masarweh, L. (2018) 'Addressing erasure, microfication and social change: age-friendly initiatives and environmental gerontology in the 21st century', in T. Buffel, S. Handler and C. Phillpson (eds) *Age-Friendly Cities and Communities: A Global Perspective*, Bristol: Policy Press, pp 51–72.

Kenkmann, A., Poland, F., Burns, D., Hyde, P. and Killett, A. (2017) 'Negotiating and valuing spaces: the discourse of space and "home" in cares homes', *Health & Place*, 43: 8–16.

Kent, S. (ed) (1993) *Domestic Architecture and the Use of Space: An Interdisciplinary Cross-Cultural Study*, Cambridge: Cambridge University Press

Kindon, S., Pain, R. and Kesby, M. (2010) *Participatory Action Research Approaches and Methods: Connecting People, Participation and Place*, London: Routledge.

King, A. and Stoneman, P. (2017) 'Understanding SAFE Housing – putting older LGBT people's concerns, preferences and experiences of housing in England in a sociological context', *Housing, Care and Support*, 20 (3): 89–99.

King, A., Almack, K. and Jones, R.L. (eds) (2020). *Intersections of Ageing, Gender and Sexualities: Multidisciplinary International Perspectives*, Ageing in a Global Context series, Bristol: Policy Press.

King, R., Warnes, A.M. and Williams, A.M. (2000) *Sunset Lives: British Retirement Migration to the Mediterranean*, Oxford: Berg.

The King's Fund (2021a) 'What will the government's proposals mean for the social care system?', 7 September, Available at: https://www.kingsfund. org.uk/publications/government-proposals-social-care-system

The King's Fund (2021b) 'Briefing on the Health and Care Bill: House of Commons report stage and third reading', London: The King's Fund. Available at: https://www.kingsfund.org.uk/publications/ briefing-health-and-care-bill-report-stage-third-reading

Kinsella, K. (2001) 'Urban and rural dimensions of global population aging: an overview', *Journal of Rural Health*, 17 (4): 314–22.

Kitwood, T. (1990) 'The dialectics of dementia: with particular reference to Alzheimer's disease.' *Ageing and Society*, 10: 177–96.

Kitwood, T. (1993) 'Towards a theory of dementia care: the interpersonal process', *Ageing and Society*. 13: 51–67.

Kitwood, T (1997) *Dementia Reconsidered: The Person Comes First*, Buckingham: The Open University Press.

Kitwood, T. and Bredin, K.C. (1992) 'Towards a theory of dementia care: personhood and well-being', *Ageing and Society*. 12: 269–87.

Kleemeier, R. (1959) 'Behaviour and the organisation of the bodily and external environment', in J.E. Birren (ed) *Handbook of Ageing and the Individual*, Chicago: University of Chicago Press, pp 400–51.

Kleemeier, R. (1961) 'The use and meaning of time in special settings', in R. Kleemeier (ed) *Aging and Leisure*, New York: Oxford University Press, pp 1–22.

Klinenberg, E. (2003) *Heat Wave: A Social Autopsy of Disaster in Chicago*, Chicago: University of Chicago Press.

Kneale, D. (2011) 'Establishing the "extra" in extra care: perspectives from three extracare providers', ILC-UK report, London. Available at: https:// ilcuk.org.uk/establishing-the-extra-in-care-perspectives-from-three-extra-care-housing-providers/

Kneale, D. and Smith, L. (2013) 'Extra care housing in the UK: can it be a home for life?', *Journal of Housing for the Elderly*, 27 (3): 276–98.

Kneale, D., Henley, J., Thomas, J. and French, R. (2019) Inequalities in older LGBT people's health and care needs in the United Kingdom: a systematic scoping review, *Ageing & Society*, 41 (3): 493–515.

Knight Frank (2018) 'Retirement housing market update, Q1 2018'. Available at: https://content.knightfrank.com/resources/knightfrank.co.uk/retirement-housing-market-update-q1-2018.pdf

Knipscheer, C.P.M., de Jong Gierveld, J., van Tilburg, T.G. and Dykstra, P.A. (eds) (1995) *Living Arrangements and Social Networks of Older Adults*. Amsterdam: Free University Press.

Kobayashi, M. (2016) 'The housing market and housing policies in Japan', ADBI Working Paper 558, 22 March. Available at: https://ssrn.com/abstract=2752868 or http://dx.doi.org/10.2139/ssrn.2752868

Komaromy, C., Sidell, M. and Katz, J. (2000) 'The quality of terminal care in residential and nursing home', *International Journal of Palliative Nursing*, 6 (4): 192–204.

Kontos, P.C. (2005a) 'Multi-disciplinary configurations in gerontology', in G.J. Andrews. and D.R. Phillips (eds) *Ageing and Place: Perspectives, Policy, Practice*, London: Routledge, pp 24–36.

Koppitz, A.L., Dreizler, J., Altherr, J., Bosshard, G., Rahel, N. and Imhof, L. (2017) 'Relocation experiences with unplanned admission to a nursing homes: a qualitative study', *International Psychogeriatrics*, 29 (3): 517–27.

Korte, S. (1966) 'Designing for old people: the role of residential homes', *The Architectural Journal*, 19 October, 144: 987–91.

KOVE (Kilburn Older Voices Exchange) (2012) 'Walking the Kilburn High Road' video. Available at: https://KOVE.org.uk

Krendl, A.C. and Perry, B.L. (2021) 'The impact of sheltering in place during the COVID-19 pandemic on older adults' social and mental wellbeing', *The Journals of Gerontology: Series B,* 76 (2): e53–e58.

Labit, A. (2015) 'Self-managed co-housing in the context of an ageing population in Europe', *Urban Research & Practice,* 8: 32–45.

Lagadec, P. (2004) 'Understanding the French 2003 heat wave experience: beyond the heat, a multi-layered challenge', *Journal of Contingencies and Crisis Management*, 12 (4): 160–9.

Laing, W. (2002) *Healthcare Market Review 2001–2*, London: Laing and Buisson.

Laing, W. (2018*) Care Homes for Older People: UK Market Report* (29th edn), London: LaingBuisson.

Laing, W. (2019) *Care Homes for Older People: UK Market Report* (30th edn), London: LaingBuisson.

Lamura, G., Mnich, E., Nolan, M., Woiszel, B., Krevers, B., Mestheneos, L., Dohner, H. (2008) 'Family carers' experiences using support services in Europe: empirical evidence from the EUROFAMCARE study', *The Gerontologist*, 48 (6): 752–71.

Langton-Lockton, S. (1998) 'Centre forward: extending Part M to new housing', *Access by Design*, 75: 72.

Laslett, P. (1989) *A Fresh Map of Life: The Emergence of the Third Age*, London: Weidenfeld & Nicolson.

Laslett, P. (1996) *A Fresh Map of Life: The Emergence of the Third Age* (2nd edn), London: Palgrave Macmillan.

Laws, G. (1994) 'Contested meanings, the built environment and ageing in place', *Environment and Planning A*, 26: 1787–802.

Laws, G. (1995) Understanding ageism: lesson from postmodernism and feminism, *The Gerontologist*, 35 (1): 112–18.

Laws, G. (1997) 'Spatiality and age relations', in A. Jamieson., S. Harper, and C. Victor (eds) *Critical Approaches to Ageing and Later Life*, Buckingham: Open University Press, pp 90–100.

Lawton, M.P. (1975a) *Planning and Managing Housing for the Elderly*, New York: John Wiley and Sons.

Lawton, M.P. (1975b) 'The Philadelphia Geriatric Center morale scale: a revision', *Journal of Gerontology*, 30 (1): 85–9.

Lawton, M.P. (1979) 'Measures of quality of life and subjective wellbeing, *Generations*, 21 (1): 45–7.

Lawton, M.P. (1980) *Environment and Aging*, Belmont, CA: Brooks-Cole.

Lawton, M.P. (1982) 'Competence, environmental press, and the adaptation of the elderly', in M.P. Lawton., P.G. Windley and T.O. Byerts (eds) *Environmental Theory and Aging*, New York: Springer, pp 33–59.

Lawton, M.P. (1983) 'Environments and other determinants of well-being in older people', *The Gerontologist*, 23: 349–57.

Lawton, M.P. (1985) 'The elderly in context. Perspectives from environmental psychology and gerontology', *Environment and Behaviour*, 17: 501–19.

Lawton, M.P. (1987) 'Foreword', in Willcocks, D., Peace, S. and Kellanher, L. (eds) *Private Lives in Public Places: A Research Based Critique of Residential Life in Local Authority Old People's Homes*, London: Tavistock Publications, pp x.

Lawton, M.P. (1989) 'Environmental proactivity in older people', in V.L. Bengston and K.W. Schaie (eds) *The Course of Later Life*, New York: Springer, pp 15–23.

Lawton, M.P. (1990) 'An environmental psychologist ages', in I. Altman and K. Christensen (eds) *Environment and Behaviour Studies: Emergence of Intellectual Traditions*, New York: Plenum Press, pp 339–63.

Lawton, M.P. (1998) 'Environment and aging: theory revisited', in R.J. Scheidt and P.G. Windley (eds) *Environment and Aging Theory. A Focus on Housing*, Westport, CT: Greenwood Press, pp 1–31.

Lawton, M.P. (2000) 'Chance and choice make a good life', in J.E. Birren and J.F. Schroots (eds) *A History of Geropsychology in Autobiography*, Washington DC: American Psychological Association, pp 619–24.

Lawton, M.P. (2001) 'The physical environment of the person with Alzheimer's disease', *Aging and Mental Health*, 5 (1): 56–64.

Lawton, M.P. and Simon, B. (1968) 'The ecology of social relationships in housing for the elderly', *The Gerontologist*, 8: 108–115.

Lawton, M.P. and Nahemow, L. (1973) 'Ecology and the aging process', in C. Eisdorfer and M.P. Lawton (eds) *Psychology of Adult Development and Aging*, Washington DC: American Psychological Association, pp 619–74.

Lawton, M.P., Winter, L. and Kleban, M.H. (1999) 'Affect and quality of life: objective and subjective', *Journal of Aging and Health*, 11 (2): 169–98.

Lawton, M.P., Moss, M. and Moles, E. (1984) 'The suprapersonal neighbourhood context of older people: age heterogeneity and well-being', *Environment and Behaviour*, 16 (1): 89–109.

Lawton, M.P., Weisman, G.D., Sloane, P., Norris-Baker, C., Calkins, M. and Zimmerman, S. (2000) 'Professional environmental assessment procedure for special care units for elderly with dementing illness and its relationship to the therapeutic environment screening schedule', *Alzheimer Disease and Associated Disorders*, 14 (1): 28–38.

Lawton, M.P., Moss, M., Hoffman, C., Kleban, M., Ruckdeschel, K. and Winter, L. (2001) 'Valuation of life: a concept and a scale', *Journal of Aging and Health*, 13 (1): 3–31.

Leamy, M. and Clough, R. (2006) *How Older People Become Researchers: Training Guidance and Practice in Action*, York: Joseph Rowntree Foundation.

Lee, V.S.P., Simpson, J. and Froggatt, K. (2013) 'A narrative exploration of older people's transitions into residential care', *Aging & Mental Health*, 17 (1): 48–56.

Leece, J. and Peace, S. (2009) 'Developing new understandings of independence and autonomy in the personalised relationship', *British Journal of Social Work*, 40 (6): 1847–65.

Lefebvre, H. (1991) *The Production of Space*, London: Blackwell Publishing.

Le Mesurier, N. (2011) *Growing Older in the Countryside*, Cirencester: Action with Rural Communities.

Le Quere, C., Jackson, R.B., Jones, M.W., Smith, A.J.P., Abernethy, S., Andre, R.M., De-Goi, A.J., Willis, D.R., Shan, Y., Canadell. J., Friedlingstein, P., Creutzig, F and Peters, G.P. (2020) 'Temporary reduction in daily global CO2 emission during the COVID 19 forced confinement', *Nature Climate Change*, 10: 647–53.

Lewin, K. (1936) *Principles of Topological Psychology*, New York: McGraw-Hill.

Lewin, K. (1951) *Field Theory in Social Science: Selected Theoretical Papers*, New York: Harper & Row.

Lewis, A., Torrington, J., Barnes, S., Holder, J., McKee, K., Netten, A. and Orrell, A. (2010) 'EVOLVE: a tool for evaluating the design of older people's housing', *Housing, Care and Support*, 13 (3): 36–41.

Lewis, A. and Torrington, J. (2012) 'Extra-care housing for people with sight loss: lighting and design, *Lighting Research and Technology*, 45 (3): 345–61.

Leyland, L.-A., Spencer, B., Beale, N., Jones, T. and van Reekum, C.M. (2019) 'The effect of cycling on cognitive function and well-being in older adults', *PLoS ONE*, 14 (2): e0211779, https://doi.org/10.1371/journal.pone.0211779

Liddle, J., Scharf, T., Bartlam, B., Bernard, M. and Sim, J. (2014)' Exploring the age-friendliness of purpose-built retirement communities: evidence from England', *Ageing & Society* 34 (9):1601–29.

Lievesley, N. (2010) 'The future ageing of the ethnic minority population of England and Wales', Older BME People and Financial Inclusion report, Runnymede/ Trust/Centre for Policy on Ageing, London.

Lipman, A. (1968) 'A socio-architectural view of life in three homes for old people', *Gerontologia Clinica*, 10: 88–101.

Lipman, A. and Slater, R. (1977a) 'Homes for old people: towards positive environments', *The Gerontologist*, 17 (2): 146–56.

Lipman, A. and Slater, R. (1977b) 'Status and spatial appropriations in eight homes for old people', *The Gerontologist*, 17 (3): 250–5.

Litwak, E. and Longino, C.F. (1987) 'Migration patterns among the elderly: a developmental perspective', *The Gerontologist*, 27 (3): 266–72.

Liu, J., Guo, M. Mao, W. and Chi, I. (2018) 'Geographic distance and intergenerational relationships in Chinese migrant families', *Journal of Ethnic and Cultural Diversity in Social Work*, 27 (4): 328–45.

Lloyd, L. (2015) 'The Fourth Age', in J. Twigg and W. Martin (eds) *Routledge Handbook of Cultural Gerontology*, London and New York: Routledge, pp 261–8.

Lloyd, L., Calnan, M., Cameron, A., Seymour, J. and Smith, R. (2014) 'Identity in the fourth age: perseverance, adaptation and maintaining dignity'. *Ageing and Society,* 34 (1): 1–19.

Lloyd-Sherlock, P. (2010) *Population Ageing and International Development: From Generalisation to Evidence*, Bristol: Policy Press.

LoBuono, D.L., Leedahl, S.N. and Maiocco, E. (2019) 'Older adults learning technology in an intergenerational program: qualitative analysis of areas of technology requested for assistance', University of Rhode Island, Kingston. Available at: https://digitalcommons.uri.edu/hdf_facpubs/63/

Local Government Association (2017a) *Housing Our Ageing Population: Learning from Councils Meeting the Needs of Our Ageing Population*, London: Local Government Association. Available at: https://www.local.gov.uk/sites/default/files/documents/5.17%20-%20Housing%20our%20ageing%20population_07_0.pdf

Local Government Association (2017b) *Neighbourhood Planning Act 2017 (Get in on the Act)*. London: Local Government Association. Available at: https://www.local.gov.uk/neighbourhood-planning-act-2017-get-act#:~:text=The%20Neighbourhood%20Planning%20Act%202017,effect%20at%20an%20earlier%20stage

Local Government Association (2021) *The future of the planning system and the upcoming Planning Bill*, House of Commons, 15 July, Available at: https://www.local.gov.uk/parliament/briefings-and-responses/future-planning-system-and-upcoming-planning-bill-house-commons

Loe, M. (2010) 'Doing it my way: old women, technology and wellbeing', *Sociology of Health and Illness*, 32 (2): 319–34.

Lofland, L.H. (2017 [1998]) *The Public Realm: Exploring the City's Quintessential Social Territory*, New York: Taylor & Francis Group.

London Assembly (2020) 'New network of sensors to tackle toxic air pollution across London', London Assembly, 14 December. Available at: https://www.london.gov.uk/press-releases/mayoral/new-network-of-sensors-to-tackle-toxic-air

London Councils (n.d.) 'Freedom Pass: eligibility', Available at: https://www.londoncouncils.gov.uk/services/freedom-pass/older-persons-freedom-pass/eligibility

Lorimer, H. (2005) 'Cultural geography: the busyness of being "more-than-representational"', *Progress in Human Geography*, 29 (1): 83–96.

Lorimer, H. (2008) 'Cultural geography: non-representational conditions and concerns', *Progress in Human Geography*, 32(4): 551–9.

Lovatt, M. (2018) 'Becoming at home in residential care for older people: a material culture perspective', *Sociology of Health & Illness*, 40 (2): 366–78.

Lowenstein, A. (2005) 'Global ageing and challenges to families', in M.L. Johnson in association with V.L. Bengston, P.G. Coleman and T.B.L. Kirkwood (eds) *The Cambridge Handbook of Age and Ageing*, Cambridge: Cambridge University Press, pp 403–12.

Lowenstein, A. and Katz, R. (2010) 'Family and age in a global perspective', in D. Dannefer and C. Phillipson. (eds) *The SAGE Handbook of Social Gerontology*, London: Sage Publications Ltd, pp 190–201.

Luborsky, M.R., Lysack, C.L. and Van Nuil, J. (2011) 'Refashioning one's place in time: stories of household downsizing in later life', *Journal of Aging Studies*, 25 (3): 243–52.

Lucco, A.J. (1987) 'Planned retirement housing preferences of older homosexuals', *Journal of Homosexuality*, 14 (3–4): 35–56.

Luck, R. (2018) 'Participatory design in architectural practice: changing practices in future making in uncertain times', *Design Studies*, 59: 139–57.

Lui, C., Everingham, J., Warburton, J., Cuthill, M. and Bartlett, H. (2009) 'What makes a community age-friendly: a review of international literature', *Australasian Journal of Ageing*, 28 (3): 116–21.

Lumby, T. (2019) 'Girls born in Cornwall face more than 20 years of poor health in old age', *The Falmouth Packet*, 29 December. Available at: https://www.falmouthpacket.co.uk/news/18125461. girls-born-cornwall-face-20-years-poor-health-old-age/

Lynch, K. (1960) *The Image of the City*, Cambridge, MA: The MIT Press.

Mackintosh, S. (2020) 'Putting home adaptations on the policy agenda in England', *Journal of Aging and the Environment*, 34 (2):126–40.

Maclennan D. and O'Sullivan, A. (2013) 'Localism, devolution and housing policies', *Housing Studies*, 28 (4): 599–615.

Madanipour, A. (1999) Why are the design and development of public spaces significant for cities? *Environment and Planning B: Development and Design*, 26: 879–891.

Madanipour, A. (2003) *Public and Private Spaces of the City*, London: Routledge.

Maggie's (n.d.) Available at: https://www.maggies.org/

Maguire, M., Peace, S., Nicolle, C., Marshall, R., Sims, R., Percival, J. and Lawton, C. (2012) *The Easier Kitchen: Making it Happen*, The Open University/Loughborough University. Available via Sheila Peace, The Open University.

Maguire, M., Peace, S., Nicolle, C., Marshall, R., Sims, R., Percival, J. and Lawton, C. (2014) 'Kitchen living in later life: exploring ergonomic problems, coping strategies and design solutions', *International Journal of Design*, 8 (1): 73–91.

Mahmood, A. and Keating, N. (2012) 'Towards inclusive built environments for older adults', in T. Scharf and N. Keating (eds) *From Exclusion to Inclusion in Old Age: A Global Challenge*, Bristol: Policy Press, pp 145–62.

Manthorpe, J. (2008) 'Dementia care quality in homes', *Community Care*, 1720, 1 May.

Manzo, L.C. (2005) 'For better or worse: exploring multiple dimensions of place meaning', *Journal of Environmental Psychology*, 25 (1): 67–86.

Manzo, L.C. and Devine-Wright, P. (eds) (2014) *Place Attachment: Advances in Theory, Methods and Applications*, Abingdon and New York: Routledge.

Marmot, M. and Bell, R. (2016) 'Social inequalities in health: a proper concern of epidemiology', *Annals of Epidemiology*, 26 (4): 238–40.

Marmot, M., Allen, J., Goldblatt, P., Boyce, T., McNeish, D., Grady, M. and Geddes, I. (2010) *Fair Society, Healthy Lives: The Marmot Strategic Review of Health Inequalities in England Post 2010*, London: Department of Health.

Marshall, M. (2001) Dementia and technology', in S, Peace and C. Holland (eds) *Inclusive Housing in an Ageing Society*, Bristol: Policy Press, pp 125–44.

Marston, H.R., Genoe, R., Freeman, S.S., Kulczycki, C. and Musselwhite, C. (2019) 'Older Adults Perspectives of ICT: Main findings from the technology in later life (TILLS) initial study', *Healthcare*, 7 (3): 86–113.

Marston, H.R. and van Hoof, J. (2019) 'Who doesn't think about technology when designing urban environments for older people?' A case study approach to a proposal extension of the WHO's age-friendly cities model', *International Journal of Environmental Research and Public Health*, 16: 3525–60.

Marston, H.R., Kroll, M., Fink, D., de Rosario, H. and Gschwind, Y.J. (2016) Technology use adoption and behaviour in older adults. Results from the iStoppFalls project, *Educational Gerontology*, 42: 371–87.

Maslow, A.H. (1964) *Motivation and Personality*, New York: Harper & Row.

Massey, D. (1993) 'Power-geometry and a progressive sense of place', in J. Bird, B. Curtis, T. Putnam, G. Robertson and L. Tickner (eds) *Mapping the Futures: Local Cultures, Global Change*, Abingdon: Routledge, pp 59–69.

Massey, D. (1994) *Space, Place, and Gender*, Cambridge: Polity Press.

Massey, D. (2005) *for space* (1st edn), London: Sage Publications.

Massey, D., Allen, J., and Pile, S. (eds) (1999a) *City Worlds*, Abingdon: Routledge.

Mathie, E., Goodman, C., Crang, C., Froggatt, K., Illiffe, S., Manthorpe, J. and Barclay, S. (2012) 'An uncertain future: the unchanging views of care home residents about living and dying', *Palliative Medicine*, 26 (5): 734–43.

Matrix (1984) *Women and the Man Made Environment*, London: Pluto Press.

Mayor of London (2015) 'Housing standards: minor alterations to the London Plan, consultation draft', May, Greater London Authority.

Mayor of London (2018) 'London Plan annual monitoring report 14 2016/17', September, Greater London Authority.

McCafferty, P. (1994) *Living Independently: A Study of the Housing Needs of Elderly and Disabled People*, London: HMSO.

McCarthy & Stone (2018) 'Generation stuck: downsizing report', McCarthy & Stone, Bournemouth.

McCormack, D. (2017) 'The circumstances pf post-phenomenological life worlds', *Transactions of the Institute of British Geographers*, 42 (1): 2–13.

McCracken, K. and Phillips, D.R. (2016) *Global Health: An Introduction to Global and Future Trends* (2nd edn), Abingdon: Routledge.

McCreadie, C. (2010) 'Technology and older people', in D. Dannefer and C. Phillipson (eds) *The Sage Handbook of Social Gerontology*, London: Sage Publications, pp 607–17.

McDowell, L. (1999) *Gender, Identity and Place: Understanding Feminist Geography*, Minneapolis: University of Minnesota Press.

McGranahan, G., Balk, D. and Anderson, B. (2007) 'The rising tide: assessing the risks of climate change and human settlements in low elevation coastal areas, *Environment and Urbanization*, 19 (1): 17–37.

McKee, K. (2012) 'Young people, homeownership and future welfare', *Housing Studies*, 27 (6): 853–62.

McKee, K. (2015) 'Community anchor housing associations: illuminating the contested nature of neoliberal governing practices at the local scale', *Environment and Planning C: Government and Policy*, 33 (5): 1076–91.

McKee, K., Muir, J. and Moore, T. (2017) 'Housing policy in the UK: the importance of spatial nuance', *Housing Studies* 32 (1): 60–72.

McKee, K., Moore, T., Soaita, S. and Crawford, J. (2017) '"Generation rent" and the fallacy of choice', *International Journal of Urban and Regional Research*, 41 (2): 318–33.

McManus, S. and Lord, C. (2012) 'Circumstances of people with sight loss': secondary analysis of Understanding Society the Life Opportunities Survey, Natcen, London.

Meacher, M. (1972) *Taken for a Ride: Special Residential Homes for Confused Old People*, London: Longman.

Meadows, R., Arber, S. and Venn, S. (2008) Engaging with sleep: male definitions, understandings and attitudes', *Sociology of Health and Illness*, 30 (5): 696–710.

Means, S and Smith, R. (1983) 'From public assistance institutions to "sunshine hotels': changing state perceptions about residential care for elderly people, 1939–1948', *Ageing & Society*, 3 (2): 157–81.

Means, R and Smith, R. (1998) *From Poor Law to Community Care: The Development of Welfare Services for Elderly People 1939–1971*, Bristol: Policy Press.

Means, R., Burholt, V. and Hennessy, C.H. (2014) 'Towards connectivity in a grey and pleasant land?', in C.H. Hennessy, R. Means, R and V. Burholt (eds) *Countryside Connections: Older People, Community and Place in Rural Britain*, Bristol: Policy Press, pp 245–76.

Menec, V., Means, R., Keating, N., Parkhurst, G. and Eales, J. (2011) 'Conceptualising age-friendly communities'. *Canadian Journal of Aging*, 30 (3): 479–93.

Mertens, D.M. and Hessbiber, S. (2012) 'Triangulation and mixed methods research', *Journal of Mixed Methods Research* 6 (2): 75–9.

Meyer, J. (2015) 'Most care homes don't have registered nurses working in them', *Nursing Times*, 25 February. Available at: https://www.nursingtimes.net/opinion/most-care-homes-dont-have-registered-nurses-working-in-them-25-02-2015/

MHCLG (Ministry of Housing, Community and Local Government) (2011) *Planning Policy Statement 3: Housing.* London: Housing LIN. Available at: https://www.housinglin.org.uk/_assets/Resources/Housing/Policy_documents/PPS3.pdf

MHCLG (2015) 'The Building Regulations 2010. Approved Document M: Access to and Use of Buildings, Volume 1: Dwellings', HMSO, London. Available at: https://assets.publishing.service.gov.uk/government/uploads/system/uploads/attachment_data/file/540330/BR_PDF_AD_M1_2015_with_2016_amendments_V3.pdf

MHCLG (2017) *Fixing Our Broken Housing Markets*, 7 February, London: MHCLG.

MHCLG (2018) *English Housing Survey: Headline report 2016–17*, London: Office for National Statistics.

MHCLG (2019a) *The Future Homes Standard. Consultation on changes to Part L (Conservation of Fuel and Power) and Part F (Ventilation) of the Building Regulations for New Dwellings*, October. London: MHCLG.

MHCLG (2019b) *Guidance: Housing for Older and Disabled People*, London: MHCLG. Available at: https://www.gov.uk/guidance/housing-for-older-and-disabled-people

MHCLG (2020a) 'English Housing Survey: housing across the life course, 2018–19', July. London: MHCLG. Available at: https://www.gov.uk/government/statistics/english-housing-survey-2018-to-2019-housing-across-the-life-course

MHCLG (2020b) 'Home ownership: ethnicity facts and figures' (updated September), London: MHCLG. Available at: https://www.ethnicity-facts-figures.service.gov.uk/housing/owning-and-renting/home-ownership/latest#by-ethnicity

MHCLG (2020c) 'Renting social housing: ethnicity facts and figures' (updated March), MHCLG, London. Available at: https://www.ethnicity-facts-figures.service.gov.uk/housing/social-housing/renting-from-a-local-authority-or-housing-association-social-housing/latest#by-ethnicity

MHCLG (2020d) 'People without decent homes: ethnicity facts and figures', MHCLG, London. Available at: https://www.ethnicity-facts-figures.service.gov.uk/housing/housing-conditions/non-decent-homes/latest

MHCLG (2020e) 'English Housing Survey: 2019–20: headline report', December, MHCLG, London. Available at: https://www.gov.uk/government/statistics/english-housing-survey-2019-to-2020-headline-report

MHCLG (2020f) 'Renting from a private landlord: ethnicity facts and figures (updated March), MHCLG, London. Available at: https://www.ethnicity-facts-figures.service.gov.uk/housing/owning-and-renting/renting-from-a-private-landlord/latest

MHCLG (2020g) 'Approved Document M volume 2 amendments': circular 02/2020, MHCLG, London. Available at: https://www.gov.uk/government/publications/approved-document-m-volume-2-amendments-circular-022020

MHCLG (2020h) *English Housing Survey. Technical Report 2018–19*. July. London: MHCLG. Available at: https://www.gov.uk/government/publications/english-housing-survey-2018-to-2019-technical-report

MHCLG (2021a) *English Housing Survey. Homeownership, 2019–2020*. July. London: MHCLG.

MHCLG (2021b) *English Housing Survey. Private Rented Sector, 2019–2020*. London: MHCLG.

MHCLG (2021c) *English Housing Survey. Social Rented Sector, 2019–2020.* London: MHCLG.

MHCLG (2021d) *English Housing Survey. Home adaptation report, 2019–2020.* London: MHCLG.

MHCLG (2021e) 'The Future Homes Standard: 2019 Consultation on changes to Part L (conservation of fuel and power) and Part F (ventilation) of the Building Regulations for new dwellings. Summary of responses received and Government response', January, MHCLG, London. Available at: https://assets.publishing.service.gov.uk/government/uploads/system/uploads/attachment_data/file956094/Government_response

MHLG (Ministry of Housing and Local Government) (1958) *Flatlets for Old People. Design Bulletin,* London: HMSO.

MHLG (Ministry of Housing and Local Government) (1960) *More Flatlets for Old People,* London: HMSO.

MHLG (Ministry of Housing and Local Government) (1962) *Some Aspects of Designing for Old People,* London: MHLG.

MHLG (Parker Morris Report) (1962) *Homes for Today and Tomorrow,* London: HMSO.

MHLG (1966) '*Old People's Flatlets at Stevenage: An Account of the Project with an Appraisal',* Design Bulletin no. 11, London: HMSO.

MHLG (1969) *Housing Standards and Costs: Accommodation Specially Designed for Old People,* Circular 82/69. London: HMSO.

MHLG and Ministry of Health (1961) *Services for Old People,* Joint Circular 10/61 and 12/61, London: HMSO.

Migration Data Portal (2021) 'Older persons and migration', last updated 6 April 2021. Available at: https://migrationdataportal.org/themes/older-persons-and-migration

Millar, D. (2001) *Home Possession: Material Culture behind Closed Doors,* Oxford: Berg.

Millar, D. (ed) (2005) 'Materiality: introduction'. Available at: https://www.ucl.ac.uk/anthropology/people/academic-and-teaching-staff/daniel-miller/materiality-introduction

Miller, D. (2008) *The Comfort of Things,* Cambridge: Polity Press.

Miller, D. (2010) *Stuff,* Cambridge: Polity Press.

Miller, E.J. and Gwynne. G. (1972) *A Life Apart: Pilot Study of Residential Institutions for the Physically Handicapped and the Young Chronic Sick,* London: Tavistock Publications.

Milligan, C. (2005) 'From home to "home": situating emotions within the care-giving experience', *Environment and Planning A,* 37 (12): 2105–20.

Milligan, C. (2009) *There's No Place Like Home: Place and Care in an Ageing Society,* Farnham:Ashgate Publishing.

Milligan, C. and Wiles, J. (2010) 'Landscapes of care', *Progress in Human Geography,* 34 (6): 736–54. http://dx.doi.org/10.1177/0309132510364556

Milligan, C. and Bingley, A. (2015) 'Gardens and gardening in later life', in J, Twigg and W. Martin (eds) *Routledge Handbook of Cultural Gerontology*, Abingdon: Routledge, pp 320–8.

Milligan, C, Mort, M. and Roberts, C. (2010) 'Cracks in the door? Technology and the shifting topology of care', in M. Schillmeier and M. Domenech (eds) *New Technologies and Emerging Spaces of Care*, Farnham: Ashgate Publishing, pp 19–38.

Milligan, C., Roberts, C. and Moret, M. (2011) 'Telecare and older people: who cares where?, *Social Science and Medicine*, 72 (3): 347–54.

Milner, J. and Madigan, R. (2001) 'The politics of accessible housing in the UK', in S. Peace and C. Holland (eds) *Inclusive Housing in an Ageing Society*, Bristol: Policy Press, pp 77–100.

Ministry of Health (1950) *Report of the Ministry of Health for the Year End 11 March 1949*. Cmd.7910, London: HMSO.

Ministry of Health (1955) *Circular 3/55*, London: HMSO.

Ministry of Health (1962) *Local Authority Building Note No. 2. Residential Accommodation for Elderly People*, London: HMSO.

Ministry and Health/Ministry of Works (1944) *Housing Manual 1944*, London: HMSO.

Minkler, M. (1996) 'Critical perspectives on ageing: new challenges for gerontology', *Ageing & Society*, 16 (4): 467–87.

Minkler, M. and Estes, C. (eds) (1991) *Critical Perspectives on Aging: The Political and Moral Economy of Growing Old*, Amityville, NY: Baywood.

Minton, A. (2017a) *Big Capital: Who is London For?*, London: Penguin Books.

Minton, A. (2017b) 'High rise living after Grenfell', *British Medical Journal*, 357: j2981.

Mitchell, F., Gilmour, M. and McLaren, G. (2010), "Hospital discharge: a descriptive study of the patient journey for frail older people with complex needs', *Journal of Integrated Care*, 8 (3): 30–6.

Mitchell, L. (2012) 'Breaking new ground: the quest for dementia friendly communities', June, Housing LIN, London. Available at: https://www. housinglin.org.uk/_assets/Resources/Housing/Support_materials/ Viewpoints/Viewpoint25_Dementia_Friendly_Communities.pdf

Mitchell, L. and Burton, E. (2006) 'Neighbourhoods for life: designing dementia-friendly outdoor environment, *Quality in Ageing and Older Adults*, 7 (1): 26–33.

Mitchell, L, Burton, E. and Raman, Shibu, R. (2004) 'Neighbourhood for life: a checklist of recommendations for designing dementia friendly outdoor environments', Housing Corporation, London, and Oxford Brookes University, Oxford. Available at: www.idgo.ac.uk/about_idgo/ neighbourhoods.pdf

Mitchell, L., Burton, E., Raman, S., Blackman, T., Jenks, M. and Williams, K. (2003) 'Making the outside world dementia-friendly: design issues and considerations', *Environment and Planning B: Planning and Design*, 30 (4): 605–32.

Mizra, R.M., Martinez, L., Austen, A., McDonald, L., Klinger, C., Hsieh, J. and Salomons, T. (2019) 'More than just a room: results from an intergenerational home sharing program in Toronto', *Innovation in Aging*, 3 (2): S154.

Montgomery, M.R. (2008) 'The urban transformation of the developing world', *Science*, 319: 761–4.

Moody, H.R. (1993) 'Critical questions for critical gerontology (and gerontologists)', in C. Wellin (ed) *Critical Gerontology Comes of Age: Advances in Research and Theory for a New Century*, London: Routledge.

Mooney, G. and Scott, G. (2011) 'Social justice, social welfare and devolution: Nationalism nationalism and social policy making in Scotland, *Poverty & Public Policy*, 3 (4): 1–21.

Moos, R.H. (1974) *Evaluating Treatment Environments: A Social Ecological Approach*, New York: John Wiley & Sons.

Moos, R.H. and Lemke, S. (1996) *Evaluating Residential Facilities*, Thousand Oaks, CA: SAGE Publications.

Morgan, M. and Cruickshank, H. (2014) 'Quantifying the extent of space shortages: English dwelling', *Building Research & Information*, 42 (6): 710–24.

Morgan-Brown, M., Newton, R. and Ormerod, M. (2013) 'Engaging life in two Irish nursing home units for people with dementia: quantitative comparisons before and after implementing household environments', *Aging & Mental Health*, 17 (1): 57–65.

Mortenson, W.B. Sixsmith, A. and Woolrych, R. (2015) The power(s) of observation: theoretical perspectives on surveillance technologies and older people', *Ageing and Society*, 35 (3): 512–30.

Mumford, L. (1928) 'Towards a rational modernism', *New Republic*, April: 797–8.

Mumford, L. (1938) *The Culture of Cities*, New York: Harcourt.

Murray, H.A. (1938) *Explorations in Personality*, New York: Oxford University Press.

Naess, A., Fjaer, E.G. and Vabø, M. (2016) 'The assisted presentation of self in nursing home life', *Social Science & Medicine*, 150: 153–9.

National Audit Office (2018) 'Adult social care & workforce in England report' (2018/19), HC 714 Session 2017–19, 8 February 2018. Department of Health & Social Care. National Audit Office, London.

National Council for Hospice and Specialist Palliative Care Services (2002) *Definitions of Supportive and Palliative Care*. London: National Council for Hospice and Specialist Palliative Care Services.

National Institute on Aging (2021) 'What is long-term care?' Available at: https://www.nia.nih.gov/health/what-long-term-care

National Institute for Clinical Excellence (2004) *Guidance on Cancer Services: Improving Supportive and Palliative Care for People with Cancer.* London: National Institute for Clinical Excellence.

National Institute for Social Work (1988) *Residential Care: A Positive Choice.* Report of the Independent Review of Residential Care chaired by Gillian Wagner, London: HMSO.

National Records Scotland (2018) 'Population density'. Available at: https://www.nrscotland.gov.uk/statistics-and-data/statistics/statistics-by-theme/population/population-estimates/mid-year-population-estimates/archive/mid-2005-population-estimates-scotland/population-density#:~:text=Population%20density%20is%2065%20persons,in%20Glasgow%20City%20Council%20area.

Netten, A., Darton, R., Bäumker, T. and Calaghan, L. (2011) 'Improving housing with care choices for older people: an evaluation of extra care housing', PSSRU, University of Kent, Canterbury. Available at: https://kar.kent.ac.uk/34666/1/PSSRUsummary_.pdf

New London Plan (2021) *London's Living Spaces and Places. Policy 7.2. An Inclusive Environment.* London: London Assembly. Available at: https://www.london.gov.uk/what-we-do/planning/london-plan/current-london-plan/london-plan-chapter-seven-londons-living-space-7

Newcomer, R.J., Lawton, M.P. and Byerts, T.O. (1986) *Housing an Aging Society: Issues, Alternative, and Policy*, New York: Van Nostrand Reinhold Company.

Newman, O. (1972) *Defensible Space*, New York: Macmillan.

Nhede, N. (2020) 'Top ten countries with the highest proportion of renewable energy', Smart Energy International. Available at: https://www.smart-energy.com/industry-sectors/smart-energy/top-ten-countries-with-the-highest-proportion-of-renewable-energy/

NHS (National Health Service) (2014) 'Community care statistics, social services activity, England – 2013–14. Final release – Annex E national tables'. Available at: http://digital.nhs.uk/catalogue/PUB16133

NHS (2020) 'Dementia guide'. Available at: https://www.nhs.uk/conditions/dementia/about/

Nicol, S., Roys, M. and Garrett, H. (2016) 'The cost of poor housing to the NHS', Briefing Paper 87741, Building Research Establishment, Watford. Available at: https://www.bre.co.uk/filelibrary/pdf/87741-Cost-of-Poor-Housing-Briefing-Paper-v3.pdf

Nicolson, A-M., Buterchi, J. and Cameron, C. (PRP) (2020) 'Safe, happy & together: design ideas for minimising the spread of infection whilst nurturing social interaction' Housing LIN, London. Available at: https://www.housinglin.org?_assets/Resources/Housing/OtherOrganisation/Minimising-infection-Later-Living-Communities.pdf

NISRA (Northern Ireland Statistics and Research Agency) (2020) 'Population'. Available at: https://www.nisra.gov.uk/statistics/population

Nocon, A. and Pleace, N. (1999) 'Sheltered housing and community', *Social Policy and Administration*, 33 (2): 164–80.

Nolan, M. and Allan, S. (2012) 'The "senses framework": a relationship-centred approach to care', in J. Katz, S, Peace and S, Spurr. (eds) *Adult Lives: A Life Course Perspective*, Bristol: Policy Press, pp 100–9.

Oakley, A. (1985) *The Sociology of Housework*, New York: Basil Blackwell.

ODPM/DH (Office of the Deputy Prime Minister/Department of Health) (2006) 'Preventative Technology Grant (2006–07–2007–08)'. Available at: http://data.parliament.uk/DepositedPapers/Files/DEP2009-0073/DEP2009-0073.pdf

OECD (2011) *Help Wanted? Providing and Paying for Long-Term Care*, Summary, Paris: OECD Health Policy Studies. Available at: https://www.oecd-ilibrary.org/docserver/9789264097759-sum-en.pdf?expires=1634923563&id=id&accname=guest&checksum=163BE237CAC6E4DA71DFDC5471F61867

OECD (2015) 'Ageing in cities: policy highlights'. Summary of the publication *Ageing in Cities*, Paris: OECD Publishing. Available at: https://ec.europa.eu/eip/ageing/file/956/download_en%3Ftoken=hEuIq7R4

Ofcom (2018) 'Adults' media use and attitudes report', April. Available at: https://www.ofcom.org.uk/__data/assets/pdf_file/0011/113222/Adults-Media-Use-and-Attitudes-Report-2018.pdf

Office of Fair Trading (2005) *Care Homes for Older People in the UK: A Market Survey*. London: Office of Fair Trading.

Ogg, J. (2005) 'Heatwave: implications of the 2003 French heat wave for the social care of older people', Young Foundation Working Paper No. 2, The Young Foundation, London.

Ogg, J. and Renaut, S. (2006) 'The support of parents in old age by those born during 1945–1954: a European perspective", *Ageing & Society*, 26 (5): 723–43.

Okamoto, N,. Greiner, C. and Paul, G. (2015) 'Lesson and learned from the older people in case of great East Japan Earthquake and Tsunami of 2011', *Procedia Engineering*, 107: 133–139.

Oliver, M. (1990) *The Politics of Disablement*, Basingstoke: Macmillan.

ONS (Office for National Statistics) (2013) 'What does the 2011 Census tell us about older people?' Available at: https://www.ons.gov.uk/peoplepopulationandcommunity/birthsdeathsandmarriages/ageing/articles/whatdoesthe2011censustellusaboutolderpeople/2013-09-06

ONS (2018a) 'Living longer: how our population is changing and why it matters'. Available at: https://www.ons.gov.uk/peoplepopulationandcommunity/birthsdeathsandmarriages/ageing/articles/livinglongerhowourpopulationischangingandwhyitmatters/2018-08-13

ONS (2018b) 'Internet access – households and individuals, Great Britain, 2018', released 7 August. Available at: https://www.ons.gov.uk/peoplepopultationandcommunity/householodchracteristics/homeinternetandsocialmediausage/bulletins/internetaccess

ONS (2018c) 'Population of England and Wales. Ethnicity facts and figures'. Available at: https://www.ethnicity-facts-figures.service.gov.uk/uk-population-by-ethnicity/national-and-regional-populations/population-of-england-and-wales/latest

ONS (2019a) 'Internet users, UK: 2019', released May. Available at: https://www.ons.gov.uk/businessindustryandtrade/internetindustry/bulletins/internetusers/2019

ONS (2019b) 'Living longer – caring in later working life'. Available at: https://www.ons.gov.uk/peoplepopulationandcommunity/birthsdeathsandmarriages/ageing/articles/livinglongerhowourpopulationischangingandwhyitmatters/2019-03-15

ONS (2020a) 'Population estimates for the UK, England and Wales, Scotland & Northern Ireland: mid-2019'. Available at: https://www.ons.gov.uk/peoplepopulationandcommunity/populationandmigration/populationestimates/bulletins/annualmidyearpopulationestimates/mid2019estimates

ONS (2020b) 'Population estimates by marital status and living arrangement, England and Wales: 2019'. Available at: https://www.ons.gov.uk/peoplepopulationandcommunity/populationandmigration/populationestimates/bulletins/populationestimatesbymaritalstatusandlivingarrangements/2019

ONS (2020c) 'People living alone age 65 years and over, by specific age group and sex, UK, 1996 to 2019'. Available at: https://www.ons.gov.uk/peoplepopulationandcommunity/birthsdeathsandmarriages/families/adhocs/11446peoplelivingaloneaged65yearsoldandoverbyspecificagegroupandsexuk1996to2019

ONS (2020d) 'Life expectancy for local areas of the UK: between 2001 to 2003 and 2017 to 2019'. Available at: https://www.ons.gov.uk/peoplepopulationandcommunity/healthandsocialcare/healthandlifeexpectancies/bulletins/lifeexpectancyforlocalareasoftheuk/between2001to2003and2017to2019

ONS (2020e) 'Regional ethnic diversity (updated 2020)'. Available at: https://www.ethnicity-facts-figures.service.gov.uk/uk-population-by-ethnicity/national-and-regional-populations/regional-ethnic-diversity/latest

ONS (2020f) 'One in eight British households has no garden'. Available at: https://www.ons.gov.uk/economy/environmentalaccounts/articles/oneineightbritishhouseholdshasnogarden/2020-05-14

ONS (2020g) 'Deaths involving COVID-19 in the care sector, England & Wales: deaths occurring up to 12 June 2020 and registered up to 20th June (provisional)'. Available at: https://www.ons.gov.uk/peoplepopulationandcommunity/birthsdeathsandmarriages/deaths/articles/deathsinvolvingcovid19inthecaresectorenglandandwales/latest

ONS (2020h) 'Coronavirus (COVID-19) related deaths by ethnic group, England & Wales: 2 March 2020 to 15 May, 2020'. Available at: https://www.ons.gov.uk/peoplepopulationandcommunity/birthsdeathsandmarriages/deaths/articles/coronaviruscovid19relateddeathsbyethnicgroupenglandandwales/2march2020to15may2020

ONS (2021) 'Deaths registered weekly in England and Wales, provisional: week ending 22 January 2021'. Available at: https://www.ons.gov.uk/peoplepopulationandcommunity/birthsdeathsandmarriages/deaths/bulletins/deathsregisteredweeklyinenglandandwalesprovisional/weekending22january2021#deaths-registered-by-place-of-occurrence

Orellana, K., Manthorpe, J. and Tinker, A. (2020a) 'Day centres for older people: a systematically conducted scoping review of literature about their benefits, purposes and how they are perceived', *Ageing & Society*, 40 (1): 73–104.

Orellana, K., Manthorpe, J. and Tinker, A. (2020b) 'Choice, control and person-centredness in day centres for older people', *Journal of Social Work*, published online 30 August: 1–24.

Orrell, A., McKee, K., Torrington, J., Barnes, S., Darton, R., Netten, A. and Lewis, A. (2013) 'The relationship between building design and residents' quality of life in extra care housing schemes', *Health & Place*, 21: 52–64.

Ortega, A. (2018) 'Globalization & technological change', Elcano Royal Institute blog, 11 December. Available at: https://blog.realinstitutoelcano.org/en/globalisation-4-0-people-centred/#respond

Orulv, L. (2010) 'Placing the place, and placing oneself within it: (dis)orientation and (dis)continuity in dementia", *Dementia,* 9 (1): 21–44.

Osborn, A. and Willcocks, D. (1990) 'Making research useful and usable', in S. Peace (ed) *Researching Social Gerontology: Concepts, Methods and Issues*, London: Sage Publications, pp 188–202.

Oswald, F. and Wahl, H-W. (2005) 'Dimensions of the meaning of home in later life', in G.D. Rowles and H. Chaudhury (eds) *Home and Identity in Later Life: International Perspectives*, New York: Springer, pp 21–46.

Oswald, F. and Wahl, H-W. (2010) 'Environmental perspectives on ageing', in D. Dannefer and C, Phillipson. (eds) (2010) *The SAGE Handbook of Social Gerontology*, London: SAGE Publications Ltd, pp 111–24.

Oswald, F. and Wahl, H-W. (2013) 'Creating and sustaining homelike places in home environments', in G.D. Rowles and M. Bernard (eds), *Environmental Gerontology: Making Meaningful Places in Old Age*, New York: Springer, pp 53–77.

Oswald, F., Wahl, H-W., Schilling, O., Nygren, C., Fänge, A., Sixsmith, A., Sixsmith, J., Szeman, Z., Tomsone, S. and Iwarsson, S. (2007) 'Relationships between housing and healthy aging in very old age', *The Gerontologist*, 47 (1): 96–107.

Ozaki, R. 2002) 'Housing as a reflection of culture: private living and privacy in England and Japan', *Housing Studies*, 17 (2): 209–27.

Paddock, K., Brown Wilson, C., Walshe, C. and Todd, C. (2019) 'Care home life and identity: a qualitative case study', *The Gerontologist*, 9 (4): 655–64.

Pain, R. (2001) 'Gender, race, age and fear in the city', *Urban Studies*, 38 (5–6): 899–913.

Pain, R., Mowl, G. and Talbot, C. (2000) 'Difference and the Negotiation of "Old Age"', *Environment and Planning D: Society and Space*, 18 (3): 377–93.

Pannell, J., Pooley, A. and Francis, S.A. (2020) *Almshouses for the 21st Century: Transformation in Progress*, Viewpoint 100, London: Housing LIN.

Park, A., Ziegler, F. and Wiggleworth, S. (2016) 'Designing with downsizers', University of Sheffield. Available at: https://dwell.group.shef.ac.uk/downsizing/

Park, J. (2017) 'One hundred years of housing space standards. what now?'. Available at: https://levittbernstein.co.uk/site/assets/files/2682/one_hundred_years_of_housing_space_standards.pdf

Park, J. and Porteus, J. (2018) *Age-Friendly Housing: Future Design for Older People*, London: RIBA Publishing.

Park, R.E. and Burgess, E.W. (eds) (1925) *The City*, Chicago: Chicago University Press.

Parker, C., Barnes, S., McKee, K., Morgan, K., Torrington, J. and Tregenza, P. (2004) 'Quality of life and building design in residential and nursing homes for older people', *Ageing & Society*, 24 (8): 941–62.

Parkhurst, G., Galvin, K., Musselwhite, C., Phillips, J., Shergold, I. and Tadres, L. (2014) 'Beyond transport: understanding the role of mobilities in connecting rural elders in civic society', in C.H Hennessy, R. Means and V. Burholt. (eds) *Countryside Connections: Older People, Community and Place in Rural Britain*, Bristol: Policy Press, pp 125–58.

Parry, N. (1996) 'The new town experience', *Town and Country Planning*, 11: 302.

Pastalan, L.A. (2013) 'The quest for a new paradigm: a need to rewire the way we think', in R.J. Scheidt and B. Schwarz (eds) *Environmental Gerontology: What Now?* Abingdon and New York: Routledge, pp 23–8.

Pastalan, L.A. and Carson, D. (eds) (1970) *Spatial Behaviour of Older People*, Ann Arbor: Institute of Gerontology, University of Michigan.

Patel, N. and Traynor, P. (2006) 'Developing extra care housing for Black and minority ethnic elders: an overview of the issues, examples and challenges', Policy Research Institute on Ageing and Ethnicity (PRIAE). Available at: https://www.priae.org/assets/aim/housing/PRIAE_BME_Extra_Care_Housing_Report.pdf

Paterson, M. (2010) 'Electric snakes and mechanical ladders? Social presence, domestic spaces, and human-robot interactions', in M. Schillmeier, and M. Domenech (eds) *New Technologies and Emerging Spaces of Care*, Farnham: Ashgate Publishing, pp 107–27.

Peace, S. (1977) 'The Elderly in an Urban Environment: A Study of Spatial Mobility and Neighbourhood Interaction in Swansea. PhD Thesis, Department of Geography, University College of Swansea, University of Wales.

Peace, S. (1986) 'The design of residential homes: an historical perspective', in K. Judge and I. Sinclair (eds) *Residential Care for Elderly People Research Contributions to the Development of Policy and Practice*. London: HMSO, pp 139–50.

Peace, S. (1993) 'The living environments of older women', in M. Bernard and K. Meade (eds) *Women Come of Age*, London: Edward Arnold, pp 126–45.

Peace, S. (1998) 'Unit 6, Places for Care, Block 2 People and Places, K100 Understanding Health and Social Care, a course at Level 1', p 24. Milton Keynes: The Open University.

Peace, S. (ed) (1999) *Involving Older People in Research: An Amateur Doing the Work of a Professional?*', London: Centre for Policy on Ageing.

Peace, S. (2002a) 'Commentary 1 to Ch. 3. "Is genuine choice a reality"', in K. Sumner (ed) *Our Homes, Our Lives: Choice in Later Life Living Arrangements*, London: Centre for Policy on Ageing/The Housing Corporation, pp 59–65.

Peace, S. (2002b) 'The role of older people in research', in A. Jamieson and C. Victor (eds) *Researching Ageing and Later Life*, London: Sage Publications, pp 226–44.

Peace, S. (2003) 'The development of residential and nursing home care in the UK', in J. Katz and S. Peace (eds) *End of Life in Care Homes: A Palliative Approach*, Oxford: Oxford University Press, pp 15–42.

Peace, S (2009) 'Reflecting on ageing and environment', inaugral lecture, March. Milton Keynes: The Open University.

Peace, S. (2013) 'Social interaction in public places and spaces: a conceptual overview', in G. Rowles and M. Bernard (eds) *Environmental Gerontology: Making Meaningful Places in Old Age*, New York: Springer, pp 25–49.

Peace, S. (2015) 'Meanings of home and age', in J. Twigg and W. Martin (eds) *The Handbook of Cultural Gerontology*, London: Routledge, pp 447–54.

Peace, S. (2016) 'Age-inclusive design – a challenge for urban living?', in C. Bates, R. Imrie and K. Kullman (eds) *Care & Design: Bodies, Buildings and Cities*, London: John Wiley & Sons, pp 18–36.

Peace, S. (2017) 'Home thoughts', in H. Chaudhury and F. Oswald. (eds) *Autobiographical Perspectives in Environmental Gerontology: Understanding the Field through Personal Reflections. 2018 Annual Review of Gerontology and Geriatrics*, 38, New York: Springer, pp 131–46.

Peace, S. (2018) 'On the interdisciplinary challenge of geographical gerontology', in M.W. Skinner., G.J. Andrews and M.P. Cutchin (eds) *Geographical Gerontology: Perspectives, Concepts, Approaches*, London and New York: Routledge, pp 307–32.

Peace, S. and Willcocks, D. (1986) 'Changing the environment in old people's homes', In K Judge and I. Sinclair (eds) *Residential Care for Elderly People Research Contributions to the Development of Policy and Practice*, London: HMSO, pp 35–48.

Peace, S. and Holland, C. (2001a) 'Housing an ageing society', in S. Peace and C. Holland (eds) *Inclusive Housing in An Ageing Society*, Bristol: Policy Press, pp 1–26.

Peace, S. and Holland, C. (2001b) 'Homely residential care: a contradiction in terms', *Journal of Social Policy*, 30 (3): 310–410.

Peace, S. and Darton, R. (2020a) 'Introduction' to the special issue 'Cross-cultural comparison of the impact of housing modification/adaptation for supporting older people at home, *Journal of Aging and Environment*, 34 (2): 103–9.

Peace, S. and Darton, R. (2020b) 'Reflections on cross-cultural comparison of the impact of housing modification/adaptation for supporting older people at home: a discussion', *Journal of Aging and Environment*, 34 (2): 210–31.

Peace, S., Kellaher. L. and Willcocks, D. (1982) 'A balanced life? A consumer study of residential life in 100 local authority old people's homes', Research Report No. 14, Social Research Unit, Polytechnic of North London.

Peace, S., Kellaher, L. and Willcocks, D. (1997) *Re-Evaluating Residential Care*, Maidenhead: Open University Press.

Peace, S., Holland, C. and Kellaher, L. (2005) 'Making space for identity', in D.R. Phillips and G. Andrews (eds) *Ageing and Place*, London: Routledge: 188–204.

Peace, S., Holland, C. and Kellaher, L. (2006) *Environment and Identity in Later Life*, Maidenhead: Open University Press/McGraw-Hill.

Peace, S., Holland, C. and Kellaher, L. (2011) 'Option recognition in later life': variations in ageing in place', *Ageing & Society*, 31 (5): 734–57.

Peace, S., Wahl, H-W., Mollenkoph, H. and Oswald, F. (2007) 'Environment and ageing', in J, Bond., F, Dittmar-Kohli., S, Peace and G, Westerhoff (eds) *Ageing in Society: European Perspectives on Gerontology*, London: SAGE Publications, pp 209–34.

Peace, S., Katz, J., Holland, C. and Jones, R. (2016) *The Needs and Aspirations of Older People with Visual Impairment*, Milton Keynes/London: The Open University/Thomas Pocklington Trust.

Peace, S., Maguire, M., Nicolle, C., Marshall, R., Percival, J., Scicluna, R.M., Sims, R., Kellaher, L. and Lawton, C. (2018) 'Transitions in kitchen living: past experiences and present use', in A. Walker (ed) *The New Dynamics of Ageing, Vol. 1*, Bristol: Policy Press, pp 257–75.

Peace, S., Katz, J., Holland, C. and Jones, R. (2019) 'The age-friendly community: a test for inclusivity', in T. Buffel, S, Handler and C. Phillipson (eds) *Age-Friendly Communities: A Global Perspective*, Bristol: Policy Press, pp 251–71.

Peek, S.T.M., Luijkx, K.G., Vrijhoef, H.J.M., Nieboer, M.N., Aarts, S., van der Voort, C.S., Rijnaard, M.D. and Wouters, E.J.M. (2017) 'Origins and consequences of technology acquirement by independent-living seniors. Towards an integrative model', *BMC Geriatric.* 17: 189.

Percival, J. (2002) 'Domestic spaces: uses and meanings in the daily lives of older people', *Ageing and Society* 22 (6): 729–49.

Percival, J. (ed) (2013a) *Return Migration in Later Life: International Perspectives*, Bristol: Policy Press.

Percival, J. (2013b) 'Charting the waters: return migration in later life', in J. Percival (ed) *Return Migration in Later Life: International Perspectives*, Bristol: Policy Press, pp 1–18.

Percival, J. (2020) 'Afterword on *Return Migration in Later Life* in the wake of COVID-19', Policy Press, Bristol. Available at: https://policy. bristoluniversitypress.co.uk/asset/8867/percival-online-afterword-final.pdf

Percival, J. and Hanson, J. (2006) 'Big brother in a brave new world? Telecare and its implications for older people's independence and social inclusion', *Critical Social Policy*, 26 (4): 888–909.

Pettersson, C., Slaug, B., Granbom, M., Kylberg, M. and Iwarsson, S. (2017) 'Housing accessibility for senior citizens in Sweden: Estimation of the effects of targeted elimination of environmental barriers', *Scandinavian Journal of Occupational Therapy*, online 24 January. Doi:10.1080/ 1038128.2017.1280078.

Phillips, D.R. and Feng, Z. (2015). 'Challenges for the aging family in the People's Republic of China', *Canadian Journal of Aging*, 34 (3): 290–304.

Phillips, D.R. and Feng, Z. (2018) 'Global ageing', in M.W. Skinner., G.J. Andrews and M.P. Cutchin. (eds) (2018) *Geographical Gerontology: Perspectives, Concepts, Approaches*, London and New York: Routledge, pp 93–109.

Phillips, J., Walford, N., Foreman, N., Hockey, A., Lewis, M., Samarasundra, E. and Del Agulia, M. (2010) 'Older people's use of unfamiliar space (OPUS) New Dynamics of Ageing Findings 4', University of Sheffield.

Phillips, J.E., Walford, N. and Hockey, A. (2011) 'How do unfamiliar environments convey meaning to older people? Urban dimension of placelessness and attachment' *Journal of Ageing and Later Life*, 6 (2): 73–102.

Phillips, J.E., Dobbs, C., Burholt, V. and Marston, H. (2015) Extracare: does it promote resident satisfaction compared to residential and home care?, *British Journal of Social Work*, 45: 949–67.

Phillipson, C. (2003) 'Globalisation and the future of ageing: developing a critical gerontology', *Sociological Research Online*, 8 (4):144–52.

Phillipson, C. (2004) 'Urbanisation and ageing: towards a new environmental gerontology', *Ageing & Society,* 24 (6): 963–72.

Phillipson, C. (2007a) 'The elected and the "excluded": sociological perspectives on the experience of place and community in old age', *Ageing & Society*, 27 (3): 321–342.

Phillipson, C. (2007b) 'Understanding the baby boomer generation: comparative perspectives', *International Journal of Ageing & Later Life*, 2 (20): 7–11.

Phillipson, C. (2010) 'Ageing and urban society: growing old in the "century of the city"', in D. Dannefer and C. Phillipson (eds) *The Sage Handbook of Social Gerontology*, London: Sage Publications, pp 597–606.

Phillipson, C. (2012) 'Globalisation, economic recession and social exclusion: policy challenges and responses', in T. Scharf and N. Keating (eds) *From Exclusion to Inclusion in Old Age: A Global Challenge*, Bristol: Policy Press, pp 17–32.

Phillipson, C. (2015a) 'Placing ethnicity at the centre of studies of later life: theoretical perspectives and empirical challenges', *Ageing & Society*, 35 (5): 917–34.

Phillipson, C. (2015b) 'Global and local ties and the reconstruction of later Life', in J. Twigg and W. Martin (eds) *Routledge Handbook of Cultural Gerontology*, Abingdon, Oxon: Routledge, pp 389–96.

Phillipson, C. and Scharf, T. (2005) 'Rural and urban perspectives on growing old: developing a new research agenda', *European Journal of Ageing*, 2 (2): 67–75.

Phillipson, C., Bernard, M., Phillips, J. and Ogg, J. (1998) 'The family and community life of older people: household composition and social networks in three urban areas', *Ageing & Society*, 18 (3): 259–90.

Phillipson, C., Bernard, M., Phillips, J. and Ogg, J. (2001) *The Family and Community Life of Older People: Social Networks and Social Support in Three Urban Areas*, London: Routledge.

Phillipson, C., Leach, R., Money, A. and Biggs, S. (2008) 'Social and cultural constructions of ageing: the case of the baby boomers, *Sociological Research Online*, 13 (3): 1–14.

Piddington, J., Nicol, S., Garrett, H. and Custard, M. (2017) 'The housing stock of the United Kingdom', Building Research Establishment, BRE-Trust, Garston, Hertfordshire. Available at: https://files.bregroup.com/bretrust/The-Housing-Stock-of-the-United-Kingdom_Report_BRE-Trust.pdf

Plouffe, K. and Kalache, A. (2010) 'Towards global age-friendly cities. Determining urban features that promote aging', *Journal of Urban Health*, 87: 733–9.

Poole, T. (2006) 'Telecare and older people. Background paper', Wanless Social Care Review, The King's Fund, London. Available at: https://www.kingsfund.org.uk/sites/default/files/telecare-older-people-wanless-background-paper-teresa-poole2006.pdf

Porter, G. (2016) 'Mobilities in rural Africa: new connections, new challenges', *Annals of the American Association of Geographer*, 106 (2): 434–41.

Porteus, J. (2018) 'Rural housing for an ageing population: preserving independence' (HAPPI 4), The Rural HAPPI Inquiry, All Party Parliamentary Group on Housing and Care for Older People, Housing LIN, London. Available at: www.housingandcare21.co.uk/about-us/appg-housing-and-care-for-older-people/

Powell, J., Mackintosh, S., Bird, E., Ige, J., Garrett, H. and Roys, M. (2017) *The Role of Home Adaptations in Improving Later Life*, London: Centre for Ageing Better.

PRB (2019) 'World population data sheet', PRB, Washington DC. Available at: https://www.prb.org/2019-world-population-data-sheet/

Preece, J., Crawford, J., McKee, J., Flint, J. and Robinson, D. (2020) 'Understanding changing housing aspirations: a review of the evidence', *Housing Studies*, 35 (1): 87–106.

Prince, M., Knapp, M., Guerchet, M., McCrone, P., Prina, M., Comas-Herrera, M., wittenberg, A., Adelaja, R., Hu, B., King, B., Rehill, D., and Salimkumar, D. (2014) 'Dementia UK: Update', Alzheimer's Society. Available at: http://www.alzheimers.org.uk/dementiauk

Prieser, W.F.F. and Ostroff, E. (eds) (2001) *Universal Design Handbook*, New York: McGraw-Hill.

Proshanksy, H.M. (1976) *Environmental Psychology: People and their Physical Setting*, New York: Holt, Rinehart & Winston.

Proshanksy, H.M. (1978) 'The city and self-identity', *Environment and Behaviour*, 10: 147–69.

Proshanksy, H.M., Fabian, A.K. and Kaminoff, M. (1983) 'Place-identity: physical world socialization of the self', *Journal of Environmental Psychology*, 3: 57–83.

Public Health England (2020) 'Dementia profile'. Available at: https://fingertips.phe.org.uk/profile-group/mental-health/profile/dementia/data#page/6/gid/1938133052/pat/46/par/E39000026/ati/165/are/E38000056/cid/4/page-options/ovw-do-0_eng-vo-0_eng-do-0

Putnam, R.D. (2000) *Bowling Alone: The Collapse and Revival of American Community*, New York: Simon & Schuster.

Putney, N.M. and Bengtson, V.L. (2005) 'Family relations in changing times: a longitudinal study of five cohorts of women', *International Journal of Sociology and Social Policy*, 25 (3): 92–119.

Ramsey-Iranah, S.D., Maguire, M., Peace, S. and Pooneth, V. (2020)'Older adults perspectives on transitions in the kitchen', *Journal of Aging and Environment*, 35 (2): 207–24. https://doi.org/10.1080/26892618.2020.1834052

Rapoport, A. (1969) *House, Form and Culture*, Englewood Cliffs, NJ: Prentice-Hall Inc.

Rapoport, A. (1985) 'Thinking about home environments: a conceptual framework', in I. Altman and C.M. Werner (eds) *Human Behavior and Environment: Home Environments* (Vol 8), New York: Plenum Press, pp 255–86.

Rapoport, A. (2005) 'On using "home" and "place"', in G.D. Rowles and H. Chaudhury (eds) *Home and Identity in Late Life: International Perspectives*, New York: Springer, pp 343–60.

Ray, M. (2007) 'Redressing the balance? The participation of older people in research', in M. Bernard and T. Scharf (eds) *Critical Perspectives on Ageing Societies*, Bristol: Policy Press, pp 73–88.

Ray, C.A., Ingram, V. and Cohen-Mansfield, J. (2015) 'Systematic review of planned care transitions for person with dementia", *Neurodegenerative Disease Management,* 5 (4): 317–31.

Read, J., Joes, N., Fegan, C., Cudd, P., Simpson, E., Mazumdar, S. and Ciravegna, F. (2020) 'Remote home visit: exploring the feasibility, acceptability and potential benefits of using digital technology to update occupational therapy home assessments', *British Journal of Occupational Therapy*, 83 (10): 648–58.

Regnier, V. (1974) 'Matching older persons' cognition with their use of neighbourhood areas', in D.H. Carson (ed) *Man Environment Interaction, Section II Cognition and Perception*, Pennsylvannia: Hutchinson and Ross, pp 64–87.

Relph, E. (1976) *Place and Placelessness*, London: Prion.

Rémillard-Boilard, S. (2019) 'The development of the age-friendly cities and communities', in T, Buffel, S. Handler and C, Phillipson (eds) *Age-Friendly Cities and Communities*, Bristol: Policy Press, pp 13–32.

of subjective well-being', *Social Indicators Research*, 128: 693–708.

Reuter, A., Liddle, J. and Scharf, T. (2020). 'Digitalising the age-friendly city: insights from participatory action research', *International Journal of Environmental Research and Public Health*, 17 (21): 8281. https://doi.org/10.3390/ijerph17218281

RIBA (Royal Institute of British Architects) (2013) *Silver Linings: The Active Third Age and the City*, London: RIBA.

RIBA (Royal Institute of British Architects) (2014) 'Design for an ageing population initiative'. Available at: https://www.architecture.com/knowledge-and-resources/resources-landing-page/design-for-an-ageing-population

Richardson, S.J., Carroll, C.B., Close, J., Gordon, A.L., O'Brien, J., Quinn, T.J., Rochester, L., Sayer, A.A., Shenkin, S.D., van der Velde, N., Woo, J. and Witham, M.D. (2020) 'Research with older people in a world with COVID-19: identification of current and future priorities, challenges and opportunities', *Age and Ageing*, November 49 (6): 901–6.

RICS (Royal Institution of Charted Surveyors) (2016) 'Dwellings & downsizing for the elderly'. Available at: https://www.rics.org/uk/training-events/cpd-foundation-subscription/cpd-foundation-on-demand/cpd-foundation-on-demand-content/dwellings-and-downsizing-for-the-elderly/

Riseborough, M., Fletcher, P. and Gillie, D. (2015) 'Extra care housing: what is it?', Factsheet 1 (update from 2008). Available at: https://www.housinglin.org.uk/_assets/Resources/Housing/Housing_advice/Extra_Care_Housing_What_is_it.pdf

Rishworth, A. and Elliot, S.J. (2019) 'Global environmental change in an ageing world: the role of space, place and scale', *Social Science and Medicine*, 227: 128–36.

Robb, B. (1967) *Sans Everything: A Case to Answer*, London: Nelson.

Roberts, H. (ed) (1990) *Doing Feminist Research*, London: Routledge.

Robertson, R. (1990) 'Mapping the global conditions: globalization as the central concept', *Theory, Culture & Society*, 7 (2–3): 15–30.

Robertson, R. (1994) Globalisation or glocalisation?, *The Journal of International Communication*, 1 (1): 33–52.

Rose, G. (1993) *Feminism and Geography*, Minneapolis: University of Minnesota Press.

Rosow, I. (1967) *The Social Integration of the Aged*, New York: Free Press.

Rowe, J.W. and Kahn, R.L. (1998). *Successful Aging*, New York: Pantheon Books.

Rowles, G.D. (1978) *Prisoners of Space? Exploring the Geographical Experience of Older People*, Boulder, CO: Westview.

Rowles, G.D. (1983) 'Geographical dimensions of social support in rural Appalachia', in G.D. Rowles and R.J. Ohta (eds) *Aging and Milieu. Environmental Perspectives on Growing Old*, New York: Academic Press, pp 111–30.

Rowles, G.D. (2000) 'Habituation and being in place', *The Occupational Therapy Journal of Research*, 20 (1): 52S–67S.

Rowles, G.D. (2018) '"Being in place": identity and place attachment in late life', in M.W. Skinner, G.J. Andrews and M.P. Cutchin (eds) *Geographical Gerontology: Perspectives, Concepts, Approaches*, London and New York: Routledge, pp 203–15.

Rowles, G.D. and Watkins, J.F. (2003) 'History, habit, heart and hearth: on making spaces into places', in K.W. Schaie., H-W, Wahl., H. Mollenkoph and F. Oswald (eds) *Aging Independently: Living Arrangements and Mobility*, New York: Springer, pp 77–96.

Rowles, G.D. and Chaudhury, H. (2005) 'Leaving Home', in G.D. Rowles and H. Chaudhury (eds) (2005) *Home and Identity in Late Life: International Perspectives*, New York: Springer, pp 379–86.

Rowles, G.D. and Bernard, M. (2013) 'The meaning and significance of place in old age', in G.D. Rowles and M. Bernard (eds) *Environmental Gerontology: Making Meaningful Places in Old Age*, New York: Springer, pp 3–24.

Rowles, G.D., Oswald, F. and Hunter, E.G. (2004) 'Interior living environments in old age', in H-W. Wahl, R. Scheidt and P. Windley (eds) *Annual Review of Gerontology and Geriatrics: Vol. 23 Environments, Gerontology and Old Age*, New York: Springer, pp 167–93.

Royal College of Occupational Therapists (RCOT) (2019) 'Adaptations without delay: A guide to planning and delivering home adaptations differently', London: RCOT. Available at: https://www.housinglin.org.uk/_assets/Resources/Housing/Support_materials/Other_reports_and_guidance/Adaptations-Without-Delay.pdf

RTPI (Royal Town Planning Institute) (2007) 'Delivering healthy communities', Good Practice Guide, No. 5. Available at: https://www.bromsgrove.gov.uk/media/751968/CD-1010-GPGN5-Delivering-Healthy-Communities.pdf

RTPI (Royal Town Planning Institute) (2017) 'Dementia and town planning: creating better environments for people living with dementia', Practice Advice (updated September 2020). Available at: https://www.housinglin.org.uk/_assets/Resources/Housing/OtherOrganisation/dementia_and_town_planning_final.pdf

RTPI (Royal Town Planning Institute) (2020) 'RTPI response to the Planning White Paper', October, London: RTPI.

RTPI (Royal Town Planning Institute) (2021) 'Planning for a better future: RTPI Proposals for Planning Reform in England', London: RTPI. Available at: https://www.rtpi.org.uk/policy/2021/march/planning-for-a-better-future/

Rubinstein, R.L. (1987) 'The significance of personal objects to older people', *Journal of Aging Studies*, 1: 225–38.

Rubinstein, R.L. (1989) The home environments of older people: a description of the psychosocial processes linking person to place. *Journal of Gerontology*, 44 (2): S45–S53.

Rubinstein, R.L. (1990) 'Personal identity and environmental meaning in later life', *Journal of Aging Studies*, 4: 131–48.

Rubinstein, R.L. and Parmelee, P.W. (1992) 'Attachment to place and representation of life course by the elderly', in I. Altman and S.M. Low (eds) *Human Behavior and Environment: Place Attachment, Vol. 12*, New York: Plenum Press, pp 139–63.

Rubinstein, R.L. and de Mederios, K. (2004) "Ecology and the aging self", in H-W. Wahl., R.J. Scheidt, and P.G. Windley (eds) *Aging in Context: Socio-Physical Environments*, Annual Review of Gerontology and Geriatrics, New York: Springer, pp 59–84.

Rubinstein, R.L. and de Medeiros, K. (2005) 'Home, self and identity', in G. Rowles and H. Chaudhury (eds) *Home and Identity in Late Life: International Perspectives*, New York: Springer, pp 47–62.

Rubinstein, R.L. and de Medeiros, K. (2015) "Successful aging". Gerontological theory and neoliberalism: a qualitative critique", *The Gerontologist*, 55 (1): 34–42.

Rusinovic, K., van Bochova, M. and van de Sande, J. (2019) 'Senior co-housing in the Netherlands: benefits and drawbacks for its residents', *International Journal of Environmental Research & Public Health*, 16 (9): 3776.

Russell, R.M., Ormerod, M. and Newton, R. (2018) 'The development of a design and construction process protocol to support the home modification process delivered by occupational therapists', *Journal of Aging Research*, 2018. https://doi.org/10.1155/2018/4904379

Ryan, A. and McKenna, H. (2013) ' "Familiarity" as a key factor influencing rural family carers' experience of the nursing home placement of an older relative: a qualitative study', *BMC Health Services Research*, 13: 252.

Sargisson, L. (2012) 'Second-wave Cohousing', *Utopian Studies*, 23(1): 28–56.

Sassen, S. (2001) *The Global City: New York, London, Tokyo* (2nd edn), Princeton, NJ: Princeton University Press.

Sassen, S. (2004) *Cities in a World Economy*, London: Sage Publications.

Saunders, P. (1990) *A Nation of Home Owners*, London: Unwin Hyman.

Savills (2020) 'Market in minutes: elderly care homes', 29 October. Available at: https://www.savills.co.uk/research_articles/229130/291740-0/market-in-minutes--elderly-care-homes---q4-2019

Saville Rossiter-Base (2019) 'Adults' media use and attitudes report'. Available at: https://www.ofcom.org.uk/_data/assests/pdf_file/0031/149872/Adults-medi-use-and-attitudes-report-2019-chart-pack.pdf

Scanlon, K., Whiteread, C., Pichler-Milancoic, N. and Cirman, A. (2004) *International Trends in housing Housing tenure Tenure and mortgage Mortgage financeFinance*, London: London School of Economics and Political Science.

Scanlon, K., Sagor, E., Whitehead, C. and Mossa, A. (2016). *New London Villages: Creating Community*, London: London School of Economics and Political Science.

Scharf, T. and Bartlam, B. (2006) *Rural Disadvantage: Quality of Life and Disadvantage amongst Older People – a Pilot Study*, London: Commission for Rural Communities.

Scharf, T. and de Jong Gieveld, J. (2008) 'Loneliness in urban neighbourhoods: an Anglo-Dutch comparison', *European Journal of Ageing*, 5: 103–15. https://doi.org/10.1007/s10433-008-0080-x

Scharf, T. and Keating, N. (2012) 'Social exclusion in later life: a global challenge', in T. Scharf and N. Keating (eds) *From Exclusion to Inclusion in Old Age: A Global Challenge*, Bristol: Policy Press, pp 1–16.

Scharf, T., Phillipson, C. and Smith, A.E. (2004) 'Poverty and social exclusion – growing older in deprived urban neighbourhoods', in A. Walker and C. Hagan Hennessy (eds) *Growing Older – Quality of Life in Old Age*, Maidenhead: Open University Press, pp 81–106.

Scharf, T., Phillipson, C. and Smith, A.E. (2005a) *Multiple Exclusion and Quality of Life amongst Excluded Older People in Disadvantaged Neighbourhoods*, London: Social Exclusion Unit, Office of the Deputy Prime Minister.

Scharf, T., Phillipson, C. and Smith, A.E. (2005b) 'Social exclusion of older people in deprived urban communities of England', *European Journal of Ageing*, 2 (2): 76–87.

Scharf, T., Walsh, K. and O'Shea, T. (2016) 'Ageing in rural places', in M. Shucksmith and D.L. Brown (eds) *The Routledge Handbook of Rural Studies*, Abingdon and New York: Routledge, pp 50–61.

Scharf, T., Phillipson, C., Smith, A.E. and Kingston, P. (2002) *Growing Older in Socially Deprived Areas*, London: Help the Aged.

Scheidt, R.J and Schwarz, B. (eds) (2013) 'Last words', in R.J. Scheidt and B. Schwarz (eds) *Environmental Gerontology: What Now?* Abingdon and New York: Routledge, pp 326–34.

Scheidt, R.J. and Windley, P.G. (2003) *Physical Environments and Aging: Critical Contributions of M. Powell Lawton*, Philadelphia, PA: The Haworth Press.

Scheidt, R.J. and Windley, P.G. (2006) 'Environmental gerontology: progress on the post-Lawton era', In J. Birren and K.W. Schaie (eds) *Handbook of Psychology of Aging* (6th edn), San Diego, CA: Academic Press, pp 105–25.

Schillmeier, M. (2008) 'Time-spaces of in/dependence and dis/ability', *Time & Society*, 17 (2–3): 215–31.

Schillmeier, M. and Domenech, M. (2010) *New Technologies and Emerging Spaces of Care*, Farnham: Ashgate Publishing.

Schwanen, T. and Ziegler, F. (2011) 'Wellbeing, independence and mobility: an introduction', *Ageing & Society*, 31 (5): 719–33.

Schwarz, B. (2003) 'M. Powell Lawton's three dimensions in the field of environment and aging', in I.R. Scheidt and P. Windley (eds) *Physical Environments and Aging: Critical Contributions of M. Powell Lawton to Theory and Practice*, New York: The Haworth Press, pp 5–22.

SCIE (Social Care Institute for Excellence) (2020) 'Dementia: at a glance', https://www.scie.org.uk/dementia/about/

Scicluna, R. (2013) 'The "Other" Side of the Domestic Kitchen: An Anthropological Approach to the Domestic Kitchen and Older Lesbians'. PhD thesis, The Open University, Milton Keynes.

Scott, I. (2017) 'Mobility, mood and place co-designing age-friendly cities: a report on collaborations between older people and students of architecture (Edinburgh School of Architecture and Landscape Architecture, University of Edinburgh)', *Arts*, 6 (3): 12.

Scott, M.J. and Canter, D.V. (1997) 'Picture or place? A multiple sorting study of landscape', *Journal of Environmental Psychology*, 17: 263–81.

Scott, T.L., Masser, B.M. and Pachana, N.A. (2014) 'Exploring the health and wellbeing benefits of gardening for older adults', *Ageing & Society*, 35 (10): 2176–200.

Scottish Government (2005) 'Guidance on free personal and nursing care in Scotland 2003'. Available at: https://www.gov.scot/publications/guidance-free-personal-nursing-care-scotland-2003/pages/2/

Seely, A. and Keep, M. (2021) *Health and Social Care Levy Bill 2021–22.* No. 9310. London: House of Commons Library.

Selwyn, N., Gorard, S., Furlong, J. and Madden, L. (2003) 'Older adults' use of information and communication technology in everyday life', *Ageing and Society*, 23 (5): 561–82.

Shakespeare, T., Zelig, H. and Mittler, P. (2019) 'Rights in mind: thinking Differently about dementia and disability', *Dementia*, 18 (3): 1075–88.

Shaw, R.L., West, K., Hagger, B. and Holland, C.A. (2016) 'Living well to the end: a phenomenological analysis of life in extra care housing', *International Journal of Qualitative Studies on Health and Well-Being*, 11 (1), https://doi.org/10.3402/qhw.v11.31100

Shankley, W. and Finney, N. (2020) 'Ethnic minorities and housing in Britain', in B. Byrne, C. Alexander, O. Khan, J. Nazroo and W. Shankley (eds) *Ethnicity, Race and Inequality in the UK: State of the Nation*, Bristol: Policy Press, pp 149–66.

Sheehan, B., Burton, E. and Mitchell, L. (2006) Outdoor wayfinding in dementia', *Dementia*, 5 (2): 271–81.

Sheldon, J.H. (1948) *The Social Medicine of Old Age*, London: Nuffield Foundation.

Shergold, I. and Parkhurst, G. (2012) 'Transport-related social exclusion amongst older people in rural Southwest England and Wales', *Journal of Rural Studies*, 28 (4): 412–21.

Sherman, E. and Dacher, J. (2005) 'Cherished objects and the home: their meaning and roles in later life', in G.D. Rowles and H. Chaudhury (eds) *Home and Identity in Later Life: International Perspectives*, New York: Springer, pp 63–80.

Shucksmith, M and Brown, D.L. (eds) (2016) *The Routledge Handbook of Rural Studies*, Abingdon and New York: Routledge.

Shucksmith, M., Brown, D.L. and Vergunst, J. (2012) 'Constructing the rural–urban interface. Place still matters in a highly mobile society', in M. Shucksmith, D.L. Brown., S. Shortall., J. Vergunst and M. Warner (eds) *Rural Transformations and Rural Policies in the US and UK*, New York: Routledge, pp 287–303.

Simpson, P., Almack, K. and Walthery, P. (2018) 'We treat them all the same': the attitudes, knowledge ad practices of staff concerning old/er lesbian, gay, bisexual and trans residents in care homes', *Ageing & Society*, 38 (5): 869–99.

Sims, R.E., Maguire, M.C., Nicolle, C., Marshall, R., Lawton, C., Peace, S. and Percival, J. (2012) Older People's Experiences of Their Kitchens: 2000 to 2010. *Housing, Care & Support,* 15(1):6–15.

Sixsmith, A. and Guttman, G. (eds) (2013) *Technologies for Active Aging*, New York: Springer.

Sixsmith, J., Sixsmith, A., Fänge, A.M., Naumann, D., Kuesera, C., Tomsone, S., Haak, M., Dahlin-Ivanoff, S., Woolrych, R. (2014) 'Health ageing and home: the perspectives of very frail old people in five European Countries', *Social Science and Medicine,* 106: 1–9. https://doi.org/10.1016/j.socscimed.2014.01.006

Skinner, M.W. and Winterton, R. (2018) 'Rural ageing contested spaces, dynamic places', in M.W, Skinner, G.J. Andrews and M.P. Cutchin (eds) (2018) *Geographical Gerontology: Perspectives, Concepts, Approaches*, London and New York: Routledge, pp 136–48.

Skinner, M.W., Andrews, G.A. and Cutchin, M.P. (eds) (2018) *Geographical Gerontology: Perspectives, Concepts, Approaches*, London and New York: Routledge.

Slaug, B., Granbom, M. and Iwarsson, S. (2020) 'An aging population and an aging housing stock – housing accessibility problems in typical Swedish dwellings', *Journal of Aging and Environment*, 34 (2):156–74.

Slaug, B., Schilling, O., Iwarsson, S. and Carlsson, G. (2011) 'Defining profiles of functional limitations in groups of older persons. How and why?', *Journal of Aging and Health*, 23 (3): 578–604.

Smith, A.E. (2009*) Ageing in Urban Neighbourhoods: Place Attachment and Social Exclusion*, Bristol: Policy Press.

Smith, A.E., Sim, J., Scharf, T. and Phillipson C. (2004) 'Determinants of quality of life amongst older people in deprived neighbourhoods', *Ageing & Society*, 24: 793–814.

Smith, R., Darton, R., Cameron, A., Johnson, E.K., Lloyd, L., Evans, S., Atkinson, T.J. and Porteus, J. (2017) 'Outcomes-based commissioning for social care in extra care housing: is there a future?', *Housing, Care and Support*, 20 (2): 60–70.

Soja, E. and Kanai, M. (2008) 'The urbanization of the world', in R. Burdett and D. Sudjic (eds) *The Endless City*, London: Phaidon, pp 54–69.

Sommer, R. (1969) *Personal Space: The Behavioural Basis of Design*, Englewood Cliffs, NJ: Prentice-Hall.

Soonthornchaiya, R., Tuicomepee, A. and Romano, J.L. (2018) 'Impacts of tsunami disaster in Thai elderly survivors', *Ageing International*, 44: 154–69. https://doi.org/10.1007/s12126-018-9324-z

Sopp, L. and Wood, L (2001) 'Consumer and industry views of lifetime homes', York: Joseph Rowntree Foundation. Available at: https://www.jrf.org.uk/report/consumer-and-industry-views-lifetime-homes

Steinman, M.A., Perry, L. and Perissmotto, CM. (2020) 'Meeting the needs of older adults isolated at home during the COVID-19 pandemic', *JAMA Internal Medicine*, 180 (6): 819–20. Available at: https://jamanetwork.com/journals/jamainternalmedicine/article-abstract/276448

Stevens, M., Biggs, S., Dixon, J., Tinker, A. and Manthorpe, J. (2013) 'Interactional perspectives on the mistreatment of older and vulnerable people in long-term care settings', *British Journal of Sociology*, 64 (2): 267–86.

Stula, S. (2012) 'Living in old age in Europe – current development and challenges', Working paper no. 7 of the Observatory for Socio Political Developments in Europe, June, Berlin. Available at: http://www.sociopolitical-observatory.eu.

Sugiyama, T., Ward Thompson, C. and Alves, S. 2009. 'Associations between neighborhood open space attributes and quality of life for older people in Britain', *Environment and Behaviour*, 41 (1): 3–21. https://doi.org/10.1177/0013916507311688

Sussman, T. and Dupuis, S. (2012) 'Supporting a relative's move into long-term care: starting point shapes family members' experiences', *Canadian Journal on Aging*, 31 (4): 395–410.

Sutherland Report (1999a) *With Respect to Old Age: Long Term Care: Rights and Responsibilities*, London: The Stationery Office.

Sutherland Report (1999b) *With Respect to Old Age: Long Term Care: Rights and Responsibilities, Research Volumes 1–3*, London: The Stationery Office.

Svensson, T. (1996) 'Competence and quality of life: theoretical views of biography', in J. Birren, G. Kenyon., J. Ruth, J. Schroots and T. Svensson (eds) *Aging and Biography: Explorations in Adult Development*, New York: Springer, pp 100–16.

Tanner, D., Ward, L. and Ray, M. (2018) ' "Paying our own way": application of the capability approach to explore older people's experience of self-funding social care', *Critical Social Policy*, 38 (2): 262–82.

Thein, N.W., D'Souza, G. and Sheehan, B. (2011) 'Expectations and experience of moving to a care home: perceptions of older people with dementia', *Dementia*, 10 (1): 7–18.

Thomas, C. and Milligan, C. (2018) 'Dementia, disability rights and disablism: understanding the social position of people living with dementia', *Disability & Society*, 33 (1): 115–31.

Thomese, F., Buffel, T. and Phillipson, C. (2019) 'Neighbourhood change, social inequalities and age-friendly communities', in T, Buffel, S, Handler and C. Phillipson (eds) *Age-Friendly Cities and Communities*, Bristol: Policy Press, pp 33–50.

Thompson, J.L., Peace, S., Astell, A., Moynihan, P. and Macdonald, A. (2014) 'Food environments: from home to hospital', in A. Walker (ed) (2014) *The New Science of Ageing*, Bristol: Policy Press, pp 155–80.

Thompson, P. (2000) *The Voice of the Past: Oral History* (3rd edition, first published 1978), Oxford: Oxford University Press.

Thompson, P. and Townsend, P. (2004) 'Reflections on becoming a researcher', *International Journal of Social Research Methodology*, 7 (1): 85–95.

Thomson, P. (2018) *Becoming an Age-Friendly Employer*, London: Centre for Ageing Better.

Thordardottir, B., Malmgren, A., Chiatti, C. and Ekstam, L. (2018) 'Participation in everyday life before and after a housing adaptation', *Journal of Housing for the Elderly*, 33 (1): 41–55.

Thordardottir, B., Fänge, A.M., Chiatti, C. and Ekstam, L. (2020) 'Participation in everyday life before and after housing adaptation', *Journal of Aging and Environment*, 34 (2): 175–89.

Thrift, N. (1996) *Spatial Formation*, London: Sage Publications.

Thrift, N. (2004) 'Intensities of feeling: towards a spatial politics of affect', *Geografiska Annaler B*, 86 (1): 57–78.

Thrift, N. (2007) *Non-Representational Theory: Space, Politics, Affect*, Abingdon: Routledge.

Thompson, J.L., Peace, S., Astell, A., Moynihan, P. and Macdonald, A. (2014) 'Food environments: from home to hospital', in A. Walker (ed) *The New Science of Ageing*, Bristol: Policy Press, pp 155–80

Thunberg, G. (2019) *No One Is Too Small to Make a Difference*, London: Allen Lane.

Timmins, M., Macdonald, A., Maganaris, C., Haslam, C., Gyi, D., van den Heuval, E., di Giulio, I., McCann, J., Maguire, M., Peace, S. and Percival, J. (2014) 'Design for living in later life', in A. Walker (ed) *The New Science of Ageing*, Bristol: Policy Press, pp 209–39.

Tinker, A. (1989) *An Evaluation of Very Sheltered Housing*, London: HMSO.

Tinker, A. and Ginn, J. (2015) '*An Age Friendly City – How Far Has London Come?*' London: Kings College London/Greater London Association.

Tinker, A., Wright, F. and Zelig, H. (1995) *Difficult to Let Sheltered Housing*, London: HMSO.

Tinker, A., Wright, F., Hanson, J., Mayagoitia, R., Wijgani, H. and Holmans, A. (2008) 'Remodelling to extra care housing: some implications for policy and practice', *Quality in Ageing*, 3 (1):1–10.

Tomassini, C., Glaser, K., Broes van Groenou, M.I. and Grundy, E. (2004) 'Living arrangements among older people: an overview of trends in Europe and the USA', *Population Trends*, 115: 24–33.

Tomata, Y., Kakizaki, M., Suzuki, Y., Hashimoto, S., Kawado, M. and Tsuji, I. (2014) 'Impact of the 2011 Great East Japan Earthquake and Tsunami on functional disability among older people: a longitudinal comparison of disability prevalence among Japanese municipalities', *Journal of Epidemiology & Community Health*, 68 (6): 530–3.

Torres, S. (2012) 'International migration: patterns and implications for exclusion in old age', in T. Scharf and N.C. Keating (eds) *From Exclusion to Inclusion in Old Age: A Global Challenge*, Bristol: Policy Press, pp 33–49.

Torres, S. (2019) *Ethnicity and Old Age: Expanding our Imagination*, Ageing in a Global Context series, Bristol: Policy Press.

Torrington, J. (1996) *Care Homes for Older People: A Briefing and Design Guide*, London: Taylor & Francis.

Torrington, J. (2006) What has architecture got to do with dementia care. Explorations of the relationship between quality of life and building design in two EQUAL projects. *Quality of Ageing and Older Adults*, 7 (1): 34–48.

Town and Country Planning Associates (2015) 'New towns and garden cities – lessons for tomorrow: creating garden cities and suburbs today', Town and Country Planning Association/Housing LIN, London. Available at: https://www.housinglin.org.uk/_assets/Resources/Housing/OtherOrganisation/New_towns_report.pdf

Townsend, L., Wallace, C. and Fairhurst, G. (2015) 'Stuck out here': the critical role of broadband for remote rural places', *Scottish Geographical Journal*, 131 (3–4): 171–80.

Townsend, P. (1957) *The Family Life of Old People*, London: Routledge & Kegan Paul.

Townsend, P. (1962) *The Last Refuge*, London: Routledge & Kegan Paul.

Townsend, P. (1981) The structured dependency of the elderly: a creation of social policy in the twentieth century, *Ageing and Society*, 1 (1): 5–28.

Tuan, Y-F. (1977) *Space and Place: The Perspective of Experience*, Minneapolis and London: University of Minnesota Press.

Tulle, E. (2008) 'Acting your age? Sports science and the ageing body', *Journal of Aging Studies*, 22 (4): 340–7.

Tulle, E. (2015) Theorising embodiment and ageing', in J, Twigg and W, Martin (eds) (2015) *Routledge Handbook of Cultural Gerontology*, Abingdon: Routledge, pp 125–32.

Turner, P., Turner, S. and Van De Walle, G. (2007) 'How older people account for their experiences with interactive technology', *Behaviour and Information Technology*, 26 (4): 287–96.

Twigg, J. (2000) *Bathing – The Body and Community Care*, London: Routedge.

Twigg, J. (2006) *The Body in Health and Social Care*, Basingstoke: Palgrave MacMillan.

Twigg, J. and Martin, W. (eds) (2015a) *Routledge Handbook of Cultural Gerontology*, Abingdon: Routledge.

Twigg, J. and Martin, W. (2015b) 'The field of cultural gerontology: an introduction', in J. Twigg and W. Martin (eds) *Routledge Handbook of Cultural Gerontology*, Abingdon: Routledge, pp 1–16.

Twyford, K. and Porteus, J. (2021) 'Housing for people with dementia – are we ready?' A report from an inquiry by the APPG on Housing and Care for Older People, February, Housing LIN.

UK Co-housing Network (n.d.) Available at: https://cohousing.org.uk/

UKRI (United Kingdom Research Institute) (2021) 'The healthy ageing challenge'. Available at: https://www.ukri.org/our-work/our-main-funds/industrial-strategy-challenge-fund/ageing-society/healthy-ageing-challenge/

UN Climate Change Conference UK (2021) COP26 Outcomes, Available at: https://ukcop26.org/the-conference/cop26-outcomes/

Union of Concerned Scientists (2020) 'Each country's share of CO_2 emissions' first published July 2008, updated August 2020. Available at: https://www.ucsusa.org/resources/each-countrys-share-co2-emissions

United Nations (n.d.) Available at: https://www.un.org/en/global-issues/ageing

United Nations (2016) 'United Nations climate change: the Paris agreement'. Available at: https://unfccc.int/process-and-meetings/the-paris-agreement/the-paris-agreement

UN DESA (2017a) 'World population ageing' Highlights from 2017. Population Division (ST/ESA/SER.A/397). Available at: https://www.un.org/en/development/desa/population/publications/pdf/ageing/

UN DESA (2017b) 'Sustainable development goals'. Available at: https://www.un.org/sustainabledevelopment/sustainable-development-goals/

UN DESA (2019a) 'World population ageing report. Peace dignity and equality on a healthy planet'. Available at: https://www.un.org/en/global-issues/ageing

UN DESA (2019b) 'Population Division. World urbanization prospects: the 2018 revision' (ST/ESA/SER.A/420), New York: United Nations. Available at: https://population.un.org/wup/Publications/Files/WUP2018-Report.pdf

UN DESA (2019c) 'Population facts'. Migration Data Portal. Available at: https://migrationdataportal.org/themes/international-migrant-stocks

UN DESA (2019d) 'International migration 2019: report', UN Population Division (ST/ESA/SER.A/438). Available at: https://www.un.org/en/development/desa/population/migration/publications/migrationreport/docs/InternationalMigration2019_Report.pdf

UNDP (United Nations Development Programme) (2017) *Ageing, Older Persons and the 2030 Agenda for Sustainable Development*. New York: UNDP.

UN Environment Programme (2020) 'Ten impacts of the Australian bushfires'. Available at: https://www.unep.org/news_and_stories/story/ten-impacts-australian-bushfires

UN-HABITAT (2016) 'Urbanization and development: emerging futures, World Cities Report, United Nations Human Settlement Programme, Nairobi.

UNHCR (United Nations High Commission for Refugees) (2018) 'Global trends. Forced displacement. Available at: https://www.unhcr.org/globaltrends2018/

UNICEF (2010) 'Children "Left Behind"', Working Paper. Available at: Https://www.unicef.org/media/61041/file

Urry, J. (2000) 'Mobile sociology', *British Journal of Sociology*, 51 (1): 185–203.

Urry, J. (2007) *Mobilities*, London: Polity Press.

van den Berg, N., Schumann, M., Kraft, K. and Hoffman, W. (2012) 'Telemedicine and telecare for older patients – a systematic review', *Maturitas*, 73 (2): 94–114.

van der Linden, V., Annemans, M. and Heylighen, A. (2016) "Architects' approaches to healing environment in designing a Maggie's cancer caring centre', *International Journal for all Aspects of Design*, 19 (3): 511–33.

van Hoof, J., Janssen, M.L., Heesakkers, C.M.C., van Kersbergen, W., Severijns, L.E.J., Willems, L.A.G. (2016) 'The importance of personal possessions for the development of a sense of home of nursing home residents', *Journal of Housing for The Elderly*, 30 (1): 35–51. https://doi.org/10.1080/02763893.2015.1129381

Van Malderen, L., Mets, T., de Vriendt, P. and Gorus, E. (2013) 'The active ageing – concept translated to the residential long-term care', *Quality of Life Research*, 22: 929–37.

Venn, S. and Arber, S. (2011) 'Day-time sleep and active ageing in later life', *Ageing & Society*, 31 (2): 197–216.

Verbrugge, L.M. and Jette, A.M. (1994) 'The disablement process', *Social Science & Medicine*, 38 (1): 1–14. Available at: https://doi.org/10.1016/0277-9536(94)90294-1

Verbrugge, L.M., Latham, K. and Clarke, P.J. (2017) 'Aging with disability for midlife and older adults', *Research on Aging*, 39 (6): 741–77.

Vesto, D.U. (2010) 'Cohousing in Sweden: history and present situation', online report. Scholl of Architecture and the Built Environment, Royal Institute of technology, Stockholm. Available at: www.kollektivhus.nu/pdf/SwedishCohousing14.pdf

Victor, C., Grenade, L. and Boldy, D. (2005) 'Measuring loneliness in later life': a comparison of different measures', *Reviews in Clinical Gerontology*, 15 (1): 63–70.

Wada, M., Canham, S.L., Battersby, L., Sixsmith, J., Woolrych, R., Lan Fang, M. and Sixsmith, A. (2020) 'Perceptions of home in long-term care settings: before and after institutional relocation', *Ageing & Society*, 40 (6): 1267–90.

Wagner, G. (1988) *Residential Care: A Positive Choice. Report of the Independent Review of Residential Care*. National Institute for Social Work. London: HMSO.

Wahl, H-W. and Weisman, G.D. (2003) 'Environmental gerontology at the beginning of the new millennium: reflections on its historical, empirical, and theoretical development', *The Gerontologist*, 43 (5): 616–27.

Wahl, H-W. and Lang, F. (2004) 'Aging in context across the adult life course: Integrating physical and social environmental research perspectives', in H.W. Wahl, R. Scheidt, and P. Windley (eds) *Annual Review of Gerontology and Geriatrics Vol. 23*, New York: Springer, pp 1–33.

Wahl, H-W. and Oswald, F. (2010) 'Environmental perspectives on ageing', in D, Dannefer and C, Phillipson (eds) *The SAGE Handbook of Social Gerontology*, London: SAGE Publications, pp 111–24.

Wahl, H-V., and Oswald, F. (2016) 'Theories of environmental gerontology: old and new avenues for person–environment views of aging', in V.L. Bengtson and R.A. Settersten Jr (eds) *Handbook of Theories of Aging* (3rd edn), New York: Springer, pp 621–41.

Wahl, H-W., Oswald, F. and Zimprich, D. (1999) 'Everyday competence in visually impaired older adults: a case for person-environment perspectives', *The Gerontologist*, 39 (2):140–9.

Wahl, H-W., Iwarsson, S. and Oswald, F. (2012). 'Ageing well and the environment: toward an integrative model and research agenda for the future', *The Gerontologist*, 52 (3): 306–16.

Wahl, H-W., Fänge, A., Oswald, F., Gitlin, L.N. and Iwarsson, S. (2009) 'The home environment and disability-related outcomes in aging individuals: what is the empirical evidence?' *The Gerontologist*, 49 (3): 355–67.

Waights, V., Holland, C., Huchet, E. and Fisk, M. (2019) 'Age-friendly standards around ICT: the challenge of co-production with older people', *International Journal of Standardization Research*, 17 (2): 1–20.

Waitzmann, E. (2021) *Extraordinary funding for Transport for London*, London: House of Commons Library. Available at: https://lordslibrary.parliament. uk/extraordinary-funding-for-transport-for-london/

Walker, A. (1981) Towards a political economy of old age, *Ageing & Society*, 1 (1): 73–94.

Walker, A. (1990) 'The economic "burden" of ageing and the prospect of intergenerational conflict', *Ageing & Society*, 10 (4): 377–96.

Walker, A. (1999) 'The future of pensions and retirement in Europe: towards productive ageing', *The Geneva Papers on Risk and Insurance. Issues and Practice*, 24 (4): 448–60. Available at: http://www.jstor.org/stable/41952494

Walker, A. (2005) 'Towards an international political economy of ageing'. *Ageing & Society*, 25: 815–39.

Walker, A. (ed) (2014) *The New Science of Ageing*, Bristol: Policy Press.

Walker, A. (ed) (2018) *The New Dynamics of Ageing, Vol. 1*, Bristol: Policy Press,

Walker, A. and Foster, L. (eds) (2014) *The Political Economy of Ageing and Later Life: Critical Perspectives*, Cheltenham: Edward Elgar Publishing Ltd.

Walker, M. (2017) 'Creating homes that people would like to live in rather than have to live in: is there a role for occupational therapists in the design of housing?' Housing LIN Viewpoint 85, January. Available at: www. housinglin.org.uk

Walsh, K., Carney, G. and Leime, A. (2015) (eds) *Ageing through Austerity: Critical Perspectives from Ireland*, Bristol: Policy Press.

Walsh, K., Scharf, T. and Keating, N. (2017) "Social exclusion of older persons: a scoping review and conceptual framework', *European Journal of Ageing*, 14: 81–98. http://dx.doi.org/10.1007/s10433-016-0398-8

Walsh, K., O'Shea, E., Scharf, T. and Murray, M. (2012) Ageing in changing community contexts: cross-border perspectives from rural Ireland and Northern Ireland, *Journal of Rural Studies*, 28: 347–57.

Wanless, D. (2006) 'The Wanless Review. Securing good care for older people', co-authored with J. Forder, The King's Fund, London. Available at: https:// www.kingsfund.org.uk/publications/securing-good-care-older-people

Ward, R., Clark, A., Campbell, S., Graham, B., Kullberg, A., Manji, K., Rummery, K. and Keady, J. (2018) 'The lived neighbourhood: understanding how people with dementia engage with their local environment', *International Psychogeriatrics*, 30 (6): 867–80.

Warnes, A.M. (1981) 'Toward a geographical contribution to gerontology', *Progress in Human Geography*, 5 (3): 317–41. http://dx.doi.org/10.1177/ 030913258100500301

Warnes, A. (1999) 'UK and western European late-age mortality: trends in cause-specific death rates, 1960-1990', *Health & Place*, 5 (1): 111–18.

Warnes, A. (2010) 'Migration and age', in D. Dannefer and C. Phillipson (eds) *The SAGE Handbook of Social Gerontology*, London: SAGE Publications, pp 389–404.

Warnes, A. and Williams, A. (2006) 'Older migrants in Europe: a new focus for migration studies', *Journal of Ethnic and Migration Studies*, Special Issue: Migrants in Europe: Expenses, Exclusion & Constructive Accommodation, 32 (8): 1257–81.

Warnes, A., Friedrich, K., Kellaher, L. and Torres, S. (2004) 'The diversity and welfare of older migrants in Europe', *Ageing & Society*, 24 (3): 307–26.

Warnes, A.M., King, R., Williams, A.M. and Patterson, G. (1999) 'The well-being of British expatriate retirees in southern Europe', *Ageing & Society*, 19 (6): 717–40.

Warth, L. (2016) 'The WHO Global Network for Age-Friendly Cities and Communities: origins, developments and challenges', in T. Moulaert and S. Garon (eds) *Age-Friendly Cities and Communities in International Comparison. Political Lessons, Scientific Avenues and Democratic Issues*, Cham: Springer, pp 37–46.

Watts, N., Amann, M., Arnell, N., Ayeb-Karlsson, S., Belesova, K., Boykoff, M. (2019) 'The 2019 report of *The Lancet* countdown on health and climate change: ensuring that the health of a child born today is not defined by a changing climate', *The Lancet*, 394 (10211): 1839–1978.

Weisman, G.D. (1997) 'Environments for older persons with cognitive impairments', in G. Moore and R. Marans (eds) *Environment, Behavior and Design*, Vol. 4, New York: Plenum Press, pp 315–46.

Weisman, G.D. (2003) 'Creating places for people with dementia: an action research perspective', in K. Schaie, H-W. Wahl, H. Mollenkoph and F. Oswald (eds) *Aging Independently: Living Arrangements and Mobility*, New York: Springer, pp 162–73.

Weisman, G.D., Chaudhury, H. and Diaz Moore, K. (2000) 'Theory and practice of place: toward an integrative model', in R.Rubinstein, M. Moss and M. Kleban (eds) *The Main Dimensions of Aging: Essays in Honor of M. Powell Lawton*, New York: Springer, pp 3–21.

Welsh Government (2020) 'Summary statistics for Wales by region: 2020'. Available at: https://gov.wales/sites/default/files/statistics-and-research/2020-05/summary-statistics-regions-wales-2020-629.pdf

Wenger, G.C. (1995) *The Supportive Network*. George Allen & Unwin, London.

Wenger, G.C. (2001) 'Myths and realities of ageing in rural Britain', *Ageing & Society*, 21 (1): 117–30.

West, K., Shaw, R., Hagger, B. and Holland, C. (2017) 'Enjoying the third age! Discourse, identity and liminality in extra-care communities', *Ageing & Society*, 37 (9): 1874–97.

Westwood, S. (2016) ' "We see it as being heterosexualised, being put into a care home": gender, sexuality and housing/care preferences among older LGB individuals in the UK', *Health and Social Care in the Community*, 24 (6): e155–e163.

Westwood, S. (2017) 'Gender and older LGBT housing discourse: the marginalised voices of older lesbians, gay and bisexual women', *Housing, Care and Support*, 20 (3): 100–9.

Which (2020) 'Extra care housing'. Available at: https://www.which.co.uk/later-life-care/housing-options/sheltered-housing/extra-care-housing-acfud8m0r7tu

Which (2021) 'Social Care reform: what's changing and how will it will affect you?'. Available from: https://www.which.co.uk/news/2021/09/social-care-reform-whats-changing-and-how-will-it-affect-you/p371,line22/23 Added citation to p203

Whitbourne, K. and Whitbourne, S.B. (2014) *Adult Development & Aging: Biopsychosocial Perspectives*, Hoboken, NJ: John Wiley & Sons.

Wiles, J.L. (2005a) 'Conceptualizing place in the care of older people: the contribution of geographical gerontology', *Journal of Clinical Nursing*, 14 (8B): 100–8. http://dx.doi.org/10.1111/j.1365-2702.2005.01281.x

Wiles, J.L. (2005b) 'Home as a new site of care provisions and consumption', in G.J. Andrews and D.R. Phillips (eds) *Ageing and Place: Perspectives, Policy and Practice*, London: Routledge, pp 79–97.

Wiles, J.L. (2018) 'Health geographies of ageing', in M.W. Skinner, G.J. Andrews and M.P. Cutchin (eds) *Geographical Gerontology: Perspectives, Concepts, Approaches*, London and New York: Routledge, pp 31–42.

Wiles, J.L., Rolleston, A., Pillai, A., Broad, J., Teh, R., Gott, M. and Kerse, N. (2017) 'Attachment to place in advanced age: a study of the LiLACS NZ cohort', *Social Science & Medicine*, 185: 27–37. https://doi.org/10.1016/j.socscimed.2017.05.006

Willcocks, D., Peace, S. and Kellaher, L. (1987) *Private Lives in Public Places: A Research based Critique of Residential Life in Local Authority Old People's Homes*, London: Tavistock Publications.

Willcocks, D., Peace, S., Kellaher, L. with Ring, A. (1982) 'The residential life of old people: a study of 100 local authority old people's homes', Vol. 1. Research Report No. 12, Survey Research Unit, Polytechnic of North London.

Williams, A. (ed) (2019) *Therapeutic Landscapes. Geographies of Health*, Abingdon: Routledge.

Willemse, B.M., Depla, M.F., Smith, D. and Pot, A.M. (2014) 'The relationship between small-scale, nursing home care for people with dementia and staff's perceived job characteristics.' *International Psychogeriatrics*, 26 (5): 805–16.

Willis, P., Raithby, M. and Maegusuku-Hewett, T. (2018) '"It's a nice country but it's not mine": exploring the meanings attached to home, rurality and place for older lesbian, gay and bisexual adults', *Health & Social Care in the Community*, 26 (6): 908–16.

Willis, P., Maegusuku-Hewett, T., Raithby, M. and Miles, P. (2016) Swimming upstream: the provision of inclusive care to older lesbian, gay and bisexual(LGB) adults in residential and nursing environments in Wales', *Ageing & Society*, 36 (2): 282–306.

Willis, R. (2020) *Too Hot to Handle: The Democratic Challenge of Climate Change*, Bristol: Bristol University Press.

Willmott, M. and Young, P. (1960) *Family and Class in a London Suburb*, London: Routledge & Kegan Paul.

Windley, P.G. and Scheidt, R.J. (2003) *Physical Environments and Aging: Critical Contributions of M. Powell Lawton*, Philadelphia: The Haworth Press.

Wiseman, R.E (1980) 'Why older people move', *Research on Ageing*, 2 (2): 242–54.

Wondrwall (2020) 'Convert standard homes into intelligent homes'. Available at: https://wondrwall.co.uk/

Wood, C. (2013) *Top of the Ladder*, London: Demos.

Wood, C. and Vibert, S. (2017) 'Unlocking the market' Demos, London. Available at: https://demos.co.uk/project/supply-and-demand/

Wood, G.A., Ong, R. and Haffner, M.E.A. (2020) 'Housing wealth and aged care: asset-based welfare in practice in three OECD countries', *Housing Studies*. https://doi.org?1080/02673037.2020.1819966.

WorldAtlas (2020) 'Megacities'. Available at: https://www.worldatlas.com/articles/what-is-a-megacity.html

WHO (2002) *Active Aging: A Policy Framework*, Geneva: World Health Organization.

WHO (2006) 'Constitution of the World Health Organization'. Available at: https://www.who.int/governance/eb/who_constitution_en.pdf

WHO (2007) 'Global age-friendly cities: a guide', Ageing and Life Course, Family and Community Health. Available at: https://www.who.int/ageing/publications/Global_age_friendly_cities_Guide_English.pdf

WHO (2015a) 'World report on ageing and health'. Available at: https://www.who.int/ageing/publications/world-report-2015/en/

WHO (2015b) 'The epidemiology and impact of dementia: current state and future trends'. Available at: https://www.who.int/mental_health/neurology/dementia/dementia_thematicbrief_epidemiology.pdf

WHO (2017) 'Global action plan on the public health response to dementia 2017–2025'. Available at: https://www.who.int/mental_health/neurology/dementia/action_plan_2017_2025/en/#:~:text=The%20Global%20action%20plan%20on,dementia%20on%20communities%20and%20countries.

WHO (2018) 'Climate change and health, fact sheet', 1 February. Available at: https://www.who.int/news-room/fact-sheets/detail/climate-change-and-health

WHO (2020a) 'Dementia factsheet'. Available at: https://www.who.int/news-room/fact-sheets/detaildementia

WHO (2020b) 'About the Global Network for Age-Friendly Cities and Communities', Age-Friendly World, World Health Organization'. Available at: https://extranet.who.int/agefriendlyworld/who-network/

WHO (2020c) 'WHO Director-General's opening remarks media briefing on COVID-19, 11 March'. Available at: https://www.who.int/director-general/speeches/detail/who-director-general-s-opening-remarks-at-the-media-briefing-on-covid-19---11-march-2020

WHO (2020d) 'WHO coronavirus disease (COVID-19) situation report – 63, 23 March'. Available at: https://www.who.int/docs/default-source/coronaviruse/situation-reports/20200323-sitrep-63-covid-19.pdf?sfvrsn=d97cb6dd_2

WHO (2021a) 'WHO statistics on the coronavirus disease (COVID-19) dashboard'. Available at: https://covid19.who.int

WHO (2021b) Dementia Factsheet, Available at: https://www.who.int/news-room/fact-sheets/detail/dementia

World Meteorological Organization (2020) 'United in Science report: climate change has not stopped for COVID19', September. Available at: https://public.wmo.int/en/media/press-release/united-science-report-climate-change-has-not-stopped-covid19/

Worpole, K. (2010) The Modern Hospice Movement: A Quiet Revolution in End of Life Care. Special Issue Annales Universitatis Apulensis Series Historica, Romainia: University of Alba Iulia, pp 529–33, Abstract available:

Worpole, K. and Knox, K. (2007) 'The social value of public spaces', Joseph Rowntree Foundation, York. Available at: https://www.jrf.org.uk/sites/default/files/jrf/migrated/files/2050-public-space-community.pdf

Youll, P.J. and McCourt-Perring, C. (1993) Raising Voices: Ensuring Quality in Residential Care, London: HMSO

Young, Iris Marion (2005) On Female Body Experience: 'Throwing like a Girl' and Other Essays, New York: Oxford University Press.

Young, M. and Willmott, P. (1957) Family and Kinship in East London, London: Routledge & Kegan Paul.

Zhou, F., Yu, T., Du, R., Fan, G., Liu, Y., Liu, Z., Xiang, J., Wang, Y., Song, B., Gu, Y., Guan, L., Wei, L., Li, H., Wu, X., Xu, J., Tu, S., Zhang, Y., Chen, H. and Cao, B. (2020) 'Clinical course and risk factors for mortality in patients with COVID-19 in Wuhan, China: a retrospective cohort study', The Lancet, 395 (10229): 1054–62.

Zimdars, A., Nazroo, J. and Gjonca, E. (2012) 'The circumstances of older people in England with self-reported visual impairment: a secondary analysis of the English Longitudinal Study of Ageing (ELSA)', The British Journal of Visual Impairment, 30 (1): 22–30.

Index

Note: References to figures appear in *italic* type; those in **bold** type refer to tables.

375

P

Paddock et al 223–4
Pain, R. 46
Pakistan 77
Pakistani people (older, all ages) 85, 115, 180
palliative care 219
PAR (participatory action research) 93, 237, 239–50
Paralympic Games 98
parenthood 9
parents, working 84
Paris 64
Paris Agreement on Climate Change 62, 268
Park, J. 3, 124, 128, 164, 168, 187–8
Parker, Barry 104
Parker Morris report 106
Park et al 131, 132
Parkhurst et al 92
Parmelee, P.W. 34–5
participatory design 109–10
participatory research 235–50, 287
participatory thinking 44
Pastalan, L.A. 250
patriarchal society 74
paving, tactile 95
Peabody Trust 103
Peace, S. xv, 17, 25, 113, 146, 159, 207, 216, 221, 238, 250
Peace et al 22, 24, 126, 133, 137, 157, 196, 198, 212, 229–30
P–E congruence 30–1, 47, 97, 270
P–E fit 27, 29, 31, 32, 33, 47, 209
P–E interaction 1, 25, 26–7, 37, 43, 225, 230
  in care homes 283
  and Carp and Carp 30–1
  definition 24
  and Environment and Identity in Later Life study 256
  and national consumer study 211
  and negotiations 47
  and prevention and care 54
  and Torrington 212–14
pelican crossings, audible/tactile signals 95
pension age 5
pensioners 12, 14–15
pensions 11–12, 12
Percival, John 17, 272
P–E relationships 29, 33, 226
performance 18
performativity 44, 45
person (P) 1, 2–12
personal agency 7, 230, 285, 286
personal autonomy 223, 283
personal care 174, 178, 191, 193, 197

personal communication 69, 129, 273
personal control 37, 283
personal history 38
personal identity 19, 192
personalisation 228
personal meaning 32, 33
personal mobility 59
Personal Social Services Research Unit, University of Kent 204
person-centred dementia care 39
person–environment exchange 42
P–E synergy 30
Philadelphia Geriatric Center Morale Scale 29
Phillips, Judith 88, 251
Phillips et al 96, 178
Phillipson, C. 49, 55, 56, 58
Phillipson et al 5, 81–2, 83–4
physical environment 30, 39, 97, 155, 175
  adapting 149
  and care homes 212, 214, 228
physical impairment 43
physical insideness 34
physical place attachment 101
place 13–17, 26, 34, 35–6, 38–9
  and dementia 248
  and home 74
  re-engagement with 47
  and self 59
  and touch 45
place-as-dwelling 14
place attachment 19, 33–4, 40, 46, 99, 100–1, 133
place detachment 34
place integration 46
place of origin, returning to 35
place roles 38
place rules 38
'Planning for a Better Future' (RTPI) 124
'Planning for the Future' White Paper 124
planning guidance 90
Poland 77
police, community 98
Policy Research Institute on Ageing and Ethnicity 180
Pollard Thomas Edwards architects 188
pollution 64, 275
the poor 56
Poor Law 196, 295
Poor Law Unions 196, 294
poor sleep 21
population
  ageing 15–16, 48, 49–59
  UK 74–8
Porteus, J. 3, 120, 122, 124, 128, 164, 168, 187–8, 292
Port Sunlight 103–4
positionality 249
positioning theory 225

.